MODERN DEBATE

ITS LOGIC AND STRATEGY

Arthur N. Kruger

PROFESSOR OF ENGLISH AND SPEECH
WILKES COLLEGE

McGRAW-HILL BOOK COMPANY, INC.

New York   Toronto   London   1960

MODERN DEBATE: ITS LOGIC AND STRATEGY

MODERN DEBATE

ITS LOGIC AND STRATEGY

McGraw-Hill Series in Speech

CLARENCE T. SIMON, *Consulting Editor*

In Memory of My Mother
1894–1958

The author took great pains to put forward the ideas clearly and simply.
... In the interest of clarity, I did not hesitate to repeat myself and did
not pay the slightest attention to the elegance of presentation; I sincerely
stuck to the prescription of the great theoretician L. Boltzmann, that the
business of elegance should be left to the tailors and shoemakers.

Albert Einstein

PREFACE

This book is based on the premise that intercollegiate debate is a valuable academic discipline, perhaps the most valuable in the curriculum, and one which therefore deserves to be taught well. Textbooks, a traditional means to this end, are often ignored by debaters and debate coaches who complain that the average text slights important debate concepts, treats logical principles superficially, emphasizes peripheral matters, and frequently gives unrealistic advice. Although such judgments may be overly critical, they have guided me in writing and organizing this book.

Part Two, *Analysis and Development*, contains much new material on such concepts as probability and truth, definition, analysis of issues, and strategy.

Part Three, *Attack and Defense*, treats in ten chapters concepts usually treated in one or two.

Part Four, *Presentation*, is, on the whole, traditional.

Part Five, *The Case in Action*, analyzes a debate in great detail to enable the student to see how principles are actually applied.

Part Six, *Special Problems*, is on the whole traditional.

In emphasizing the practice as well as the theory of debating, I have chosen many examples from actual debates. Also, I believe the book is comprehensive enough for both elementary and advanced debate classes as well as for coaches and extracurricular debaters.

ACKNOWLEDGMENTS

Besides those to whom specific reference is made in the footnotes, I am indebted in a general way to the authors of certain books on logic which have helped shape my thinking. For some of the illustrations culled from actual debates I am indebted to the many intercollegiate debaters whom I have taught and judged. For valuable suggestions I am indebted to my colleagues Stanko Vujica and Robert Tener, to my former students and debaters Gwen Evans, Jesse Choper, and Fred Roberts, and especially to my friend and former student John Bucholtz. For any errors or shortcomings, of course, I alone am responsible.

Arthur N. Kruger

CONTENTS

PART ONE

INTRODUCTION

FIRST PRINCIPLES

> It is better to debate a question without settling it than to settle it
> without debating it.
>
> *Joubert*

To understand why logic, analysis, case construction, attack and defense, and related matters have been emphasized in this book, the reader
should know the writer's philosophy of academic debate. This is summarized in the following paragraphs.

1. THE QUALITY OF ACADEMIC DEBATE

Despite the importance of academic debate as an educational device,
the over-all quality of academic debate is not very high. Except for comparatively few debaters, often from the same schools every year, most
debaters are guilty of ill-conceived cases, fallacious reasoning, and poor
organization, faults which indicate a poor grasp of logical principles.
This inadequacy may be attributed to three factors: personal limitations,
inadequate instruction, and poor textbooks. Let us consider each briefly.

Many students can blame only themselves for being mediocre debaters,
since they are unwilling to devote the necessary time and effort to develop
sound cases and effective debating skills. Some, of course, are unable to
master so complex an activity as debating; but, if motivated and properly
taught, most students can become competent debaters.

Some blame for the uneven quality of academic debate must also fall
on the instruction many students receive. Drafted unwillingly by the
administration, some debate coaches serve reluctantly without either the
required knowledge or the desire to acquire it. The more conscientious
bone up and learn as they go along, but, owing to the complexity of the
subject and the pressure of time, their knowledge frequently remains
fragmentary and misconceived. Also, since the debate program is often
delegated to a teacher of speech, many coaches believe that academic
debate is primarily an exercise in public speaking. Using the criteria of

effective public speaking, they deemphasize the more important aspects of academic debate both in teaching and judging debate.

Unqualified or misinformed coaches do a disservice not only to their own students but also to those of other institutions. Since their teaching is predicated on certain false assumptions, so too is their judging. By stressing the wrong criteria and rewarding debaters accordingly or by de-emphasizing the proper criteria and penalizing debaters accordingly, they discourage some serious students from continuing in academic debate or, worse, encourage those bent on winning at any cost to adopt the false standards apparently expected of them.

Finally, most textbooks on debate seem to slight the very subjects they should emphasize, namely, analysis and argumentation. Many offer abstractions difficult to grasp and are thus bypassed by many coaches and debaters, except for very elementary matters.

The mediocre quality of debating due to the foregoing factors prompts discerning coaches to remark at the end of many a debate tournament, "I've heard only one good debate during the past two days."

2. SOME MISCONCEPTIONS OF ACADEMIC DEBATE

Perhaps the most common misconception of academic debate is that it is primarily training in mass persuasion by means of effective delivery. From this premise it follows that a debater must have convictions, which in turn are incompatible with debating both sides of a question. Such a view confuses the goals of academic and political debate. If there is any analogy between academic debate and other kinds, it is between academic debate and that carried on in expert administrative and legislative government committees, before those "whose training and specialized experience give them superiority in the technical aspects of the problem." As Pennock says, "One does not need to be a social psychologist to know that the man-in-the-street is not equipped to judge whether or not processor subsidies are a desirable means of price control or whether the 'prudent investment' theory of evaluating public utility properties is superior to the 'reproduction cost' formula." [1] Since such subjects are usually chosen for academic debate, the latter clearly is not directed to the general public or man-in-the-street audience.

Griffin and Linkugel make the same point in the following terms: [2]

In the tournament debate situation we are training future junior executives, sales managers, high-school superintendents, etc., to be able to go before

[1] J. Roland Pennock, *Liberal Democracy: Its Merits and Prospects* (New York: Rinehart & Company, Inc., 1950), p. 221.

[2] Kim Giffin and Will Linkugel, "The Place of Debate in Modern Education," *The Bulletin of the National Association of Secondary School Principals*, XLII, 241 (November, 1958), p. 182.

their boards of directors, school boards, or whatever their decision-making group may be, and effectively advocate a proposal—for example, the expenditure of $200,000 for a new sales campaign or the construction of a new high-school building. Such policy-forming groups are much more interested in solid reasons backed by specific evidence than they are in a boyish smile, human interest stories, after-dinner jokes, or dramatic innuendoes.

But even the analogy between academic debate and that engaged in before experts is imperfect because in the latter type the emphasis is on convincing others to accept views presumably arrived at after a long period of investigation and thought; the speakers have acquired convictions, which though important, academic debaters need not have because their goal is different.

3. THE VALUES OF ACADEMIC DEBATE

The paramount goal of academic debate is to train the student in the tools of argumentation, to train him how to construct logical arguments and to detect weaknesses or lapses from logical standards in the arguments of others. (An argument, as the term is used here, is a form of discourse having a conclusion and a reason for believing it.) Thus, the student debater and the student of logic perform basically the same task. Training in academic debate is more valuable than a course in logic, however, because it offers the student many additional advantages. In academic debate logic is not studied in a vacuum but in relation to current social, political, and economic problems. Debate arguments and the application of logical principles are more realistic.

Academic debate also provides many subsidiary advantages.

1. It provides training in how to think quickly as well as critically.

2. It provides training in how to express ideas clearly so that they may be understood and evaluated by others.

3. It provides training in organizing and integrating many arguments into a coherent whole.

4. It (particularly the practice of debating both sides of the same question) develops tolerance for different points of view, and is thus a valuable means for seeking the truth. As Pennock observes: "In all walks of life, the most useful debates are not those which are designed with the idea that one of the contenders will convince his opponent, but rather those where the idea is to enable third parties to come to sounder conclusions than they might otherwise reach." [3]

A second group of advantages is:

1. It provides training in how to speak effectively before a group. The confidence developed in acquiring this ability leads in turn to greater poise and self-assurance.

[3] Pennock, p. 222.

2. It motivates the student to learn much about current social, political, and economic problems, which in turn leads to better reading habits.

3. It provides healthy competition and helps cultivate a sense of fair play.

4. It affords the student an opportunity to travel and to meet interesting people.

4. THE QUESTION OF PERSONAL BELIEFS

If the goal of academic debate is primarily training in clear thinking, it follows that the persuading involved is that of persuading a judge that one has argued, or reasoned, better than the opposition and not that one's beliefs should be accepted. It also follows that the coach-judge is not an average man in the street but an expert in argumentation and familiar with the question. As we shall see, both qualifications are necessary, for even expert logicians require much time (not available in debate) to evaluate an intricate chain of arguments unless they know many of them beforehand.

The charge that academic debate is unrealistic because the audience usually consists of a single judge follows from the same misconception of academic debate as a medium of mass persuasion. But as Griffin and Linkugel point out: [4]

Tournament debating as we know it puts a special premium on an integrated series of arguments (generally known as a "case") with each argument backed by pertinent and carefully documented data. A judge, trained to put emphasis where it belongs, provides a correlative for a serious-minded board of directors or a sincerely perplexed school board. If we can assume that such a judge is properly trained and well-qualified, no further audience should be necessary in the laboratory or practice situation.

It is true that viewing academic debate chiefly as an academic discipline to train the mind may have the drawback that the problems debated tend to lose their significance for the student. For as Dunham says,[5]

Now it is the fate of principles to lose their content in proportion as they become mere devices of argument. So used, a principle begins to appear in so many different contexts that any strictness of original meaning is relaxed, and a multitude of meanings, corresponding to a multitude of contexts, takes its place. The resulting ambiguity is fatal to accurate thought. The principle becomes simply a counter which is moved about in an effort to forestall defeat.

[4] Giffin and Linkugel, *loc. cit.* Even if the charge weren't misplaced it would be unfounded; for, as the writers remind us, "Our best audience debaters are generally those who do the best job in tournament debating." *Ibid.,* p. 184.

[5] Barrows Dunham, *Man against Myth* (Boston: Little, Brown & Company, 1947), p. 123.

Though admittedly a risk in academic debate, this is more than balanced by the fact that many students, if they did not debate, would not be aware of the problems in the first place and almost surely not to the degree that they become aware of them in debate. Moreover, after they have debated a question, particularly both sides, they are less likely to make snap judgments or rationalize an unfounded conviction. Thus, when beginning to debate a question, students should be encouraged *not* to form a strong attachment to the point of view advocated but to develop the soundest possible case and to understand that their convictions are not at stake. Convictions should come only after one has given *both* sides the same fair test. The student must understand that he is learning valuable techniques and that his performance will be judged not by the earnestness or intensity of his beliefs but primarily by his ability to reason.[6]

Thus, academic and nonacademic debate have entirely different goals. Where nonacademic debate aims at getting others to share one's convictions, academic debate stresses the learning of certain skills, primarily the skill of thinking critically. What the student does with these skills after acquiring them should not be confused with the means of acquiring them. All teachers hope, of course, that he will put them to good use after he graduates, and he is likely to, if his academic-debate training has been sound, for he will then be more aware of irrational appeals, more likely to expose them, and more logical in his own arguments.

[6] A. N. Kruger, "Is It Educational? Yes," *Bulletin of the DAPC*, XXII (December, 1956), pp. 4–9.

PART TWO

ANALYSIS AND DEVELOPMENT

CHAPTER 2

THE DEBATE PROPOSITION

As absolute certainty is seldom obtainable in human affairs, reason requires that men form their opinion of the truth on the superior number of probabilities on one side or the other.

Paraphrased from Lord Mansfield

1. THE NATURE OF A PROPOSITION

To understand why men in a free society resort to debate and why some propositions are debatable while others are not, we must inquire into the nature of sentences and discourse in general, and into the nature of facts and inferences in particular. Most of us learned in grade school that, classified according to meaning, sentences which assert something are *declarative,* those which question *interrogative,* those which command or request *imperative,* and those which express emotion *exclamatory.* Of these four kinds of sentences, only the declarative can provide the basis for debate, and then only certain types of declarative sentences. Let us see why this is so by considering examples of the other three kinds of sentences.

Interrogative Sentences: What grade did you make in history? Do you think that the Yankees will win the pennant again? What caused the downfall of the Roman Empire?

Imperative Sentences: Keep off the grass! Thou shalt love thy neighbor as thyself! No talking in the library!

Exclamatory Sentences and Expressions of Personal Taste, Feeling, or Emotion: What an exciting game! Hooray for Smith! I like strawberry shortcake. I'm sorry you can't go to the movies with us.

Although this last category contains declarative sentences, these sentences express emotional reactions or tastes, likes and dislikes, and thus resemble exclamations in that both essentially express how our nervous system reacts to different stimuli. Since reactions vary with different people and different nervous systems, and since we ordinarily have no other choice but to take at face value a person's insistence that his own nervous system is reacting this way rather than that way, there is no

11

point in arguing whether his reaction is right or wrong, good or bad. That human reactions occur as they do is a fact which we must accept. Thus the ancient Romans were given to saying, "*De gustibus non est disputandum*" ("There is no disputing about tastes").

Questions, commands, exclamations, and expressions of personal taste and feeling are not debatable because it would not make any sense to reply to them "I agree" or "I disagree," which is another way of saying that they are neither true nor false. Declarative sentences, on the other hand, with the exception of those expressing personal feeling or emotion ("I am unhappy," etc.), are of a different order. If someone remarks, "It's been raining all day," or "Smith is a good debater," one can believe or disbelieve, doubt or deny, what is asserted, depending upon whether he believes such statements to be true or false. Most declarative sentences, therefore, possess one necessary characteristic of a debatable subject: they must be either true or false. However, this characteristic by itself is not sufficient to make a declarative sentence debatable. Before considering some of the other necessary characteristics, we may now define the term "proposition" as any declarative sentence or statement which must be either true or false.

2. THE NATURE OF TRUTH

To determine why some propositions are debatable and why some are not, we must inquire into the nature of truth and into some of the problems involved in arriving at it. Without becoming too technical or philosophical, we shall define "truth" or rather a "true proposition (or statement)" as one which corresponds to the facts. Thus, the statement that "the world's longest covered bridge is the Hartland Bridge over the Saint John River in New Brunswick, with a total length of 1,282 feet" is true because it corresponds to the facts, i.e., there actually is in existence at this moment such a bridge of such length which is longer by actual measurement than any other known bridge of this type.

A fact, as we have used the term in the foregoing context, is anything known to exist, known in the sense that it is or can be directly perceived and verified; that is, a fact is a known or discovered truth. Although "fact" and "truth" may seem synonymous, they are not; a fact, as we have defined the term, is a discovered, directly verifiable, truth, but not all truth is factual, just as all bears are mammals but not all mammals are bears. That is to say, not all truth is known or has been discovered. For example, what happened on earth one million years ago is true in the sense that it actually happened but is not a fact in the sense that it can be directly perceived or verified.

One may ask, can the truth of what happened one million years ago or at any time in the past ever be known? Are direct perception and verification the only means of arriving at the truth? Though direct perception and verification are an important means of discovering the truth, experience has shown that there are also indirect means, namely, perception or observation plus reasoning; i.e., one may infer or "guess" the truth about a given situation without directly perceiving it. One may reason, for example, that because of some known truths, or facts, such as fossils that have been discovered, a certain type of plant and animal life existed on this earth one million years ago; and it may very well be true that such life did exist though we can never be certain of this truth. In other words, we cannot say that it is a fact that such-and-such life existed, for facts are certain truths, but we can say it is probably true and proceed from that assumption to discover other probable and even certain truths.

Nuclear physicists, to name but one group of people, do this very thing every day. Even though they have never actually seen the individual components of an atom, their assumption, based on certain facts, that there are protons, electrons, and neutrons has led to such tangible developments as hydrogen bombs and atomic-powered submarines. The point is, truth is often elusive and there is more than one way of discovering it. Furthermore, in our search for the truth we cannot always be sure that we have discovered it. Occasionally, with the passage of time some probable truths become certain truths, or facts, as witness predictions concerning eclipses of the moon, the coming of Halley's Comet, or the movement of the tides. However, many probable truths remain in the realm of probability and can never become certain—subject to direct perception. This does not mean that they cannot be depended upon as a guide for intelligent belief or action. Clearly, "probable truths," or "educated guesses" as they are sometimes called, are a better basis for action and belief than no basis at all. When two or three doctors agree that a certain patient has acute appendicitis, their diagnosis may not be classed as "certainly true," but it would be the imprudent patient who failed to take steps for an immediate operation.

3. PROBABILITY AND DEBATE

Certain types of probable truths, as the reader may have guessed by now, fall into the realm of the debatable. But before considering some of these types, we need to look more closely at this concept of probability. And in this connection we shall introduce the term "inference," which we have really defined and illustrated already. For an inference is a statement or conclusion based upon facts and reasoning but not at the moment directly perceivable; in other words, an inference is a probable truth. As we shall see subsequently, the amount of faith that may be placed in an inference depends upon the data which support it. Since all inferences are not supported in the same manner, they may be rated all the way from "almost certainly true" to "certainly false," with such categories as "true beyond a reasonable doubt," "probably true," "inconclusive," "probably false," "false beyond a reasonable doubt," and "almost certainly false" coming in between these extremes.

For example, an inference—though most people don't think of it as such—which is almost certainly true is that the earth is spherical but flattened at the poles. And one which is almost certainly false is that there is a correlation between the color of a person's skin and his intelligence. Between these two extremes, in the so-called "inconclusive" category, fall the propositions which lend themselves most readily to debate. They are debatable because, owing to the complexity of the topic with which they deal, or owing to a lack of corroborating evidence, there seem to be good reasons supporting both their truth and falsity simultaneously. This does not mean, of course, that they *are* both true and false simultaneously or that they are half true and half false. (As we shall see, a proposition can only be *either* true *or* false; there is no middle ground between the two.) It is simply that at the moment the truth or falsity of a debatable proposition is not clearly ascertainable.

If it were ascertainable "beyond a reasonable doubt," the proposition would hardly be debatable. It is precisely *because* a proposition is not clear-cut that debate may become necessary—in order to determine where the probable truth or wisest line of action lies. Once that has been established, the goal of persuading others to accept that truth or line of action may be pursued; for usually some course of action or belief is required at the time. And sound reasons, as we said, are a better basis for action or belief than no reasons at all. In passing, it should be mentioned that in academic debate the goal of influencing belief or action in others is subordinate to that of familiarizing the student with the means for doing so, namely, logical argumentation. In other words, academic debate is analogous to a laboratory situation where the student becomes familiar with certain valuable tools and techniques which may be put to many constructive uses later on.

4. TYPES OF DEBATABLE PROPOSITIONS

For purposes of study, debatable inferences may be classified as of four types: the proposition of fact, the proposition of explanation, the proposition of value, and the proposition of policy. The reasoning used in connection with each will subsequently be discussed in some detail, but for the present each type will be identified and briefly explained.

The Proposition of Fact

To use the term "fact" to designate a type of inference may be confusing, for, as defined, a fact is a known truth, something directly perceivable and verifiable. Why then should the term be used to designate an inference, or probable truth? It is so used because inferences of fact are those which once were or may yet become directly verifiable but, at the moment of discussion, are not. Thus, questions of fact pertain to events that have happened, are happening, or will happen, e.g.,

"Sacco and Vanzetti Were Innocent of the Crime for
Which They Were Executed."   (has happened)
"Russia Does Not Desire War."   (is happening)
"A Third World War Is Inevitable."   (will happen)

Many court cases revolve around questions of fact: Did X commit such and such a crime? Does Y owe Z the sum of money claimed by Z? It is interesting to note that in civil cases the verdict goes, or is supposed to go, to the side which has shown "a preponderance of evidence," i.e., the side which has demonstrated its position to be more probably true than the other side's, the same criterion for deciding a winner in academic debate. But in criminal cases, where a man's life or liberty is at stake, the defendant must be proved guilty "beyond a reasonable doubt" before he can be convicted of a crime. A much higher degree of probability must be shown than that which suffices for civil suits or academic debates.

The Proposition of Explanation

Closely related to questions of fact are questions of explanation, or those which affirm a reason *why* something has happened, is happening, or will happen, e.g.,

"The Versailles Treaty Was Largely Responsible for Hitler's Rise to Power."
"The Present Uprising in Lebanon Is Communist-inspired."
"The Hydrogen Bomb Has Rendered War Obsolete as a Means of Settling International Disputes."

Such questions deal with complex cause-and-effect relationships, which by their very nature are not subject to direct verification. As we shall see, although the absence of a given factor as a possible cause can be determined empirically, its presence as a cause cannot be so determined. To put it another way, although it may be empirically determined that something is *not* a cause of a given effect, it cannot be so determined that something *is* a cause of that effect. This, of course, does not mean that we should not try to determine the probable truth or falsity of such propositions, for as we can see, important decisions must often be made on this basis.

The Proposition of Value

Questions of value are those which assert that some individual, institution, program, or policy possesses or lacks a certain desirable or undesirable characteristic, e.g.,

"Franklin Delano Roosevelt Was a Great President."
"United States Policy in the Middle East Is Bankrupt."
"The American Press Is Free."

An evaluation is a special kind of judgment, or inference, which implies the existence of a standard, namely, "anything taken by general consent as a basis of comparison; an approved model." Something is thus rated good or bad, harmful or beneficial, attractive or unattractive, by comparison with some approved model. Implicit in most evaluations, particularly of policies and programs, is how something functions to accomplish a desired end. That is, most evaluations involve means-end or cause-and-effect relationships. A teacher, for example, may be rated good or bad, effective or ineffective, in accordance with how effectively he communicates ideas or motivates students. A political act or program is judged on how it promotes the general welfare, a generally accepted criterion of a democratic society.

Although a debatable characteristic cannot be empirically verified (for again, if it could be, there would be no debate), it can be determined indirectly by logical reasoning. One purpose of debate is to explore the logical ramifications of a given evaluation so as to determine how probably true or false it is.

The Proposition of Policy

Questions of policy, also called normative statements, are the most complex type of proposition, for they involve all three of the preceding types. Such questions assert that a new program or policy should be instituted, e.g.,

"The United States Should Recognize Red China."
"All Colleges Should Use the Honor System."
"A National FEPC Law Should Be Enacted by Congress."

Propositions of policy are actually implied evaluations of a given policy and may be paraphrased as "such-and-such a policy is the best of available means to a certain desired end." They are more complex than other questions of value since they involve a comparison between the policy recommended and the policy in use or other potential policies. Like all evaluations they entail a cause-and-effect or means-end relationship, the means being the policy itself (world government, Federal grants, etc.) and the end usually being implicit. Sometimes the end is explicit, as in the proposition "Resolved, That the Federal Government Should Give Annual Grants to the States *To Equalize Educational Opportunities in Tax-supported Schools.*"

As we shall see, determining the end implied in policy questions is an important step in analyzing such questions.

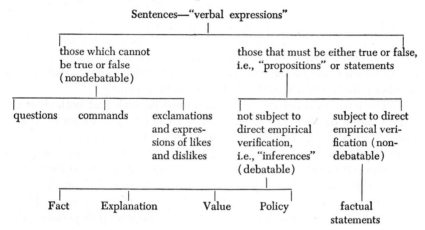

5. ADDITIONAL CHARACTERISTICS OF A DEBATE PROPOSITION

Up to now we have primarily considered debatability. Although this is the most important, there are other characteristics of a good debate proposition, namely,

1. The proposition should contain but one judgment. For example, the proposition "Resolved, That the President of the United States Should Be Elected by a Direct Vote of the People and Should Not Be Limited to Two Terms in Office" violates this criterion because it contains two distinct proposals, each of which could be debated separately. A similar error would be to append an epithet to the proposed policy. For example, in the proposition "Resolved, That the Pernicious Practice of Installment Buying Should Be Illegal," "pernicious" entails a judgment which must be proved. Thus, the proposition affirms two evaluations: installment buying is pernicious and making this practice illegal would be logically desirable.

Because of their connotations some terms suggest an evaluation, e.g., the term "socialized," which has unfavorable connotations and therefore suggests something bad. Thus, a proposition like "Congress Should Enact a Program of Socialized Medicine" would present an affirmative with the dilemma of contending that an undesirable program would be desirable, and the negative with contending that an undesirable program would be undesirable, a proposition which assumes what must be proved. Using neutral language, namely, "Resolved, That Congress Should Enact a National Compulsory Health Insurance Law" would eliminate this problem.

Still another related error is the use of terms so broad that the policy encompasses several important programs. For example, the proposition "Resolved, That the American People Should Reject the Welfare State" calls for rejecting several important programs—the compulsory social security program, the program of government price supports for farm commodities, a national compulsory health insurance program, etc.—any one of which could be the subject for a debate. This example violates still another criterion of a sound debate proposition, namely,

2. The terms of a debate proposition must be such that both sides can readily agree on their meaning. They must not be too vague or ambiguous. Thus, since a "welfare state" is very hard to define, two opposing teams might disagree on its meaning and argue about different programs.

3. Propositions of policy must call for a major change from the present policy. This would rule out a proposition like "Resolved, That the American People Should Reject a National Program of Compulsory Health Insurance" since it calls for maintaining the present policy rather than changing it.

6. TYPES OF POLICIES

Since policy questions are used extensively in academic debates, let us consider the nature of policies a little more closely. A new policy may be a program for something that is lacking ("Resolved, That Congress Should Appropriate Funds for Building a Second Canal Across the Isthmus of Panama"), an alternative program for one that exists ("Resolved, That the Non-Communist Nations Should Form a New International Organization"), or simply a discontinuation of the present policy ("Resolved, That the United States Should Discontinue Giving Direct Economic Aid to Foreign Countries").

Whenever possible, policy questions should be phrased to contain a specific program, for when the new policy is merely a discontinuation of the present one there may be some ambiguity. In debating the question "Resolved, That the United States Should Discontinue Giving Direct Economic Aid to Foreign Countries," for example, most affirmative teams went beyond the change called for in the resolution and offered such policies as free trade, free trade combined with private investment, and granting aid indirectly through the medium of the United Nations or through some regional organization like the Columbo organization. Thus, negative teams had to come prepared to debate many different policies. Such ambiguity could have been avoided had the proposition been phrased as "Resolved, That the United States Should Grant Its Economic Aid to Foreign Countries Indirectly Through an Agency of the United Nations," which contains one specific proposal.

7. THE FALLACY OF POPULAR SUPPORT

Some writers have expressed the view that the policy advocated in the resolution must be supported by some significant group of people. This criterion, however, defeats one of the paramount purposes of debate, which is to create a climate of opinion that makes change from the majority view possible democratically. The misconception that the policy debated must have some popular support is related to the more common misconception that the fact of popular support argues in favor of a given policy. Though this error is touched upon elsewhere, we shall consider it here briefly.

Since the affirmative is advocating a change from the status quo, it is presumably in the minority, since in a democratic society the status quo presumably represents the majority view. However, a crucial concern of debate is, is the majority always right? Does it always support the best program? Obviously not, for history is full of examples where the majority of people have on occasion supported foolish policies or held erroneous beliefs. We need only recall that people once thought that the earth was flat and the sun revolved around the earth. Since debate on a policy is resorted to in the first place to determine by reasoning whether the minority or majority view is true, the negative would be guilty of circular reasoning if it assumed that the majority view were true while trying to prove it.

Several years ago the students of the United States Military and Naval Academies were not permitted to debate the question concerning the recognition of Communist China because nonrecognition, they were told, was the official government policy. If this were a legitimate reason for not debating a given question, clearly no questions concerning current governmental policies could be debated. All such existing policies, whether good or bad, would have to remain. But the fact that a policy exists or is favored by the majority is not necessarily a reason why it *should* exist, for the policy may be unreasonable. Since debate is resorted to in the first place to question its reasonableness, to argue that popular support favors its retention is to be guilty of circular reasoning. Such remarks, of course, should not be construed as an attack upon popular government. The point is, the man in the street is not a qualified expert on the policies debated and, since his views are not authoritative, they do not constitute valid evidence concerning the merit or demerit of a complex policy. This does not mean, of course, that the ultimate determination of such policies should not be his.

Incidentally, in attacking the argument that "what is approved should be approved" one should be careful not to antagonize a judge who might not see the distinction between such an attack and one upon democracy itself. He should not say bluntly, as one well-meaning debater once said, "It doesn't make any difference what the people want; the question here is, what would be best for them?" The next speaker spent his entire rebuttal on this point and apparently convinced the judge that the affirmative program was totalitarian. Thus did a tactless answer to an irrelevancy lose a debate. What the first debater might have said was,

Our friends tell us that the majority opposes the affirmative policy. But what does this mean? That a policy should be opposed because it is opposed? If so, what would be the point of debating? The status quo could never be changed except by force. On the other hand, if they mean that the affirmative policy would be enacted against the will of the majority, they have given no proof. Since we must assume that people can be persuaded by reason, the real question is, is the affirmative policy contrary to their best interests? We have shown that it is not and we say, prove that it is.

EXERCISES

1. Define "proposition," "fact," and "inference."

2. Why are some propositions debatable? What is the relationship between probability and debatability?

3. Which of the following sentences are propositions? Which of the propositions may be designated as "factual statements" and which as "inferences"? What inferences, if any, are suggested by the factual statements?

a. Should we continue to give economic aid to the underdeveloped nations of Asia?

b. We should continue to give economic aid to South Korea.

c. Our development assistance program for the fiscal year 1957 was reduced to 27 million dollars.

d. Send your CARE package now!

e. The countries of Latin America have enjoyed much prosperity and progress during the past ten years.

f. Why should Americans be taxed to support slavery in Saudi Arabia?

g. I think that Nehru is a very distinguished-looking man.

h. Does United States economic aid promote the best interests of the United States?

i. But for the Marshall Plan, the French would have revised their constitution and built a sound economy.

j. I'm suspicious of Chou En-lai's overtures.

k. In the provinces where Italian per capita income is the highest, the Communists received 52 per cent of the total vote in the 1951–1952 elections.

l. Defense support is just another name for economic aid.

m. Although there is some waste in the present aid program, most aid goes where it will do the most good for the United States.

n. In the fiscal years 1955 and 1956, financial assistance to South Korea, the Indochinese states, Taiwan, and Pakistan accounted for over 60 per cent of all United States economic aid to less developed countries.

o. What is the purpose of United States economic aid?

p. Support our aid program! Write your congressman!

q. I'm especially fond of Brazilian coffee.

r. The Soviet Union plans to expand its industrial output by 65 per cent over the next five years, whereas even the most optimistic economists are not willing to forecast more than a 25 per cent advance in United States industrial output by the end of 1965.

s. Economic aid will strengthen the will of the underdeveloped nations to resist communism.

t. I believe that Congress will extend the Reciprocal Trade Agreements Act.

4. Classify the following propositions according to the four basic types:

a. Spiritual progress is a counterpart of economic progress.

b. Truman's foreign policy was basically sound.

c. Congress should enact a uniform divorce law.

d. Russia does not want war.

e. The United States is as much to blame for perpetuating the cold war as the Soviet Union.

f. The United States press is not free.

g. The jury system should be abolished.

h. Labor should have a direct share in management.

i. Abner Doubleday did not invent baseball.

j. Hitler's rise to power may be attributed largely to the Versailles Treaty.

k. Discontinuing direct economic aid would be in the best interests of the United States.

l. Public housing has been a failure.

m. Formal religions will eventually disappear.

n. Tension in the Formosa Straits is caused mainly by United States refusal to recognize Communist China.

5. Which criterion or criteria of a sound debate proposition do the following propositions fail to meet? Suggest suitable debate propositions for each.

a. Juvenile delinquency is harmful to society.

b. Congress should enact legislation to curb inflation.

c. The President should be empowered to make treaties with other nations.

d. The immoral practice of capital punishment should be abolished.

e. Direct price and wage controls should be instituted in times of economic emergency.

f. NATO should be reorganized.

g. Unemployment results in losses to the economy of the United States.

    h. Eighteen-year-olds should not be permitted to vote.

    i. The inefficient jury system should be abolished.

6. Phrase suitable debate propositions of policy for the following topics:

TVA	The Presidency
Price supports	United States trade
The educational system	Nuclear weapons
American Communists	Labor

7. Discuss the "fallacy of popular support."

CHAPTER 3

INTERPRETING AND DEFINING
THE TERMS OF THE PROPOSITION

A man that seeketh precise truth had need to remember what every name he useth stands for, and to place it accordingly, or else he will find himself entangled in words as a bird in lime twigs—the more he struggles the more belimed.

Thos. Hobbes

1. THE IMPORTANCE OF DEFINITION

How a team interprets and defines the terms of the resolution can greatly influence the development of its case. Some debaters, and even coaches, believe that the affirmative team, the first to deal with the problem of definition, may interpret terms in a way that facilitates winning debates, as if the framers of the question, like the oracle at Delphi, deliberately chose ambiguous terms to enable debaters to show some skill in word manipulation. However, the national high school and college debate topics chosen over the past ten years deal with real national and international problems and fairly specific proposals for solving them; and debaters are not individuals "bombinating in the void" or engaged in sophistical word play. Although the phrasing of a resolution is occasionally awkward or ambiguous, the intended meaning can usually be determined with a little effort. In no instance is there any reason to suppose that the framers intended to encourage the loose and equivocal definitions frequently conceived by debaters to win debates. To prevent quibbling and confusion, debaters should define their terms as honestly and logically as possible. After all, the truth and not the meaning of a resolution should be debatable.

2. AIDS IN DEFINITION

The best aids in definition are dictionaries, textbooks, and encyclopedias. A general dictionary may be used for common terms, but specialized dictionaries and textbooks (plus some study and research) must be used for such terms as "the guaranteed annual wage," "price and wage control," and "the law of comparative advantage."

3. THE CONTEXT OF THE QUESTION

To determine the meaning of a term, one must examine its complete context—social, political, economic, and historical as well as verbal. Since the debate resolution is almost invariably chosen because it embodies an issue of concern among certain groups of thinking people, the question will have for some time engaged some of the very best minds. Thus, the debater's problem usually is to find out what the terms have meant when used by certain experts. Presumably these people will have agreed upon a fairly precise definition of the terms well before the debater finds himself thinking about them. In the past twelve years, for example, every national college and high school debate topic had been previously discussed in public forums (in Congress, over radio and television, in the United Nations, etc.) or in periodicals and textbooks. Such is the underlying context or "climate" of the question that must be considered and that prevents one from stipulating private meanings.

Frequently debaters will ignore the underlying context to avoid defending what they believe to be a difficult position. For example, in 1953 most affirmative teams debating the question of permanent price and wage controls defined "controls" as a "restraining influence" or "price and wage controls" as a program which "permits prices and wages to fluctuate between certain floors and ceilings." Completely overlooked in the definition was the program which had been in effect during World War II—the Wage Stabilization Board, the OPA, and the OPS—as well as the meanings expressed in most elementary textbooks on economics. Besides being poor debate strategy, as we shall see in a moment, such definitions failed to meet the most important criterion of a logical definition, the criterion of equivalence, which we shall now consider.

4. THE CRITERION OF EQUIVALENCE

When we say that a definition must meet the criterion of equivalence, we mean that the term defined, known technically as the *definiendum*, must be equivalent in meaning to its definition, or *definiens;* i.e., we must be able to reverse the positions of the *definiendum* and the *definiens* in a sentence and still get a true statement. For example, the terms of the statement "All men are mammals" could not be reversed, for it is not true that all mammals are men. However, one could reverse the terms of the statement "all triangles are three-sided plane figures," for it is also true that all three-sided plane figures are triangles. The latter example, therefore, meets the test of equivalence, whereas the former does not.

To say that a definition must meet the test of equivalence is another way of saying that a logical definition must be neither too broad nor too narrow. If we were to define a hat as "an article of clothing worn on the head," the definition would be too broad, for bandannas and shawls are also worn on the head; if we defined it as "an article of clothing made of felt, worn on and shaped to fit the head, and having a crown," the definition would be too narrow, for it would exclude hats made of cloth or straw. In neither case would it be possible to reverse the positions of the *definiendum* and the *definiens* and still get a true statement. Now consider the definition of price and wage control as "anything which exerts a restraining influence on prices and wages." Reversing the terms, we get "anything which exerts a restraining influence on prices and wages is price and wage control." Thus, if the housewives of the country refused to buy meat for a week and thereby "restrained" the rising price of meat, this action, according to the definition given, would be "price control." Thus, we see, the definition is illogical because it is too broad.

5. THE PROBLEM OF RELATIVE TERMS

A special problem of definition is raised by the presence of relative terms in the debate proposition, terms like *fair, free, new, share, resist, welfare, advantage, development,* etc. Such words are inherently vague in that the realities to which they refer are not clear-cut; thus, the words, which merely signify the realities, have no sharp limits of meaning and therefore cannot be precisely defined. Take the characteristics, for example, frequently applied to water. Precisely when is water cold, cool, tepid, lukewarm, warm, hot, and very hot? It is apparent that these characteristics are imprecise and overlapping. However, the fact that they cannot be precisely defined does not mean that they cannot be defined at all or that such characteristics are meaningless. They are meaningful enough as anyone knows who has tried shaving with cold water. The point is, even though one cannot set exact limits to the meanings of such words, one must try to set approximate limits to them.

To say that a term is relative is not to imply that it has different meanings for different people but rather that its meaning is relative to some fixed frame of reference, namely, some standard of measurement. This standard is supposed to be the same for all, for if it varied from person to person communication would be impossible. If everyone had his own personal standard for warm water, for example, the concept "warm" would lose its meaning by having too many meanings. We define terms, set limits to their meaning literally, to make sure that there will be agreement upon their meaning, for only when there is such agreement can an intelligent exchange of ideas ensue. If the same words mean different things to two people, as they would with different frames of reference, the two people might just as well be talking to one another in two different languages.

6. THE PROBLEM OF VALUE TERMS

Of particular importance in debate are the relative terms which signify value judgments, words like *good, harmful, practical,* etc. To guard against the confusion which results from giving the same value words different meanings, debaters must agree beforehand on the meaning of the value words used, and this means agreeing on the standard of evaluation which determines the meaning. For example, before two teams can argue whether or not "price controls are beneficial" or "free trade is harmful," they must first agree on what they mean by "beneficial" or "harmful," and this means agreeing on a certain standard of measure, namely, beneficial or harmful to what end, for whom, and to what degree? If each had its own meaning for "beneficial" or "harmful," they obviously would not be debating the same proposition and the ensuing argument would be pointless. Since most debate questions affirm an evaluation, finding a common standard of measure or common goals is, as we shall see in the next chapter, a most important step in analysis.

If, in arguing a question of policy, an affirmative team deliberately ignores the implied goals or substitutes unwarranted ones, much wrangling over definition will result, especially if the negative interprets the new policy logically. Several years ago the national college debate topic was "Resolved, That the Non-Communist Nations Should Form a New International Organization." Although the phrase "a new international organization" seems vague, it really isn't when one considers the related term "non-Communist nations" and the underlying political context— the growing antagonism between the United States and the Soviet Union, their conflicts in the United Nations, and former President Hoover's speech proposing such an organization. Thus, the new organization was clearly an alternative to the United Nations and the common goal, world peace. By ignoring this goal, an affirmative team might argue for a new international chess association or, as some teams did, for a new international labor organization. In other words, these teams misdefined the key term and forced negative teams to debate their interpretation. Rather than argue the merits of an unwarranted policy, the negative should explain why the affirmative interpretation is illogical and evasive and then debate the proper policy. Though this does not make for a very interesting debate, a perceptive judge would penalize the affirmative.

7. THE MEANING OF "SHOULD"

The word "should," which identifies a policy resolution, embodies a basic concept presumably understood beforehand and thus should not have to be defined. However, many debaters do not understand the concept and define it erroneously. Many define it simply as "ought to," which is pointless since this term is no clearer than "should." Briefly, "should" means that the proposed policy is the best of available means to a certain desired end and is therefore logically desirable.

Frequently confusion arises when the negative team argues that the affirmative plan "will not" or "would not" come into existence or "will not" or "would not" be enforced, and the affirmative answers, "But we are arguing 'should' and not 'will' or 'would.'" In arguing against an international prohibition of nuclear weapons tests, a negative team might contend that the affirmative plan is impracticable because the Soviet Union and France would not join such an agreement or because the Soviet Union would not abide by its stipulations. This is a legitimate argument, which the affirmative may not glibly dismiss by stating, "But we are arguing that the Soviet Union and France should join, not that they would." For what can this mean? That the Soviet Union and France *should* join because by doing so they will help the affirmative to win the debate? Obviously not.

The only alternative is that "they should join" means that "they should want to join" or "they will realize it is to their best interest to join"—and it thus becomes an affirmative obligation to demonstrate that joining is indeed in these countries' own best interest. Admittedly, this interpretation assumes that people and nation-states are motivated chiefly by self-interest. But if debate did not take into account such realities, it would tend to be sterile. Of course, one might contend that "they should want to join" can also be translated into "they will want to promote the peace of the world and therefore will join"—which is an appealing but utterly quixotic argument. Other variations of the translation are possible, depending on the standard selected to establish why "they should want to join," but the standard selected here is undoubtedly the most realistic.

The "would"-"should" argument sometimes comes up in connection with public opinion polls introduced by the negative to show that a majority opposes the affirmative proposal. This argument is legitimate only if it aims to show that since the majority opposes the proposed legislation, the latter would not be enacted by Congress or would not be enforced. However, such arguments are weak since they overlook the factor of intensity. To disobey a law, people must oppose it *intensely;* and one must prove that this intensity exists. Congressmen are also influenced as much by intensity as by numbers, as evidenced by their occasionally enacting certain laws mildly opposed by the majority but intensely favored by a minority.

If a negative team argues that Congress would not enact the proposed legislation because a poll indicates that most Congressmen oppose it, the affirmative may answer that, since the legislation is in the best interests of the people, Congress can be persuaded to pass it. As long as the goals of Congress and those of the proposed legislation are the same, congressional opposition would not be an insurmountable obstacle. Congress has been known to enact legislation rejected in previous sessions.

On the other hand, if an affirmative team arguing for an international ban on nuclear weapons tests contended that such a ban would give the United States an advantage over the Soviet Union, the negative could legitimately argue that the Soviet Union would refuse to join since one objective of the affirmative plan (United States superiority over the Soviet Union) is contrary to that of one of the proposed members of the plan, the Soviet Union. In other words, the affirmative argument would be self-defeating. More will be said on this subject in Chapter 5.

8. OBTAINING LOGICAL DEFINITIONS

Now that we have seen some of the pitfalls of interpretation and definition, let us consider some actual propositions and see how one might go about interpreting and defining their terms. Since the problem of definition varies somewhat with the three different types of policy question, we shall consider each type separately. In each case the following outline will serve as a guide:

1. What is the new policy?
2. What type of policy is it? How does it relate to the status quo?
3. What is the key term, or essential feature, of the new policy? What is lacking at present?
4. What does the key term mean?

 a. What are the common objectives of the new and present policies?

 b. How does the essential feature of the status quo compare with that of the new policy?

 c. How has the key term been interpreted by professors, textbooks, debate handbooks, publicists, public officials, special dictionaries, and other assorted experts? What is the underlying context of the question?

5. Do any other terms require clarification?
6. How should the definitions be expressed?

Proposition 1: "Resolved, That the United States Should Extend Diplomatic Recognition to the Communist Government of China."

New Policy: Diplomatic recognition of Communist China.

Type of Policy: "Something-or-nothing" type, or, symbolically, *P* or not-*P;* i.e., the program advocated is for something nonexistent.

Key Term: Diplomatic recognition. The key term or characteristic of the new policy should not be difficult to recognize, for it identifies what is presently lacking.

Meaning of Key Term: Consulting authoritative sources, one finds in Smith and Zurcher's *New Dictionary of American Politics* that "recognition" is "acknowledgment by one state of the existence of another state or government. The President may recognize a foreign country by receiving its diplomatic envoy, sending a diplomat to it, negotiating a treaty with it, or issuing an appropriate proclamation." [1] One reads further in *White's Political Dictionary* that "recognition" is "acknowledging the independence and equality of a state and its right to be admitted into the family of nations." [2] Other sources, like the Institute of International Law,[3] say substantially the same thing. From these sources one concludes that "diplomatic recognition" is recognition involving an exchange of diplomats.

Other Terms: "United States," "Should," "Extend," "Communist Government of China" seem to be self-explanatory. There might be some question about "extend," which, according to a general dictionary, means "offer."

Expressing the Definitions: One should define only those terms which are not entirely clear. Sometimes paraphrasing the resolution is desirable. Here one might say: "We feel that the terms of the question are self-explanatory, with the possible exception of 'extend,' by which we mean 'offer'; and 'diplomatic recognition,' by which we mean 'the acknowledgment of a new political regime and its right to represent the state of China in the family of nations.' This would, of course, include the exchange of diplomatic agents with that government."

Proposition 2: "Resolved, That the Federal Government Should Adopt a Policy of Permanent Wage and Price Control."

New Policy: Permanent wage and price control.

Type of Policy: Alternative, or symbolically *P* or *Q.* Since wages and prices are determined by some policy at present, this is an alternative policy.

Key Term (What is presently lacking?): "permanent control."

Meaning of Key Term: How does the proposed policy compare with

---

[1] Edward C. Smith and Arnold J. Zurcher, *New Dictionary of American Politics* (New York: Barnes and Noble, Inc., 1949), p. 320.

[2] Wilbur W. White, *White's Political Dictionary* (Cleveland: The World Publishing Company, 1947), p. 241.

[3] *American Journal of International Law,* XXX, Supplement (1936), p. 185.

the present one? How are prices and wages determined at present? From economics professors and textbooks we learn: (1) They are influenced by the law of supply and demand, (2) They are influenced by certain governmental monetary and fiscal policies. (Both influences may be called "permanent indirect controls.") (3) In times of emergency, particularly during wartime, they are directly fixed or set by certain governmental agencies, like the OPA, the OPS, and the National Wage Stabilization Board during World War II. (These are the temporary "direct controls.")

Since the status quo consists of permanent indirect controls and temporary direct controls, the term "permanent control" must mean "permanent direct control," or the direct fixing of prices and wages by the government for an indefinite period of time, not just during emergency periods. Further analysis reveals that "control" (in the resolution) cannot mean "indirect control," for if it did the affirmative would have to support the status quo, which is contrary to established procedure. Further proof that "control" here means "direct control" is furnished by economists, who, in discussing "price control" or "wage control," clearly indicate they mean *direct* price control or *direct* wage control. Professor Seymour E. Harris of Harvard, for example, says: "Price control is a method for establishing prices by legal means, thus to circumvent the law of supply and demand, which if allowed to take its course in wartime, would lead to high prices and low supplies—to economic collapse and defeat." [4] White's *Political Dictionary* defines "price control" (or "price stabilization") as "the process of setting a whole scale of maximum prices to prevent all from rising, and to maintain the fairness of prices in relation one to another." [5] Thus, the main issue is: man-made (or direct) law versus economic (or indirect) law.

Do Other Terms Need to be Defined? No; the meaning of terms like "Federal Government," "Should," "Adopt," and "Policy" is self-evident.

Expressing the Definition: "A policy of permanent wage and price control may be defined as a program under which wages and prices would be directly fixed by a governmental agency or agencies for an indefinite period of time."

Some of the blame for the confusing definitions given by affirmative debaters when debating this proposition in 1951–1952 must fall on the framers of the question because they omitted the word "direct." Although logical analysis reveals that "direct" was clearly implied, debaters should not be unnecessarily burdened.

Unfortunately, the framers of the national high school and college topics are sometimes careless in other respects. For example, the 1956–

---

[4] Seymour E. Harris, *Price and Related Controls in the United States* (New York: McGraw-Hill Book Company, Inc., 1945), p. 43.

[5] White, p. 225.

1957 college topic, "Resolved, That the United States Should Discontinue Giving Direct Economic Aid to Foreign Countries," is ambiguous. The term "discontinue giving direct economic aid" may mean that indirect economic aid should be given instead or that no economic aid should be given. Actually, the context favors the former interpretation. Verbally, the suggestion is like that contained in the statement, "It's about time you stopped reading such books," the suggestion being that you should start reading other types of books and not that you should stop reading altogether. The underlying intellectual context also implies indirect aid since simple discontinuance would be politically suicidal. However, debaters should not be burdened by having to seek out such implications. If the terms of a resolution are too vague, misinterpretations are bound to arise.

Proposition 3: "Resolved, That the Further Development of Nuclear Weapons Should Be Prohibited by International Agreement."

New Policy: The prohibition of the further development of nuclear weapons.

Type of Policy: Since the new policy is simply a rejection or discontinuation of the present policy, it is the "nothing-or-something" type, or, symbolically, not-*P* or *P*. The clue to recognizing this type of policy is a negative concept, like "discontinue," "prohibit," "make illegal," "reject," and "abolish."

Key Term: Since the new policy is a negative concept, the chief concern here is with the essential feature of the present policy. In other words, what is to be stopped or discontinued? "Further development."

Meaning of Key Term: Since the new policy is expressed directly in terms of the present one, its essential characteristic should be well known and thus relatively easy to define. In the present instance, however, the term "development" is not only comparatively unfamiliar but also quite vague, being preferred for some reason to the commonly used and more specific term "tests." Unfortunately, there is no formula for coping with a poorly phrased resolution. One must use some imagination and common sense. The best course here would probably be to try to relate the two terms, which, as it happens, can be done. Consulting several expert sources, one finds that in 1957, Dr. Willard F. Libby, Chairman of the Atomic Energy Commission, said, "Cessation of tests would, to all intents and purposes, end shortly our developmental work"; [6] in 1958, the Advisory Committee on Biology and Medicine of the American Science Association stated, "No such development [of nuclear weapons] can be carried out successfully without tests"; [7] and other scientists writing in the *Bulletin of the Atomic Scientists* have expressed essentially

[6] *Foreign Policy Bulletin,* XXXVI (July 15, 1957), p. 163.

[7] "Statement on Radioactive Fallout," *American Scientist,* XLVI (June, 1958), p. 149.

the same view.[8] Thus, one would be justified in interpreting the development of nuclear weapons as a process dependent upon testing and unlikely to occur if testing were prohibited.

Do Other Terms Need to be Defined? Possibly the term "nuclear weapon" since there might be some confusion between a weapon and a weapons carrier like an atomic submarine. Consulting the *United States Air Force Dictionary* (1956, p. 564), one would find the distinction clearly made. If he preferred not to define this term in his introduction, he should have the definition ready in case the opposition asked for it.

Expressing the Definition: "The affirmative interprets development as a process involving observation, hypothesis, and testing. Since testing is an integral part of this process, we feel that by stopping tests, we would effectively stop development; for, as the Advisory Committee on Biology and Medicine of the American Science Association indicated in June, 1958, no development of nuclear weapons 'can be carried out successfully without tests.'"

If a negative team chose to argue that stopping tests would not completely stop development since there is nothing to prevent observation and forming hypotheses, a judge might resent this attack as quibbling, or "splitting hairs," since the affirmative definition is logical.[9] That is, the negative should attack only unrealistic or evasive definitions.

9. HANDLING FAULTY DEFINITIONS

Evasive and illogical definitions not only reduce academic debate to a form of sophistry but are actually poor debate strategy. Such definitions are usually resorted to by teams who want to defend a more moderate position than that called for by the resolution. Many affirmative teams— and the charge is particularly true of them—undoubtedly feel that by offering a watered-down interpretation of the affirmative policy they can avoid an extreme or difficult position and defend a moderate one. However, evasive definitions, though sometimes successful, are usually poor strategy not only because they leave one open to the charge of being illogical but also because cases built upon them are usually much weaker than those based upon logical definitions.

For example, if an affirmative team debating the question of "Perma-

[8] See L. W. Nordheim, "Tests of Nuclear Weapons," *Bulletin of the Atomic Scientists,* XI (September, 1955), p. 253, and Eugene Rabinowitch, "Science and the Affairs of Men," *ibid.,* XII (May, 1956), p. 139.

[9] Such an attack might be self-defeating in another way, for the negative could not later claim that the affirmative program would be disadvantageous because the United States would be unable to develop small tactical nuclear weapons. That is, it would not be consistent to claim that the affirmative program would simultaneously not stop and stop development.

nent Price and Wage Controls" interpreted this policy as a permanent provision for a program to be used temporarily (a definition used by practically every affirmative which debated this question in 1951–1952), it would find itself defending the present policy and thus without a real "need for a change" issue. And without such an issue, it would be hard to win. The best it could do would be to invent a problem or present a trivial one, whereas a logical definition would at least make possible a significant "need for a change" issue (as shown on pp. 48–50). Turning to an actual debate, let us see how the minor problem concocted by the affirmative—a so-called "time lag"—was handled by the opposition:

Now to get into this debate immediately, I would like to say that the difference between the affirmative and the negative today is not very great. There is practically no difference between the plan envisaged by the gentlemen of the opposition and the status quo. It leaves us wondering if we traveled about three thousand miles by plane to debate whether we should have a board that would sit around to wait to do the same things that Congress does now. Now why do I say that? Let's look at some of the objections leveled against the status quo, and see what the gentlemen of the opposition have proposed to meet them. The gentleman has said that we are going to have a time lag because Congress has to identify the inflation; then it has to get together the controls. What does the plan envisage for the board to do? They will study the economy; they will identify the bad inflation when it comes, tailor a plan to fit it, and then put it into operation. According to the status quo, Congress does it; according to the new affirmative plan, a centralized board in Washington waits for the inflation to rise, studies it, and tailors a plan to meet it.[10]

To take another example, in 1952–1953, most affirmative teams had a field day manipulating the terms of the question, "The United States Should Adopt a Policy of Free Trade." The commonest evasion involved "exceptions" to a policy of free trade: exceptions for vital defense industries, for the farmer, for the merchant marine, and for whatever an affirmative team thought it could get away with. Another type of evasion involved the time when this program would go into effect, this being anywhere from five to twenty-five years. Other affirmative teams excluded Russia and her satellites from the program, and some even advocated reciprocal free trade, that is, free trade only with those countries willing to reciprocate. Such evasions were not only a confession of weakness and a lack of confidence in the affirmative position but also made that position more vulnerable to contradictions and undermined its "need for a change."

The "exceptions" raised the question, is the affirmative really advocating "free trade"? With agriculture, probably the nation's number one

[10] Holt Spicer, University of Redlands, debating in the final round of the West Point Tournament, April 25, 1952.

industry, and "defense industries" (where is the line drawn here?) excepted, a judge might have some real doubts. Moreover, such exceptions admit that trade restrictions (tariffs, quotas, subsidies, etc.) are desirable in certain important areas, which of course is the negative position.

The five, ten, or twenty-five-year time lag is also a fairly obvious equivocation, for, unless otherwise stated, a resolution always calls for adopting a policy *now*. This provision also undermines the affirmative case since a future program suggests the lack of a present problem. A negative team might ask, how serious can the problem be if the affirmative is willing to wait several years, or where is the proof of a future problem? Moreover, since the affirmative wishes to retain the present program for several years, it suggests that this program is in some way desirable, once again the negative position.

Certain minor "exceptions" or qualifications are legitimate if they are in keeping with the spirit of the resolution. In arguing for a cessation of all nuclear bomb explosions, for example, an affirmative team might allow nuclear explosions for economic purposes—the building of harbors, dams, etc. Though a legitimate exception, even this could be self-defeating since the negative could argue that the task of enforcing the ban on nuclear explosions for other purposes would now be greatly complicated. An alternative course would be to make no exceptions and simply concede that the affirmative plan would not be perfect. Since this approach is quite realistic, it would not be very damaging.

10. EQUIVOCATION

When both sides agree to the meaning of a term, neither side may now employ a second meaning for it. Giving a term two different meanings, whether intentionally or not, is called *equivocation*. For example, if the meaning of "job discrimination" has been established as "the act of depriving an individual of gainful employment because of race, religion, or national origin," one may not subsequently argue that "discrimination" is "selection on the basis of sound judgment" and therefore justified. This would be evasion by equivocation. Ironically, in debates on permanent price and wage controls negative debaters were often accused of equivocating when they objected to the affirmative's equivocal definitions of "control" as "any restraining influence" and "a permanent program" as "a permanent provision for a program which would be used temporarily." When debaters use illogical definitions, the ensuing debate becomes one on semantics rather than on the comparative merits of two programs.

In conclusion, to build sound cases debaters must know the criteria of a sound definition, the nature of evaluations, and how to interpret a question logically. Ignorance of these matters leads to faulty analysis and in turn to faulty strategy, weaknesses apparent in many debate cases.[11]

EXERCISES

1. Discuss Voltaire's statement: "If you would converse with me, define your terms."

2. What are the most useful aids to a debater for interpreting and defining the terms of the resolution?

3. How does the context of the question relate to the meaning of its key terms?

4. Define "equivalence" as a criterion of a sound definition.

5. What is the meaning of "should" in a proposition of policy? How is this concept related to "will," "could," "can," and "would"?

6. What is the meaning of (a) a "relative" term, (b) a "value" term? Give three examples of each type and indicate how you would go about defining them. Write a brief definition for each of your examples.

7. Indicate which of the three general types of policy is involved in the following questions. Identify and define the key term of each question.

a. "Price Supports for the Farmer Should be Abolished."

b. "The President of the United States Should be Elected by a Direct Vote of the People."

c. "Gambling Should be Legalized in the United States."

8. Evaluate the definitions involved in the following statements or arguments. Explain why they are sound or unsound.

a. Freedom of speech is the right of an individual to say whatever he pleases.

b. The national debt is money owed by the United States government to private individuals and companies.

c. Intoxicating beverages are those which contain alcohol.

d. Foreign economic aid consists of sending technicians abroad to help train the people of other countries in the fields of agriculture, forestry, fisheries, health and sanitation, and education.

e. A fair employment practices law is one which guarantees workers suitable or fair working conditions.

f. Discrimination is the rejection of an individual because of his color.

g. Free trade is the right of one country to trade with any other country it chooses.

h. The unemployment compensation program is that program which has been designed to supplement the income of workers when they are unemployed.

i. Our friends contend that Senator D . . . has a liberal voting record. But

[11] Some of the foregoing material appeared originally in two articles by the writer: "Interpreting the Debate Question," *DAPC Bulletin*, XVIII (December, 1952), pp. 13–19; and "Honest Definitions Are the Best Policy," *ibid.*, XIX (December, 1953), pp. 4–11.

what do they mean by "liberal"? Some of our best minds have been unable to define the term precisely.

j. By an international agreement (to suspend nuclear weapons tests) we mean an agreement between the United States, Great Britain, and France.

k. Affirmative arguing for the adoption of a guaranteed annual wage: To be eligible for twelve months of a guaranteed annual wage a worker would have to be employed a minimum of two years and four months by the company.

l. Then they ask us, how are we going to get all industries to adopt a guaranteed annual wage in the first place? But you will note that the topic reads that they "should," that they ought to, not that they will, and so this objection is not pertinent to the debate.

m. (See *k*) If a worker doesn't become eligible until after four months and then gets one month's wage for every two worked, he must work two years and four months to get a guaranteed annual wage. This doesn't meet the terms of the resolution.

n. (See *l*) But the point is, why should they adopt this plan if it is not to their best interests to do so? We have seen the disadvantages that would accrue to them if they did adopt it. Therefore, they should not want to adopt it and would not. Moreover, since such a program would bankrupt many companies, as our statistics show, many of them could not adopt it. Thus we see that many industries should not, should not want to, will not, and could not adopt the affirmative plan. To dismiss this argument by saying simply we are arguing "should" or "ought to" and not "will" is to evade the entire issue.

o. Our friends speak of aid to underdeveloped nations. But just what exactly is "underdeveloped"? Economists and political scientists don't always agree on the meaning of this term.

CHAPTER 4

ANALYSIS: IS THERE A NEED FOR CHANGING THE STATUS QUO?[1]

> It requires a very unusual mind to undertake the analysis of the obvious.
>
> *A. N. Whitehead*

Analysis may be described as the process of breaking down an entity into its component parts and examining the relationships among them. Accordingly, analysis of a debate resolution may be described as the process of determining the main points or arguments which, when developed, "prove" the truth or falsity of the resolution. Since such points when contested by the opposition are called the basic issues, analysis of the debate resolution may be said to be primarily a search for the basic issues inherent in the resolution. Since all questions of policy involve two causal hypotheses, such questions can be analyzed quite systematically by inquiring into and applying the principles of causation. Before doing so, however, let us recall the nature and meaning of a question of policy, or what logicians call a "normative proposition."

First, it will be recalled that questions of policy contain the word "should" or its equivalent: "Resolved, That all Electric Power Facilities in the United States *Should* be Operated by Private Enterprise"; second, that "should" in this context means logically desirable or that the proposed policy is the most logical or the best of available means to a certain desired end. Thus, policy questions involve a means–end relationship, the means being the policy advocated, the policy in existence, or other available policies, and the end being certain mutually desired goals.

[1] Since policy questions are the most complex type of question and involve all other types, the following discussion will deal exclusively with policy questions.

1. COMMON OBJECTIVES

Before we can explore the various means-end relationships, we must know specifically the means and ends involved. As to the means, the resolution provides the answer directly, for it is the policy advocated and, by implication, the policy in existence, also called the status quo. Occasionally, the negative team may introduce still another policy (in lieu of the existing policy) and call it a counterplan or substitute plan, in which case, this, too, must be considered. So that there may be agreement on the meaning of the policies to be discussed, they are usually defined at the outset unless their meaning is self-evident. Since we have already considered the problems involved here, let us turn to the second consideration, the mutually desired end, or the common goals sought.

On rare occasions the resolution will specify this end (e.g., "Resolved, That Congress Should Grant Subsidies to the Various States *For the Purpose of Equalizing Educational Opportunities Throughout the Nation in Tax-supported Schools*," the end being the italicized phrase), but usually the student must determine it himself. In doing so, he is limited by the same factors which limit any definition. Thus, he must consult textbooks and other authoritative commentaries and consider the underlying social, political, economic, and historical context of the question. In most debates between American students the political context must be interpreted in terms of the major goals of a democratic society. Set forth in the Preamble to the Constitution, these are "to form a more perfect union, establish justice, insure domestic tranquility, provide for the common defense, promote the general welfare, and secure the blessings of liberty to ourselves and our posterity." These goals must be considered for questions of national, state, and local character. For questions involving the United States and other countries, "to promote the best interests of the United States to the greatest possible extent" is a desirable and readily agreed upon goal.

In debates between American students the aforementioned goals may be designated as self-evident truths which do not have to be justified or defended. On the other hand, a different context calls for different goals. If, for example, the proposition "Communist China Should be Admitted to the UN" were debated by American and Russian delegates to the UN, the goal obviously could not be "to promote the best interests of the United States to the fullest possible extent" but would have to be a commonly sought goal like "to promote and maintain international peace." If the opposing debaters insisted upon different goals, the ensuing debate would actually be on two different interpretations and would thus make little sense. Theoretically, there are situations where debate would be impossible because of utterly irreconcilable goals. For example, if someone held the destruction of the human race as a desirable goal, debate with him would normally be impossible. However, debate is usually possible even with those whose immediate goals differ radically from one's own, for immediate goals are themselves usually means to other goals, which in turn may lead to a mutually agreed on goal.[2]

The common goal, also called "rationale," often embraces several factors. For example, in a debate on an international trade policy for the United States, the common goal might be:

1. Maximizing United States consumer satisfaction (or providing goods and services for the American people at the lowest possible prices)

2. Maintaining harmonious relations with our allies

3. Strengthening the free world against the threat of Communist aggression

The important point is, the meaning of the end as well as of the means must be agreed on before any intelligent discussion of the relationship between end and means can occur.

Having identified the means (or policies) and the end (or goals), we can now inquire into the basic components, or the "stock issues," of a policy question. These issues revolve around the questions "Is there a need for changing the status quo?" and "Would the affirmative plan meet the need?" Each involves several subissues, which shall now be considered.

2. AFFIRMATIVE APPROACH TO THE NEED ISSUE [3]

The need issue is probably the most important and least understood of the various issues and subissues. It is important, for it is the foundation for other issues; a poorly conceived need issue results not only in a weak affirmative case but in a poor debate. The many misconceptions concerning this issue suggest that it is also the least understood.

The Underlying Logic of the Need Issue

To understand the need issue, one must understand the underlying logic that requires this issue in the first place. Since the new policy is

---

[2] For an interesting discussion of this subject, see Lionel Ruby, *Logic: An Introduction* (Philadelphia: J. B. Lippincott Company, 1950), pp. 485ff. To illustrate the point that "cases where discussion [or debate] must *necessarily* fail are rare," Ruby indicates the line of argument that a humanitarian and a Nazi discussing the question "Is Naziism Morally Wrong?" might pursue in arriving at some agreed-upon goal.

[3] For convenience, we shall use the abbreviated term "need issue" whenever referring to the issue initiated by the question "Is there a need for changing the status quo?"

presumably the best of available means, it is presumably better than the present policy or any other policy the negative may choose to introduce. Thus, the affirmative policy must be compared with other available policies. Since the only other available policy the affirmative presumably knows about at the outset is the status quo, it must begin its comparison by evaluating the status quo. Should the first negative speaker advocate a different policy, the affirmative would then have to stop evaluating the status quo and begin evaluating the negative's alternative policy. However, since the first affirmative speaker doesn't know the negative strategy, he must begin by evaluating the status quo.

The Presumption Favoring the Negative

Since the affirmative is contending that its own policy is better than the present one, it must prove it. If the affirmative could do no more than show that its policy was as good as the present one, then the latter presumably should be retained since it is already in existence and presumably has worked, however imperfectly, for some time.[4] In this regard, most writers on debate speak of "a presumption in favor of the negative," by which they mean that, before a debate on a new policy begins, the negative in being able to defend the status quo has an advantage over the affirmative. The reason given is that most people inherently resist change. This explanation, however, is somewhat misleading. That people inherently oppose change under normal circumstances is a well-founded generalization. But to a large degree this intrinsic conservatism is irrational, reflecting an emotional attachment to what already exists—what is, is right. A consideration like this can only be irrelevant (logically) to any burden carried by an affirmative team. What is relevant, however, is that change involves some work or readjustment. Thus, it must be proved that the affirmative policy will work not only as well as or even slightly better than the status quo, but much better in order to compensate for the difficulty of changing the status quo and for the inevitable readjustments.

Most important of all, perhaps, is that the status quo is *known* to be functioning, however imperfectly, whereas in advocating a new policy one can only argue what *will probably* happen; and, as the saying goes, a bird in the hand is worth two in the bush. Thus, the affirmative burden is a burden of *proof*; and since the status quo is almost never a total

---

[4] Only under extraordinary circumstances does it become clear that an extant policy has failed almost totally. The economic catastrophe of the early 1930s might be cited as a case in point. During those years the feeling was widely prevalent that the economic system was radically disordered. Then, if ever in American history, a quite clear presumption lay in favor of the advocates of change, justifying Franklin Roosevelt's assertion, "The country needs, the country demands, bold experimentation." But the circumstances were, as earlier suggested, truly extraordinary.

failure, affirmative teams will almost always have a presumption (varying with the degree of the status quo's failure) to overcome. The extent of the presumption will vary also with the nature of the question and its susceptibility to being proved affirmatively.[5] The two factors (first, that the status quo has been somewhat—and determinably—successful; second, that the affirmative policy can hardly be presented in such a way as to eliminate all doubt that it will be successful) seem to interact to make up the negative presumption. Needless to say, if a negative team chose not to defend the status quo, it would forego its initial advantage.

Summing up, the affirmative team must first consider, is there a need for changing the status quo? In answer, it must prove that the status quo is not only inferior to the proposed policy but so inferior that minor changes could not make it equal to the new policy. For, again, if minor changes could, the advantage would lie with a status quo requiring only minor changes as against a new policy requiring major ones. Thus, proving that the status quo is inherently defective or defective beyond practical repair constitutes the affirmative need.

Common Misconceptions of the Need

Before considering how the affirmative proves a need, let us consider some common misconceptions, or how not to prove it.

Confusing Need with "Need for the Affirmative Plan"

A very common confusion is to interpret the term "need" as "need for the affirmative plan," an entirely separate issue. Clearly, one could show that the status quo is not working or that a problem exists without taking the further step of showing that a particular plan will solve the problem. A need-for-plan issue could follow a need-for-changing-the-status-quo issue, but the two should be kept distinct. To avoid unnecessary confusion or equivocation, the term "need for the affirmative plan" should be avoided.

Confusing Need with Common Objectives

Another misconception, held usually only by very inexperienced debaters, is that of interpreting the "need" to mean the common goals.

[5] For example, if one were advocating the erection of a new school, there would be less of a presumption in favor of the status quo than if one were advocating lowering the voting age to eighteen. This is so because it would be appreciably easier for the affirmative to "prove" that a school with the appropriate specifications could be built than it would be to anticipate all the consequences of lowering the voting age. There would be, in short, less left to doubt about the new school proposition. The affirmative here could virtually guarantee (so high is the probability) that it will deliver what it says it will (on the school), while lowering the voting age touches upon so many other economic, political, and social questions as to leave one wondering just what would happen if an alteration were made.

Thus, the entire issue is sometimes dismissed in a phrase or two, like "The need is obvious. We need peace in the world." Or "As to the need, it is clear that the worker needs security." Since this interpretation begs the question—i.e., it assumes that the goals are not being presently achieved, which is precisely what must be proved—it dooms an affirmative team at the very outset.

The "Comparative Advantage" Need

Another confusing approach to the need is the "comparative advantage need." In effect, the approach here is that no serious problem exists— the status quo is working well—but the affirmative program would be more advantageous than the existing one. As one debater once put it, "Although we didn't know what we were missing when there were no electric lights, the world was a much better place to live in when Edison finally invented the incandescent bulb." Actually, this is an indirect and somewhat confusing attempt to show that there really is a need for changing the status quo; for if the affirmative program would result in some important gain, the absence of that gain is really a defect of the status quo. Thus, the suggestion that the status quo is working well is contradicted by the subsequent claim made for the affirmative plan. This "negative" approach to the need may well be lost on both the opposition and the judge, with the opposition contending that, if the present program is wholly adequate as the affirmative claims, why institute a completely new program on such tenuous grounds that it might be better than what we have; why chance something untried and unproved? And the judge will probably agree and vote accordingly.

Confusing Need with "Not Necessary"

Still another confusing and strategically weak approach to the need is the contention that "the status quo is not necessary," the reasoning here being that if the status quo is not needed, it should be discarded (or changed). In effect, this approach also concedes that there is no real problem at present but argues that the desired goals could be achieved without the present policy. However, if present results are desirable, a judge isn't likely to accept the notion that an important change should be made because it would do no harm. For, again, the presumption favors what is *known* rather than what *might be.*

Clearly, "not necessary" or "not needed" does not mean the same as "there is a need for a change." If an appendix, for example, did not perform any necessary function in the body, one could say that it was not needed; but one would hardly be justified in advocating that for this reason it should be removed. Why hazard a serious operation if no harm is being done?

When an affirmative team argues that the status quo is "not necessary," it is really anticipating negative objections to its proposal. For the negative will probably argue that the status quo performs certain necessary functions which will be eliminated by the removal of the status quo. However, when the affirmative first argues that the status quo is not necessary, this argument does not constitute any compelling need for a change; the argument merely says that a change would not be objectionable.

Realizing that this approach is weak, some affirmative teams go one step further and claim that the status quo has a minor defect which would be eliminated by the affirmative proposal. In effect, this argument reduces to: both programs are desirable, but the affirmative program is slightly more desirable. As already pointed out, this approach is very weak and would hardly counteract the presumption favoring a program admittedly working well.

Equating Need with Existing Evils

Finally, many debaters erroneously equate the need with certain existing evils. This approach, as we shall see in a moment, overlooks an important aspect of the need, namely, that the evils are caused by the present policy. To assume this causal connection is fallacious reasoning, specifically the *post hoc ergo propter hoc* fallacy (discussed in Chapter 11).

In ignoring the cause of existing evils, affirmative debaters often find themselves with "evils" that are unrelated to and therefore cannot be eliminated by their proposal. In advocating the diplomatic recognition of Communist China, for example, some affirmative teams contended that there was much unrest in the world—in Kashmir, Morocco, Algeria, Indochina, Burma, and Tibet. How this evil was related to nonrecognition or could be eliminated by recognition could not be demonstrated, as alert negative teams were quick to point out.

Affirmative debaters will also find the negative agreeing that evils exist but arguing that, since they are unrelated to the status quo, there is no need for changing the latter. In other words, some *other existing policy* might be at fault, but that would be no reason for changing the policy at issue. For example, in debates on Federal aid to education affirmative teams often consumed the entire first affirmative speech vividly pointing out the shortcomings of our educational system, whereupon an alert negative team would respond, "Yes, we agree; our educational system is far from perfect. But that is not the real issue. The real issue is, are insufficient funds always the cause and, if so, should additional funds be provided by the Federal government or by state and private agencies?" This answer clearly indicated the affirmative's failure to show a real need for changing the present system of financing education, a need which it now had to prove after consuming one whole constructive speech.

Defects of the Status Quo

As we have seen, the criterion for evaluating a policy is the goals sought. In evaluating the status quo, therefore, the affirmative must first consider the question, "Is the present policy achieving certain desired goals, or are the established goals being met under the status quo?" The answer must be no (for if it were yes, there would be no point to the debate) and must be supported with evidence, i.e., facts and expert testimony. Since the goals in question are by mutual consent desirable, any failure to reach them must be considered undesirable, or "evil." In effect, then, this step consists of citing certain existing evils. For example, if domestic tranquility were the desired goal, any manifestation of domestic strife would be undesirable or evil; if the most effective allocation of economic resources were the desired goal, any manifestation of wasted resources would be undesirable or evil; or if harmonious relations between the United States and her allies were the desired goal, any manifestation of friction would be undesirable or evil.

Since evils vary in size, the evils cited by the affirmative must be significant, or constitute a serious problem. If not, there wouldn't be much need for changing the present policy. Actually, a serious problem may also encompass potential rather than actual evils. For example, if during recess a group of school children habitually congregated in a dangerous area, a worried parent might argue that it should not be permitted to because of what might happen rather than what has happened. Similarly, in debating the question "The Continued Development of Nuclear Weapons Should Be Prohibited by International Agreement" (the 1958–1959 national college topic), an affirmative team had to consider not so much existing evils as the threat of future ones (from increased radioactive fallout and the danger of small irresponsible nations getting nuclear weapons).

Since effects are in turn causes of other effects, an affirmative may also show, if time permits, that certain evil effects have led to other evil effects, like unemployment leading to lowered health standards. Sometimes, an affirmative must do this, when the main "evil" does not appear too significant. For example, affirmative debaters advocating the guaranteed annual wage (the national college topic for 1955–1956) had the problem of showing that unemployment was serious in our economy when there was relatively full employment. Actually, there are several ways of dealing with this type of situation:

1. Show related effects which are not too well known or realized
2. Show that the evil is preventable but not under the status quo

3. Show the existence of certain factors which are holding the evil in check but only temporarily

4. Show the probability of new factors entering which will change the picture shortly

(In other words, in steps 3 and 4 try to prove a potentially significant evil.)

Let us see how all four might be applied to the G.A.W. question:

We are aware that there are some people who would discount the gravity of the unemployment problem in the United States today. After all, they say, average unemployment for 1955 was only 2¾ millions. We believe this optimism to be unjustified and the problem to be serious for four reasons:

1. The problem is serious because these 2¾ millions of workers are not statistics but human beings with human sensibilities. Since not only the worker is affected but also his dependents, and since the average family has four persons, there are actually about eleven million people bearing the hardships of unemployment.

2. The present problem is also serious because a great deal of the unemployment that occurred could have been prevented. As Under Secretary of Labor Arthur Larson said: "Any avoidable unemployment is unfortunate, and we should never rest as long as these figures can be reduced." In other words, any avoidable unemployment constitutes a serious problem.

3. As serious as the unemployment problem is, it would be even more serious were it not for the fact that defense expenditures are artificially stimulating our economy; and there are indications that such expenditures are to be decreased in the near future. [Proof.]

4. Moreover, the situation promises to become worse in the immediate future for two other reasons: automation and the return of certain normal seasonal and cyclical patterns.

a. As to automation, we read in *Traffic World*, etc.

b. As to seasonal and cyclical patterns, Economist Richard Lester of Princeton University has said in 1954: "Etc." The recent sharp downturns in production and employment in the automobile industry bear out the validity of Professor Lester's statement.

Citing significant evils, then, existing or potential, is the first part of the affirmative need.

Inherency

As to why the preceding step does not suffice for the entire need, consider the following analogy: Suppose that my automobile had two flat tires, a dented fender, a set of faulty sparkplugs, and a broken window but was basically sound otherwise; would I be justified on the basis of these evils in getting another car? No. Why not repair these existing defects instead of going to a much greater expense of getting another car or taking the chance of getting a used car with an inferior motor? In other words, to justify a change, one must prove that the status quo cannot be repaired or is not worth repairing, that it is inherently defective or so bad that repairs would be impractical, that no amount of patching would eliminate the serious flaw. To prove this, one must consider the question, "Why are the established goals not being met under the status quo, or what has caused the evils?" To this question the answer must be, the present policy. Only thus can the affirmative show a need for changing the present policy. For, according to the law of cause and effect, an effect can be eliminated only by eliminating its cause; thus, if evil effects are caused by the present policy, they can be eliminated only by eliminating their cause, the present policy. In other words, there is a need for changing the present policy.

In speaking of the present policy, what we really mean is its essential characteristic, and this, as we have seen, is not always easy to determine. If the affirmative policy is the "something-or-nothing" type, i.e., P or not-P, the present policy is essentially the lack of P—and the lack of P's essential characteristic must be identified as the cause. For example, if the affirmative policy is a compulsory program, like compulsory FEPC, then voluntary behavior, or the lack of compulsion, must be shown as the cause of the problem. On the other hand, if the affirmative policy is the "nothing-or-something" type, i.e., not-P or P, then P's essential characteristic must be identified as the cause. For example, if the affirmative policy is a voluntary program, like voluntary unionism, then compulsion, or compulsory unionism, must be shown as the cause of the problem.

In identifying the essential characteristic of the status quo as the cause, an affirmative need not contend that it is the entire cause but rather an important part of the cause or an insurmountable obstacle to solving the problem. For example, if a landlord were taking advantage of his tenants and a certain law prevented the civil authorities from interfering, one might argue that, though the law was not the direct cause of the abuses suffered by the tenants, it prevented the authorities from acting and was thus an insurmountable obstacle to solving the problem. In one sense, the law may be considered a contributing causal factor of the abuses and in another, *the* cause of the authorities' inability to remedy them. In debating the question "Resolved, That Membership in a Labor Organization as a Condition of Employment Should Be Illegal" (the 1957–1958 topic), affirmative teams had to decide whether to try proving that compulsory unionism was a contributing causal factor of certain union abuses or the major cause of the inability to eliminate these abuses. Doing the latter would probably be clearer to a judge.

Equating the essential characteristic of the status quo with the cause of existing or potential evils is frequently complex and calls for careful analysis. Although it is probably the most important phase of the affirmative case, many affirmative teams either ignore it or muddle through it in such a way that their case collapses under the first impact of the negative attack.

Sample Analysis of Need

To tie up some of the preceding points, let us consider how the need for a complex question like price and wage controls might be developed. It will be assumed here that the affirmative has already investigated and identified the present policy and has determined the desired goals. The following questions will be used to pinpoint the need issue and its two subissues:

1. Is there a need for changing the status quo (as previously identified)?

a. Are there indications that the desired goals (also identified) have not been (are not being, or will not be) achieved? Has the status quo produced (is it producing, or will it produce) significant evils?

b. Why have these evils resulted? What, specifically, has caused them?

Stated affirmatively, the need issue and its two subissues will be developed in accordance with the following outline:

1. There is a need for changing the status quo.

a. The status quo has failed (is failing, or will fail), for

b. The status quo has failed (is failing, or will fail) because

In the foregoing substeps attention is called to the important distinction between the words "for" and "because." Confusion may arise because in some contexts the two terms are synonymous, but as used here their meanings are distinctly different. This difference may be explained thus:

"For" indicates that the statement which follows it contains a specific instance (or instances) of the more general assertion which precedes it; i.e., it indicates that the subsequent statement exemplifies and thus constitutes a reason for believing the general point made in the preceding one;

"Because" indicates that the statement which follows it names the cause of the effect mentioned in the statement which precedes it.

This distinction is more readily seen in the following sentences:

John is a good student, *for* his grades are all B's or better, he is consistently on the Dean's List, and he was recently elected to Phi Beta Kappa.

John is a good student *because* he is always attentive in class, does his assignments conscientiously, studies hard, and has a quick keen mind.

In the first sentence an illustration is given to show that a general effect has occurred; in the second an explanation is given of why it occurred. The first, as we shall see, is a descriptive hypothesis, the second, a causal hypothesis.

Let us now consider the development of our sample case.

1. There is a need for changing the status quo
a. The status quo has failed, for. . . .

Since evils are always translated in terms of failures to achieve desired goals and the desired goals are to maximize the output of consumable goods and services and the efficiency of distribution, all instances which appear contrary to these goals would be cited as evils of the status quo. Thus, the evils here would be expressed in terms of economic losses in goods, services, and purchasing power and of their inadequate distribution. Typical evidence would consist of statistics on the business cycle, depressions, inflations, unemployment, loss of purchasing power, etc.— all indicating economic losses and/or inadequate distribution and thus contrary to the desired goals. This first step then might look like this:

I. *Need*

A. The present system of price and wage determination has failed to ensure most American people a consistently adequate supply of goods and services at fair consistent prices, for
1. Depressions—eight major ones [give dates]
   a. Unemployment, breadlines, and soup kitchens [give statistics]
   b. Loss of national income [cite estimated amount]
   c. Additional effects [if time permits]: increased labor unrest and violence, increased social maladjustments, undermining of faith in the free enterprise system, and growth of fascism and communism
2. Inflations—stress the present [compare purchasing power of the present dollar with that of the 1939–1941 dollar]
   a. Fixed income groups hurt [specify]
   b. Savings depleted [specify]
   c. Labor unrest: strikes and stoppages [specify]

Now let us consider how the second step might be developed:

B. The status quo has failed because. . . .

In this step the affirmative must identify as the cause (or an important part of it) the lack of direct controls on prices and wages, or the inherent weakness of the present indirect influences (the law of supply and demand and governmental monetary and fiscal policies). In a question as complicated as this, one must be careful not to oversimplify the cause nor claim that the present policy alone is the cause of the problem. Rather, one may argue that the present policy is an important factor of the cause, the elimination of which would go far in solving the problem. Of course, not all cases are as involved as this. In some, it can be shown that the present policy directly causes the evils, like continued nuclear weapons tests directly causing radioactive fallout. However, in the present case one cannot cite evils caused directly by the status quo, for they would not be recognized as serious evils except by an economist. Thus, the evils cited are caused by factors which in turn are presumably caused by the present policy; i.e., the evils are a link in a complicated chain of cause and effect, action and interaction. To get some idea of the many factors involved, consider this relatively simple hypothesis which an economist might offer to account for the rapid and extreme fluctuations of the business cycle, the evils in question:

During normal periods, lacking a consistently dependable basis for planning future consumption needs, manufacturers periodically create an imbalance between economic goods (including services) and purchasing power. Motivated by a desire for more profits and having miscalculated consumption trends or needs, they proceed to create this imbalance (of more goods than purchasing power) by overspeculation, overexpansion, overcapitalization, and overproduction. The law of supply and demand and certain governmental monetary and fiscal policies, which theoretically are supposed to restore the balance, work too slowly to do so because they are too indirect. Because of their slowness, the consumer is affected psychologically by what seems to him the continuing imbalance (as reflected by an increase in unemployment), and the accelerator and multiplier factors inherent in our economy then come into play. As a result, the imbalance starts to grow more rapidly and excessively, with all industries being affected because of less buying, less production, and more unemployment, and the continued interplay among these factors. And since there is no effective mechanism for checking this spread or rapid growth, the end result is a depression, or an excessive amount of goods and services over purchasing power.

During wartime, on the other hand, an imbalance between goods (and services) and purchasing power results because manufacturers must sharply curtail production for civilian use in order to supply the armed forces. If the government did not step in and directly fix wages and prices (and ration certain commodities), owing to practically the same factors described above, this imbalance would grow, its growth would accelerate, and the end result would be a serious inflation, or an excessive amount of purchasing power over goods and services. By taking off direct controls prematurely after World War II, the government permitted these factors to come into play and the country experienced a rather serious inflation.

If an affirmative team decided to adopt the foregoing thesis, it might develop the second part of its need as follows:

B. The present system has failed (or depressions and inflations occur frequently in our economy) largely because

1. In normal periods the law of supply and demand in conjunction with certain governmental monetary and fiscal policies is too indirect and therefore too slow to adjust imbalances between economic goods and purchasing power brought about partly by the present lack of a consistently dependable basis for planning future consumption needs.

2. The indirectness and slowness of the present wage and price mechanism, coupled with the lack of an effective mechanism for checking the accelerator and multiplier factors of the economy, are largely responsible for the rapid growth of these imbalances and for their extreme nature.

[Thus, though many causal factors are involved, the important role played by the present policy is clearly underscored.]

Suggestive Outlines of Need Issues

The following outlines are presented for further study:

"*Resolved, That the Nonagricultural Industries of the United States Should Guarantee Their Employees an Annual Wage.*" [1955–1956 college topic.]

Status quo: Workers receive employment and wages determined by the law of supply and demand; unemployed receive benefits from a variety of state unemployment compensation programs.

Goals: Worker security, or a good steady income.

I. Need

A. Workers lack security (a good steady income) under the status quo, for
   1. Unemployment is either prevalent or constantly threatened [facts].
   2. Most unemployed workers have a substandard income [facts].
B. Workers lack security because
   1. Certain economic factors cause unemployment.
      a. Seasonal
      b. Technological
      c. Cyclical
   2. The unemployment compensation program is inadequate.
      a. Amount of benefits is too low.
      b. Duration of benefits is too short.
C. The economic factors causing unemployment are inherent in the competitive enterprise system, for
   1. Much seasonal unemployment results partially from the desire for immediate profits, and sufficient financial incentive to stabilize production is lacking.
   2. Much technological unemployment results partially from the desire for immediate profits, and sufficient financial incentive to regulate the introduction of automation is lacking.
   3. Cyclical unemployment trends are necessarily severe because the government's monetary and fiscal measures designed to counteract the cycle take time to prepare and to function; and an immediate cushion for a declining economy is lacking.
D. The unemployment compensation program is inherently inadequate, for
   1. The law stipulates limits to the amount and duration of benefits.
   2. Various states, to attract new industry, vie with each other in keeping benefits low.

3. The farm bloc in many state legislatures prevents improvements because farmers do not share in the program.

[*C* and *D* might be termed the cause of a cause, or the underlying cause. As we shall see, the affirmative must subsequently prove that all "inherent defects" of the status quo would be eliminated by the affirmative program.]

"Resolved, That Governmental Subsidies Should Be Granted According to Need to High School Graduates Who Qualify for Additional Training." [1955–1956 high school topic.]

Status quo: The private financing of a college education by parents, loans, part-time employment, state aid, private corporation grants, and existing scholarships.

Goals: To make a college education available to all high school graduates who have the capacity to acquire one, or to utilize the country's manpower resources to the greatest possible extent for purposes of economic stability and growth and for national defense.

[Actually, here we have a fairly specific goal leading to a more general one. However, neither is likely to be contested by the opposition.]

I. Need

A. Every year many high school graduates capable of acquiring a college education cannot afford to get one, for [facts].
   1. This situation in turn is partially responsible for shortages of trained personnel in many areas of our society, for [facts].
B. Many capable high school graduates cannot afford a college education because available funds are inherently inadequate, for

[Since there are so many factors to consider, some quite obviously inadequate, like loans and part-time employment, one would probably emphasize family income, state aid, private grants, and existing scholarships; and attempt to show why these sources, separately and together, are inherently inadequate, why, in a word, they cannot provide the needed funds.]

"Resolved, That the United States Should Discontinue Direct Economic Aid to Foreign Countries." [1956–1957 college topic.]

Status quo: The granting of economic aid by the United States directly, or unilaterally, to various foreign countries.

Goals: To provide higher standards of living for the people of underdeveloped countries and thus to promote economic and political stability in these countries so that communism will appear less appealing as a solution to their problems.

[Here again we have one immediate objective (higher standards of living), one intermediate objective (economic and political stability), and one end objective (to forestall the growth of communism). Even this in turn is really a means to still another objective, to promote the best interests of the United States. The objectives chosen as immediate, besides depending largely on the proposed policy, depend partly on the evils one decides to emphasize; and these in turn often depend on a preliminary study of the relevant facts. In other words, immediate objectives are subject to change. In this case, one might initially have worked down from the ultimate objective, United States self-interest, to resisting the spread of communism to winning friends among the uncommitted nations. Needless to say, the evils related to this last goal would differ from those related to the goal of promoting economic stability. After some analysis, however, one might have decided that economic stability was a sounder immediate objective than winning friends. Although more than one objective may be cited, these two might be incompatible, so in choosing one or the other, one must decide which will make for the strongest case.]

I. Need

A. Our present economic aid program has failed to raise living standards and thus to promote economic and political stability in the recipient countries, for [facts]. In many instances our aid has actually had the opposite effect, for [facts].

B. Our aid program has failed because no conditions requiring essential reforms (such as land reforms, tax reform, and the provision of agricultural credit facilities) can be attached to the aid; for if conditions were attached, aid would be either refused or bitterly resented as an attempt by the United States "to meddle in internal affairs." Thus, our aid has been used by corrupt governments to perpetuate themselves in power rather than to improve the living standards of the people.

"Resolved, That the Further Development of Nuclear Weapons Should Be Prohibited by International Agreement." [1958–1959 college topic.]

Status quo: Continuing nuclear weapons development.

Goals: To promote the best interests of the world and thus indirectly of the United States to the greatest possible extent.

I. Need

A. Continuing nuclear weapons development would not be in the best interests of the world, or of the United States, for
  1. There is a hazard to all people from radiation, for [facts].
  2. There is a danger that small nations may develop nuclear weapons and eventually precipitate a nuclear war.
  3. These is a danger that continued nuclear weapons development may result in a technological breakthrough by one of the major powers which would upset the present balance of power and thus make war more likely.

B. [Unnecessary since the effects cited in step A are alleged to be directly caused by the status quo]

[In this particular case step B is unnecessary; i.e., no elaborate causal analysis is needed, for the evils cited in step A are the direct effects of the status quo. Because of this relationship, the two steps are actually telescoped into one; step A really says, the status quo is causing (or would cause) three evils. In most cases, as we have seen, this proposition has to be treated as two distinct propositions: (1) there are evils, and (2) the status quo is causing them.]

From the preceding outlines it can be seen that the key point of the need is usually that of equating the cause of existing evils with the essential characteristic of the status quo. Only thus can a real need for a change be shown. If other than an essential characteristic of the present policy is identified as the cause, the negative can claim that this characteristic can be removed without basically altering the policy. For example, if misadministration of funds were cited as a cause of the failure of direct economic aid, the negative could point out that this characteristic is accidental, or not inherent, and could therefore be eliminated without eliminating the program; in other words, why burn down the house to get rid of a few rats? But if the defect is an essential characteristic of the present policy, it can be removed only by changing the policy itself.

Occasionally, affirmative teams make the mistake of introducing "accidents" as an evil of the status quo. Though accidents are undoubtedly an evil, they are not an inherent evil; for an accident, by definition, is a chance occurrence, "one outside the regular order of things," thus, one which does not occur by design, or which is not inevitable. An inherent evil, on the other hand, is inevitable, one which does occur by design as a regular and necessary consequence of the status quo.

We come now to the negative team's approach to the need.

3. NEGATIVE APPROACH TO THE NEED

The Underlying Logic of the Negative Position

Where the affirmative must prove that the affirmative policy is the best of available means to a given end, the negative must either cast doubt on the truth of this proposition or prove the contradictory proposition that the affirmative policy is not the best of available means. Some critics object to debate because it involves a pair of contradictory propositions and debaters are presumably forced to choose either a white or black solution whereas some intermediary solution is probably best. In the somewhat affected language of one group of critics, debate is said to have a "two-valued orientation" whereas a "multivalued orientation" is called for in solving most problems. This criticism is based on a misunderstanding of certain basic laws of thought, particularly the Law of the Excluded Middle and the Law of Contradiction. Since these are discussed elsewhere, it will suffice for the present to say that the negative team has many available alternatives in trying to disprove the affirmative proposition. In other words, debate is not a question of "white" or "black" but of "white" or "not white," where "not white" may be any shade of gray up to and including black. Or, in terms of solutions, debate is a question of the affirmative solution as opposed to *any other* solution and is thus not necessarily confined to two, and only two, solutions.

Of the many alternative propositions which it may uphold to prove the affirmative proposition false, the negative usually chooses a combination of the following:

1. The present policy is effectively achieving the desired goals.

2. The present policy is effectively achieving the desired goals but for some minor flaws which could be eliminated by minor changes.

3. A third policy would effectively achieve the desired goals.

4. Certain insurmountable obstacles would prevent the affirmative policy from coming into existence; i.e., it would not be available.

5. The affirmative policy could not be implemented or enforced and would thus not achieve the desired goals.

6. The affirmative policy would not eliminate the cause of the present problem and would thus not achieve the desired goals.

7. The affirmative policy would cause certain undesirable effects, or do more harm than good.

If any one of the foregoing propositions were true, it would follow that the affirmative proposition is false. (From a logical standpoint, propositions 1, 2, 3, and 7 are contrary propositions; and 4, 5, and 6, contradictory propositions. For a discussion of contrariety and contradiction see pp. 116–118.)

Burden of Proof

Because the affirmative has but one choice—to prove the affirmative resolution to be true—while the negative has many choices in proving the affirmative resolution false, it is said that the affirmative's burden of proof never shifts; i.e., the affirmative is more restricted than the negative. To illustrate this point, let us suppose the negative argues that the status quo or a counterplan is the best policy. Though the affirmative might succeed in disproving this proposition, it would not have proved its own; for the truth relationship between the affirmative and negative propositions in this case is such that both propositions may be false though both cannot be true. Thus, proving one false does not prove the other true. On the other hand, if the negative proposition is proved true, the affirmative proposition must be false. (For a fuller discussion of the truth relationships among propositions, see pp. 116ff.)

Negative Alternatives

Theoretically, a negative team need prove only one of the seven foregoing propositions to win; but since proof is rarely conclusive in debate, a negative team usually tries to prove several in the hope that at least one will stand up under affirmative attack. In making its choice, the negative must be careful to choose propositions that are consistent with one another. This point will become clearer in the subsequent discussion.

Conceding the Need

A negative team may concede the need, i.e., ignore the first two propositions and concentrate on the others. If it believes that existing evils are serious and deep rooted, it may offer a counterplan (proposition 3) and also try to prove propositions 4 to 7; or it may simply concentrate on these propositions without offering any counterplan. Let us consider the latter strategy first.

To ignore the first three propositions and concentrate on the other four is to admit that a serious problem exists but to argue that the affirmative policy would not solve it. Logically, this approach is justifiable, but strategically and psychologically it is weak. Strategically, it considerably lightens the affirmative's burden of proof, enabling the affirmative to concentrate on fewer points. Psychologically, most judges are prejudiced against this approach because it doesn't try to solve a problem conceded to exist. Since this prejudice is rather strong and fairly prevalent, the debater who ignores it takes a great risk.

Now let us consider the other strategy, the counterplan.

Counterplan

A counterplan should not be confused with modifications, or minor changes, of the status quo (proposition 2). A counterplan is an alternative solution to a serious problem conceded to exist and, since it differs essentially from the present policy, concedes the need for changing it. Counterplans, even when superficially conceived, sometimes succeed because of the element of surprise. However, this is not a valid reason for introducing a counterplan; it should be used only when the negative is truly convinced that the status quo is inherently defective.

In defending a counterplan, the negative should introduce it in the first constructive speech so that the affirmative need not waste any more time discussing a proposition ("there is a need for changing the status quo") which is not going to be an issue in the debate. (Actually, the rules of debate should be such that when the negative intends to propose a counterplan, it should be compelled to announce this fact before the debate starts so that the first affirmative speaker need not spend any time on an uncontested proposition.)

A counterplan must be tailored to eliminate the inherent defect of the status quo. Thus, in proposing such a plan, a negative team must analyze the cause of existing evils as carefully as the affirmative. Otherwise, the affirmative will point out that its own plan would eliminate the inherent defect whereas the negative counterplan would not.

In weighing the advantages of a counterplan, the negative should remember that it lightens the affirmative's burden and neutralizes any initial presumption favoring the negative position. Also, as we have seen, since circumstances rarely justify the assumption that the present policy is inherently bad, a counterplan should rarely be used.

Clashing on the Need

To clash on the need is generally the most logical and thus the soundest strategy since there is usually much evidence favoring the retention of the status quo. Also, this strategy forces the affirmative to carry its full burden of proof. A good attack on the need can stymie the affirmative since its other issues grow out of the need. Finally, in defending the status quo, the negative isn't simply being "negative" in its approach but is advocating a constructive policy as a means to certain desired ends.

Achievements of the Status Quo. In developing its attack on the need, the negative must consider the same preliminary points as the affirmative: the specific policy advocated by the affirmative, the specific nature of the status quo, and the mutually desired ends. With these points determined, the negative's treatment of the need somewhat parallels the affirmative's.

First, it must consider the questions: "Are there existing evils? If so, are they serious?" Theoretically, the negative may choose to answer no to the first question, arguing that the status quo is completely effective (proposition 1). This approach, however, is usually illogical and thus imprudent; for in the face of the affirmative's factual evidence to the contrary, so sweeping a proposition is ostensibly not true. Owing to the circumstances out of which debate arises in the first place and to the nature of proof, debaters should avoid such words as "always," "never," "all," "no," "every," and "surely." Being more realistic, the more moderate approach is not only more persuasive but also easier to defend. Since few systems, if at all complex, are perfect, one can admit that the status quo has certain defects. The important question, however, is, "How serious are they?" and the negative's answer here is, "Minor or insignificant." Restated, the negative's first point would be:

A. There is no need for (drastically) changing the status quo, for. . . .

Since the negative is seeking to establish a favorable evaluation of the status quo, it may deny the existence of certain alleged evils and show others to be insignificant in relation to the achievements of the status quo, achievements, like evils, being considered in relation to the desired goals. Typical evidence for the case of "Price and Wage Controls," for example, would consist of facts about America's exceptionally high standard of living. This approach really redefines the problem by putting it into a context where it can't be regarded as very significant. Eventually it will be argued that the affirmative program is uncalled for because it is a drastic approach to an insignificant problem; in other words, why develop a sledge hammer to crack a peanut?

Cause of Achievements. The negative should next consider the cause of existing achievements. Although seldom introduced at this time, this point should be considered by the negative in its preliminary analysis, for it is the basis of certain negative objections which may later be introduced. Restated, this point would be:

B. There is no need for changing the status quo because. . . .

Here the essential feature of the present policy should be identified as the cause of existing achievements. In effect, one tries to prove that these achievements are not accidental but inherent in the status quo. Taking the case of "Price and Wage Controls" again, the negative would identify the free enterprise competitive system as the cause of America's high standard of living, pointing out perhaps that other economic systems, like Russia's, despite abundant natural resources, do not effectively allocate those resources because free competition is lacking.

In actual practice, negative teams usually separate the two steps of "achievements" and "their cause," being content simply to deny or minimize alleged evils. For example, "As for the affirmative claim that India resents our aid, she actually welcomes it." Or "As for the 3½ million unemployed, the affirmative fails to consider the fact that 55 million are employed." But few teams consider at this time *why* India welcomes our aid or *why* 55 million are employed. Instead, they consider this question later when arguing the disadvantages of the affirmative policy or "compelling reasons" for keeping the status quo. ("Compelling reasons" are really achievements which would become disadvantages with the removal of the status quo.) However, for the sake of unity the two steps should probably follow one another. Together, they seek to prove that the status quo is for the most part effective and that existing gains would be lost if the present policy were removed.

Repairs of the Status Quo. Concerning the admitted imperfections, the negative should first identify their cause and then show how it can be eliminated. With the present policy thus repaired so that it is practically perfect, there is no need for changing it; for why change perfection?

Restated, these two points would be:

C. Cause of existing minor imperfections. . . .

Here the cause is explored to show that it is accidental or circumstantial and not inherent.

D. Modifications of the status quo, or minor repairs which would mitigate the imperfections. . . .

Since an effect is eliminated by eliminating its cause, the repairs are designed to eliminate the cause as determined in the previous step. In terms of the "Price and Wage Control" case, these points might be:

C. In the past, fluctuations in the economy have been caused by
    1. A sharp disparity between purchasing power and goods, this disparity in turn being caused by a lack of effective measures to control the flow of money. This lack of control is not an inherent flaw of the status quo. Certain measures which exist today for regulating this flow, like the increased powers of the Federal Reserve System and certain investment regulations, did not exist during past depressions; others, such as antitrust laws, are not enforced as strictly as possible; and still others, such as taxation, the Federal Reserve quota, credit restrictions, and other Governmental monetary and fiscal policies, are sometimes not used to the limit of their effectiveness. Individual shortcomings can be corrected if all these measures are properly used; there is no need to eliminate the system as a whole. If monopoly, for example, is bad, why do away with the competitive enterprise system? Do away with monopoly by means of better antitrust legislation and enforcement powers. If economists running the Federal Reserve System do not use its powers quickly or fully enough, put in economists who will. Why get rid of a good system just because it isn't always managed as well as it might be? Why condemn a good automobile because the driver occasionally is careless?
    2. As for inflation, outside factors like war or threats of war are responsible; the blame cannot be placed on a given economic system. Any system would have to contend with such factors. Ours does so by means of emergency controls, which, though unattractive, are the best means under the circumstances.

D. Explanation of how the flow of money can be regulated by various indirect controls, slightly modified and strengthened, and by direct controls in emergency periods. (Frequently steps C and D are telescoped into one.)

The Proper Emphasis

Since a team usually has more material than it can use, it must decide what to emphasize. Emphasis depends upon two factors: the nature of the case and the emphasis given certain points by the first affirmative speaker. Let us consider each briefly.

The Nature of the Case

Some cases are inherently strong or weak in certain respects, e.g., strong in need or weak in practicability. Like all good strategy, good debate strategy calls for exploiting the potential weakness of the opposition while capitalizing on one's own strong points. For example, the question of a compulsory fair employment practices law is, from the affirmative standpoint, probably stronger in need than in practicability, and, from the negative standpoint, vice versa. (A debater learns this by studying both sides of the question.) Thus, a good strategy for the negative would be to cut down on the need and emphasize impracticability. (An affirmative, on the other hand, anticipating this strategy, would diligently prepare suitable answers to such objections.)

Adaptation

The second factor influencing the negative strategy is the emphasis given certain points by the first affirmative speaker. In a way, the latter sets the tempo for the entire debate. Being first to speak, he does not have to answer previous arguments but delivers a completely prepared, or "canned," speech.[6] All succeeding speakers, however, must adapt their material to the preceding presentation. Adaptation calls for quick thinking, thorough familiarity with both sides of the question, and facility in extemporaneous speaking. Relying on canned speeches, or failing to adapt, not only makes for a dull debate—like two boxers fanning the air in different directions—but also is poor strategy since it prevents a team from properly defending its own case or attacking weaknesses of the opposition's. Thus, if the first affirmative speaker fails to consider inherency, the negative should emphasize this omission.

Asking Questions

Unfortunately the first negative speaker is sometimes advised to conclude his presentation with a series of canned questions so as to get the second affirmative speaker to waste valuable time answering them. However, this strategy is illogical and ill-advised. A debater is entitled to ask the opposition only one type of question, that which asks for information or clarification of a key point introduced by the opposition. If the date of a given piece of evidence is considered important and the opposition has neglected to give it, one may ask for the information. Or, if an af-

[6] For this reason the first affirmative position is the easiest one on a four-man squad. The first negative and second affirmative positions are probably next in difficulty, and the second negative probably the most difficult.

firmative team arguing for a world bank failed to indicate the nature of
the loans or the conditions under which they would be granted, or failed
to consider how the bank was to be administered or capitalized, a negative team could legitimately ask for such information since it pertains to
the essential characteristic of such a bank and would thus be needed by a
negative to evaluate the affirmative proposal properly. On the other hand,
questions calling for detailed information unrelated to any basic issue—
such as, how many members of the governing board would there be, how
often would they meet, or how much salary would they receive?—are
irrelevant and could be dismissed as such by the opposition.

Completely illogical also are questions which are really unsupported
conclusions, or assertions disguised as questions. "But is it at all likely that
the nations belonging to such an organization could remain fully sovereign?" This question clearly suggests that the nations in question would
probably *not* remain fully sovereign. If it were preceded by some proof,
it would be a conclusion stated rhetorically as a question and thus
legitimate. Standing alone, however, without proof, it is equivalent to
mere assertion. Generally, the motive for asking a question can be determined by the tone in which it is asked. Consider the questions "Who
will join this agreement?" and "What sanctions will be used to enforce
it?" If the tone indicates that information is being sought, the questions
are legitimate. But if the tone suggests that few will join ("Who will *join*
this agreement?") or that sanctions will be ineffective ("What *sanctions*
will be used to enforce it?"), they are mere assertions. Thus, the important consideration regarding questions is why and how they are asked.
(For handling fallacious suggestive questions, see pp. 198–199.)

To summarize briefly to this point, we have considered the affirmative
and negative aspects of the need issue. The affirmative must try to prove
that the status quo is inherently defective and therefore needs to be
changed. The negative may concede the point by introducing a counterplan and attempt to defeat the affirmative on other issues or simply do
the latter. Or it may contest the point by arguing that the status quo is
completely effective or almost completely effective, containing minor
flaws which can be eliminated. This latter strategy is usually the most
logical and most common one. In the next chapter we shall consider the
second basic issue which hinges on the question "Would the affirmative
plan meet the need?"

EXERCISES

1. Define the term "issue."
2. What are "common objectives" and what is their significance in debate?
3. Formulate acceptable common objectives for the following debate ques-

tions. Indicate what might be considered irrelevant, minor, or contrary objectives.

    a. This college (or high school) should have an honor system.

    b. A board of judges should replace the present jury system.

    c. The United States should considerably increase its trade with Communist nations.

    d. The United Nations should have a police force to implement its decisions.

    4. What is the "presumption favoring the negative"? What is its underlying logic and why does it vary with different questions? How does this presumption relate to the affirmative's need for a change?

    5. Define the term "need" as used in debate and explain the two basic components of an affirmative need.

    6. Discuss the five common misconceptions of an affirmative need.

    7. What is meant by the "essence of the status quo"? What is its significance? What is meant by an "inherent evil"?

    8. Using the following outline, sketch in an affirmative need for one of the resolutions listed in question 3:

    a. Status quo

    b. Common objectives

    c. Defects of the status quo

    d. Cause of defects

    9. What is usually the negative's most logical approach to the affirmative need? Why?

    10. What is the negative's purpose in considering achievements of the status quo? the cause of achievements?

    11. When should a counterplan be considered? When do "repairs" or modifications of the status quo constitute a counterplan?

    12. What is meant by "burden of proof"? What is the burden, or obligation, of the affirmative and negative positions?

    13. If the following questions were asked in a debate, which would you consider legitimate, which inappropriate or illogical? Why?

    a. Does the affirmative team actually believe that a compulsory F.E.P. law could get through Congress?

    b. Does the negative team feel that the individual state governments can provide better legislation to insure individual citizens of fair employment practices than can be provided by the Federal government?

    c. Twice in the Eighty-second Congress votes were taken to limit debate on F.E.P.C. bills. Both times the measure was defeated. We ask, what would prevent the Southern senators from filibustering a compulsory F.E.P. proposal and thus prevent it from coming up for a vote?

    d. We ask the affirmative, isn't it more probable that F.E.P. laws will be passed by the state legislatures than by the Federal Congress?

    e. We should like to know, what would constitute discrimination, how would it be determined, and who would determine it?

    f. What guarantee do we have that violence would not erupt in the South with the passage of such a law?

    g. How do we know that discrimination can be determined in every case?

h. Minority group workers were protected against discrimination during the war by President Roosevelt's measure. Should the guarantee of fair employment practices be merely a war emergency measure?

i. Do you agree that the objective of the Communist organizations throughout the world is to overthrow free governments, destroy liberties, and bring the countries under the domination of the Kremlin?

j. Where would this F.E.P. board meet, how often would they meet, who would pay their salaries, and how much salary would they receive?

k. What sanctions does the affirmative team propose to enforce their law?

l. What is to prevent an industry from closing its doors in protest against such a law?

m. Does the negative team believe that a compulsory F.E.P.C. would increase the prestige of the United States in foreign countries?

n. How would the members of an F.E.P. board be selected and who would select them?

o. Do you agree that Communist organizations throughout the world are a menace to future peace?

CHAPTER 5

ANALYSIS: WOULD THE AFFIRMATIVE PLAN MEET THE NEED?

> If there is agreement on certain goals and values, one can argue ration-
> ally about the means by which these objectives may be attained.
>
> *Einstein*

1. AFFIRMATIVE APPROACH: ITS UNDERLYING LOGIC

After proving that a serious problem exists, the affirmative now tries to solve it, its solution being the affirmative policy. A true solution elimi-nates evil effects by eliminating their cause. A doctor in treating a rash tries to determine the cause of the rash—the eating of tomatoes, perhaps —and accordingly prescribes a change in diet. Though he may also prescribe an ointment to ease the irritation, this would be only a tem-porary expedient since it would not treat the underlying cause of the problem. Similarly, if the affirmative has shown that United States eco-nomic aid has failed because it is bilateral and conditions therefore can't be attached, the affirmative plan must be nonbilateral so that conditions can be attached. Or, if the affirmative has shown that workers are dis-criminated against because employers are not compelled to hire solely on ability, the affirmative plan must compel them. If the need has been logically analyzed, the affirmative should have little trouble showing that its plan would eliminate existing defects, or "meet the need." This second basic issue embraces three subissues, namely, practicability, desirability, and additional advantages.

Practicability

Ordinarily, an affirmative team may not contend that the principle alone embodied in its policy would eliminate the problem, for principles are quite distinct from the specific programs which embody them. The principles that made an artificial satellite possible, for example, were known for some time before they could be successfully embodied in a mechanism that would actually work. In other words, many practical obstacles—developing the proper fuel, thrust, design, etc.—had to be overcome before the principles could become operational. Theoretically a man can be landed on Mars, but practicably he cannot. Similarly, the affirmative policy, though theoretically sound in some respects, must also be shown to be workable. (The terms "practicable" and "workable" are used synonymously, "practicable" meaning literally "able to be put into practice.") Thus, since the affirmative is presumably considering a real problem, it must offer a concrete, or realistic, program to solve it. If not, it could be charged with being "visionary," with considering only an abstraction and ignoring reality.

The number of details of the affirmative plan depends largely on the proposed policy. Occasionally the policy itself may almost be the plan. This would be true for propositions like "Resolved, That Eighteen-year-old Citizens Should Be Allowed to Vote" and "Resolved, That the United States Should Extend Diplomatic Recognition to the Communist Government of China." Usually, however, the affirmative must explain its solution, as with questions advocating a guaranteed annual wage plan or a compulsory fair employment practices law. Wherever possible, the affirmative should guide itself by consulting actual plans that have been advocated or used.

As we shall see, in considering practicability, the negative may attack the affirmative plan by alleging that it would be either unavailable or unenforceable. Although the affirmative need not deal with this argument until introduced, its plan should anticipate this and other objections. Consider the following plan for the question "Resolved, That Governmental Subsidies Should Be Granted According to Need to High School Graduates Who Qualify for Additional Training":

1. To qualify for aid a student would have to be of college calibre, as determined by his high school record and performance in college entrance examinations.

2. A student would be aided according to need, as determined by his family's income.

3. A student would have to attend an accredited college or university.

4. A student would have to attend a college or university that did not practice racial or religious discrimination.

5. A student would have to maintain a "C" average to be eligible for continued aid.

6. A student would be free to choose his own course of study.

7. The university or college selected by the eligible student would

receive funds directly from the government and be free from interference, as it was under the G.I. Bill.

In examining these provisions we see that the first two are needed to meet the terms of the resolution "high school graduates who qualify for additional training" and "granted according to need." The others, however, besides elaborating upon the affirmative principle, are designed to counter potential negative objections. The third provision anticipates the negative objection that many fly-by-night schools interested in quick profits would come into being, as they did under the G.I. Bill after World War II. The fourth, that taxpayers' money would sometimes be used to support undemocratic institutions; the fifth, that many "free loaders" would take advantage of the program; and the sixth and seventh, that government interference or control would result from governmental financial support.

In choosing its provisions the affirmative must be sure that they are directly related to the proposed policy. If not, the negative can adopt them as minor repairs. Also, the affirmative need not reject the entire status quo so long as it rejects its essential characteristic. If it decides to retain parts of the status quo, it must show that the affirmative innovations would constitute the main solution. For example, in advocating a fair employment practices law, an affirmative team might accept existing educational techniques as part of its program provided it showed they are insufficient to solve the problem. The affirmative may also adopt negative repairs if it can show they are consistent with the affirmative program and insufficient to solve the problem. In debating the topic "Resolved, That the United States Should Adopt a Policy of Free Trade," a negative team might contend that complicated custom regulations hamper the flow of trade and offer, as a repair, the simplifying of such regulations. The affirmative may agree with the negative and adopt this repair provided it explains that the major obstacles to trade are tariffs, quotas, and subsidies, which only the affirmative plan could eliminate.

Desirability

An affirmative plan is desirable if it can solve the problem. Thus, "desirability" in this context means the ability to eliminate the cause of the problem. When the need is complex, considering separate aspects of the problem and their particular solution is usually clearer than considering the entire problem and then explaining the solution.

Additional Advantages

Theoretically, an affirmative team need not go beyond solving the problem. However, if it can show additional advantages of its plan, these will strengthen its position. (The term "additional" is used here since the main advantage of the affirmative plan is its ability to meet the need.)

Direct and Indirect Advantages

Additional advantages may result directly or indirectly from the affirmative program. For instance, in advocating the discontinuance of direct economic aid to foreign countries, an affirmative team might argue that its program would cost less money and end Russia's unscrupulous competition with the United States in the area of foreign aid. Since these additional advantages would result directly from the affirmative program, they would be "direct" advantages. On the other hand, in advocating that Federal aid should be granted to deserving high school students, an affirmative team might argue that turning out more college graduates, the major goal, would result in other desirable effects, like increasing the country's gross national product and tax potential. Since these would result indirectly from the affirmative program, i.e., from its major effect, turning out more college graduates, they would be "indirect" advantages.

Direct advantages are undoubtedly less vulnerable than indirect, for a negative team defending the status quo or a counterplan may claim the same indirect advantages. However, direct advantages, being the unique effects of a particular program, are much more difficult to handle. The negative may try to show that such effects would not occur but it is often forced to admit that they would. How can it be denied, for example, that if aid were stopped, less money would be spent? The only answer the negative could give here would be that such advantages are insignificant or would be offset by serious disadvantages.

Advantages and Need

Additional advantages are really undeveloped need points, ignored in the need because they are not too significant. For example, in the question of direct economic aid to foreign countries, since saving money and ending Russian competition are not major goals, the affirmative would not consider them in developing its need unless it had enough time to consider minor goals.

By failing to consider explicitly any goals, affirmative teams sometimes base their need on minor ones. If an affirmative team advocating legalized gambling argued that the loss of revenues to the state from taxes on legalized gambling was the major evil of the status quo, by inference its major goal would be to increase state revenues. But how relevant is such a goal for a moral question? A negative team might point out that legalizing and taxing any number of illegal activities, such as prostitution, would also increase state revenues but would not necessarily be desirable. In other words, increasing state revenues, a minor goal, should be used only as an additional advantage.

Sample Analysis

The following suggestive outline for the question "Resolved, That Congress Should Enact a Compulsory Fair Employment Practices Law" illustrates the affirmative's second basic issue:

II. Affirmative Plan Would Meet the Need
  A. Plan explained:
    1. General organization and enforcement procedure: five-man national board plus regional boards within the various states; steps in handling bona fide complaints: review, attempt at conciliation, court review, cease-and-desist order, fine or imprisonment. [An actual plan, like the New York State Plan, or some proposed plan, like the Norton-Chavez Bill proposed in Congress, should be taken as a model.]
    2. Portion of status quo (if any) to be retained: educational program. [Explain briefly.]
  B. Practicability (to be used only if the negative argues impracticability).
    1. Bringing the plan into existence:
      a. Constitutionality: the law would not be unconstitutional; on the contrary, it would enforce a constitutional principle, the right of every individual to earn a living commensurate with his ability (the right to "life, liberty, and the pursuit of happiness").
      b. As to a conflict between this right and the rights of association and contract or certain states' rights, the former, being more fundamental, would take precedence. If it is argued that the Constitution does not specify this right to fair employment practices, it may be said that it is in accord with the spirit of the Constitution or that a constitutional amendment would bring it within the letter of the law.
    2. Enforcing the plan: there would be no insuperable obstacles, for successful integration (without violence) has already occurred in many Southern firms, notably International Harvester. Further proof is in the numerous instances where the South has accommodated itself to Supreme Court rulings against various forms of discrimination—the large number of Negroes in Southern white universities, the abolishment of "intelligence" tests as a voting requirement in Alabama, etc.
  C. Desirability (how plan would treat the cause of problem):
    1. The plan would eliminate the immediate cause of the harmful effects of discrimination: the freedom to discriminate without fear of reprisal. This freedom would be curtailed by severe penalties.
    2. The plan would also treat the underlying cause of discrimination,

namely ignorance and conditioning; for integration would lead to better understanding and more tolerance. Moreover, an expanded educational program would still be carried on to combat ignorance.

D. Additional advantages:

1. Better understanding and greater harmony among the people in the United States.
2. A higher standard of living for all.
3. An effective answer to damaging Soviet Union propaganda.
4. Strengthening the United States position among the uncommitted "colored" nations of the world, like India, Burma, Ghana, etc.

2. THE NEGATIVE APPROACH

Negative Alternatives

The negative approach to the second basic issue embodies negative propositions 4 through 7:

4. Certain insurmountable obstacles would prevent the affirmative plan from coming into existence; i.e., it would not be available.

5. The affirmative plan could not be implemented or enforced and would thus not achieve the desired goals.

6. The affirmative plan would not eliminate the cause of the present problem.

7. The affirmative plan would cause undesirable effects, or do more harm than good.

These propositions give the negative the three subissues: impracticability (propositions 4 and 5), undesirability (proposition 6), and disadvantages (proposition 7).

Before considering these points, if the negative feels that the affirmative plan is not clear or sufficiently detailed, it should request the desired information, being careful not to ask for irrelevant details.

Impracticability

The aspects of impracticability which are discussed here from both the affirmative and negative standpoints were not treated earlier because the affirmative would not have to consider them until the negative introduced them.

Although the issue of impracticability is usually minor, it can be major when topics like a compulsory Fair Employment Practices law or an international ban on nuclear weapons tests are debated. The issue usually embraces two questions: (1) Can the affirmative plan be brought into existence? (2) Can the affirmative plan be enforced long enough to solve the problem?

Both questions pertain to difficulties that may prevent the plan from meeting its objectives. If a plan cannot be brought into existence or made to function until it meets its desired objective, it is really not available as the affirmative alleges. Thus, practicability is largely a question of availability. Now let us consider both aspects of the issue.

Ease or Difficulty of Bringing the Plan into Existence

A new plan may have much to recommend it but, to merit serious consideration, it must be one that can be brought into existence. For if it were otherwise sound but unavailable, one would hardly want to dispense with the old plan, however imperfect. The latter at least does some good whereas the former would do nothing.

Miscellaneous Obstacles. To prove that a plan would not come into existence, one must prove that there are insurmountable obstacles to it; e.g., an obstacle which involves reversing some physical law would be insurmountable. Thus, building air bases on Mars now presents an insurmountable obstacle. In a social, political, economic, moral, or religious sense, an obstacle which involves overturning a deep-seated belief of the group required to enact the plan may also be considered insurmountable. Thus, trying to get a law enacted giving the President absolute powers almost surely involves the insurmountable obstacle of overcoming congressional opposition. Similarly, a law to permit nude bathing on American beaches would encounter the practically insurmountable obstacle of changing deeply rooted mores.

Again, a plan that is patently contrary to the self-interest of the parties involved will almost surely be blocked by them. Or if a plan involves an agreement between several members, whether individuals or nation-states, and its purpose is diametrically counter to that of one of the parties involved, the latter would almost surely not enter into it; i.e., the agreement would not be consummated. For the affirmative to argue that the party should join is, as we have seen, illogical, for "should" in this context means "should want to," which in turn means "it would be in its best interest to." And this the affirmative could not prove if it were not true. For example, when the affirmative argues that the prohibition of further nuclear weapons development by international agreement would give the United States an advantage over the Soviet Union, it is simply proving that the Soviet Union would not enter into such an agreement.

Unconstitutionality. Negative teams sometimes try to establish unconstitutionality as an insurmountable obstacle, particularly in questions dealing with proposed national legislation, like Federal aid to education, compulsory FEPC, TVA, Tidelands Oil, and national compulsory health insurance. That is, the negative tries to show that the proposed legislation would violate certain constitutional precepts and would therefore be blocked by the Supreme Court. However, since most affirmative policies chosen for academic debate would not violate the Constitution, the negative is usually on slippery ground here. Many negative teams realize this and treat unconstitutionality as a disadvantage of the affirmative policy rather than as an obstacle to its adoption. But even this argument is usually tenuous since constitutional rights vary in importance, with some taking precedence over others. Thus, to argue that a certain right will be abridged is not very convincing when it can be shown that a more important right will be restored in the process, as, for example, to argue that preventing employers from hiring twelve-year-old children to work fifty hours a week violates the freedom of association and contract when a more fundamental right is obviously restored. To take a more timely example, arguing that a national compulsory FEPC law would be unconstitutional (disadvantageous) because it would violate certain states' rights would be effective only if one could convincingly answer the affirmative charge that its program would restore a more basic right now being abridged in many states, namely, an individual's right to fair consideration in trying to earn a living.

Sometimes the negative will argue that a plan would be unconstitutional because the Constitution contains no provision upon which congressional authority for it can be founded. This argument, too, is weak unless the negative can also show that the proposed legislation is contrary in principle to the tenets of the Constitution. If it cannot, the affirmative can reply that a constitutional amendment would bring its proposal within the letter of the law. On the other hand, an affirmative team cannot claim that its proposal is constitutional because the Constitution says nothing specifically against it. Many believe that the late Chief Justice William Howard Taft erred in declaring that obtaining evidence by secretly wire tapping a telephone was constitutional since the Fourth Amendment refers only to the bodily search of a house. In each case the issue must be decided not by the letter but by the spirit of the Constitution.

If the proposed legislation is already operative in certain states and has been upheld by the Supreme Court, obviously one cannot argue unconstitutionality as an obstacle. To claim it as a disadvantage is not very convincing either since the opposition has the Court on its side. For example, in arguing against the adoption of a national compulsory F.E.P. law, a negative should think twice about arguing unconstitutionality (as a disadvantage) since compulsory F.E.P. state laws have already been upheld by the Supreme Court. On the other hand, the affirmative should rarely argue for the repeal of an existing law because it violates the Constitution if the Supreme Court has ruled otherwise. For instance, in advocating the repeal of compulsory unionism, an affirmative team should think twice about arguing that the present law infringes upon certain constitutional rights of the worker, for the Supreme Court has said otherwise. This does not mean that the Supreme Court is always reasonable, but it usually is. Sometimes, where the Court has split 5 to 4 or 6 to 3 and the minority view seems especially cogent, one may side with the minority, as with the minority view of Brandeis in the wire-tapping case which seems more reasonable than the majority view of Taft. But usually a debater should not argue against the majority view.

Thus, unconstitutionality must be handled very carefully and is usually not a real issue in intercollegiate debates.

Cost. Another obstacle frequently introduced as insurmountable is the cost of the plan. However, this obstacle is usually not insurmountable, for money is usually available, the real problem being to convince people that it should be spent. For this reason cost is treated more often as a disadvantage of the plan rather than as an obstacle to it.

In countering this argument, the affirmative should try to prove that the cost would be insignificant, that its program would produce revenues which would ultimately offset the cost, or that other advantages would offset it. In answering the argument that the cost of Federal aid to high school students would be exorbitant, an affirmative team might point out that the cost would be relatively small by comparison with annual gross national earnings, that the initial cost would eventually come back to the government in increased revenues from taxes since college graduates earn an average of a hundred thousand dollars more during their lifetime than high school graduates, or that national security cannot be measured in terms of cost. As a rule, cost should be introduced as a negative disadvantage rather than an insurmountable obstacle, the issue being, is the program worth what it will cost?

To sum up the question of obstacles, both sides should guard against using specious arguments, and, since convincing obstacles are usually lacking, the negative should concentrate on other lines of attack.

Enforceability of the Plan

The second aspect of impracticability is, can the affirmative plan be properly enforced to solve the problem? If, after being brought into existence, the plan will not operate, it will accomplish nothing. Here the negative usually considers specific provisions of the plan concerning personnel, organization, and enforcement procedures. To prove the plan impracticable, the negative must prove that difficulties in these areas are inherent, something quite difficult to do. As one example, one might argue that a national prohibition law would be impracticable, for, owing to deeply rooted custom, it could not be enforced. An affirmative team might answer that people could be persuaded to cooperate if they knew the benefits involved, the assumption being that reason can change deeply rooted attitudes. Whether this assumption is true or not, an opposing debater can hardly argue that it is false without tacitly admitting that he is engaged in a futile activity, for convincing others by reason is, of course, the purpose of debate. Nevertheless, popular opposition is a legitimate argument if it can be shown that people would probably not change their minds in the near future, whatever the reason, but would intensely oppose the operation of the proposed plan. Thus, when the question of prohibition was debated many years ago, negative advocates were undoubtedly right in contending that the Volstead Act would be unenforceable, as later events proved. However, this contention is usually difficult to establish. Today negative debaters often cite the repeal of the Volstead Act as proof that the affirmative program would be unenforceable, but the analogy is usually weak because the factor of intensity is overlooked.

Popular Opinion Polls. In arguing popular opposition as an obstacle to enforcement, negative debaters sometimes introduce public opinion polls. Usually, however, they neglect to explain how the polls are being used, a serious omission since popular opinion polls as evidence may be interpreted in four different ways. Briefly:

1. The affirmative policy is bad, for most people say so. This argument assumes that the majority is always right, which, of course, is a false assumption. Even the people in question would admit that they are not authorities. Thus, this interpretation would be an example of unqualified testimony.

2. The present policy should be retained, for most people want it. This argument boils down to: the present policy should be kept because it is the present policy, or policies which are favored should be favored. If true, no existing policies in a democratic society would ever be changed since existing policies are presumably favored by the majority. Thus, debating would be pointless. But what is, is not always what should be. To settle the question of whether what is should be is the purpose of debate; to assume the truth of this proposition while trying to prove it would be circular reasoning, or assuming what must be proved.

3. The affirmative policy is undemocratic, for most people oppose it. This argument assumes that the affirmative policy would be bad because it would contravene the principle of majority rule, that people are not amenable to reason, and that the policy would be brought in against their will. Such assumptions, however, must be proved, and, as we have seen, the difficulties involved here are considerable.

4. The affirmative policy would be unenforceable, for most people would disobey it. This argument assumes that the majority would prevent the affirmative policy from being enforced (or possibly from even coming into being). Once again, this assumption must be proved, and to prove it a negative debater must show that popular opposition is intense. To

prove this in turn, he must show that some basic right would be abridged or deeply rooted custom overturned, the same type of proof required for the preceding interpretation.

Thus, of the four interpretations, the first two are clearly illogical and the last two contain hidden assumptions which must be proved. Before answering an argument based on a public opinion poll, the affirmative should determine how the negative is using the poll. If the negative does not or cannot say, the affirmative answer should resemble that given on page 20.

Sanctions. To be enforceable, a plan or law must have sanctions—coercive measures (fines, punishment, loss of reward or privilege, etc.) which normally deter would-be violators. If an agreement or law can be violated without any harmful consequences, violations will probably occur and, practically speaking, the law would be unenforceable. If a negative charges unenforceability, the affirmative must indicate specific sanctions which would make its proposal enforceable. Sometimes affirmative teams dodge the issue because they do not understand it. For example, in arguing for the prohibition of nuclear weapons development by international agreement, many affirmative teams countering the charge that sanctions would be lacking to enforce the agreement blandly replied that the agreement would be voided if a violation occurred. In effect, they were tacitly admitting that their plan was unworkable; for if the agreement had no enforcement sanctions and were voided by the first violation, the affirmative would soon be back to the same status quo which allegedly needed changing; i.e., the problem which allegedly existed would still exist in the absence of a plan to solve it.

On the other hand, negative teams should not argue that a law or plan has to be "foolproof," or perfectly enforced, to be effective. Actually, very few man-made laws, if any, can meet this criterion, but this does not mean that most of our laws are unworkable. If the provisions of a law are sufficiently clear that most violations of it can be determined and if the penalties for such violations deter most would-be violators, the law may be considered workable.

Undesirability

Paralleling the affirmative's argument of desirability is the negative argument of undesirability; i.e., the affirmative plan would not solve the problem because it would not treat the cause. In handling this argument, the negative must be careful not to appear inconsistent. It must first make clear that the problem in question is not the major problem alleged by the affirmative but the minor imperfections conceded by the negative. Actually, it may even discuss the problem as major if it first indicates that the argument is hypothetical—"*Even if* such a problem existed—which we deny—the affirmative plan wouldn't solve it." Again, if the negative has previously argued impracticability, it must treat undesirability as hypothetical—"Even if the affirmative plan could come into existence and be enforced—which we deny—it would not solve the problem."

Since causal factors are usually complex and extremely important, the negative should ordinarily spend much time on this step, introducing it in its first constructive speech so that it can be dealt with in the remaining speeches and thus receive much emphasis.

Just as the affirmative need not reject the entire status quo or all negative repairs, the negative need not reject the entire affirmative plan. If certain affirmative provisions are consistent with the essence of the status quo, the negative may adopt them as repairs, as, in arguing against a policy of free trade, a negative team may agree with the affirmative that certain petty tariffs, like those on almonds, pipes, and figs, are undesirable and should be repealed, as long as it explains that such changes can readily be made within the framework of the status quo.

Disadvantages of the Affirmative Plan

Finally, paralleling the affirmative argument of "additional advantages" is the negative argument of "disadvantages." However, where the former is relatively minor for the affirmative, the latter is usually major for the negative. Significant disadvantages are often alone enough to win the debate.

Like advantages, disadvantages are effects which would result from adopting the affirmative program and may be direct or indirect. Direct disadvantages are direct effects whereas indirect disadvantages are effects of effects. For example, a negative team might contend that a disadvantage of the affirmative program would be decreased productivity and that this in turn would lead to increased costs, which in turn would lead to labor unrest. The first disadvantage, decreased productivity, would be a direct disadvantage, since it would be a direct effect of the affirmative program, while the latter two disadvantages, increased costs and labor unrest, would be indirect disadvantages. This example shows why indirect disadvantages do not usually carry much weight; for if the direct disadvantage did not occur, the others would not. Thus, when disadvantages depend upon one another, the affirmative can conveniently handle them as a single point. In debates on the guaranteed annual wage many negative disadvantages were based on the factor of cost; and alert affirmative teams, recognizing this fact, were able to deal with these many disadvantages as one. Thus, whenever possible, the negative should concentrate on individual direct disadvantages.

The negative should choose from three to five significant disadvantages, being careful not to include contradictory points. One cannot argue that the affirmative program would lower wages and depress the market and simultaneously increase wages to a point where serious inflation would occur. Again, if the negative has previously argued impracticability, it must treat disadvantages as hypothetical; for if the affirmative program would not work, it would not produce any effects, evil or otherwise. Certain distinctions, however, may be made here. Even if an affirmative program were not effectively enforced, it could still cause certain disadvantages; but these could not be the effects of the affirmative program itself but rather of attempts to enforce it. A negative team might argue, for example, that voluntary unionism could not be properly enforced and that attempted enforcement would result in violence. As long as the negative clearly indicates *attempted* enforcement, there is no inconsistency. Another distinction is that enforcement may occur in some areas and thus lead to disadvantages but would be unlikely in most.

The negative must also be careful not to claim disadvantages unrelated to the desired goals, for to argue that a policy will fail to achieve other goals is irrelevant. To argue that discontinuing nuclear weapons tests would be disadvantageous because it would not ease the tension over the Berlin crisis or lessen the effects of a war if one came is irrelevant. An affirmative program will not accomplish many things, but this is immaterial since it seeks to accomplish only certain goals; and negative disadvantages must be related to these.

In introducing their disadvantages, negative teams frequently appear to be taking "pot shots" at the affirmative case, or using what is popularly known as the "shotgun" attack, to befuddle the opposition. Since most judges resent this type of attack, the negative should carefully support and document each disadvantage and, instead of presenting seven or eight disadvantages, group them into two or three significant categories, such as political, military, and economic. The impression that two or three important points have been well developed carries more weight than the impression that seven or eight have been sketchily developed.

Sample Analysis

To give the student a clearer picture of the various components of the argument "Plan Would Not Meet the Need," the following suggestive outline of a case against a compulsory national fair employment practices law is given:

II. The Affirmative Plan Would Not Meet the Need [1]
  A. Request for clarification of the affirmative plan: what is the provision for enforcing cease-and-desist court orders in the South?
  B. Impracticability
    1. There are significant obstacles which would prevent a national compulsory F.E.P. law from coming into existence:

[1] Cf. affirmative treatment of the same issue, same topic, pp. 67–68.

       a. Filibuster in the Senate. Southern senators would filibuster to prevent the law from being voted on.

       b. Unconstitutionality. If a filibuster didn't block the law, the Supreme Court would probably declare it unconstitutional because it violated states' rights.

  2. Even if the law were enacted and declared constitutional, significant obstacles would prevent its enforcement, particularly in the South:

       a. Members of boards of appeal in the South would probably be partial to the employer.

       b. Most Southern employers as well as law-enforcement agencies in the South would probably ignore the law. (Analogies may be drawn with the national prohibition law and with various Supreme Court rulings against segregation.)

       c. The criteria for determining discrimination are inherently vague and often could not be accurately applied.

  C. Undesirability

  1. The affirmative plan would not treat the underlying cause of discrimination, which is basically ignorance as manifested by:

       a. A mistaken belief in the inherent superiority of some races.

       b. Unenlightened self-interest.

       c. Irrational customs, mores, and folkways, particularly the unfounded fears of miscegenation.

      (A national compulsory F.E.P. law would at best treat only effects, not the underlying cause of the problem.)

  2. Negative repair: a broader and more intensified educational program (in the school, church, and home). Appeal to reason, persuasion, and counterpropaganda are the only effective ways to combat ignorance and thus discrimination.

  D. Disadvantages

  Attempted enforcement by the national government would produce the following evils:

  1. It would endanger the considerable progress toward harmonious race relations already made voluntarily in the South.

  2. It would lead to the closing down of certain industries and possibly of certain public schools in the South.

  3. It would lead to violence and bloodshed like that which occurred throughout the South during the Reconstruction Period after the Civil War and in Florida, Alabama, and Louisiana during the operation of a World War II F.E.P. law designed by President Roosevelt.

(The order used in presenting the various subpoints does not always have to be that followed here.)

Summary

    In summing up the obligations of the affirmative and negative positions, the affirmative, in trying to prove the truth of the resolution, must prove the subpropositions "there is a need for changing the status quo" and "the affirmative plan would meet that need." This affirmative burden, or obligation, never changes. The negative on the other hand must create doubt about or disprove the resolution. Although this obligation never shifts, the negative has many choices in carrying it out and thus its approach or analysis may vary from case to case. It cannot be overemphasized that successful debating depends largely on logical analysis, i.e., on selecting and emphasizing the right issues.[2]

EXERCISES

1. How detailed should the affirmative plan be? What is the initial affirmative obligation regarding practicability?

2. Devise a plan for one of the following resolutions and indicate why each provision was included:

   a. "Resolved, That the United States Should Adopt a Policy of Free Trade."

   b. "Resolved, That the Federal Government Should Adopt a Permanent Program of Direct Price and Wage Controls."

   c. "Resolved, That the Nonagricultural Industries of the United States Should Guarantee Their Workers an Annual Wage."

[See *Debate Handbooks* published by J. Weston Walch.]

3. Explain "desirability."

4. Explain "additional advantages." What is the difference between "direct" and "indirect" advantages? Which are more effective and why?

5. Cite one possible direct advantage and one indirect advantage for each of the following questions:

   a. "Euthanasia Should Be Legalized."

   b. "The United States Should Give Its Economic Aid Indirectly through an Agency of the United Nations."

   c. "Compulsory Union Membership Should Not Be a Condition of Employment."

   d. "Nuclear Weapons Tests Should Be Prohibited by International Agreement."

6. Explain "impracticability." What does it encompass?

7. Discuss "self-interest," mores (deeply rooted customs), cost, and unconstitutionality in relation to impracticability.

8. Discuss the possible interpretations of public opinion polls favoring the status quo, or opposing the affirmative policy. What is the relationship, if any, of such polls to impracticability?

9. Explain "undesirability."

10. Explain "disadvantages." What is the difference between "direct" and "indirect" disadvantages? Which are more effective and why? What is an irrelevant disadvantage?

11. Cite one possible direct disadvantage and one indirect disadvantage for each of the propositions listed in question 5.

---

[2] Some of the material appearing in the last two chapters appeared earlier in two articles by the writer: "Logic and Strategy in Developing the Debate Case," *The Speech Teacher*, III, 2 (March, 1954), pp. 91–106; and "Teaching Analysis to a Debate Squad," *The Gavel*, XXXIX, 1 (November, 1956), pp. 9–11.

CHAPTER 6

GATHERING INFORMATION AND EVIDENCE

There is nothing more frightful than ignorance in action.

Goethe

1. GATHERING INFORMATION

Successful debating requires not only sound analysis but also much work in gathering materials to support the framework of the case—facts, statistics, and expert testimony. Fortunately, much material is available if one knows where to look for it.

Following a Plan

In gathering knowledge and tracking down evidence one should work according to a general plan. To read or collect evidence at random may result in wasted effort and neglect of certain issues. Therefore, before doing any research the squad should meet several times to discuss the interpretation and general issues of the question. These discussions, based on the principles considered in the previous two chapters, will provide the student with a frame of reference to guide his reading. As the reading progresses the initial outline will be modified and expanded.

Sources of Information

Among the most useful sources of information and evidence for the debater are the following:

Previous Knowledge

Oftentimes the student will find that he is majoring in the field of the debate topic or has studied aspects of it in one of his courses. However, previous knowledge, though helpful for orientation, doesn't usually take one very far and is not required for successful debating.

Interviews and Discussions with Professors

These are helpful primarily for getting started—acquiring some background and possibly some good leads on available materials. At the start of the season the director of debate occasionally invites certain professors to address the entire squad so as to orient it on the topic.

Individual Research

For background and general orientation:

Current Textbooks. These are useful for getting acquainted with the subject. Occasionally, the pros and cons are discussed. Texts also contain useful bibliographies—lists of works used in preparation of the book —which may be helpful as sources of evidence.

Encyclopedia Articles. These serve the same purpose as current texts— being used primarily for background material. The best known encyclopedias are *The Encyclopedia Britannica, Encyclopedia Americana,* and the *New International Encyclopedia.* Both the Britannica and Americana publish annual supplements called, respectively, *Britannica Book of the Year* and *The Americana.*

For evidence:

Reference Works. Books, magazines, and newspapers are indexed in separate standard reference works as follows.

Books: Card catalogues in college and city libraries. These are useful in locating books (or chapters of books) on the subject. There are usually three separate entries for a book, listed alphabetically by title, author, and general field of knowledge. Some cards contain a book's table of contents, which enable one to tell at once if the book is useful.

Magazine Articles: The most important reference works for magazine articles are *The Reader's Guide to Periodical Literature* and *The International Index.* These are valuable reference works containing alphabetical listings by author, title, and general field of study of articles which have appeared in a selected group of periodicals. Another reference work of much value to the debater is the *Public Affairs Information Service Index,* which includes not only magazine articles but also government documents indexed by title and subject.

Newspaper Articles: The New York Times Index is an index of articles which have appeared in the *New York Times,* the newspaper most frequently used by debaters.

In locating pertinent books and articles in the foregoing reference works, particularly the magazine indexes, one must use some imagination, for the references usually will not be directly to the debate proposition. Thus, one must look for topics suggested by key words of the proposition. For example, with the proposition "Resolved, That the Requirement of

Membership in a Labor Organization as a Condition of Employment Should Be Illegal," one would look for such topics as "Labor Unions," "Compulsory Unionism," "Right-to-Work Laws," "Organized Labor," "Racketeering in Labor Unions," "AFL-CIO." Frequently the various indexes themselves list related topics.

Miscellaneous Reference Works and Sources:
1. General
   Agricultural Index
   Education Index
   Encyclopedia of the Social Sciences
   Public Affairs Committee, Inc., 22 East 38th Street, New York. Issues more than 100 pamphlets at 20¢ each.
   Public Affairs Pamphlets. A bulletin of the U.S. Office of Education; index to many inexpensive pamphlets on social, economic, political, and international affairs problems.
   Public Affairs Information Service. A similar index published by H. W. Wilson Company.
   Statistical Abstract of the United States
   The Statesman's Yearbook
   World Almanac. Lists 25,000 organizations, most of which publish pamphlets.
2. Biographical
   American Men of Science
   Biography Index
   Current Biography
   Debate Handbook published annually by J. Weston Walch.
   Directory of American Scholars
   Who's Who
   Who's Who in America
   Who's Who in the East
   Who's Who in the South
   Who's Who in the West

Direct Sources. In addition to materials which have already been indexed, one should periodically check the current issues of such works as the following:

Newspapers:
Christian Science Monitor
New York Herald-Tribune
New York Times and
New York Times Magazine (Sunday)
Wall Street Journal
Weekly News Magazines:

Newsweek
Time
U.S. News and World Report
Monthly and Quarterly Journals:
Academy of Political Science Proceedings
American Bar Association Journal
American Economic Review
Annals of the American Academy
Atlantic Monthly
Business Week
Congressional Digest
Congressional Record
Current History
The Economist (London)
Foreign Policy Bulletin
Fortune
Harper's
Harvard Business Review
Journal of Political Economy
Labor Law Journal
Law Reviews (Columbia, Harvard, Iowa, Michigan, Mississippi, NYU,
    Northwestern, Pennsylvania, St. John's, Wisconsin, Yale, etc.)
Monthly Labor Review
Nation
Nation's Business
New Republic
New Statesman and Nation
Reporter
UN Review
U.S. Department of State Bulletin
Vital Speeches
Yale Review

Special Aids: There are a number of valuable sources of information which, upon request, will furnish, either free of charge or for a very nominal sum, materials and bibliographies pertaining to the current debate topic and in some cases an analysis of the question, which, though not definitive, can prove suggestive and helpful. Some of these sources are:

1. *Government Sources.* Most of the annual national high school and college debate topics deal with national problems, and the debater will find many government sources willing to supply him with relevant materials. Among these are:

a. *Congressmen*. One should write one's representative or senator early in the season requesting all available materials on the current topic. The response is invariably helpful.

b. *Special Agencies*. Among the most useful of these are:

The Library of Congress, Division of Bibliography, or Legislative Reference Service, Washington, D.C.

U.S. Office of Education. Publishes Public Affairs Pamphlets, an index to many inexpensive pamphlets dealing with social, political, and economic problems.

Government Printing Office, Washington, D.C.

Miscellaneous agencies dealing with matters related to the topic. If the topic were "Federal Aid to Education," one might write to the U.S. Department of Education, NEA of the United States, and the National Advisory Commission on Education.

2. *Private Sources*. There are many private organizations which, to promote certain economic or political views, will supply the student free of charge with materials on the particular side of the question they wish to promote. Examples of such organizations are the American Medical Association; the AFL-CIO; the Foundation for Economic Education, Inc., Irvington-on-the-Hudson, New York; the National Association of Manufacturers; the National Education Association; and the United States Chamber of Commerce. Many others are listed in the *World Almanac*. In using materials sent by such organizations the student must be careful to eliminate those which appear unreliable or written by known propagandists.

3. *Miscellaneous Aids*. Into this category fall some of the most useful materials available to the debater. For this reason particular attention should be paid to the following list:

a. *Annals of the American Academy of Political and Social Science*. This bimonthly journal covers several controversial topics in each issue, occasionally the current high school and college national topic. Representative topics from recent issues are: *Higher Education under Stress, Internal Security and Civil Rights, Contemporary Africa: Trends and Issues*, and *Future of the United Nations*. Since only recognized authorities are represented, they may be quoted freely.

b. *Congressional Digest*. This journal, published monthly except for July and August, is an independent publication and is not to be confused with the *Congressional Record*, a publication of congressional proceedings published by the Government Printing Office. The *Digest* devotes each issue to a single controversial subject, including one issue each year to the current high school debate topic and one to the current college topic. Besides pro and con arguments on the topic, each issue contains a history and an impartial analysis of the question. Subjects covered in recent issues include: "Federal Civil Rights Legislation," "Reciprocal Trade Act Renewal," "Congress and the 1958 Farm Program," and "Required Union Membership."

c. *Debate Handbooks.* These are special compilations of material on the current high school and college debate topics, published early in the school year, usually around October, and costing about $2.50 each. A typical handbook contains a history of the question, suggested interpretations of the terms, an analysis of the issues, briefs for both sides of the question, bibliographies, a considerable amount of evidence pro and con pertaining to each issue, and biographical data on the authorities quoted. If used to supplement independent analysis and evidence, such books are quite helpful. Unfortunately, too many debaters use them exclusively and do poorly, for the analyses are often fragmentary and illogical and the evidence limited or soon outdated. For a start, however, debate handbooks are quite useful if one recognizes their limitations. Two of the most popular and widely used handbooks are those published by J. Weston Walch, Publishers, Portland, Maine, and by the Midwest Debate Bureau, Normal, Illinois. Supplements containing more recent evidence on the current debate question are published about midway in the debate season.

d. *The NUEA Debate Handbook.* This work, edited by Bower Aly and published by the National University Extension Association as a service to high schools, consists of a set of paper-backed booklets —usually two a year—containing articles by prominent authorities on the annual high school topic. It also contains an introductory analysis of the topic and a selected bibliography.

e. *The AFA Register.* This publication of the American Forensic Association devotes one issue a year to analyses, suggested briefs, and bibliographies of the current high school and related topics.

f. *The Reference Shelf Series.* This is a collection of works, each one devoted to a single controversial topic and containing pro and con articles by well-known authorities on that topic, as well as an extensive bibliography. Each year a new book is added to the series. Typical titles include: *Should the Communist Party Be Outlawed?*, *The Censorship of Books*, and *Free Medical Care.* The Series, published by H. W. Wilson Company, New York, can be located in the reference section of most libraries.

g. *The University Debaters' Annual.* This is a collection of books published annually by H. W. Wilson Company from 1915 through

1952, each book being a compilation of college debates, discussions, and symposiums on various subjects, usually from five to seven different subjects in a single issue. The later issues contain debates recorded verbatim with some minor editing.

h. *Weekly Television and Radio Programs.* Several such programs bring together well-known authorities, controversial figures, and advocates of various controversial views. Among the better known are Meet the Press, Chicago Round Table, and Northwestern University Reviewing Stand. Transcripts of these programs may be purchased for a nominal sum, usually 10 or 15 cents. Often an account of the Meet the Press program appears the following day as a news item in the *New York Times.*

2. RECORDING EVIDENCE

Following a Plan

To avoid duplication, neglecting certain issues, or overburdening any one member of the squad, a plan should be followed for recording as well as for tracking down evidence. One such plan might be to draw up a tentative bibliography, assign certain readings to each squad member, and require him to make notes on this material covering the general divisions of the case ("evils," "inherency," "disadvantages," etc.). Concerning handbooks containing several hundred pieces of evidence, one should first discuss this evidence at a general meeting or meetings and check off what is usable. The work of transcribing this evidence is then divided equally among all the members. Eventually all notes should be typed, put into a common pool, sorted, and placed in small metal filing cans, one can for the affirmative case and one for the negative.

Note Cards

In recording evidence, one should use 3- by 5-in. or 4- by 6-in. note cards, preferably the latter. Each card should contain the following:

1. *Main topic heading* on upper left corner of card. These headings should correspond to the main headings of the case, like "Evils," "Impracticability," etc.

2. *Subtopic heading* at upper right corner of the card. This should identify more specifically the contents of the note.

3. *The note itself* should be recorded accurately and usually verbatim. Care must be taken not to misrepresent the writer's views by recording phrases out of context.

4. *Source of the note* should appear at the bottom of the card and should include the author's name, title of article or book, place and date published, and page number.

5. *A phrase to identify author,* if needed, should appear under the source.

A typical note would look like this:

EVIL   Aid Discourages Initiative

In Lebanon we spent during 1954 about 6 million dollars to increase agricultural production and to build roads. That country refused to contribute any of her own money to pay expenses of work there because she claimed that in so doing she would have to operate in the red.

A. J. Ellender, "Text of Address by Senator Ellender of Louisiana," *Congressional Record,* Vol. 101, June 9, 1955, p. 4140.

Note: No identifying phrase for author is necessary here since identification is made in the title of the work from which the note is taken.

Card File

When notes have been sorted and filed, divider cards marked with appropriate headings should be used to divide the various issues and subissues. A typical card file is illustrated on page 86.

Needless to say, research should continue throughout the entire debate year, with new notes being added regularly and old ones periodically removed. Many squads also find it expedient to add attack and defense (or "rebuttal") cards to the file, particularly as the season progresses and various counterarguments are used against the original case. Also, it is a good idea to file attack and defense arguments which grow out of the practice sessions preceding the actual debate season. In sum, the more experience one gains the more one realizes that solid preparation and constant practice are the keys to successful debating.

EXERCISES

1. Compile a bibliography of twenty items for one of the following questions:

a. "The United States Government Should Aid Deserving High School Students."

b. "Capital Punishment Should Be Abolished."

c. "Congress Should Enact a Compulsory Fair Employment Practices Law."

2. Bring in one piece of evidence on each of the following topics (use the same subject chosen in question 1):

a. defects of status quo
b. cause of defects
c. desirability, or plan would meet need
d. practicability
e. additional advantages
f. achievements of status quo

g. cause of achievements
h. undesirability, or plan would not meet need
i. impracticability: obstacles and unenforceability
j. disadvantages

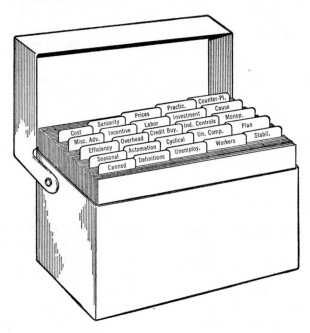

Sample evidence file. The following topics should be used as a guide for the various headings and subheadings:

Definitions
Evils of status quo
Achievements of status quo
Cause of evils (inherency)
Cause of achievements
Present machinery
Modifications of status quo

Affirmative plan
Counterplan
Plan meets need
Plan won't meet need
(Im)practicability (obstacles)
(Im)practicability (enforceability)
Additional advantages

Disadvantages

CHAPTER 7

OVER-ALL STRATEGY: ORGANIZING INDIVIDUAL SPEECHES

Science is built up of facts, as a house is built up of stones; but an accumulation of facts is no more a science than a heap of stones is a house.

Henri Poincaré

1. THE PREARRANGED SCHEDULE

In the orthodox form of debating the following format is used:

	Minutes
1st affirmative constructive	10
1st negative constructive	10
2nd affirmative constructive	10
2nd negative constructive	10
1st negative rebuttal	5
1st affirmative rebuttal	5
2nd negative rebuttal	5
2nd affirmative rebuttal	5

We are now ready to consider the organization of the individual speeches, which, taken together, constitute what is known as "the case."

Since there are many arguments and counterarguments in an average debate, a debater is continually confronted with the problem of deciding when and how long to deal with a particular issue. Leaving this matter to chance or following a very rough outline, as debaters often do, results in poor organization and neglecting important arguments. Although very careful planning is called for, debaters usually do less planning here than elsewhere. One might think that careful planning as to arrangement and emphasis of materials is impossible since one can't always predict the opposition's reaction to an argument or the way an issue will develop. While no one fixed plan can be made and followed,

87

two or three flexible plans can and should be. The order in which potential issues will be treated and for approximately how long should be decided beforehand, the plan being subject to change, of course. Such planning insures a logical, coherent development of the case and also the proper emphasis on the various issues. Most debaters tend to spend either too much or too little time on an issue, particularly on issues they are well or poorly prepared on. Since only so much time is allotted to a team, this must be used to the best possible advantage. If a debater spends too much time on one point, he takes away time from another; if one partner does not cover certain ground, he may burden the other. Optimum effectiveness comes from adhering closely to a prearranged schedule.

To carry out this plan a debater must watch the timekeeper regularly. If the latter does not have minute-by-minute cards, he should be supplied with a set, which every team should carry for just such an emergency.

The prearranged schedule not only is indispensable for good organization and proper emphasis but also aids the debater psychologically, particularly the inexperienced debater, who worries about not having enough to say or about presenting his points haphazardly. Knowing beforehand the organization of his material and knowing that he will not become entangled in a mass of arguments give him confidence.

2. ORGANIZATION, EMPHASIS, AND TIMING

Constructive Speeches

First Affirmative Constructive

This speech is wholly constructive since it is concerned not with attack or defense but with building the affirmative case. The points developed in this speech influence greatly the course of the entire debate. Since there is no adaptation to a previous speech, this speech can be completely prepared in content and phrasing, or "canned." One should make the most of this advantage. Many first affirmative speakers tend to waste much time—their speeches being rambling and diffuse, and covering too few points. Almost the entire affirmative constructive case should be developed in this speech, i.e., all the important affirmative points with the exception of additional advantages of the affirmative plan. These include a definition of key terms, an explanation of the affirmative plan, evils of the status quo, the cause of or inherency of these evils, and a demonstration of how the plan would meet the need. The affirmative need not consider impracticability or possible disadvantages of the plan until the negative introduces these points. In a few cases, where inherency does not require much causal analysis, even additional advantages may be included in the first speech. Though covering many points may decrease the over-all effectiveness of inexperienced debaters, it increases the effectiveness of good debaters. Since much has to be done in this first speech, every word and every piece of evidence must be carefully chosen for their maximum effect; anything extraneous to the case should be suppressed. A debate is often won or lost in this first speech. It should be compact, meaty, and organized along the lines shown in Chapter 4. To recapitulate, this speech should contain the following:

Brief Greeting. Typical: "We are happy to have this opportunity to debate with our friends from Bucknell on the timely question 'Resolved, etc.'" One should avoid the formal salutation "Honorable judge, worthy opponents, etc."

Definition of Terms. Only the key terms, usually those which identify the new policy, should be defined. Words like "Congress," "the United States," "discontinue," "enact," and "should" need not be defined. One may preface his definitions by remarking "We feel that the terms of the question are self-explanatory, with the possible exception of [term which designates new policy]." Sometimes a paraphrased version of the resolution will suffice; thus, the question "Resolved, That the Requirement of Membership in a Labor Organization as a Condition of Employment Should Be Illegal" might be paraphrased as "a worker should not have to join a union either to get or to keep a job." After defining terms, one may explain the affirmative plan, the arrangement preferred by this writer, though one may also explain the plan after the "need" has been established.

In the past first affirmative debaters traditionally included a brief history of the question in their introductory remarks. For good or evil, however, this practice has been discontinued. Since the first affirmative speaker has much to do, he has no time for a history of the question, unless the history can be used as an argument to support an issue. On the question of government aid to education, for example, one might show that the government has contributed to public education since 1865 and that the concept of government aid, therefore, is not so radical as it might seem or that government aid in the past has not led to government control. Unless they can use a history of the question in this way, most college debaters omit it.

A Brief Statement of Affirmative Issues and Division of Labor between Partners. Typical: "I will show that the union shop is inherently defective and that a maintenance-of-membership provision would remove the inherent defect. My colleague will show that, besides meeting the need, the affirmative proposal would result in additional advantages for the economy as a whole."

A Brief Statement of Common Objectives. Example: "In order to evaluate the status quo properly, we must first consider its objectives. We believe the negative will agree with us when we say that the overriding objective of any labor legislation should be to promote the welfare of the worker to the fullest possible extent."

Evils of the Status Quo. Example: "Has the present program, then, achieved this goal? The fact is, it has not. Undemocratic practices, Communist domination, and widespread corruption in the labor movement today indicate that the status quo is failing to meet this objective. Let us consider these evils individually. First, etc."

Cause of Evils, or Inherency. [If the evils cited are not caused by the present policy, they can be eliminated without eliminating this policy. One must therefore relate the evils directly to the present policy.] Example: "All of these facts indicate that compulsory unionism has been attended by many serious evils and consequently has failed to meet its objective. The next logical question is, is it not possible to modify the status quo in some way and thus eliminate such evils? The answer is no. We cannot eliminate these evils under the status quo because of compulsion. Now let us see why compulsory unionism is fundamentally wrong, wrong in essence, or inherently defective, why it is a major causal factor of the evils we have cited." [Such repetition is often necessary because the point is very important and because both the opposition and the judge frequently do not understand the reasoning here.]

Inability of Existing Program to Meet the Need. This step consists of a fairly detailed examination of the existing program or of available recourses under the status quo to mitigate the aforementioned evils. In a sense, this step is unnecessary since the existing program has already been shown to be wrong in principle. Time permitting, however, this step should be included since it reinforces the previous one. In some cases, like the guaranteed annual wage and Federal aid to education, it must be included before inherency is considered. If one has to omit the step because of time, the negative will undoubtedly introduce it and the affirmative will then have to discuss it in subsequent speeches, tying it always to inherency. Typical introductory remarks to this step might be: "To pursue the point further that compulsion is the insurmountable obstacle to the elimination of these evils, we need only consider the possibilities and actual attempts under the status quo to reform the labor movement, both from within and from without, certainly the only two alternatives." And typical concluding remarks might be: "Thus, reform of the status quo, both from within and from without, is impracticable. Both have failed to eliminate the evils of the present program. Why? Because it is only by eliminating compulsion, the inherent defect of the status quo, that we can eliminate these evils. We must give workers the right to withdraw their support from a union in order to provide them with the only effective way to check the autocratic power of their leaders and thus to make these leaders responsive to their will."

Explanation of the Affirmative Plan. As pointed out, this step may also follow the definition of terms. The time devoted to the plan would depend upon the particular question.

Explanation of How Plan Would Meet the Need. Depending upon the case, this step may be very brief—merely a statement that the affirmative proposal, by eliminating the inherent defect of the status quo, or cause, would therefore eliminate the evil effects—or fairly detailed— a point-by-point demonstration of how the affirmative plan would treat the various evils of the status quo. If a detailed explanation is necessary, the more effective procedure usually is to break up the speech into a series of units containing "evil 1—cause—plan would meet need," "evil 2—cause—plan would meet need," etc. However, experience is the best teacher here.

Brief Summary. Here the main points of the speech are reviewed. "In summary, then, what have we seen?" or "To sum up, let us see what the affirmative has done," or "In conclusion, we have shown, etc."

To recapitulate, the 1st affirmative constructive speech usually contains the following:

Topic	Approximate time limits
1. Greeting	
2. Definition and specific plan	
3. Statement of issues and division of labor	1½–2 min
4. Common objectives	
5. Evils of status quo	2–4 min
6. Cause or inherency of evils	1–2 min
7. Inability of existing program to meet need. (Optional)	1–2 min
8. Affirmative plan would meet need	1–2 min
9. Summary	½ min

First Negative Constructive Speech

Every speech after the first affirmative constructive speech must be constructed with the previous speech in mind; that is, it must be adapted to counter previous arguments of the opposition. This means that for the most part it must be constructed extemporaneously. The task is not so difficult as it might seem. With careful preparation, thorough familiarity with the arguments and counterarguments of both sides, and a certain amount of practice in extemporaneous speaking, a debater soon learns to master the techniques of composing on the spot a speech tailored to answer the preceding one. Failure to adapt involves the risk of directing one's attack at nonexistent arguments and of ignoring those which have actually been presented by the opposition, like an army directing its fire into an empty field while the enemy advances unscathed from another direction. The practice of "canned" constructive speeches, except for the first affirmative, justifiably is passé.

Although the main purpose of the negative is to attack or tear down the affirmative case, the negative should not argue solely on affirmative points; it should also initiate the issues of impracticability and disadvantages of the affirmative plan.

Although the negative has several alternatives, as we have seen, the most effective generally is to minimize the affirmative evils, attack inherency (i.e., question the causal relationship between the evils cited and the status quo), and create doubt as to whether the affirmative plan would meet the minimal need. All of these points should be covered in the first negative speech as well as several well-prepared disadvantages (including impracticability when feasible) of the affirmative proposal, unless such disadvantages are directed against a specific type of plan not yet introduced by the affirmative. If the first affirmative speaker did not introduce any plan, the negative should introduce certain general disadvantages of the underlying principle of the affirmative policy, delaying its attack on the plan until after it has been explained.

Many negative teams prefer to delay their objections until the second constructive speech and to attack the affirmative points more thoroughly in the first speech. Some negative teams use this strategy on the theory that the affirmative will not have enough time to deal properly with negative objections since only two five-minute speeches remain for the affirmative after the second negative constructive speech. Like all stratagems or ruses, however, this has its drawbacks. Aside from the question of sportsmanship, this delaying tactic reduces the emphasis received by an important component of the negative case. In preventing the affirmative from dealing adequately with negative objections, the negative also prevents itself from resupporting and fixing them in the judge's mind. An issue initiated late in a debate receives less attention and therefore less emphasis than one initiated earlier. If the negative's objections are any good, they should be able to stand up under affirmative crossfire; and if they are not good, they should be omitted entirely. Even though it means being less thorough temporarily in handling the affirmative points and possibly leaving oneself open to the charge of omissions, the advantage of introducing objections and thus orienting the judge early in the debate to the negative case offsets any disadvantage, which can be neutralized in any event in the next negative speech. Thus, the recommended procedure is to introduce all the negative objections in this first speech. If time runs out, as it sometimes does, and an objection or two remains, the second negative speaker should develop it at the start of his speech, after briefly reviewing the objections developed by his partner. When the negative, through no fault of its own, is forced to delay introducing certain disadvantages because the first affirmative speaker did not explain the affirmative plan, the negative is still in a relatively advantageous position because the affirmative by its delay usually puts itself into a deeper hole.

Thus, the following is a recommended breakdown of the first negative constructive speech:

Topic	*Approximate time limits*
1. Greeting	½ min
2. (Optional) Definition of terms. If the negative disagrees with any of the affirmative's definitions, it should say so and why right at the outset. If it accepts the affirmative's definitions, it need say nothing about them.	—
3. Brief statement of negative issues.	½ min
4. Attack on affirmative case: on evils, inherency, and plan would meet need (if plan was introduced by first affirmative). Some of this material can be canned.	5–7 min
5. Negative objections. These encompass impracticability and disadvantages of the affirmative plan. At least three disadvantages should be developed if possible. Occasionally one's partner may introduce two others. The time given this step depends upon whether the objections are divided between the partners. All negative objections should be introduced here if possible, and this material should be canned.	2–4 min
6. Brief summary.	½ min

Second Affirmative Constructive Speech

If the preceding speaker has done his job well, much doubt has now been cast on the affirmative case. The main purpose of this speech, therefore, is to reconstruct the affirmative case and to bring the judge back to the affirmative point of view. As in all debate speeches, the speaker must use his time wisely, adapting his material to the previous speech and emphasizing issues in accordance with the emphasis they received in the preceding speech. Thus, if the preceding speaker spent all his time on the affirmative issues (introducing no negative objections), the emphasis of this speech will also be on the affirmative issues. If the preceding speaker spent relatively little time on the affirmative evils and most of his time on inherency, impracticability, and disadvantages, the second affirmative need spend little time rebuilding the evils. First, he should point out negative omissions—i.e., failures by the negative to attack, question, or deny conclusions introduced by his partner—and emphasize their significance. He should then spend most of his remaining time on the points stressed by the first negative speaker. As a rule, he should reserve some time toward the end of the speech for introducing additional advantages of the affirmative plan—canned material which can be condensed or elaborated upon, depending upon the available time. This new constructive material not only puts an additional burden upon the next speaker, particularly if the negative objections were held in abeyance for him, but also concludes the speech on a solid affirmative note. A further advantage, psychological rather than strategic, of having prepared material in reserve is that inexperienced debaters, if they become flustered or temporarily lost, can always call upon this reserve to pull them out of an embarrassing situation.

The following is a suggested breakdown of the second affirmative constructive speech:

| | *Approximate* |
| *Topic* | *time limits* |

1. Greeting. Optional step. Typical of greetings used: "I would like to reiterate the comments of my partner and say that it is a real pleasure to be debating our friends from Bucknell this evening." If the preceding speaker was very effective, one might compliment him by stating "We should like to thank the preceding speaker for a very clear and effective presentation of the negative point of view in this debate." . . . .   ½ min

2. Reiteration of affirmative issues. "You will recall that the affirmative predicated its case on the following issues: etc." This serves to remind the judge that the affirmative also has a case. . . . .   ½ min

3. Omissions and tacit admissions by the negative, and their significance. "Before considering what the gentleman from Bucknell has said concerning the affirmative case, let us consider what he has not said. Etc. And thus we see a substantial portion of the affirmative case still unanswered and still standing." Incidentally, a team is guilty of omissions only when it fails to consider conclusions of arguments, not the supporting evidence. As we shall see, one may ignore the evidence of an argument but still attack the conclusion. . . . .   1–1½ min

4. Rebuilding issues introduced by first affirmative. This should be done with reference to the negative attack. . . . .   3½–4½ min

5. Answers to negative objections. If no objections were offered in the previous speech, this time should be spent on the previous step. . . . . . .   2–3 min

6. Additional advantages of the affirmative plan. This is canned constructive material. For novices this step may be expanded. If the negative attack was unusually strong, this material can be condensed or even eliminated and the time spent on steps 4 and 5. . . . .   —

7. Summary of entire case. If time permits, this should be made with passing references to the negative case. . . . .   ½–1 min

Second Negative Constructive Speech

This speech should be coordinated with the next one, the first negative rebuttal speech, which immediately follows it, so that the over-all effect is that of one fifteen-minute speech. A good practice is to announce at the outset the intention to make the two speeches one and to specify what each partner will cover, e.g., "My partner and I shall consider the next fifteen minutes as one speech. I shall deal with the affirmative need and with the so-called affirmative advantages; my colleague will consider once more the impracticability of the affirmative plan and the disadvantages which would accrue from such a plan." Some debaters prefer to reserve such a remark for the conclusion of the speech, when they know with greater certainty what each partner will be able to cover. However, it is more effective at the beginning of the speech, with a reminder at the conclusion of what the second speaker will discuss.

As a rule, this speech should be mainly an attack upon the reconstructed affirmative case and upon any additional advantages that may have been introduced by the preceding speaker, with the next speaker devoting himself almost exclusively to reinforcing and rebuilding negative objections. As previously noted, some negative teams, however, prefer to devote about half of the speech to an attack upon the affirmative issues and the concluding half to negative objections, introducing them here for the first time. In keeping with this strategy, the next speech would have to be devoted exclusively to countering the affirmative defense of its own case, in other words, to attacking affirmative issues, since the affirmative has not yet had an opportunity to counter negative objections. Some negative teams go to an even further extreme in this speech, abandoning the affirmative issues completely and opening instead with an attack on the practicability of the affirmative plan—particularly if the latter was introduced in the preceding speech—and then solidly building negative objections for the remainder of the speech. This strategy would also call for the next speaker to spend his entire speech attacking the reconstructed affirmative case.

The strategy of postponing the introduction of negative objections has already been discussed. This writer does not recommend it but prefers the following breakdown, predicated on the supposition that all negative objections were introduced in the first negative constructive speech:

Time limits

1. Brief greeting. Optional. ....   —
2. Statement of intention and division of labor between partners. ....   ½ min
3. Attack upon reconstructed affirmative points and additional advantages (if any). If time permits, reconstruct impracticability if it is an issue in the debate and was introduced by partner and answered by the last speaker. ....   8–8½ min
4. Brief summary of speech. This should conclude with a statement of negative objections, "which my partner will further discuss." ....   ½–1 min

If, for some reason, the first negative was not able to get in all the negative objections, the second negative should allude to those developed by his partner and then develop the remaining ones himself. This should be done before step 3.

Rebuttal Speeches

It is a rule of debate that no new issues may be introduced by either team in the rebuttal speeches. This rule, however, does not preclude the introduction of new evidence to support issues previously introduced. Such evidence is most desirable. Sometimes, it is difficult to determine if a new issue has been introduced in the rebuttals. An issue, it must be remembered, is a point in contention, a point about which there is disagreement. Although a proposition introduced in the second negative constructive speech does not become an issue until the first affirmative rebuttal speaker considers it, the latter is not guilty of introducing a new issue in the rebuttals since his side had no opportunity to consider the point until the rebuttals. Thus, if the second negative speaker argues that the affirmative plan is impracticable and the first affirmative speaker considers this argument in his rebuttal speech, which is his first opportunity to do so, the affirmative is clearly within its rights.

A different situation exists, however, when one team delays answering an important point until the rebuttals; that is, it does not avail itself of the opportunity to answer in the constructive speeches. Suppose, for example, that a negative team decides to question the affirmative's definition of terms for the first time in one of its rebuttal speeches; it would be guilty of introducing a new issue in the rebuttals since it had the opportunity of making an issue of the opposition's point in its constructive speeches.

Occasionally, a team may seem guilty of introducing a new issue in the rebuttals because it did not clearly indicate in its constructive speeches the relationship of one of its arguments to a point introduced by the opposition. It is conceivable, for example, that a negative team in a constructive speech may attack an affirmative's definition of terms without pointing out the significance of its argument. If the negative then clarified its stand in the rebuttals, it should not be penalized for introducing a new issue; it might be penalized for not being clear, perhaps, but not to the extent of having its argument disregarded, which is the rule if the argument is thought to have raised a new issue.

First Negative Rebuttal Speech

As previously noted, the negative has fifteen consecutive minutes of speaking. For maximum effect the second negative constructive and first negative rebuttal speeches should supplement each other and, ideally, should constitute one speech with no repetitions. After the second negative constructive speech, the affirmative case should be in shreds. At this point the first negative rebuttalist should open with a brief summary of what has gone before, pointing out, perhaps, that he need not deal with the affirmative case as nothing new has been said since his partner dealt with it. He should then devote the remainder of his speech to further substantiating the negative's objections. There have now been almost five minutes of negative "constructive" presentation; and the judge should have the impression that not only has the affirmative been met on its own grounds and refuted but that the disadvantages of the affirmative program far outweigh any accruing advantages.

The following is a suggested breakdown of this speech:

Time limits

1. Brief review of negative attack on affirmative case. .... ½ min
2. Resubstantiation of negative objections. .... 4 min
3. Brief summary, stressing negative case. .... ½ min

In debates where practicability is a big issue, negative teams sometimes find this breakdown effective:

Second constructive: (10 minutes)	1. Attack on affirmative need	5 min
	2. Impracticability	5 min
First rebuttal: (5 minutes)	3. Disadvantages	5 min

The order of the three parts is not fixed, with some teams preferring to discuss impracticability and disadvantages in the constructive speech and the affirmative need in the rebuttal speech.

First Affirmative Rebuttal Speech

This speech is perhaps the crucial affirmative presentation, crucial from the standpoint that the debate can easily be lost here. Assuming the teams are fairly evenly matched, the negative is further ahead at this point than at any other in the debate and the judge is "negative oriented." Although clearly behind, the affirmative *must not go on the defensive.* The mind of the judge must be brought back to the affirmative position. As a start, one should open the speech with a brief restatement of the affirmative issues ("You will recall that the affirmative predicated its case on, etc., etc."), simultaneously pointing out negative omissions, evasions, and implicit admissions, or "areas of agreement." Then, assuming that the negative objections were first introduced in the first negative constructive speech and that his partner dealt with them in his constructive speech, one should rebuild the affirmative case in the light of the negative attack, reserving approximately the final minute for an attack upon the chief negative objection. The important thing to remember is that the bulk of the speech should be devoted to rebuilding the affirmative case.

On the other hand, if the negative objections were first introduced by the second negative speaker, the first affirmative rebuttalist should deal with them since his is the first opportunity to do so.[1] The problem for the affirmative now becomes to discuss the negative case without appearing to be on the defensive or to have abandoned the affirmative case. However, it should be remembered that if the negative delayed its objections until the second negative constructive speech, the second affirmative constructive speaker was able to concentrate entirely on the affirmative case—actually, he was able to spend from three to four minutes more on his own case than he would have been had the first negative introduced the negative objections. Thus, to this point in the debate the affirmative case would be on a firmer footing than it otherwise would be. Still, the affirmative speaker must cope with fifteen minutes of consecutive negative presentation, and particularly with the negative's objections, without appearing to be on the defensive.

A discerning judge realizes that the negative tactic has forced the affirmative to deal with the negative constructive material at this time and does not penalize the affirmative for doing so. However, the affirmative can further its own cause immeasurably by considering the negative's objections in relation to the affirmative issues and by retorting to these objections at every possible opportunity. For example, "The negative tells us that the affirmative plan will weaken the UN." After denying this contention with appropriate proof, the affirmative should retort, "On the contrary, the affirmative plan will strengthen the UN, for, as such-and-such has pointed out, etc., etc. Thus we see that instead of a negative disadvantage, we actually have an affirmative advantage." In other words, the affirmative should make every effort to turn the negative's disadvantages into positive affirmative advantages. With the proper preparation, this is not too difficult to do and is most effective. (See next chapter for a full discussion of the retort.)

Suggested breakdown of first affirmative rebuttal speech:

Time limits

1. Restatement of affirmative issues. .... ½ min
2. Rebuilding of affirmative case, countering negative attacks on affirmative constructive material; i.e., negative attack should be viewed in the light of affirmative issues. .... 3–3½ min
3. Attack on outstanding negative objection (on two or more objections if time permits). .... 1–1½ min
4. Brief summary from affirmative point of view. .... ½ min

[1] Occasionally the writer's own debaters will remind the judge that the affirmative has been given little time to consider objections introduced by the second negative constructive speaker, as, "Unfortunately several negative objections were introduced when we have but two short speeches remaining in which to consider them as well as the previous negative arguments and the affirmative case. However, we shall do our best to consider them in the short time that remains." This reminder is even more effective if, by contrast, the affirmative introduced most of its case in the first speech and thus gave the negative its full thirty minutes in which to consider it.

Alternate Strategy against "Delayed Negative Objections" Tactic

Time limits

1. Restatement of affirmative issues. .... ½ min
2. Countering of negative objections, retorting wherever possible, i.e., turning negative disadvantages into affirmative advantages. (If this step doesn't take four minutes, the remaining time should be spent on the affirmative case.) .... 4 min
3. Brief summary from affirmative point of view. .... ½ min

(If negative objections are divided between partners, i.e., if half of the objections are introduced in first negative constructive and the other half in second negative constructive, the first breakdown should be used.)

Second Negative Rebuttal Speech

Final speeches are always important since they represent the last opportunity to influence the judge. Unfortunately, a final impression often nullifies previous impressions, for the judge, being human, tends to forget much of what transpired earlier. This is especially true of judges who don't carefully record the progress of the debate or who lack special training in argumentation. In any event, the final speech should bring into focus the main lines of argument which have been pursued throughout the debate, with emphasis upon one's own case. As a rule, final speeches are mainly summary and review—a summary of the main issues and a review, first, of the opposition's case, showing how each argument was dealt with, and, second, of one's own case, showing how arguments attacked by the opposition were successfully defended or rebuilt, or how in certain areas the opposition was forced to yield, agree, or failed to attack. In sum, the final rebuttal speaker should leave the impression that the opposition has been successfully refuted and that his own case has been successfully defended.

In opening the final negative speech, one should not start with minor points or analyze the debate from the negative position. Since a good first affirmative rebuttalist will have pulled almost, but not quite, even at this point in the debate, one should begin by analyzing and attacking the important affirmative contentions, citing en route affirmative evasions and omissions. One of the most effective final negative rebuttals this writer ever heard began with a lengthy summary of points that the affirmative had yet to deal with, i.e., with a review of the obligations still remaining to the affirmative. When appropriate, one should point out tactfully that the affirmative has declined to deal with certain negative arguments and that if it does so in the final affirmative rebuttal the negative will be without rejoinder, thus, "And early in the debate my colleague pointed out, etc., a point still not dealt with by the affirmative. Perhaps the next speaker will consider it when we are without rejoinder." Or "And at this late stage in the debate, the affirmative still have not considered our contention that, etc."

The foregoing step should cover roughly the first half of the speech. The final half should be devoted to a complete but precise summary of the debate from the negative point of view, including a resubstantiation of the negative objections wherever needed.

Suggested breakdown of speech:

Time limits

1. Point-by-point summary of negative attack on affirmative constructive arguments, citing affirmative failures to counter (evasions and omissions) and bolstering a negative counterargument here and there with new evidence. ....   2½ min

2. Point-by-point summary of negative objections, citing affirmative evasions and omissions and bolstering a point here and there with new evidence. ....   2½ min

Second Affirmative Rebuttal Speech

As in the preceding speech one must concentrate on the essential issues. One should avoid getting on the defensive and should refuse to be diverted by last-minute questions and challenges. One should begin with an attack upon the negative objections, answering any suggestion, if made in the preceding speech, that one is using this last speech to make points that wouldn't stand the fire of negative counterattack. In the last part of the speech one should consider the affirmative issues one by one and show how they have stood up under negative attack. Closing remarks should contain a good summary and leave the impression that the affirmative has shown a strong probability that its proposal would improve existing conditions.

Suggested breakdown of speech:

Time limits

1. Statement of affirmative issues; point-by-point summary of affirmative answers to negative objections, reinforcing a point here and there.   2½ min

2. Point-by-point summary of affirmative issues, indicating negative omissions if any and reinforcing a point here and there with new evidence. ....   2½ min

Although the suggested time limits for the various points are approximate, they should be adhered to as closely as possible. Shifts in emphasis will occur periodically, but one should always have a plan carefully worked out *before getting up to speak.* The preceding plans are flexible enough to be modified right up until the time of the speech itself and should provide a good basis for planning any debate.

3. TEAMWORK

Since academic debate usually involves opposing teams of two debaters each, good teamwork or cooperation between the members of a team can contribute much to its success. As a rule, when two people work together for a while, they develop certain techniques for helping one another. As a start the following suggestions should prove useful.

Before and after Debating

1. Establish a close association with partner so that each will know the other's abilities, fields of knowledge, and personal weaknesses. Eating lunch together regularly may be one means to this end.

2. Develop a friendly intimacy and understanding of each other, for debating together can easily cause tensions and misunderstanding.

3. Work on arguments, evidence, and file divisions together so that both know the case and can remind each other of arguments and evidence quickly during a debate or can find evidence cards for each other. If a team debates both sides of the question, usually one of the partners specializes in one side and one in the other, that is, to the extent of adding new evidence to the file and of knowing its contents a little more thoroughly.

4. Discuss often strategy and the use of time so that in a debate adaptation to various situations can be made quickly.

5. Develop a set of signals so that one partner can signal the other to speed up or to slow down, to increase or to decrease volume, to cover a particular issue or to leave it, etc.

6. Do not avoid disagreements, however unpleasant they may seem at the time; it is better to settle issues than leave them stewing. However, do not argue with partner in the middle of a debate.

7. Use the time between the rounds of a debate tournament for friendly but frank criticism of each other's performance during the round just concluded. These critiques of one another's performance are usually the best you will receive.

8. Develop a system for carrying materials, setting up before a debate, and meeting the judge and the members of the opposing team. This contributes to smoothness and efficiency of operation.

While Debating

1. Listen as attentively as your partner to what is being said by the opposition, even though you yourself may not be called upon to reply to this particular set of arguments. If an original point is made, try to analyze it for weakness and pass the suggested line of attack on to your

partner in a note. It's a good practice to enable your partner to concentrate on understanding and analyzing the case as it is presented by searching out yourself the evidence cards that he will need and setting them in order for him.

2. If, for any reason, the line of attack or defense you want to follow is different from that which you and your partner have agreed upon beforehand, clear the changes with him before you get up to speak. It does teamwork no good at all to have one partner steal the other partner's points. He should know as clearly as possible what arguments he will be expected to present and refute. Otherwise he can hardly organize his own speech.

3. If, in the course of your own speech, you have occasion to refer to an especially telling point made by your partner, credit him with it by name. It was, after all, *his* point.

4. Listen carefully to your partner's speech, while at the same time trying to assess its effect on the opposing team and the judge. Is he making his points effectively, speaking loudly enough and at the right pace? Is he spending too little or too much time on some specific point? Try to answer these questions and signal to him accordingly.

4. ATTACK AND DEFENSE: A SUMMARY OF "DO'S" AND "DON'T'S"

1. Listen carefully; record accurately the substance of your opponent's arguments; record paraphrased argument, not verbatim, unless it is a crucial admission or absurd claim.

2. When answering opponent's arguments, don't distort them by manipulating their context, misquoting, or exaggerating. At all times be moderate, fair, and polite, even if opponents misquote you; assume the misquotation was unintentional and say so.

3. Be friendly in your attitude; compliment opponents if they have done a good job. Be sincere in your compliment. Refer to opponents as "our friends of the negative" or "the gentlemen from Princeton," not as "our negative friends," "our opponents," or "the members of the opposition." Never be insulting, sarcastic, belittling, or condescending.

4. Pick the most significant arguments to attack, significant to the over-all case and, as well as you can determine, to the judge. Answer the whole case, not just the easy arguments. Attack the causal relationships between the basic issues. Don't set up "straw men" to knock down; it is a waste of time and alienates perceptive judges.

5. Don't try to answer too much; you only dissipate time and energy, create confusion as to what are the main issues, and give undue weight to the opposition's case. Above all, never let the opposition get you arguing their case exclusively on their ground. This is especially im-

portant if you're on the affirmative, for if the negative can get you to spend all your time arguing back and forth about their objections, you may whip them decisively on these points, but they will correctly point out in their final rebuttal that you abandoned the affirmative burden of proof—and that it never shifts [2]—and hence they are entitled to the decision.

6. Don't answer too little, or you will be guilty of omissions and evasions.

7. Don't refute arguments not advanced by the opposition. Don't credit the other side with arguments merely stated or inadequately developed. Answer the "shotgun" attack by pointing out its superficiality and lack of supporting evidence. However, don't glibly or automatically dismiss a "big" case, i.e., one with many ramifications, as "shotgun." (The technique for dealing with such a case is to attack its interrelationships, particularly causal.) Handle suggestive questions ("What guarantee do we have that this plan will succeed?") as though they were assertions and explain your reasoning.

8. Hit significant omissions and failures of the opposition to deal with your arguments. Point up the significance of their omissions.

9. In the rebuttal speeches, don't "divide" arguments with your partner; answer thoroughly as much as time permits. Neither partner should be a specialist; each should be completely familiar with all rebuttal material.

10. In the rebuttal speeches, use new evidence, unless that used in the constructive speeches is very good or has been specifically challenged. Don't discuss totally new issues in the rebuttal speeches unless they have been raised by the opposition in their rebuttals. If the opposition raises a new issue in its rebuttal speeches, point out that although, according to the rules of debate, you are not obliged to deal with it, you will deal with it anyway. As a rule, keep introducing new evidence to support the main issues; don't rely on mere assertion.

11. Don't wait until the final rebuttal to answer negative objections

---

[2] To say that the affirmative burden of proof does not shift means that the affirmative must directly prove the truth of the resolution. For it to disprove the proposition that the affirmative proposal would be predominantly disadvantageous does not prove the contrary proposition that the affirmative proposal would be predominantly advantageous, for contrary propositions may both be false. On the other hand, for the negative to prove that the affirmative proposal is predominantly disadvantageous does disprove the contrary proposition that the affirmative proposal is predominantly advantageous, for contrary propositions cannot both be true.

In the foregoing explanation, the reader should not be confused by the terms "not prove" and "disprove." They have entirely different meanings. "Not to prove" a proposition means that no conclusion can be drawn as to its truth or falsity because of inadequate proof; "to disprove" a proposition, on the other hand, is to prove that the proposition is false.

which the negative raised early in the debate because a discerning judge will wonder why you waited until the negative was without rejoinder to deal with the issue and will discount your answer accordingly. Some judges may even ignore your answers entirely and consider the negative objections as still standing. Should the affirmative fail to answer any negative objection, the final negative speaker should stress this fact by tactfully reminding the judge that perhaps the affirmative will consider the argument in its final rebuttal speech when the negative is without rejoinder.

12. Keep in mind the basic differences between the two sides. The affirmative must not develop a "defensive complex," particularly after the first negative rebuttal speech. To avoid the impression of being on the defensive after fifteen consecutive minutes of negative argument, the affirmative should retort wherever possible or relate its answers to affirmative constructive arguments. On the other hand, the negative should attack primarily, its main purpose being to undermine the affirmative case. In its attack the negative should do more than deny affirmative conclusions; it should also retort by initiating the issues of impracticability and disadvantages.

13. Summarize frequently, not only at the end of each speech but within each speech as well. These summaries should be grouped under the main issues. For instance, the negative may deliver a brilliant four-minute attack on the affirmative's failure to show a genuine need. But all may be for naught unless you pause to explain to a slow-thinking judge that it is a duty of the affirmative to show a genuine need and that your superior analysis of the flaws in the status quo demonstrates their failure to do so. Otherwise, after four minutes even a perceptive judge may not be quite sure of what you started out to attack and instead of regarding your argument on that issue as decisive, he may merely throw it into the scales.

14. Never make any speech a choppy series of small points. Everything must be clearly related to a main issue. Never become disorganized. Keep pointing up the main issues and the failure of the opposition to deal adequately with what you regard as the crux of the debate.

15. Plan and proportion your time intelligently. Don't be "taken in" by the opposition or "carried away" by your own oratory or arguments. Guide yourself closely by prearranged order and time schedules, such as those suggested in this book. *Above all, tell them what you're going to say —say it—then tell them what you've said.*

EXERCISES

1. From the suggestions given in this chapter, construct introductory remarks for the various components of the affirmative constructive case. Pick your own subject.

2. From the standpoint of the schedules discussed in this chapter, analyze the organization of a debate appearing in the *University Debaters' Annual*, or a similar volume, or from a recording. Check the time or estimate the emphasis given to the main divisions of each case. Comment on the strategy used by each team in this respect.

PART THREE

ATTACK AND DEFENSE

CHAPTER 8

THE LOGIC AND STRATEGY OF ATTACK AND DEFENSE

I would have you realize very clearly that all discussion, all criticism, whether wise or unwise, is reasoning. The blunderers who warn you against reason are simply bad or temporarily confused reasoners. There is no getting away from reasoning, save by way of insanity, and insanity stimulates the process of reasoning.

J. M. Robertson

1. THE UNDERLYING LOGIC OF DEBATE

Intercollegiate debate is or should be primarily an exercise in logic. Consider the debate proposition itself. To uphold the affirmative and contend that the proposition is true is really to draw an inductive inference or conclusion. For example, "Resolved, That the United States and Russia Will Not Go to War in the Foreseeable Future" is a causal hypothesis, one whose affirmative validity depends upon whether it can be demonstrated that there are causal factors operative which are likely to prevent the United States and Russia from going to war in the foreseeable future. Similarly, "Resolved, That the Present United States Trade Policy Damages the Prestige of the United States" would be a descriptive hypothesis, and "Resolved, That the Nations of the World Should Outlaw Atomic Weapons" would be a causal hypothesis. All such general propositions must be "proved" or "disproved" by means of evidence and logical reasoning; in short, by effective arguments.

Although the debate proposition is a presumed inference or conclusion of an inductive argument, the process of establishing this argument involves many subsidiary arguments, or smaller units of logical thought.

2. THE MEANING OF ARGUMENT

The term "argument" has at least two common meanings. One, a heated exchange between two disputants, usually involving bickering, squabbling, and oftentimes vigorous emotional reactions. This is the more common meaning. To the logician an argument is the basic unit of thought, or a discourse containing a conclusion (or inference) and evidence from which the conclusion is drawn. Thus, "I failed the course because I loafed all semester" would be an argument to a logician. We have a conclusion ("I failed the course") and a reason for the conclusion ("I loafed all semester"). No disagreement or conflict between individuals is necessarily involved. Throughout this book the term "argument" is used in the logician's sense.

3. THE NATURE OF ARGUMENT IN DEBATE

From the preceding chapters, we have seen that the fundamental concern of the debater and the logician is the same: to construct sound arguments and to evaluate all arguments critically; more specifically, to examine the grounds upon which conclusions are based and to consider the relationship between the grounds and the conclusion. First of all, however, one must be familiar with the nature of argument, and to this end the following points should be remembered:

The General Structure of an Argument

Every argument consists of two parts: a conclusion (or inference) and supporting evidence. There is no fixed order in which the parts must be presented. In some instances the evidence will follow the conclusion; in others, the reverse will be true. And, occasionally, the conclusion will be sandwiched in between parts of the evidence.

Also, frequently either the conclusion or some of the evidence may be implied rather than stated. To evaluate the argument properly, a debater must fill in what he thinks are the missing parts. On the other hand, if a debater is not explicit in presenting his argument, he runs the risk of having the opposition misinterpret it.

Recognizing an Argument

Sometimes the structure of an argument is obscured by excess verbiage which the debater must strip away to get at it. Certain language clues indicate not only the presence of an argument but also the direction in which it is going. As Beardsley has conveniently pointed out, the following terms show that the statement following them is a conclusion: [1]

therefore	entails
which shows that	allows us to infer that
proves that	I conclude that

[1] Monroe C. Beardsley, *Thinking Straight* (Englewood Cliffs, N.J.: Prentice-Hall, Inc., 1956), pp. 15–16.

hence	we may deduce that
thus	points to the conclusion that
so	suggests very strongly that
indicates that	leads me to believe that
consequently	bears out my point that
you see that	from which it follows that
implies that	

On the other hand, the following terms show that the statement following them is a reason for a conclusion:

since	as shown by
for	as is substantiated by
for the reason that	on the correct supposition that
as indicated by	in view of the fact that
assuming as we may that	may be inferred from the fact that
may be deduced from	

The Relationship between Evidence and Conclusion

The two parts of an argument should be so related that the conclusion necessarily follows from the evidence. Actually few debate arguments measure up to this criterion. Most arguments can be classed on a "truth" continuum as almost certainly true, true beyond a reasonable doubt, probably true, inconclusive, probably false, false beyond a reasonable doubt, almost certainly false, and certainly false.

The Relationship of an Argument to the Rest of the Case

No argument in a debate stands alone; it is always related to some other argument or conclusion, sometimes to two or more simultaneously, for purposes either of support, attack, defense for resupport, or defense for counterattack.

Complex Arguments

Many arguments which appear to be simple arguments (those with only one conclusion) are often really multiple or complex arguments (those with two or more conclusions) with only one conclusion supported by evidence. This is particularly true of causal arguments, where either the cause or the effect is unwarrantedly assumed. For example, the argument that United States economic aid to Burma is causing considerable resentment against the United States among the Burmese because they suspect us of imperialist motives assumes that there *is* considerable Burmese resentment against the United States, a proposition which must first be proved before the cause of such resentment is established. The reason (Burmese suspicion of imperialist motives), if it could be adduced with documentation, might be a good one to explain *why* the Burmese resent United States aid, but it must first be established that they actually do resent such aid. Actually, the preceding argument contains three conclusions: (1) there is considerable resentment against the United States in Burma, (2) this resentment is caused by United States economic aid, and (3) United States economic aid is resented because the Burmese suspect the United States of being imperialists. As we shall see, debaters are often guilty of ignoring certain links in a chain of reasoning.

4. PRELIMINARY ANALYSIS OF AN ARGUMENT

In approaching an argument, a debater should (1) reconstruct the argument as simply and accurately as possible, eliminating all excess verbiage, and (2) determine the related argument, or issue. Let us consider each step individually.

Reconstructing the Argument

In reconstructing an argument, the debater must determine specifically the conclusion and its supporting grounds. If this preliminary analysis reveals a conclusion without grounds, the "argument" is not really an argument at all but an assertion, which he can dismiss by merely pointing out this fact. If the analysis reveals a multiple argument, with each conclusion supported, the debater should point out this fact and deal with each argument separately. If one of the conclusions is not supported, he may handle it as he would any assertion or unsupported conclusion.

Frequently, a conclusion is supported by another conclusion. This is legitimate so long as the last conclusion in the link is supported by evidence. For example, "Our educational system is deficient. Many of our teachers are poor because they are not properly qualified. According to a survey in 1958 by the United States Office of Education, more than a half million teachers today do not have a college degree." Without considering the merit of this argument, we see that one conclusion may validly support another, thus:

Conclusion 1: Our educational system is deficient.
Conclusion 2: Many of our teachers are poor.
Conclusion 3: They are not properly qualified.
    Evidence: According to a survey in 1958 by U.S. Office of Education, more than a half million teachers do not have a college degree.

Thus, we see that conclusion 1 is supported by conclusion 2, which in turn is supported by conclusion 3, which in turn is supported by evidence. The point to remember is that one conclusion may be supported by another provided the last one is supported by evidence.[2]

[2] Actually, an argument with more than one conclusion is a multiple argument in which several arguments (corresponding to the number of conclusions) have been

Determining the Related Argument

As previously mentioned, every argument in a debate is related to some other argument, all arguments being ultimately related to the debate proposition itself. In the previous example, the argument concerning poorly qualified teachers would be related to the broader argument of evils in the status quo, which in turn would be related to the still broader argument of need for a change, which in turn would be related to a debate proposition like "The Federal Government Should Support Public Education."

5. FUNCTIONS OF AN ARGUMENT

Although all arguments are supposed to contribute to proving or disproving the debate resolution, they also perform more specific functions while contributing to this general end. These may be described as follows:

To Construct

Basically, this means using an argument to prove or support another argument. The task of constructing usually falls with the affirmative, although in a sense the issues initiated by the negative ("impracticability" and "disadvantages") may be considered "constructive" arguments.

To Answer an Opposing Argument

Basically, this means using an argument to weaken, tear down, or disprove an opposing argument. One may answer to weaken a constructive argument or to counter an attack on it, i.e., to attack or defend. Since these functions greatly overlap, there is little to be gained by calling one refutation and the other rebuttal, as is customarily done. To avoid confusion, the term "refutation" will be used here occasionally as being synonymous with "answer," and the term "rebuttal" will be reserved to designate the second speech delivered by a debater under the orthodox plan of debating.

6. LOGIC AND STRATEGY

Debate is a contest between two parties, the purpose of which is to convince a third party (a judge or audience) that the more logically tenable attitude toward the debate proposition is that of the one side rather than the other. There are many ways of convincing someone— ranging from the one extreme of giving sound reasons to the other of

---

telescoped into one by the omission of certain premises or assumptions. This point will become clearer in Chapter 15.

clubbing someone over the head with a baseball bat. Unfortunately, much "persuasive" discourse falls more into the latter category than into the former, being characterized by what is euphemistically called "non-logical," "extralogical," or "psychological" factors: constant repetition, suggestion of all kinds, the confident or confidential manner, and subtle or crude appeals to the gullibility of the audience. Such means of persuasion are entirely outside the scope, and foreign to the spirit, of this book. In academic debate we are interested in legitimate arguments, in being reasonable or logical. We try to convince by giving reasons for our conclusions, by giving proof or evidence, by stating facts from which we draw inferences. Thus, when we speak here of strategy in attack and defense, we are not thinking of stratagems or tricks, or of spurious devices to befuddle the opponents or mislead the judge. On the contrary, by "strategy" we mean the most logical way to construct or answer arguments, and to organize many arguments into a unified whole, called the "case."

To use a trick which may succeed is actually poor strategy for a good opponent will presumably reveal it for what it is and thus gain a point in his own favor. The best strategy is to be logical, for logical arguments are the most difficult to attack.

7. HANDLING AN OPPOSING ARGUMENT

Since a large part of debate consists of answering opposing arguments, let us consider some techniques for doing so. In dealing with opposition arguments, a debater tries to expose some weakness. He may try to create doubt concerning the truth or relevancy of the evidence, or the reasoning involved; he may deny the conclusion and offer other evidence to support his stand; he may try to establish a contrary conclusion; or he may accept the truth of the conclusion but attack it as being insignificant, irrelevant, or inconsistent. In sum, he may attack directly by expressing doubt, denying, or retorting to the conclusion; or he may attack indirectly by accepting the conclusion but arguing that it is insignificant, irrelevant, or inconsistent. And sometimes he may combine two different attacks.

As an illustration, let us see how the various forms of direct and indirect attack might be used against the following argument: "Recognition of Communist China would be advantageous to the United States, for we could then have a chargé d'affaires in Peiping who would be in a position to get and transmit valuable information to our State Department."

[This argument says, the proposition that the United States will benefit from the recognition of Communist China is true.]

The Direct Attack

Expressing Doubt

We wonder if such an advantage would result. Britain has had a chargé d'affaires in Peiping for six years, and, according to the British Under Secretary of Foreign Affairs, he hasn't been able to see anyone higher than an office boy in that time.

[This answer says, there is a reasonable doubt that the conclusion of the argument answered is true.]

Denial

We don't think such an advantage would come about, for, judging from Britain's example, she had to wait three years after recognizing Communist China before China recognized her and permitted her to send a chargé d'affaires to Peiping. We don't believe Chou En-lai—and Mr. Dulles agrees—would let us send a chargé d'affaires to Peiping even if we recognized Communist China.

[This answer says, the conclusion of the argument is not true.]

Retort

If we send a chargé d'affaires to China who will have his finger on the pulse of Chinese affairs, remember that they will send representatives to this country who may well have their fingers on our throat. As Richard P. Stebbins and the Research Staff at the Council on Foreign Relations stated in 1952: "Diplomatic recognition would entail the stationing of Chinese Communist representatives on American soil, a possibility which some Americans view with alarm because of the attendant opportunities for espionage and sabotage."

[This answer goes one step further than the previous one and says not only is the conclusion false but a contrary conclusion is true.]

The Indirect Attack

Showing Insignificance

We are told that having a chargé d'affaires in China would be an advantage. However, this seems pretty insignificant when compared with the damaging effect recognition would have on the people of the Far East. As Walter P. McConaughy, writing in the U.S. Department of State Bulletin, January, 1954, expressed it: "Even Chinese who are not particularly in sympathy with the Chinese National Government tell us that recognition of the Communist dictators in Peiping would be the greatest single nonmilitary triumph for the Communist cause and the hardest psychological blow against the will to resist the further spread of communism that could be devised."

[This answer says, the conclusion may be true, but it is insignificant in relation to other conclusions.]

Showing Inconsistency

Earlier it was conceded that a diplomatic exchange between Communist China and the United States would be unlikely for some time, even after recognition. Now it is argued that a chargé d'affaires is going to transmit information to the United States.

[This answer says, the conclusion may be true but it is inconsistent with a previous conclusion of the same case.]

Showing Irrelevancy

We fail to see what bearing this point has on how an international ban on nuclear weapons development could be enforced.

[This answer says, the conclusion may be true but it is irrelevant to the proposition at issue.]

The Underlying Logic of the Retort

One of the most effective types of answer is the retort. To understand its underlying logic we must consider what logicians call the truth relations among propositions, or how the truth or falsity of one proposition may affect the truth or falsity of another. Although there are many possible relations among propositions, for the moment we are interested in only two, contradiction and contrariety.

Contradiction

Contradiction has a very precise meaning for the logician. One proposition is said to be the contradictory of another when the truth of one involves (or entails) the falsity of the other and when its falsity involves the truth of the other. Both propositions cannot be true and both cannot be false. Thus the proposition P: "Franklin D. Roosevelt was the thirty-second president of the United States," and the proposition not-P: "Franklin D. Roosevelt was not the thirty-second president of the United States" are contradictory, for they satisfy or meet the terms of the foregoing definition. Symbolically:

If P is true, then not-P is false.
If P is false, then not-P is true.
If not-P is true, then P is false.
If not-P is false, then P is true.

Both cannot be true, but both cannot be false. Consider another example:

P: All United States Senators were at least forty years old when they took office.

Q: Some United States Senators were under forty when they took office.

If *P* is true, then *Q* must be false; if *P* is false, then it must be true that some United States senators were under forty when they took office. If *Q* is true, then *P* must be false; and if *Q* is false, *P* must be true. Thus, when one debater contends that *P* is true and another denies that *P* is true (or contends that *P* is not true), a pair of contradictory propositions is involved.

Contrariety

The relationship of contrariety must be carefully distinguished from that of contradiction. The propositions "Everyone in the United States is employed" and "No one in the United States is employed" are not contradictory, for although both cannot be true, both may be false. In fact, both are false, though the important consideration here is that, even if we lacked this knowledge, we would still know that both may be false. On the other hand, if one of these propositions were true, the other would have to be false. These, then, are called contrary propositions, or propositions which are so related that both cannot be true, but both can be false. Contrariety is the relationship involved in a retort. For our purpose, the big difference between contradictions and contraries is that the former exhaust all possible alternatives while the latter do not.

Perhaps the following example will make this last point clearer. Suppose by agreement between two parties, *A* and *B,* a "rich man" were defined as one having assets of one hundred thousand dollars or more. Now suppose that *A* contended that Jones was rich. *B* might now answer that Jones was not rich, since his assets were less than one hundred thousand dollars. In using this alternative form of reply (denial), *B* is not at all concerned here with *how much* Jones is actually worth, whether as much as $99,000 or as little as $1,000. Rather, he is concerned only with whether or not Jones meets the specific criterion agreed upon and is worth $100,000. Thus, *B's* denial of *A's* allegation involves but two —no more, no less—alternatives: either Jones is or he is not worth at least $100,000. The alternatives are contradictories. If, however, *B* had decided to use the retort rather than the denial in replying to *A,* he would have supported a contrary contention, that Jones was perhaps only "moderately well off," with assets say of $10,000, or that Jones was very poor, with no assets. Using the retort as his reply, that is to say, *B* had several different specific contrary allegations available to him; for there are several different ways of making the same general point that Jones was "not rich." The specific contrary allegations that could be made can, in fact, be ranged along a continuum:

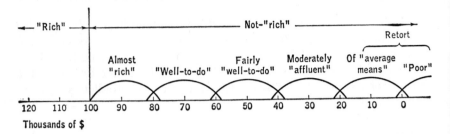

"Not rich" would be *any* point to the right of 100, including 99¾, or "very nearly rich"; but a category on the other end of the scale, "almost poor" or "poor," would have to be specified in a retort. Thus, a retort not only denies but also reverses the point in contention. In terms of our example, "Jones is not only not rich (denial); he is actually poor (retort)." Since it represents a more extreme position, a retort, though very effective, is always more difficult to substantiate than a denial.

Whenever relative terms (those denoting characteristics which may be possessed by something in varying degrees) are involved in an argument, a retort should always be considered as a possible answer. For example:

A: John is brilliant.
B: (Retort)   John is stupid.

A: A G.A.W. would help to pull us out of a depression.
B: (Retort)   A G.A.W. would cement us in a depression.

A: Recognition of Communist China would weaken the UN.
B: (Retort)   Recognition of Communist China would strengthen the UN.

Lest the retort be used indiscriminately, one should remember that both the opposing team's proposition and one's retort in the form of its contrary may be false. Honesty, which is the best strategy after all, might dictate the use of the less extravagant denial. For example, the recognition of Communist China might neither strengthen nor weaken the UN but leave it materially as it is, in which case simply denying A's contention in the above example would be the proper answer.

Turning the Tables

One of the most dramatic types of retort is known as "turning the tables," an answer which consists not only in reversing the conclusion of a given argument but also in using the very same evidence of that argument to do so. This is usually accomplished by adding a new ingredient to the evidence, some fact or circumstance overlooked by the original argument, and drawing an opposite conclusion based upon the new combination of evidence. For example:

A: The turnout of only twelve thousand spectators at last Sunday's game between two teams in contention for the championship indicates that Detroit fans have lost interest in professional football and that it is time for Detroit's franchise to be shifted to another city.

B: A neglects to mention that on the day of the game there was a near-blizzard. In view of this fact, it is incredible that as many as twelve thousand turned out for the game. This number would indicate that not only have Detroit fans not lost interest in professional football but their interest is probably greater than can be found anywhere else in the country.

A: We have a serious unemployment problem at present, as indicated by the fact that last month 2¾ millions were listed as unemployed.

B: A fails to consider that our current work force is now around 70 millions and that 2¾ millions unemployed is considered by economists as practically "full employment" in a dynamic and expanding economy such as ours.

A: Under the Hobbes Act only three convictions were obtained last year. This would indicate that the act is failing to punish violators.

B: A tells us that under the Hobbes Act only three convictions were obtained last year and that this indicates that the act is failing. On the contrary, this would seem to indicate that the act is working very well, for apparently would-be violators are afraid of its consequences.

In all of the foregoing examples B uses the same evidence as A, adds a new fact,[3] and comes up with a contrary conclusion.

As we have said, the retort is one of the most effective types of answer to an opposing argument and should be used whenever possible. All negative disadvantages of the affirmative plan are retorts to affirmative advantages and should be a prominent feature of any negative case. Although the negative can win by effectively denying or casting doubt on the affirmative points, that is, by arguing solely on affirmative grounds, it should also retort by introducing its own "constructive" material in the form of disadvantages of the affirmative plan.

Certain independent propositions superficially resemble contrary propositions and should not be confused with them. Independent propositions are those whose truth or falsity has no bearing whatsoever on each other; both may be true and both may be false. The point is, one is in no way an answer to another. Thus, answering a given proposition with

[3] In the last example A assumes that many violations go unpunished; B assumes the contrary: that very few or no violations go unpunished. This latter assumption is the new ingredient in B's argument. Both, however, are guilty of making unwarranted assumptions.

an independent proposition is to be irrelevant. For the present, it is sufficient for debaters to recognize that propositions like the following pairs are independent and not contrary:

A: There are many corrupt union officials today.
B: There are many honest union officials today.

A: There are approximately 200,000 high school graduates every year who can't afford to go to college.
B: America has the largest college enrollment of any country in the world.

A: American prestige is falling in the Far East.
B: Communist China's prestige is falling in the Far East.

In each pair of examples, both propositions may be true and both may be false, whereas in a contradictory or contrary pair of propositions, if one is true, the other must be false.

To summarize briefly, there are two general types of attack on an opposing argument; the *direct* attack and the *indirect* attack. A direct attack is on the substance and form of the argument itself, that is, on the evidence and reasoning (the relationship between the evidence and conclusion). An indirect attack is on the relationship between the conclusion of one argument and that of another. The direct attack involves the truth of the conclusion. In effect, it says, this conclusion is not true. The indirect attack accepts the truth of the conclusion but attacks its effectiveness in relation to another conclusion. In effect, it says, this conclusion may be true, but it proves little or nothing.

In Chapters 10 through 15 we shall deal mainly with the direct attack, and in Chapter 16 the indirect attack.

EXERCISES

1. Define "argument." Is an assertion supported by an assertion an argument?

2. Which of the following are arguments and which are assertions? Of the arguments identify the conclusion, the reason for believing it, and the term, if any, which links the two. For the assertions supply hypothetical data which would make them arguments.

a. The average income of all families living in low-rent projects in 1956 was $1,691, and their average monthly rent was $29.96. Do these averages indicate that the type of people living in the projects are getting high incomes? We think not.

b. Every third American family lives in a home below the minimum standards of decency.

c. According to the National Education Association, over 2 million children of school age don't attend school because there aren't enough classrooms or because bus facilities to neighboring schools are lacking.

d. Social insurance, free education, and subsidized housing are not new. In Britain these programs have been in effect for many years.

e. If a free society is to win the allegiance of its members, it must provide certain minimum basic securities.

f. As Senator Wayne Morse has pointed out, "Labor is no more entitled to exceptions from legal checks upon its excesses than are employers, businessmen, or corporations."

g. More juvenile delinquents come from homes where the parents are divorced than from homes where the parents are living together.

h. The Communists today do not pose any serious ideological threat to the world, for on a world basis about one person in 115 is a Communist.

i. Since all matter is subject to the law of gravity and since this book is matter, it will fall to the floor if I release my hold on it.

j. Outlawing the Communist Party would violate the constitutional rights of some American citizens.

k. In hearings before the Senate Committee on Finance, it was brought out that the cotton textile industry is still exporting goods equivalent to 500,000 bales of cotton.

l. The Russian people are being told by Khrushchev that the Soviet Union now believes in the peaceful coexistence of capitalism and communism, and peaceful competition between the two systems. War in the near future, therefore, seems most unlikely. Moreover, the nuclear weapons possessed by both sides are a powerful deterrent.

m. If we have faith in democracy and in the ability of our students to make sound judgments, we should not fear that an occasional Communist teacher will subvert the student body.

n. Our imports last year amounted to little more than 3 per cent of our gross national product. If we lowered our trade barriers so that imports could amount to 5 per cent of our gross national product, as they did from 1925 to 1929, there would be no "dollar gap."

o. The Army reports that three nuclear bombs in the megaton range would be enough to destroy all of Moscow.

3. Explain the difference between the direct and indirect attack. Specify the type or types used in the following answers:

a. In answer to the charge that unions have become powerful, it is significant, for example, that whereas the United Steel Workers of America have assets of 20 million dollars, United States Steel Corporation has assets of 3 billion. In fact, the assets of this one corporation are greater than the combined assets of all unions.

b. Despite their so-called power, unions are finding it harder to organize and win strikes because of the government's hands-off policy.

c. We're told that labor unions have become powerful. Since power has to reside somewhere, it is better in the hands of the representatives of 17 million workers than in the hands of a relatively few members of management.

d. How powerful can unions be with two-thirds of our present labor force still outside union ranks?

e. They speak of economic sanctions, and yet the affirmative plan is one gigantic economic sanction designed to isolate the East from the West.

f. It is doubtful if visits by Soviet dignitaries to the United States will give the Soviet Union a better understanding of the United States or ease cold war tensions. It may be recalled that the many Japanese students who studied in American colleges later led their country to Pearl Harbor. If anything, the visits may result in the Soviet Union's becoming more covetous of American wealth.

g. Our friends tell us that voluntary unionism would depress wage rates. On the contrary, wages in right-to-work states have been rising at a much faster rate than in the rest of the country.

h. We're told that wages in right-to-work states are rising at a much faster rate than in the rest of the country. This is so only because the wages in these states were much lower than those in the rest of the country to begin with and were due to rise in any event. It is significant that they are still much lower on the average than wage rates in non-right-to-work states.

i. Thus we see that not only is there no need but even if there were, the affirmative plan couldn't meet it.

j. And to combat Soviet propaganda they propose an enlarged Voice of America program. What is international about that? In fact, what is new about it?

k. What if an attempt to set up such an organization should prove abortive, should fail? The harm done to the United Nations would be incalculable.

l. Compulsory unionism is not needed, we are told. The unions would do as well without compulsion. But even if compulsion were not needed, this would not constitute a need for a change. If unions are prospering under the present law, why change that law? The truth is, however, the union shop is needed to prevent management from undermining the unions and weakening their power to bargain collectively.

m. Although money wages and real wages have both risen considerably over the past few years, there is no conclusive evidence that they would not have risen without compulsory unionism.

n. They tell us that voluntary unionism would hurt the unions, and yet unions have continued to grow in right-to-work states.

o. Then the negative contends that the guaranteed annual wage would not necessarily produce utopian conditions between labor and management. We never said that it would. Frankly, we don't see the point here.

p. As for the claim that right-to-work laws would mean fewer labor disputes, actually the reverse is true. The best labor-management relations exist when the union feels secure and when management knows it is dealing with a strong, dependable union.

q. England cannot claim to be the parent country, for more than half of the colonists come from other countries. But even if she were the parent country, her actions toward the colonies would be all the more reprehensible. Even the wolf doesn't devour its young. (Adapted from Thomas Paine.)

r. First they tell us that 97 per cent of all union members approve of unions, and in the next breath they contend that there would be many free-riders—members who would desert the union if given the chance. These two conclusions do not seem to be consistent with one another.

s. We are told that seasonal workers suffer, but this is not so. Workers in seasonal industries get higher wages on the whole than those in more stable industries.

t. Even if some workers did leave the union, they could still be taxed to cover costs of their representation, without being assessed full union dues.

u. Small nuclear weapons are not strategically important, but even if they were, the United States has plenty of them.

v. And then on the basis of two states they claim that the present unemployment compensation program is being misadministered. But if this program were eliminated, valuable employment service bureaus would be eliminated.

w. (1) We are told that economic aid provides a higher standard of living for the people and that this in turn combats the spread of communism. But this is not true. In the provinces where Italian per capita income is the highest, the Communists received 52 per cent of the total vote in the 1951–1952 elections, a much higher percentage than in the lower per capita income areas.

(2) However, in the provinces referred to, the average per capita income is the highest only because of a handful of very wealthy families. The median per capita income is actually lower than in the surrounding provinces, which means that most of the people have lower incomes and explains why communism is so attractive to them, the very point we made originally.

4. Define "contradiction" and "contrariety."

5. Which of the following pairs of propositions are contradictory, which are contrary, and which are neither?

a. We must trust Tito.
We must trust Nehru.

b. Nuclear weapons are a deterrent to war.
Nuclear weapons are not a deterrent to war.

c. Strontium-90 poses a great threat to human life.
Strontium-90 poses practically no threat to human life.

d. Children assimilate strontium-90 to a greater degree than adults.
Adults assimilate strontium-90 to a greater degree than children.

e. Nuclear bomb tests high above the earth's atmosphere could be detected.
Nuclear bomb tests high above the earth's atmosphere could not be detected.

f. Russia would secretly violate a test ban.
The United States would not violate a test ban.

g. The Democrats favor large expenditures for national defense.
The Republicans favor large expenditures for national defense.

h. Tariffs will be increased next year.
Tariffs will be diminished next year.

i. Tariffs impede trade.
Tariffs do not impede trade.

j. The Democrats favor lowering the tariff.
The Republicans favor raising the tariff.

6. Explain "retort" and "turning the tables."

7. What would the retort be to the following propositions? In which instances might it be appropriate? What type of answer might be used in the other instances?

a. The spread of nuclear weapons to other nations would be harmful.

b. A major nuclear war could well mean the end of our civilization.

c. As a result of fallout, more people will die from leukemia and bone cancer.

d. The United States has great need of small tactical nuclear weapons.

e. The nuclear powers have no right to inflict fallout on the rest of the world.

f. Military preparedness is a deterrent to war.

CHAPTER 9

SOME BASIC DEFINITIONS

Men will continue to commit atrocities as long as they continue to believe absurdities.

Voltaire

Throughout the next several chapters we shall frequently use such terms as "prove," "disprove," "fail to prove," "believe," "disbelieve," and "doubt." So that the reader may understand how they are used here, they will now be explained.

1. "PROVE"

To prove is to show that a proposition is true by virtue of its being the consequence of one or more propositions which are themselves true. As used throughout this book, the term "proof" is a relative concept which may be described as ranging along a continuum from "conclusive" to "extremely doubtful." In other words, there are many degrees of proof and thus many degrees of probable truth. "Conclusive proof" would be proof that left no doubt as to the truth of the proposition being proved; or, to express it another way, "to prove conclusively" is to show that a proposition is *certainly* true by virtue of its being the *inevitable* consequence of one or more propositions which are themselves true. An example of a proposition conclusively proved is the following:

Proposition: The unmeasured angle of a given triangle is 45 degrees.
    Proof: Two angles of the triangle are known to add up to 135 degrees, and all three angles are known to add up to 180 degrees.

A proposition conclusively proved merits complete belief by thinking men. In debate, a proposition is rarely capable of such proof, and, of course, the debate proposition itself never should be. However, propositions need not be conclusively proved to merit belief. In debate, a proposition merits belief if its proof is such as to indicate that the proposition is at least "probably true." More convincing proof, though it may be offered,

125

is not required. An example of a proposition "probably" proved is the following:

Proposition: The South, if not compelled by national troops, would refuse to enforce a national compulsory fair employment practices law.

Proof: The South has refused to enforce voluntarily a number of Supreme Court edicts against segregation, notably the recent ruling against segregation in the public schools.

To say that a proposition is "probably proved" is to say that it is "probably true," or that there is a greater likelihood that it is true than that it is false. Such a proposition merits the judge's belief unless or until the other team either demonstrates that the proof given does not warrant this belief or proves the proposition to be "probably false."

2. "DISPROVE"

To disprove is to demonstrate that a proposition is false by proving the truth of a contradictory or contrary proposition. For if a contradictory or contrary proposition is proved true, the proposition in question is automatically proved false since, as we have seen, neither a pair of contradictories nor a pair of contraries can both be true. The qualifications regarding "prove" apply to "disprove" since the latter really involves proving another proposition. A proposition which is disproved merits disbelief, or the belief that the proposition in question is false.

The simplest way to disprove a proposition is to prove its contradictory, though perhaps a more effective way to secure disbelief from others is to prove its contrary.

The contradictories of the four possible forms of a proposition can be seen in the following table:

Proposition: All S is P;
Contradictory: Some (even one) S is not P.

Proposition: No S is P;
Contradictory: Some (even one) S is P.

Proposition: Some S is P;
Contradictory: No S is P.

Proposition: Some S is not P;
Contradictory: All S is P.

In proving the contrary of a proposition, the choices are theoretically limitless.

3. "FAIL TO PROVE"

To fail to prove is to offer either the wrong kind of proof or insufficient proof to merit the belief that a proposition is probably true. Although belief is not merited in this case, neither is disbelief but rather *unbelief*, or doubt; for although proper proof has not been given to show the proposition to be probably true, one may not conclude that the absence of such proof is proof that the proposition is probably false. One can only "suspend belief," or doubt. An example of a proposition which has not been proved and which thus merits doubt as to its truth is the following:

Proposition: Recognition of Communist China by the United States would weaken the Nationalist Chinese Army.

   Proof: Recognition by the United States would enhance the prestige of Communist China in the eyes of Burma, India, and other neutralist countries in the Far East.

The Prima Facie Case

In debate, failure by the affirmative to prove the debate resolution (to be probably true) obliges a judge to vote for the negative. Because of the initial presumption favoring the negative, the affirmative must initially present what is known as a prima facie case, that is, a case which on the face of it proves, or appears to prove, the resolution (to be probably true). The negative then has the obligation of showing, by one means or another, that the affirmative has failed to prove the resolution (to be probably true). In fact, as we have seen, it may try to go further and not only create doubt, or cause the judge to suspend belief, but even furnish enough proof to merit disbelief. Throughout the course of the debate each team deals with its particular obligation, and at the conclusion of the debate the judge must decide whether or not the affirmative has proved the resolution. Once again, we can see that the negative has a decided edge over the affirmative, for if both teams were of equal or nearly equal skill, the judge would be in doubt concerning the probable truth of the resolution and would therefore be obliged to vote for the negative. In other words, a tie is not possible. If the affirmative fails to prove the resolution, the negative wins.

4. "BELIEVE" AND "DISBELIEVE"

To believe means to accept a proposition as true. To disbelieve means to accept a proposition as false. In debate, as in all logical thinking, belief that a proposition is true is merited when that proposition has been proved to be probably true or when a recognized expert says it is true or probably true. Disbelief, or the belief that a proposition is false, is merited when that proposition is disproved, i.e., proved to be probably false, or when a recognized expert says that it is false or probably false. When two recognized experts disagree concerning the truth or falsity of a given proposition, neither belief nor disbelief is merited but only doubt, or a suspension of belief. As we have seen, such a state of mind on the part of the judge concerning the debate proposition would favor the negative.

Nonlogical "Proof"

The primary objective of nonacademic debate is, from the affirmative standpoint, to create the belief that the debate resolution is probably true and, from the negative standpoint, to create doubt that the resolution is probably true and/or the belief that it is probably false. More often than not, these objectives are attained by means other than logical proof or expert testimony, the only basis of belief for thinking people and thus the only basis which should be considered in academic debate. These other means are called by various names such as "nonlogical," "nonrational," "psychological," "emotional," "psychic," "ethical," "verbal," etc., but all have one thing in common: all are devices for securing belief by means other than reason. In an attempt to dignify them, some writers call them a kind of proof; thus, even as far back as Aristotle we read of "psychic proof," "ethical proof," "emotional proof," etc. In their cruder forms these devices consist of such activities as hiring brass bands, kissing babies, posing with pretty girls, waving patriotic banners, wearing short sleeves, providing free barbecues or clambakes, calling people by their first names, shaking hands firmly, slapping backs, grinning broadly, speaking loudly and confidently, making rash promises, villifying the opposition, using glittering generalities or catchy slogans, telling anecdotes, and establishing some identification with American heroes of the past. In their more sophisticated forms they consist of appearing attractive, sincere, likable, earnest, intense, courageous, confident, learned, and competent.

Since logical analysis is difficult and man tends to be intellectually lazy—or as some one once said, "To think about anything is hard work; but to have a prejudice is a pleasure"—the unreasonable appeals listed above unquestionably succeed in securing belief from most people, often to their detriment. The task of education in a democratic society is to expose such devices for what they are—the tools for exploiting man's weakness and, more often than not, the tools of unscrupulous people. Academic debate is certainly one of the best forms of training in the recognition of such devices.

Unfortunately, many writers on the subject of debate and persuasion, including Aristotle, one of the first, tacitly or openly condone such devices,[1] apparently because they succeed with uncritical audiences. To

---

[1] Although he is credited with being the father of logic, Aristotle could be very illogical at times. In defending the institution of slavery, for example, he says, "He then is by nature formed a slave, who is fitted to become the chattel of another person, and on that account is so." In other words, the slaves of Aristotle's society

extricate themselves from the dilemma in which such approval places them as educators, many writers rationalize their approval by citing Aristotle's theory of what he called "ethos," the theory that a speaker must be morally good if he is to be effective, a theory refuted many times throughout history.[2] Would that this appealing theory were true, but, unfortunately bigots, demagogues, and dictators speak with as much earnestness, intensity, confidence, assurance, and courage as do men of good will—and with much more, as a rule, than do thinking men. As Hoffer points out, the requirements for effective mass persuasion—witness Lenin, Hitler, Mussolini, *et al.*—seem to be "audacity and a joy in defiance; an iron will; a fanatical conviction . . . ; a capacity for passionate hatred; contempt for the present; a cunning estimate of human nature; a delight in symbols"; and a brazen "disregard of consistency and fairness. . . . Exceptional intelligence, noble character and originality seem neither indispensable nor perhaps desirable." [3] One can only speculate on the amount of suffering that has resulted because people have been persuaded by such irrelevant factors as the appearance and manner of a man rather than by his ideas and his reasoning, the only relevant factors.

Personality and Persuasion

That a speaker's personality is a "cause of persuasion" is a well-founded generalization. To a thinking person, however, there is an important distinction between what is and what should be. Whether a doctrine or a proposition is true or false should be determined by relevant factors, and a speaker's personality cannot, by the widest stretch of imagination, be classed as a relevant factor. One would hardly dispute Cicero when

---

were slaves because nature intended them to be slaves, and nature intended them to be slaves because they were slaves. In this circular argument the real question, whether the slaves were intended by nature to be slaves, is completely evaded.

[2] The theory also finds expression in the romantic words of Emerson, "What you are speaks so loud that I cannot hear what you say," words often quoted by apologists for this theory. To understand what Emerson meant, however, one must know something of his philosophy. Emerson believed that all men were good and that evil was nonexistent. Since every man contains within him a spark of the Divine, man need merely rely on his intuition and live by whim or impulse from day to day. This he called "self-reliance." From such a philosophy it follows that man can do no wrong. Man is part of the divine creation and therefore divine. What he says, therefore, is not important; all that matters is what he is. The danger of such an unrealistic approach to human affairs should be apparent. It is not surprising that Emerson was hostile to reasoning, formal education, intelligent planning, and many of those disciplines and institutions which have raised man above the level of animals. (For an excellent summary and analysis of Emerson's ideology, see Ivor Winters' *In Defense of Reason,* New York: The Swallow Press and William Morrow & Company, Inc., 1947.)

[3] Eric Hoffer, *The True Believer* (New York: Harper & Brothers, 1951), p. 112.

he says that "attributes useful in an advocate are a mild tone, a countenance expressive of modesty, gentle language. . . . It is very helpful to display the tokens of good-nature, kindness, calmness, loyalty, and a disposition that is pleasing and not grasping or covetous." However, such attributes should not be a cause of persuasion just because they happen to be with most people. To teach the doctrine that such attributes should be persuasive because they are is both illogical and educationally indefensible. Although such attributes should be endorsed, they should not be endorsed as a form of proof but rather as a safeguard against antagonizing or distracting an audience and thereby preventing it from concentrating on the content of the speech. The crucial consideration is one's motive in teaching students to be pleasant and agreeable speakers. To teach them that such attributes should be cultivated as a form of proof, i.e., a factor relevant to truth, is both illogical and meretricious.

Many writers attempt to justify "emotional proof," i.e., persuasion by emotional factors, by arguing that certain situations call for action and that the best way to get a worthwhile proposal acted on is to appeal both to the emotions and intellect of the audience. (The argument, of course, assumes that the speaker knows what is "worthwhile.") From a long history of speech making, no one can deny that emotional and psychological appeals are much more effective than logical appeals. But this fact only emphasizes man's unthinking nature. It is hardly a fact to be complacent about, however, let alone one to be made the cornerstone of an educational theory.

The notion that action is frequently desirable regardless of how it is motivated is really another way of saying that the end justifies the means. Now, it is true that in rare situations, where a person's or a country's very existence is at stake, the end does justify the means; but to generalize from such exceptional instances that the end always justifies the means, or that a "good" program always merits support regardless of how that support is obtained, is dangerous, both politically and educationally. Advocates of emotional persuasion would do well to apply Holmes' criterion of "a clear and present danger" to instances where belief or action is desirable on other than purely rational grounds. In academic debate, where no such danger exists, belief must be justified on the grounds of reason.

5. "DOUBT"

Doubt is that state of mind which accepts neither the truth nor the falsity of a given proposition. In debate, a proposition which is in doubt carries weight for neither side, unless that proposition is the resolution itself, in which case the decision would go to the negative since, as we have seen, there is an initial presumption in favor of maintaining the status quo rather than of making the extreme change called for in the resolution. In other words, if the affirmative has been unable to merit the belief that the resolution is true, specifically, that a change should be made, the judge can only doubt the truth of the resolution, or perhaps, with the help of the negative, disbelieve it. This principle would apply even if the negative were supporting a counter plan, the point being that the central question in every debate is: Has the affirmative proved the resolution (to be probably true)? If it has, it wins; if it has not, it loses. Thus, in one sense, when the negative wins, it does so *because* the affirmative loses.

EXERCISE

1. From the standpoint of the affirmative, the negative, and the judge, discuss the following terms: "prove," "disprove," "fail to prove," "prima facie case," "nonlogical proof," "belief," and "doubt."

CHAPTER 10

EVIDENCE

We may stare at facts every minute of our waking day without being a whit the wiser unless we exert our intellects to build upon them or under them.

William Minto

Evidence is the basis of an argument, the substance from which the inference, or conclusion, is derived, the "proof" of the conclusion (which itself is not directly verifiable), or a reason for believing the conclusion.

1. EMPIRICAL EVIDENCE

The best evidence is empirical, i.e., facts, or statements which are directly verifiable and thus inarguable. For example, "For the first six months of 1953, Ford Division sold 475,000 cars. For the last six months, it sold 640,767." "The U-235 bomb dropped on Hiroshima had the explosive force of approximately 20,000 tons of TNT. The U-238 bomb exploded at Bikini, March 1, 1954, had the explosive equivalent of approximately 15 million tons of TNT." "Except for three loans to Thailand totaling $25,400,000, the International Bank for Reconstruction and Development has provided no economic development capital for Southeast Asia."

2. AUTHORITATIVE EVIDENCE

Since we cannot often get the facts, we must rely on experts, or authorities, who presumably have them. Not only in debating but in everyday affairs we often find ourselves forced to rely on the word of specialists—doctors, physicists, economists, etc.—since we have neither the time nor the wherewithal to get the facts ourselves. Often we must accept a conclusion because an authority says it is true. Actually, an authoritative opinion does not prove a proposition, but it is a reasonable basis for *believing* it. When we accept an authority's word for something, we accept the fact that the authority has the evidence. But, as

Ruby says, "if we wish to *know,* rather than merely to believe, we should inquire into the evidence on which his conclusions are based."[1]

In debate a truly authoritative opinion is reasonable as a means of influencing belief, though it has its limitations. Whenever possible, a debater should give not only the authority's conclusion but also the proof used in arriving at it. Otherwise, arguments from authority (*P* is true, for *X* says so) can easily be undermined, for in the areas of intercollegiate debate—concerned as they are with political, social, and economic problems—authorities often express conflicting views. A conflicting view doesn't necessarily prove or disprove anything, but it does create doubt as to which of two views is true; and a sensible person will accept neither until he has more information.

3. CRITERIA FOR EVALUATING EVIDENCE

In evaluating evidence, a debater should consider three criteria: clarity, accuracy, and reliability. Evidence which fails to measure up to these is faulty, or fallacious. In the following discussion we shall consider some of these fallacies.

4. FALLACIES OF EVIDENCE

Unclear Evidence

Evidence may be unclear because it is too vague, ambiguous, or implicit rather than stated.

Vague Evidence

Vague evidence is that which contains terms that are very indefinite. The following categories are typical:

Vague Source or Authority. Typical examples of this error are:

"Recent statistics show...." Whose statistics? Where and when did they appear?

"Leading nuclear physicists contend...." Who specifically? When? Where?

"A survey taken last year indicates...." Whose survey? What was surveyed? Where was the survey published?

Improperly Defined Terms. All relative terms—like "free," "serious," "great," "small," "progress," and "control"—are by nature vague and must therefore be defined. Evidence containing the word "control," for example, would be meaningless unless the degree of control was indicated,

[1] Lionel Ruby, *Logic: An Introduction* (Philadelphia: J. B. Lippincott Company, 1950), p. 128.

for there are many degrees of control, ranging from complete control to no control.

Very general or abstract terms are also vague and must be defined —words like "average," "democracy," "foreign aid," and "guaranteed annual wage." Such words may refer to different members of the general class named. For instance, foreign aid may or may not include military aid, defense support, technical assistance, or long-term loans. A guaranteed annual wage plan may refer to any one of several different plans—the Hormel Plan, the Nunn-Busch Plan, or the Procter and Gamble Plan.

Poorly Classified Data. Sometimes data are poorly classified or erroneously compared. For comparison, data must be expressed in the same terms. To compare the 1924 divorce rate in terms of the number of marriages that year with the 1959 divorce rate in terms of divorces per one thousand people is confusing. Or to compare teachers' salaries of 1940 with those of 1959 without taking into account the relative cost of living during those years is misleading.

Ambiguous Evidence

Ambiguous evidence is that which contains terms subject to more than one interpretation. Thus, ambiguity is closely related to vagueness since vague terms also tend to be ambiguous. "By 'fallacies' of ambiguity," to quote Ruby, "we refer to cases where the reader or speaker fails to recognize the existence of ambiguity and draws unwarranted conclusions because of this neglect. The errors occur either in use or interpretation. The speaker may use ambiguous words in an illegitimate manner; the hearer may incorrectly interpret a speaker because of failure to note the existence of ambiguity." [2] The following errors are typical:

Equivocation. This error consists of using a word in two different senses in the same argument. "The mayor and his council are not permitted to strike, for they are public servants. Thus, the bus drivers should not be allowed to strike, for they are also public servants." Here "public servant" is used in two senses: one who is elected to public office and one who serves the public.

Improper Accent. This error consists of improperly emphasizing certain words or ideas so that their meaning is changed. "The Fourth Amendment protects the individual against illegal searching or seizure of his private property. Since no one entered this man's house or office, wiretapping his telephone did not violate his rights." Here "searching private property" is too narrowly interpreted or improperly emphasized. The interpretation resembles that in the argument "Since the Bible says,

[2] Ruby, p. 55.

'Thou shalt not bear false witness against thy neighbor,' I guess it's all right to do so against others."

Ambiguity of Emphasis. This error consists of presenting evidence subject to more than one interpretation because certain facts are missing. For example, to state that three million are unemployed at present is to present an isolated fact subject to several different interpretations. To interpret the fact properly we need other facts: does this figure represent a significant increase or decrease over last month's? How does it compare with last year's figure? What is considered normal unemployment in periods of relatively full employment? Also, the term "unemployment" tends to be ambiguous. Does it cover those willfully unemployed, incapacitated, in the process of shifting to other jobs, or in seasonal industries?

Implicit Assumptions. Ambiguity may also result when evidence is implied rather than stated. Speakers often present arguments elliptically, omitting certain assumptions on which their conclusion has been based. Thus, one cannot always identify these assumptions. In the argument "Since Jones is opposed to extending the Reciprocal Trade Agreements, he must be a Republican" the underlying assumption may be either "everyone who is opposed to extending R.T.A. is a Republican" or "All Republicans are opposed to extending R.T.A." Since the underlying assumption, which is really part of the evidence, is ambiguous, the argument cannot be properly evaluated until this ambiguity is cleared up.

Stating implicit assumptions often reveals also that they are probably false. For example, the argument "intercollegiate debating is not educational because most debaters lack an audience" is based on the unstated assumption that no academic activity which lacks an audience can be educational, which is patently false.

False Evidence

Since a debater depends upon secondary sources—newspapers, speeches, periodicals, reference works, etc.—for his evidence, he sometimes records the wrong data, overlooks significant data, ignores fine distinctions, or makes unwarranted assumptions about the evidence. Thus, his evidence may be inaccurate or false. The following errors are typical:

Simple Inaccuracies

This error is usually due to carelessness or outdated evidence. To state that Harry Truman served two full terms as president is untrue, for it is a matter of historical record that he did not; or to state that Japan does not recognize Communist China is untrue for the same reason. When encountering such inaccuracies, a debater should tactfully point them out and never impute dishonest motives to the opposition. He might even preface his answer by saying, "Our friends are in error—unintentional, I am sure—when they state, etc." If the error is of minor significance, little more need be said about it, for to dwell on it would make one guilty of an irrelevancy (diversion by attack on a minor point). If the error is of major significance, this should be pointed out vigorously—but, again, without attacking the opposition's motives or character.

Overlooking Significant Factors

This error consists of citing part of the truth but not the whole truth, of ignoring facts which, if introduced, would change the meaning of the evidence cited. The error resembles ambiguity of emphasis. For example, "According to the Association for Higher Education, last year (1956) approximately 200,000 high school graduates capable of doing college work could not afford to go to college." It was further reported, however, that of this number approximately 100,000 had no desire to go, a fact which alters the significance of the previous one. The error is pointed up by the story of the night watchman who swore on the witness stand that he had waved his lantern to signal the on-coming train but who neglected to mention that the lantern wasn't lighted. Affirmative teams tend to commit this error in developing their need, by exaggerating or oversimplifying the evils of the status quo, whereas negative teams often exaggerate the achievements of the status quo.

Quoting Out of Context

This error consists of omitting portions of a quotation so that a meaning not intended by the person quoted is conveyed. Usually the portions omitted are conditional statements or qualifying terms. In arguing against compulsory unionism, for example, many affirmative teams quoted the late Supreme Court Justice Brandeis as having said, "I am against compulsory unionism." What Brandeis really said was, "I am against the closed shop; I am against this type of compulsory unionism. But I am also against the open shop. What I favor is the preferential union shop." Thus, Brandeis was quoted as saying just the opposite of what he had really said.

The best defense against this tactic is to be familiar with as much evidence as possible on both sides of the question. If one encounters a particularly damaging quotation in one debate, he will probably encounter it in another. The best practice is to go to the original source and read the entire passage from which the quotation was taken. If the quotation has not been lifted out of context, the next best attack is to introduce a conflicting authoritative opinion if possible or other evidence supporting a contrary conclusion. Thus, "Though Brandeis may be against the union shop, our evidence indicates that the union shop has benefited both the worker and management in many ways, etc."

False Assumptions

Although the best evidence is empirical, or factual, evidence may legitimately consist of certain self-evident truths. In discussing implicit assumptions we saw that these aren't always self-evidently true but rather false. In this section we shall consider typical misinterpretations of an assumption basic to all reasoning, namely, Aristotle's Law of the Excluded Middle, which may be stated as: everything in the universe is either *A* or not *A*, or a proposition *P* is either true or false. Thus, the moon is either made of green cheese or it is not; or the proposition that a man known as Shakespeare from Stratford-on-Avon wrote *Hamlet* is either true or false.[3] There is no middle ground, or alternative, between truth and falsity. Despite its simplicity, this assumption is frequently misinterpreted, the following errors being typical:

False Alternatives. This error results from confusing contradiction with contrariety. Although one may correctly assume that something is either *A* or not *A*, one may not assume that something is either *A* or *B*, where there are alternatives between *A* and *B*. For example, one may correctly assume that all existing institutions are either perfect or not perfect, but one may not assume that all existing institutions are either perfect or very faulty; for the choices, being contraries rather than contradictories, do not exclude all other alternatives. Sometimes a debater erroneously assumes two alternatives that do not even exclude each other let alone all other possibilities. An example would be "*X* government official was either dishonest or foolish; since he was foolish, he was not dishonest." Actually, he could have been both or neither.

Black-or-white Fallacy. This error consists of erroneously assuming that a sharp line can always be drawn between two categories designated as contradictories. Although such qualities as "bald" and "not bald," "passing" and "failing," and "hot" and "not hot" are expressed as contradic-

---

[3] Some one may object, "But suppose Shakespeare wrote only half of *Hamlet* and Ben Jonson the other half. Then your proposition would be neither true nor false." Not, however, if we made the proposition sufficiently precise. When we say that some one wrote something, we usually mean that he alone wrote it. If this were the intended sense, the proposition would be false. As Ruby says (p. 259), "The failure to note the necessity for precision is responsible for the belief that some propositions are neither true nor false. 'I am happy' and 'We are enjoying prosperity' are examples of propositions which may be regarded as neither completely true nor false. But when words are defined precisely, then in some determinate respects the propositions will be either true or false. If we cannot define 'happiness' or 'prosperity,' then we are not stating completely meaningful propositions, and truth and falsity apply only to meaningful propositions." As we have already seen, anything "half true" is false.

tories, they may be contiguous or overlapping categories. For example, "not hot," though the contradictory of "hot," may be anything from cold to warm. If the latter meaning were intended, no sharp line could be drawn between this category and "hot" since the lowest temperature for "hot" merges into the highest temperature for "warm," just as "warm" merges with "lukewarm," "lukewarm" with "cool," etc. As the diagram below shows, these are overlapping categories, even though they may be expressed as contradictories in relationship to one another.

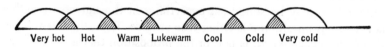

Very hot   Hot   Warm   Lukewarm   Cool   Cold   Very cold

Thus, terms like "hot," "mature," and "free," are by their nature vague and cannot ordinarily be sharply defined. This does not mean that such terms are meaningless or should be avoided. On the contrary, they are useful in designating those realities which by their nature are not clear-cut. As Beardsley points out, "It is handy to be able to report that the room was 'crowded' without having to calculate the number of people per square foot. . . . [or] to be able to speak of the 'context' of a word without having to specify exactly and for all cases how many words before and after a given word we shall include in its context." [4]

One creates an obstacle to clear thinking by insisting that a characteristic be sharply marked off when in reality it cannot be. As Stebbing observes, "If we do make this mistaken attempt, we are very likely to substitute clear-cut abstractions for untidy facts. . . . We . . . run the danger of losing contact with those matters of fact about which we desire to think effectively." [5]

An example of this error in debate is the insistence upon a too rigid definition of such terms as "conservative," "reactionary," and "liberal." Although their general limits of meaning can be indicated, their precise limits cannot be.

Sometimes a sharp line is drawn arbitrarily between contiguous categories to administer a law. In the United States twenty-one is the legal voting age, though a person who has reached twenty-one is hardly more mature than he was a week before. Since a line must be drawn somewhere, however, it is arbitrarily drawn at twenty-one. Stebbing cites an act passed by the British Parliament at the end of World War I drawing the line between legitimate and illegitimate profit-making at $33\frac{1}{3}$ per cent. Critics scoffed at the notion that a man who made 33 per cent was

[4] Monroe C. Beardsley, *Thinking Straight* (Englewood Cliffs, N.J.: Prentice-Hall, Inc., 1956), p. 169.

[5] L. Susan Stebbing, *Thinking to Some Purpose* (Baltimore: Penguin Books, Inc., 1951), p. 85.

not a profiteer. However, although "profiteer" could be defined precisely for legal purposes, it is generally not used in this legal sense. On the other hand, as we shall see in considering the next error, it does not follow that we cannot distinguish between excess profits and reasonable profits. As Stebbing says, "We shall all, I hope, agree that there is a *clear* distinction, and further, that it is in the *nature of the distinction* that no sharp line can be drawn between the extremes, except in an arbitrary manner for the practical purposes of administration." [6]

Argument of the Beard. Although one cannot insist upon drawing a sharp line between overlapping categories, it is equally fallacious to contend that there is no significant difference between them. Those who commit this error blur all distinctions, small or large, their reasoning being that since no *sharp* line can be drawn, *no* line at all can be drawn; black becomes white; one is the same as many; there is "no logical stopping off" on any continuous series of intermediate degree. In effect, the argument denies that there is any difference between categories or even between two extremes because they are connected on a continuum. The fallacy is called the "argument of the beard" because some of the ancient Greek philosophers were fond of propounding such puzzles as how many hairs constitute a beard: one, ten, fifty, five hundred, a thousand? The proper answer, of course, is that there is no definite number, a beard being a category that cannot be *precisely* defined.

Typical of the "beard" error is the following argument: "In opposing the admission of Alaska as a forty-ninth state, Senator George Malone of Nevada said, 'Once you take in Alaska you've broken the ice. Two more senators from Hawaii, then Puerto Rico comes in. Why not take Formosa?'" The Senator's argument boils down to: "One is the same as two, which is the same as three, which is the same as four; and you see how bad four would be." However, is one the same as four? [7]

Another example is the following: "You don't have to stretch your imagination very far to believe that if they can take the profit out of housing, the next logical step is to take the profit out of the manufacture of automobiles or whatever else you manufacture. You cannot stop with housing; public housing borders on socialized housing, which in turn borders on the complete socialization of industry." [8] Here the speaker runs the gamut from public housing to the complete socialization of

[6] Stebbing, pp. 186–187.
[7] Marshal Tito of Yugoslavia once commented to an American journalist that there really wasn't much difference between the political systems of America and Yugoslavia. After all, America has two major political parties and Yugoslavia one, a difference of only one party.
[8] Paraphrased from Edward R. Carr, "Is Private Enterprise Doing an Adequate Housing Job?" *Vital Speeches*, XIV (May 1, 1948), p. 438.

industry without seeing any difference between the two extremes. Indeed, black is the same as white.

Another manifestation of this error is the argument that differences in degree cannot be very significant. For example, "Our friends concede that some type of ban is desirable; now it is merely a question of degree." Here "merely" suggests that a difference in degree cannot be very significant (and that the opposition has thus made a big concession). However, if sufficiently large, differences in degree are actually differences in kind, as seen by the difference between cold and hot water.

Denying Complex Realities. This error consists of erroneously assuming that realities which can't be precisely defined or precisely determined empirically don't exist. Thus, since terms like "capitalism," "monopoly," "freedom," and "due process" can't be precisely defined, they are meaningless abstractions or the realities which they signify don't exist. Stuart Chase argues that "fascism," since it can't be precisely defined, is really an evil spirit and "the student of semantics is not afraid of evil spirits and takes no steps to fight them." In other words, fascism doesn't exist. In debates on a compulsory FEPC law, many negative debaters argued that "discrimination" is too elusive to be combatted by designing a law. In other words, it is more of a "spirit" than a reality.

Another manifestation of this error is the argument that causes do not exist or are "mere theory" because they cannot be directly verified. Thus, there is no such thing as a cause of war, juvenile delinquency, or cancer. In other words, problems are really insoluble because, to solve a problem, one must first determine its cause and then eliminate it. If true, this argument would defeat one of the basic purposes of debate, to solve a problem.

Still another manifestation of this error is the argument that value judgments are meaningless or that terms like "good" and "bad," "right" and "wrong," "effective" and "ineffective" merely signify emotional reactions. Thus, statements like "Full employment is desirable" and "an economic system which permits millions to starve is bad" are neither true nor false but merely expressions of emotion. This argument, however, is self-contradictory since its major premise is a value judgment. Thus, if all value judgments are meaningless, this very judgment itself is meaningless. Fortunately, in debate one doesn't encounter this latter argument very often.

Misuse of the Mean. This error consists of falsely assuming that the mean between two extremes is always the best course, a misconception that probably stems from Aristotle's philosophy of the "golden mean." While the mean is often the best course, it isn't necessarily always; sometimes an extreme is best. In offering a counterplan, negative teams sometimes commit this error by arguing that it should be adopted because it is a middle-of-the-road plan, i.e., not so extreme as the affirmative plan or so conservative as the status quo. However, a plan must be judged only on how effectively it meets the need; any other criterion is irrelevant.

Doubtful Evidence

Though not conclusively false, some evidence may be classed as doubtful, namely, that which is inconsistent with other known evidence or apparently outdated.

Inconsistent Evidence. If the opposition presents evidence which is inconsistent with other known evidence, the inconsistency should be pointed out. Thus, if the opposition argues that at present 250,000 workers are members of Communist-dominated unions and one's own evidence indicates 150,000, one should point out the discrepancy between the two figures and ask for the date and source of the opposition's evidence.

Apparently Outdated Evidence. Since debating today involves contemporary problems, evidence more than two years old, particularly factual, should be examined carefully. After all, what the United States exported in 1957 is not what it exported in 1959. This, of course, does not apply to basic principles, which are presumably true for all time—murder, for example, being as evil in Caesar's day as today. But it usually does apply to facts and opinions about specific situations. If a debater cites a 1943 statistic about democracy in unions, one may legitimately ask, how applicable can this be to a situation now? Similarly with authoritative opinion. If one argued against NATO because George Washington warned against "entangling alliances," a debater should point out that what might have been a good policy in Washington's day is not necessarily good today, what with intercontinental bombers and ballistic missiles.

To impress the judge or opposition, many debaters cite evidence from a newspaper published on the same day as the debate, and some even quote from "next week's" news magazines (which usually appear several days before the date on their cover).

Occasionally, "dated" evidence can be effective in showing cumulative effects. For example, "According to..., strontium-90 had already reached a dangerous level in 1955. Since there have been many nuclear explosions since that time, we can only conclude that the situation is much worse today." Generally, however, debaters should keep their evidence up to date and scrutinize any evidence which seems outdated.

Unreliable Evidence

The third criterion for evaluating evidence is reliability. Evidence, especially authoritative, can be discredited if it can be shown that its source is unreliable. Unfortunately, for one reason or another certain institutions and men in high places make false statements or express opinions on matters about which they know very little. Thus competent scholars have demonstrated that the late Senator Joseph McCarthy "employed the big lie or the 'multiple untruth,' not as an occasional expedient, but as a studied and deliberate instrument of policy." [9] Everywhere we encounter testimonials—by big league ball players, actresses, and other public figures—concerning products which many of them do not even use. Since what is published or publicized is not always true, a debater must always consider the source of his own evidence and that used against him.

Unqualified Source

An authority is considered competent by virtue of his training and experience in a given field. He is one who has been able to get the facts and to think about them consistently, and is usually of demonstrated ability in his particular field. Thus, Einstein was an authority in the field of nuclear physics; Professor Sumner Slichter of Harvard may be considered an authority in the field of economics. Being an authority in one field, however, does not make one an authority in another. In fact, competence in one field is usually a presumption against competence in another, for specialization tends to narrow one's interests. Professor Slichter undoubtedly would not consider himself an authority in the field of classical music, and one would be guilty of an error to cite him as such. Most testimonials are unreliable because their source is unqualified.

In debate authorities may be considered unqualified if they are inconsistent. Now, a person may legitimately change his mind, especially where time has elapsed and new factors have been introduced; but if he does so regularly, his integrity is suspect, particularly when he keeps changing his facts, as did Senator McCarthy on the number of "subversives" in the State Department. Men who have been known to perjure themselves, like many ex-Communists, are always suspect as sources of information, and one should seek out others.

Biased Source

A source that is apparently biased or strongly motivated by self-interest may also be considered unreliable. Accordingly, a source which is paid to

[9] Barnet Baskerville, "Joe McCarthy, Brief-case Demagogue," *Today's Speech*, II, 3 (September, 1954), p. 10. In substantiating this point Dr. Baskerville writes, "Hornell Hart, Professor of Sociology at Duke University, spent several months during the summer and fall of 1951 checking McCarthy's charges of communism in the State Department—the charges that made him famous as an exposer of subversives. Professor Hart found that McCarthy's assertions had been radically at variance with the facts in fifty specific instances." Cf. Hornell Hart, "McCarthyism versus Democracy," *New Republic*, CXXVI (Feb. 25, 1952), p. 12.

endorse a product or policy may be considered biased. Thus, all testimonials for cigarettes, razor blades, breakfast cereals, etc., would be disqualified. In debate one may encounter prejudiced testimony by paid lobbyists for various special interest groups, i.e., men who are paid to represent and promote the interests of such groups as the real estate operators, farmers, veterans, teachers, Nationalist China, etc.

Equally suspect is the testimony of individuals or groups known to be apologists for, or intimately associated with, certain movements or programs, who would stand to lose either money, prestige, or power if contrary programs were adopted. Thus, the Polish or Nationalist Chinese ambassador to the UN would hardly be expected to be objective on an issue like, Should Communist China be admitted to the UN? In a debate on National Compulsory Health Insurance one negative team argued:

According to Secretary Lull of the AMA, the record in Germany and Great Britain shows that governmentally dominated medical systems burden doctors with much red tape and paper work, thus robbing them of the valuable time needed for careful diagnosis and treatment of patients.

A suitable answer might be:

We wonder, how qualified is Secretary Lull? Though he may be a competent physician, he is not necessarily an expert on administration. And since the AMA, of which Dr. Lull is a member, has long opposed the affirmative program, we wonder also, how objective is his testimony?

Finally, certain groups, institutions, and publications, like the NAM, the United States Chamber of Commerce, *The New Masses, Freeman's Magazine, The Daily Worker*, etc., are known to be very biased and thus should be ruled out as sources of evidence.

On the other hand, evidence which is prejudicial to the testifier is very effective. If Dr. Lull, for instance, favored a program which his group opposed or the NAM had kind words to say about labor unions, such evidence would be very effective since one would expect the source to say just the opposite.

As a word of caution, in attacking the source of evidence one must be careful to avoid an irrelevant, or *ad hominem*, attack, i.e., an attack on some characteristic of the source unrelated to its ability or willingness to tell the truth. For example, an attack on someone's testimony concerning world government because he has a mistress or is homosexual would be irrelevant, or *ad hominem*, since this characteristic is unrelated to his ability or willingness to tell the truth. (More will be said about this error shortly.)

In conclusion, evidence must be probably true, and to meet this criterion, it must be clear, accurate, and reliable. If not, the foregoing fallacies will be committed, all of which are ultimately self-defeating.

EXERCISES

1. Classify the following evidence, using these categories: factual or empirical, authoritative, partly factual and authoritative, and self-evident or acceptable premise:

a. Sumner Slichter has said, "It is evident that the foreign-aid program would have to be several times larger than the proposed 8½ million dollars before it would reduce the established levels of consumption or bring about a decrease in capital per worker."

b. Since depressions and inflations are undesirable. . . .

c. According to Paul H. Appleby, former Under Secretary of Agriculture: "Contrary to a prevalent impression, people in the government do not yearn for the responsibility of extensive and intensive control over economic activity."

d. A good educational system is one of the pillars of a democratic society.

e. William Green, writing in the *Congressional Digest:* "The latest available returns filed by labor unions with the Bureau of Internal Revenue show that the total receipts for all American labor unions in 1946 amounted to only $477,701,000. Contrasted with this, receipts for one corporation—General Motors—in 1948 amounted to $4,700,000,000."

f. As Professor Eugene V. Rostow has pointed out, "High wages do not cause inflation; sharp wage increases, not matched by changes in productivity, can be realized only because inflationary profits permit them to be paid."

g. A just and honorable peace serves the best interests of the United States.

h. The economy includes about 6 million farmers, most of whom are individual enterprisers.

i. Either the farmers want price supports or they don't.

j. From *Fortune* magazine we read: "Over the past two decades steel as a whole has probably not earned much more than 3 per cent on invested capital. And even today steel-making does not compare favorably with other forms of industrial endeavor."

2. Point out any weaknesses in the evidence used in the following selections:

a. More than 70 per cent of the people in the United States live in mediocre dwellings.

b. Since stealing is a means of obtaining money wrongfully, advertisers who make false claims and thereby get money wrongfully may be designated as thieves.

c. The Bible itself has said "There is no God." [Full quotation: "The fool has said in his heart, 'There is no God.'"]

d. Nationalizing the railroads will mean nationalizing the entire transportation industry and ultimately all industries in the United States. One cannot draw the line at railroads.

e. The United States produces 43 per cent of the world's steel whereas the Soviet Union produces only 35 per cent of the world's coal.

f. All bills may be initiated by either house of Congress.

g. Since maintenance of membership is neither completely compulsory nor completely voluntary, it is the desirable mean between the union shop and voluntary unionism.

h. If editorial policies are occasionally influenced by certain advertisers, the American press can't be described as free. One can't make distinctions where freedom is concerned.

i. It is logical to assume that either the Soviet Union is ahead of the United States in nuclear weapons development or the United States is ahead of the Soviet Union. Therefore, neither side would want to be a party to such an agreement.

j. Ely Culbertson, one of the world's greatest bridge players, writing in the *Reviewing Stand,* has said: "There are fatal defects in the structure of the United Nations."

k. As Wellington Koo, Nationalist Chinese Ambassador to the UN has pointed out, to admit Communist China to the UN would demoralize many Asian nations.

l. If the United States yields her sovereignty to the UN in this area, she may as well yield it completely; for a nation is either sovereign or it is not.

m. Since prices either rise or fall. . . .

n. Ask thirty different people what they mean by communism and you'll get thirty different answers. Thus, we wonder if all this talk about foreign aid to combat communism in underdeveloped countries isn't just so much talk about something that's really a figment of the imagination.

o. Investigations have been made which reveal that one-third of the people were ill housed.

p. For a man who is supposed to be a champion of democracy it is odd that Lincoln said, "You can fool all of the people some of the time." This certainly doesn't show much faith in the judgment of the people.

q. Since he received the largest popular vote in history, Eisenhower must be considered the most popular president of all time.

r. It isn't surprising that Senator K . . . favors a liberal tax policy for the oil industry. He himself is one of the richest oil men in the country.

s. Free trade was endorsed by no less a statesman than Thomas Jefferson.

t. "If we are going to give medical care free to all people, why not provide them with free transportation, free food, free housing and clothing, all at the expense of the taxpayer. . . . Socialization is a question of degree, and we cannot move much farther in that direction unless we do wish a completely socialistic state." (Robert A. Taft)

u. Right-to-work laws have been endorsed by the NAM.

v. Who is to say what discrimination is? How can it be known with certainty on what basis an employer hires and fires? Discrimination is too elusive to be identified. Thus, a law designed to combat a phantom cannot possibly work.

CHAPTER 11

THE DESCRIPTIVE HYPOTHESIS
AND
DESCRIPTIVE GENERALIZATION

In the testing of hypotheses lies the prime difference between the investigator and the theorist. The one seeks diligently for the facts which may overthrow his tentative theory, the other closes his eyes to these and searches only for those which will sustain it.

G. K. Gilbert

In the last chapter we considered certain weaknesses of evidence. In the next four chapters we shall consider how the relationship between the evidence and conclusion or the underlying reasoning of an argument may be evaluated.

The soundest type of argument is that in which the conclusion *necessarily* follows from the evidence, or where the evidence *forces* the conclusion. Very few arguments are of this nature. Most, as was pointed out earlier, fall somewhere on a continuum between "very probably true" and "very probably false." Before the reasoning process can be evaluated, it must first be understood.

1. THE NATURE OF REASONING

Reasoning is a process of the mind which begins with something known or believed to be true and reaches other supposed truths which cannot be, or have not been, directly determined by sense perception. We are reasoning when we give reasons or evidence for a particular conclusion. The French astronomer Leverrier was reasoning when he put certain facts together—Newton's Law of Gravitation (presumed to be true) and the regular deviation of the planet Uranus from its predicted orbit (observed)—and concluded that there must be a planet, therefore undiscovered, which was causing Uranus to deviate. That his

146

reasoning was sound is indicated by the discovery of the planet Neptune where Leverrier reasoned it should be.

2. THE ASSUMPTION OF UNIFORMITY AND REGULARITY

Unfortunately, the only way we know that sound reasoning is sound is that it works, that it leads to new knowledge, as in Leverrier's case. And it is assumed that what has worked in the past will work in the present. Underlying this assumption is still another: there is regularity and order in the universe; all phenomena operate in accordance with certain invariant laws. In other words, it is assumed that things just don't happen haphazardly, that everything is in some way related to something else, that everything can be placed in a system [1] with other things, and that all systems can be placed into one great system, the universe of fact. As Stebbing, commenting on the "faith of the scientist"—and, by extension, all reasonable men—puts it: "What happens happens in accordance with laws, and these laws are such that we can discover them." [2]

3. THE STUDY OF REASONING

The study of reasoning, or the method of logical inference, is the study of the techniques and principles which have been successfully employed in ferreting out the relationships between seemingly disconnected facts, i.e., in discovering systems of fact and relationships between various systems. Logical reasoning is essentially the recognition of true relationships. The logical thinker sees connections and relationships where others do not. The average person, for example, seeing passengers on a train thrown forward when the train suddenly stops, a shell explode when it strikes a hill, liquid being agitated when hauled in a tank over a rough road, and a dog futilely trying to catch a dodging rabbit, would not think of relating such phenomena. But a scientist would see them all as manifestations of Newton's First Law of Motion.[3]

The better informed one is the more likely one is to see relationships, or to recognize patterns like the preceding one. Only after one has acquired much knowledge does one begin to recognize signs of order and interrelatedness; and only after much study do seemingly isolated facts and

[1] A system is an arrangement among things so that the properties of one member of the system bear upon the properties of another. Thus a college, a human being, a machine is each a system.

[2] L. S. Stebbing, *A Modern Introduction to Logic* (New York: Thomas Y. Crowell Company, n.d.), p. 401.

[3] This law states that a body will continue to move with its present speed in a straight line until acted upon by an external force.

fragments of fact begin to fit together like the pieces of a jigsaw puzzle. Without knowledge there can be no effective thinking, either creative (discovering new relationships) or critical (questioning the relationships which others have affirmed). Reasoning and knowledge are thus inseparable.[4] One reasons only by means of evidence; one does not reason in a vacuum. Thus, as a general rule, the more evidence the better the reasoning will be.

How do such observations apply to debate? They apply, first of all, when one is constructing a case. The more one knows the better the case, and the better the defense of it. They apply also when one clashes with the opposing case. In this phase of debate one must know not only the principles of reasoning but also the subject so thoroughly that he can point out less damaging interpretations of the facts than those put forward by the opposition.

4. INDUCTIVE AND DEDUCTIVE REASONING

In formulating the principles of logical reasoning, logicians speak of two general types, inductive and deductive. Actually, the terms are not very important and are rarely used by a debater. As Ehninger has said, "What the debater needs to know is . . . the nature of the thought relationship" manifested in a particular argument and "the conditions under which that thought relationship may be said to produce a valid conclusion." [5] In the following discussion we shall deal mainly with these matters, but for the purpose of study we shall keep the traditional classification.

Inductive reasoning is a process of reasoning whereby it is inferred that what is true of some members of a class is true of all, or some determinate proportion of all, members of that class. For example, all mules known to man are sterile (observed or known); therefore, all mules, including those unknown, are sterile (conclusion). This type of reasoning is also known as generalizing.

Inductive reasoning clearly involves an extension of fact, a leap, so to speak, into the unknown or unproved. This leap, called the "inductive leap," is justified by the assumption of regularity and uniformity in nature. One assumes that the structure of the argument, the way the facts are related, known to unknown, duplicates a previously accepted pattern or system of fact; i.e., one assumes that the principles thought to be true in the past continue to be true in the present and will continue to be true in the future.

---

[4] Occasionally, a debate judge will admonish a debater to use "less evidence and more reasoning," not realizing that this statement is a contradiction in terms.

[5] Douglas Ehninger, *Argumentation and Debate*, in David Potter, ed. (New York: The Dryden Press, Inc., 1954), p. 104.

Deductive reasoning is a process of reasoning whereby it is inferred that what is presumed true of all the members of a class is true of some members of that class. For example, all mules are sterile (presumed true); these animals are mules (specific members of the class; observed, known, or presumed true); therefore, these animals are sterile (conclusion).

The relationship between inductive and deductive reasoning may be seen in the following diagram:

Inductive Reasoning

| 1. Evidence—Experience—Observation: Human being *A* is mortal. Human being *B* is mortal. Human being *C* is mortal. Human beings *D, E, F, G, H* are mortal. | + | 2. The assumption of the uniformity and regularity of nature: certain relationships are invariant and recurrent throughout the universe. | → | 3. Generalization: an assumption or inference resulting from the combination of 1 and 2: All human beings are mortal.
 +
 4. Further observation: Jones is a human being.
 ↓
 5. Conclusion resulting from the relationship between 3 and 4:
 Jones is mortal. |

Deductive Reasoning

5. OTHER KINDS OF REASONING

For purposes of study, there are said to be two other kinds of reasoning, namely, reasoning by analogy and reasoning by hypothesis. Let us consider each briefly.

Reasoning by Analogy

Reasoning by analogy actually embraces all five steps as set forth in the preceding diagram, with this distinction: step 1 usually consists of a single instance with additional characteristics enumerated, and steps 2 and 3 are implicit. Thus the earth has an atmosphere, rotates on an axis, revolves around and derives its energy from the sun, experiences temperatures in which life can be sustained, and contains living organisms (step 1, observation); Mars has an atmosphere, rotates on an axis, revolves around and derives its energy from the sun, and experiences temperatures in which life can be sustained (step 4, observation); therefore, Mars contains living organisms (step 5, conclusion).

Although reasoning by analogy is both inductive and deductive, it is treated (and will be treated here) as a distinct type.[6]

Reasoning by Hypothesis

Reasoning by hypothesis is actually deductive reasoning; it consists of steps 4 and 5, with step 3 being implied. There is also this distinction: step 4 usually consists of an instance with more than one characteristic enumerated, as in reasoning by analogy. Here is an example: the lock on the door has been jimmied, the drawers have been opened and their contents strewn on the floor, and the silver is missing (step 4, observation); therefore, the house has been robbed (step 5, conclusion). Implied is step 3, namely, the situation described in step 4 generally indicates that a robbery has occurred.

There are, as we shall see, two types of hypothesis, descriptive and causal. Because the emphasis in this type of reasoning is on empirical data (step 4) and truth, as it is in inductive reasoning (step 1), whereas deductive reasoning as traditionally studied is concerned only with the relationships among steps 3, 4, and 5 and not with their truth,[7] reasoning by hypothesis is studied as a form of inductive reasoning.

Now that we have considered briefly the nature of reasoning and some of the forms which it takes, we are ready to consider in greater detail two of these forms, the descriptive hypothesis and descriptive generalization, and their application in debate.

6. DESCRIPTIVE HYPOTHESIS

The descriptive hypothesis may take several forms. It may be an allegation of fact, past or present, concerning a single event or entity. (Examples: Brutus stabbed Caesar; the Soviet Union is plotting to get a foothold in the Middle East.) It may be a statement concerning a quality or characteristic of an event or entity. (The United States is now experiencing a recession; the Franco government in Spain is a dictatorship; this program is costly and wasteful.) Like the conclusion of all arguments, the descriptive hypothesis is not directly verifiable. Either the event has already occurred and thus cannot be directly witnessed or the characteristic is by nature not directly observable or subject to precise verification. Thus, the conclusion goes beyond observed fact; to be sound it must be consistent with the facts to which it is related or from which it is derived. As Stebbing says, "The function of the de-

---

[6] Actually, all reasoning involves analogy, i.e., the comparison of one structure or system with another.

[7] The distinction between truth and a valid relationship will be treated more fully in Chapter 15.

scriptive hypothesis is to symbolize the ordered connection of the facts"; [8] i.e., it connects seemingly unrelated facts into a coherent whole or system of fact by describing the relationship between them. To put it another way, the descriptive hypothesis sums up certain facts in a terse descriptive phrase or word.

A sound hypothesis may be used deductively to uncover other facts which support it. For example on the basis of certain facts one might construct the hypothesis that the Soviet Union is suspicious of the Western democracies. If this hypothesis is sound, other instances than those used originally can now probably be found to support this hypothesis or even predictions made concerning future moves by the Soviet Union. In this manner, the hypothesis would be used deductively to uncover new facts.

In discussing the use of the descriptive hypothesis in science, Stebbing says: "The essential characteristic of descriptive hypotheses is that they are not put forward as generalizations from experience; they are not anticipations of natural laws awaiting confirmation. On the contrary, they are descriptions that serve the function of models enabling the scientist to understand the mode of connection between the facts for which he is trying to account. Such hypotheses must be regarded as being essentially provisional and temporary." [9]

Examples from science of descriptive hypotheses are Copernicus' hypothesis concerning the structure of the solar system and Mendeleev's hypothesis that the properties of elements could be explained as periodic functions of their atomic weights; i.e., each hypothesis describes a relationship theretofore unperceived. Both have proved to be extremely valuable, for they have led to the discovery of new facts, which further supported the truth of the hypotheses.

In debate, the following arguments illustrate the use of the descriptive hypothesis:

1. The existing unemployment compensation program is inadequate. [The hypothesis, or conclusion.] The average maximum weekly unemployment benefit is still less than $30—even after the recent increases. Coverage is only for about one-half of the unemployed, even in a period of comparatively light unemployment as in 1954. Finally, payments continue for a maximum of 26 weeks, and some states, like Mississippi, Virginia, and Florida, have a maximum duration of a mere 16 weeks. [Evidence.]

2. In conducting the War, Lincoln was often dictatorial. [Descriptive hypothesis, or conclusion.] In May, 1861, he issued orders, which transcended his authority, to increase the regular army and to organize a volunteer army of three-year men; he suspended the writ of habeas corpus without congressional consent, an act deliberately defying Chief Justice Taney, who had said

[8] Stebbing, A Modern Introduction to Logic, p. 308.
[9] Ibid.

the President had no right to such action on his own. He permitted citizens to be arrested by military orders and tried by Army courts-martial, outside and within the regions where fighting occurred. And he approved the arrest and courts-martial conviction in May, 1863, of his leading Democratic critic Vallandigham. [Evidence.]

7. DETECTING WEAKNESSES IN THE DESCRIPTIVE HYPOTHESIS

Insufficient Facts

In debate the important consideration in evaluating a descriptive hypothesis is usually the number of facts cited to support the hypothesis, or conclusion. One fact is rarely sufficient, though it may be. This would depend upon the kind of fact it is. A few examples will illustrate these points.

India resents direct economic aid from the United States. [Conclusion.] Early in February, 1956, Prime Minister Nehru suggested that "wealthy" countries channel all of their economic aid to underdeveloped areas through agencies of the UN. India and other sensitive Asian nations would prefer to be indebted to an international organization rather than to any specific country. The source of this evidence is Marshall Windmiller, political scientist at the University of California, writing in the *Far Eastern Review*, March, 1956.

Here, only one fact is given to support the conclusion that India resents direct economic aid from the United States. When only one fact is given, it is usually possible to construct an equally plausible hypothesis to account for that fact. Thus, one might answer this argument by offering the contrary hypothesis that India likes United States aid even though Nehru, if given a choice, would prefer to receive it through the UN. One may doubt the validity of the original conclusion, in other words, by showing that an equally reasonable conclusion may be inferred from the same evidence. This point is perhaps better illustrated by the following argument:

Jones is a Communist. He has gone on record as favoring the nationalization of all basic industries.

However, it is equally reasonable to suppose that Jones is a socialist.

In rare instances a fact may be such that it alone may strongly establish the truth of the hypothesis, as for example:

Jones is almost certainly a card-carrying Communist. He has gone on record as saying that he has never deviated from the accepted Communist "line" and doesn't intend to.

In this case, no other hypothesis can account for the evidence so well as the one given.

Relevant Data Missing

In considering other possible attacks on a given descriptive hypothesis, let us return to the previous argument concerning India and United States economic aid. Besides casting doubt by pointing out the insufficiency of the evidence or by offering a contrary hypothesis which may account for the evidence, one may deny or retort to the conclusion by citing other relevant facts which have not been accounted for in the argument. Thus,

Not only is it false that India resents United States economic aid, but the truth is that it greatly appreciates such aid and would like more. Quoting from *U.S. News & World Report,* December 28, 1956: "Prime Minister Nehru in his talks with President Eisenhower made known that he would like 'substantially more' United States aid with which to finance his new Five-Year Plan."

And A. M. Rosenthal, foreign correspondent for the New York *Times,* writing in that paper, January 23, 1956, said: "It is a fact that aid has made considerably more friends than enemies and that in both countries [India and Pakistan] demands to eliminate aid are fringe affairs. In the smaller cities and villages of India and all over Pakistan an American feels among friends. The overwhelming opinion among national and United States specialists in both countries is that the programs have been heavily on the credit side and should be continued."

(Rosenthal's views also support what one might have offered as a contrary hypothesis, namely, that Nehru's stand does not necessarily reflect the feelings of all the people in India, or that what is true of the part [the government] is not necessarily true of the whole [the people].) [10]

8. DESCRIPTIVE GENERALIZATION

The descriptive generalization differs from the descriptive hypothesis in that the individual facts upon which the conclusion is based are all members of the same class; i.e., they all have in common a certain essential or significant characteristic. The descriptive generalization itself is a

---

[10] To conclude that a system, or a whole, may be characterized after the character of one of its parts or, vice versa, to conclude that a part may be characterized after the character of the whole is to be guilty of the fallacies known traditionally as "Composition" and "Division." The fallacy in each case arises from overlooking the fact that different kinds of parts usually make a whole and that the latter has an identity of its own, one which stems from the interrelationships among the various parts. Thus, that which we call a radio differs in character from the various parts which work together to make a radio. The descriptive hypothesis, incidentally, identifies the character of the whole.

statement which asserts that all or some determinate portion of all the members of a given class possess or lack a certain characteristic, the basis for the conclusion being that some members of the class are known to possess or to lack this characteristic. We generalize that all men are mortal, including those of future generations, on the basis that all men in the past have been known to be mortal. Thus, generalization is the process of inferring that what has been found true of all observed members of a given class is true of all or some determinate portion of all members of that class, including those unobserved; or of inferring that what has happened on all known occasions will in similar circumstances always happen. (The latter are causal generalizations, which we shall consider in a moment.) The following are typical descriptive generalizations:

> Water freezes at a temperature of 32 degrees Fahrenheit.
> Light travels at a speed of 186,000 miles per second.
> Lead has a greater density than water.
> Harvard Law School graduates are usually successful lawyers.
> Wars are usually followed by periods of inflation.
> Most men are motivated by self-interest.

9. PARTIAL GENERALIZATIONS

For practical purposes, generalizations are possible about some determinate part of a class as well as about the whole class. (These might be called "partial generalizations.") If on actual count in a given classroom we learn that 55 per cent of the students have blue eyes, no generalization is involved; for all the components involved are perceived and the conclusion that 55 per cent of the students in this class have blue eyes does not go beyond the facts. In other words, the statement is a statement of a directly perceived fact. If, however, we infer on the basis of this fact that 55 per cent of all the students in the college have blue eyes, we have a "partial generalization." In a sense, it is a generalization concerning all the students in the college, namely, 55 per cent have blue eyes and 45 per cent do not. Similarly, generalizations are possible about "most," "nearly all," "about half," and "very few," but not about vague proportions of the whole, like "some" or "many." Predictions on the outcome of an election based on public opinion polls are partial generalizations, for here a prediction of how the entire voting population will vote is based on how a very small percentage (usually much less than 1 per cent) have said they would vote. (Before one concludes that such polls are worthless because they fail occasionally to predict the winner of a presidential election, he should remember that a small error of 2 per cent in a presidential election can often be the difference between a true and false prediction.)

10. DETECTING WEAKNESSES IN THE DESCRIPTIVE GENERALIZATION

Before considering the criteria of a sound descriptive generalization, we must differentiate between the generalizations of the physical sciences and those of the social sciences. In debate we deal with and are therefore primarily interested in the latter. A social science—examples being social psychology, anthropology, political science, economics, and sociology—may be defined as a study which deals with men in their relations to one another. A physical science—examples being physics, chemistry, biology, and astronomy—is one which deals with matter and its relations to other matter.

There are two important differences between these two major fields of study: first, the data studied in the social sciences are considerably more complex than those in the physical sciences; second, the data in the physical sciences may be derived from experiment; i.e., conditions can be carefully controlled and duplicated for subsequent experiments, whereas in the social sciences investigation, or exploration, usually replaces experiment.

Because of these differences, generalizations in the social sciences are usually far less dependable than those in the physical sciences. Since a debater ordinarily deals with the former, he must be careful not to make his generalizations too inclusive or too categorical. Rather, in accordance with the nature of the data dealt with he should qualify his generalizations with such terms as "it would appear," "it seems," "most," "the great majority," "all tend to," "would seem to have," and "it is quite probable that." Such qualifications do not mean that the generalizations are unreliable; they merely remind one that these conclusions cannot be classed as "almost certainly true" or even as "true beyond a reasonable doubt." In debate one cannot expect to do more than prove most propositions to be "probably true" for if a higher degree of probability could be shown, the question itself would probably not be debatable.

11. CRITERIA OF A SOUND GENERALIZATION

In evaluating generalizations, one should apply the following criteria; the failure of a generalization to measure up to them would justify one in designating it as "hasty" or false.

Number of Cases Cited

The precise number of cases required to make a generalization sound cannot be stipulated. As a general guide, the more cases cited, the more confidence one can have in the generalization. In physical science two cases may be enough to warrant generalizations classed as "almost certainly true"; but in social science a great many are usually required for a conclusion with a lower degree of probability, such as "probably true." Two or three cases would be quite useless. Consider the following arguments, for example:

1. The proposed increases in unemployment compensation and social security benefits may very well destroy man's incentive to get ahead. History has shown that it is usually those of humble origin and without security who make the greatest successes. We need only look at Lincoln, Ford, George Washington Carver, and Owen Roberts, to name but a few.

2. Most workers feel the need for security. F. C. Smith, in *Personnel Journal*, February, 1951, writes: "Professor E. Wight Bakke found in his detailed study that out of every 100 employees interviewed, 90 preferred lower but regular wages to high but irregular wages."

Both arguments contain descriptive generalizations: (1) men of humble origin are usually very successful in later life; (2) most workers feel the need for security. Applying the test of numbers, one could attack the first argument as citing only four cases, though others are hinted at, as a basis for a conclusion about millions. On the basis of numbers alone, there is great doubt concerning the truth of the conclusion. In the second argument there is ambiguity concerning the numbers interviewed ("detailed study"). However, the assumption, which seems reasonable, is that Professor Bakke is a competent and fair-minded individual and that he interviewed several hundred workers, adequate for such a poll. Thus, on the basis of numbers, this generalization could be regarded as sound, or "probably true." (Both arguments can be attacked in other ways, but for the moment we are considering one type of attack.)

Homogeneity of Cases Cited

As pointed out, two or three cases in the physical sciences could be enough to make a generalization reliable. This is so because of the homogeneity or similarity of the cases. For example, two careful tests concerning the boiling point of water would be sufficient to generalize that water, at a certain atmospheric pressure, boils at 212° F, for one molecule of water is like any other molecule of water. But in the social sciences the classes dealt with are much more general, which means that their members are much more complex and heterogeneous. Although individuals may be put into a class called "workers" or "voters" or "students" because they share a common characteristic, they nevertheless differ in more ways than they are alike.

To allow for differences and still arrive at a useful generalization about a very heterogeneous class, such as human beings, one must get a cross section or a "fair sampling" of the class, i.e., one must choose typical or representative instances and seek them out in as wide a variety of circumstances as possible. The greater the cross section and variety of circumstances, the greater the confidence one can have in the generalization. A familiar example of what may happen when this criterion is ignored is the experience of the now defunct *Literary Digest*, a weekly news magazine, which conducted a poll in 1936 to predict the winner of the Landon-Roosevelt presidential election. Although the magazine more than met the test of numbers by polling over two million people, a number far greater than that needed for a fairly accurate prediction, it restricted the poll to persons listed in telephone directories. The sample, in other words, was "loaded"; it did not represent the many classes of people in the United States. On the basis of its survey, the magazine predicted 370 electoral votes for Alfred Landon and 161 for Franklin Roosevelt. The actual result—Roosevelt 523 and Landon 8—caused the magazine to go out of business. Thus, in citing as evidence the results of a poll by an economist or sociologist which purports to show certain national trends, a debater should make sure that the poll has not been confined to people in large cities like New York and Chicago, or to those in rural areas of the South and Middle West; it must be representative—must cover a wide cross section of the people involved.

Going back, we see that the argument concerning "men of humble origin" can be attacked on the ground that Lincoln, Ford, Carver, and Roberts are not representative of the class of men who have achieved outstanding success in life; it could be pointed out that they are isolated examples, which therefore prove very little. The argument concerning the workers' need for security can be presumed to meet the test of representativeness, unless one has a valid reason for suspecting that the poll was "loaded."

Absence of Conflicting (Contradictory or Contrary) Instances

A true generalization must be consistent with all known facts. If there are known facts inconsistent with the generalization, the generalization must be false for contradictories or contraries cannot both be true. The old saw that "the exception proves the rule" makes sense only if we add the words "to be false." The common interpretation that "it proves the rule to be true" involves a contradiction and is thus nonsensical. We cannot say, for example, that *all* mothers are unselfish if we know one who is selfish; the propositions "all mothers are unselfish" and "one is selfish" are contradictories, so that if the latter is known to be true, the former must be false. Exceptions, however, do not mean that a generalization need be completely abandoned. Exceptions are often useful in indicating the direction in which the truth lies, or in suggesting how the generalization may be modified to make it compatible with the exceptions, i.e., exceptions may lead to useful qualifications. Instead of "all mothers are unselfish," the generalization could be revised to "almost all mothers are unselfish" or "all mothers tend to be unselfish." Also, a careful examination of exceptions can lead to a more specific generalization than the original. The mother who is selfish, for example, may be found to be neurotic or unbalanced, which fact would enable the original generalization to be qualified as "emotionally stable mothers tend to be unselfish."

The more thorough the search for conflicting instances and the fewer the number of such instances, the greater the confidence one can have in the generalization which is qualified to account for these instances.

Returning once more to the generalization about "men of humble origin," we see that it can be attacked on the basis of conflicting instances. One could retort:

Not only do men of humble origin not generally become eminent, but a survey by sociologists Krech and Crutchfield indicates that men of humble origin tend to occupy humble positions in later life and that those who rise above their humble beginnings do so not because of, but in spite of, such beginnings. Thus, men like Lincoln and Carver were able to rise only because of exceptional fortitude, intelligence, and dedication and not because of motivation due to their humble origin. So we see that men of ordinary endowments with humble origins tend to occupy lowly positions in later life, as the survey bears out.

Here a contrary generalization is supported by data overlooked by the original argument. Furthermore, exceptions to the new generalization (Lincoln and Carver) are explained as "nontypical" and the new generalization is qualified ("men of ordinary endowments") so as to be compatible with these exceptions. [Actually, they are no longer "exceptions" but are outside the scope of the new generalization.]

Another possible attack might be the retort that a successful career is usually preceded by an affluent beginning; and conversely, a poor beginning usually means a poor ending.

In conclusion, the prime consideration in dealing with the types of reasoning discussed in this chapter is "what are the facts?"

EXERCISES

1. Discuss briefly the different kinds of reasoning and the relationship between them.

2. Identify the descriptive hypothesis in the following arguments and indicate possible weaknesses or lines of attack:

a. The Soviet Union is not a military threat in Europe, for she cannot depend upon her European satellites, as evidenced by the revolt in Hungary and the unrest in Poland.

b. Big business in the United States is too big. As Senator O'Mahoney points out, "Three milling corporations produce 38 per cent of all flour consumed in the United States; 3 meat packing companies produce 43 per cent of all processed meat; 3 dairy companies produce 44 per cent of all condensed and evaporated milk and 63 per cent of all cheese."

c. The Soviet Union doesn't want to start a major war. In recent years all of her important leaders from Khrushchev on down have been preaching peaceful coexistence. They realize that in an atomic war neither side will be the winner. Besides, they believe that the capitalist system will eventually collapse on its own. So there is no need to pour billions each year into armaments.

d. The UN has been an important force for world peace. It has helped to solve conflicts in Israel, Egypt, Iran, Greece, and Indonesia—conflicts involving about one-fourth of the human race.

e. The Russians are not prepared to fight a major war, for they are still short of such strategic materials as oil, coal, and steel.

f. Since being committed to St. Elizabeth's Hospital, Pound has been studying Chinese and writing verse. A man sane enough to perform such activities is sane enough to stand trial for treason.

g. The Soviet Union seems to be well on the road to democracy, for members of the High Presidium are now often chosen in a democratic manner.

3. Why are two or three instances enough for a sound generalization in some cases and a thousand or more not enough in others?

4. Identify the descriptive generalization in the following arguments and indicate possible weaknesses or lines of attack:

a. Judging from the films exhibited here last year, it must be concluded that British films are more adult and more artistic than American films.

b. McClelland's committee received forty thousand letters protesting various abuses in unions. It seems clear that most workers are dissatisfied with unions.

c. Since the cost-of-living index is supposed to go up again next month, housewives can expect to pay more for meat and clothing.

d. In the last seven national elections the American press taken as a whole was against the winning presidential candidate five times, a fact which indicates that the American press as a whole does not reflect the political views of the American people.

e. "I think eighteen-year-olds today have more maturity of judgment than eighteen-year-olds did one or two generations ago. I have a daughter who is now twenty, and I feel at eighteen she was at least as well equipped to decide who she wanted to have for governor and what her position should be on public affairs, as I was at twenty-one." (Representative Kenneth B. Keating, *Congressional Digest*, March, 1954.)

f. Out of twenty letters to the editor, eighteen complained of the inconvenience caused by the strike. The public clearly is against the strike.

g. In recent years several college professors have invoked the Fifth Amendment. The teaching profession ought to clean itself up before asking for more money.

h. The heads of strong labor unions tend to perpetuate themselves in power.

Look at Lewis, Bridges, Reuther, Carey, Dubinsky, and MacDonald, to name but a few.

i. All eight offenses reported during the past month were committed by men previously convicted for such offenses and subsequently released. Once a sex offender, always a sex offender.

j. The Democrats must be reckoned as the War Party. The last three major wars in which the United States was involved started with a Democrat in the White House.

k. "Pythagoras was misunderstood, and Socrates, and Jesus, and Luther, and Copernicus, and Galileo, and Newton, and every pure and wise spirit that ever took flesh. To be great is to be misunderstood." (Ralph W. Emerson)

l. In a recent poll taken among eighteen-year-olds 6 per cent were undecided as to whether eighteen-year-olds should be enfranchised. This shows that many eighteen-year-olds can't make up their minds and would therefore make poor voters.

m. All generalizations are false, including this one.

CHAPTER 12

THE CAUSAL HYPOTHESIS AND CAUSAL GENERALIZATION

The social sciences, like the natural sciences, proceed upon the one great premise that the intricate flux of events can in some way be explained.

Allyn A. Young

1. THE CAUSAL HYPOTHESIS

Where a descriptive hypothesis merely describes the relationship between certain facts, or affirms the existence of a certain state of affairs or the occurrence of a given event, a causal hypothesis is an inferred explanation of why this relationship has occurred, why a certain state of affairs existed or exists, why a certain event has happened, is happening, or will happen. Thus, a causal hypothesis may be described as an explanatory hypothesis. Such is the hypothesis of burglary to account for the disappearance of money. In debate the attempt to account for the inadequacy of a given policy involves a causal hypothesis. For example, consider the following argument:

Now let us see why a program of direct economic aid has failed. It has failed because the United States has been forced to give its aid without essential conditions attached—conditions which would regulate the use of aid by corrupt governments and which would require that land reform, tax reform, and agricultural credit facilities be instituted. If we had attempted to impose these conditions on recipient governments, some nations, like the Arab states, would have flatly refused our aid, while other nations, such as the Asian countries, would have accused the United States of meddling in internal affairs or imperialist domination. Thus, the United States was forced to give its aid without essential conditions attached, with the result, as we have seen, that living standards have not been noticeably improved.

In the foregoing argument we see that a causal hypothesis may go in both directions: it may be an inference concerning why a certain state of affairs, or effect, has occurred; i.e., it may cite a cause (lack of conditions

161

with respect to the aid); and it may also be an inference concerning what would happen if a certain state of affairs, or cause, existed; i.e., it may cite an effect of a given cause (refusal of aid or charge of imperialism). The prediction of advantages or disadvantages of a certain policy thus involves a causal hypothesis, e.g., "If we stopped aid to Saudi Arabia, we would lose valuable air bases in that country."

All policy questions are, as we have seen, causal hypotheses, whose truth or falsity must be demonstrated by proof. As previously explained, all such propositions mean that the affirmative proposal is the best means (or cause) to a certain agreed-upon end (or effect). As was shown in Chapters 4 and 5, the structure of a policy case is basically causal. Typical examples of causal arguments are:

Asians distrust the United States because of her discrimination against colored peoples. [Why something is happening.]

Communist China entered the war in Korea because she felt that American troops were menacing her vital interests in Manchuria. [Why something happened.]

Recognition of Communist China would enable United States diplomats there to gain vital information about the inner workings of the Chinese regime. [Why something good would happen.]

Recognition of Communist China would enable Chinese diplomats in the United States to gain vital information about the United States. [Why something bad would happen.]

2. THE CAUSAL GENERALIZATION

A causal generalization is essentially the same as a causal hypothesis, the only difference being that the latter affirms a causal relationship between fairly specific components, whereas the former affirms a causal relationship between abstract, or very general, components. This difference is illustrated by the following two arguments:

Causal Hypothesis: The conflict between the "have nots"—such as the Puerto Rican, Negro, and underprivileged white students—and the "haves"—students from middle and upper middle class families—has led to increased juvenile delinquency in the New York City schools.

Causal Generalization: Whenever large numbers of privileged and underprivileged children are thrown together in the same school, an increase in juvenile delinquency is likely to result.

Actually, behind every causal hypothesis is an implicit causal generalization. Other examples of causal generalizations would be:

Depressions are caused mainly by overexpansion of plant facilities, overextension of credit, and overproduction.

Depressions usually cause a decreased birth rate.
Success is usually due to hard work, singleness of purpose, and intelligence.

Since a causal relationship is presumed to be an invariant, or never-changing, relationship, it follows that what is true of two causally related components is true of all essentially similar components, provided no new condition is introduced which might conceivably affect the outcome. Thus, if fire causes dry wood to burn on one occasion, it may be presumed that under similar circumstances fire always causes dry wood to burn because of the invariant relationship between fire and dry wood. Since the causal hypothesis and causal generalization are essentially alike, we shall treat them as one in the subsequent discussion.

3. THE NATURE OF CAUSATION

Causal relationships differ from other constant relationships in that they involve a time sequence; i.e., theoretically, a cause always precedes its effect, however brief the interval of time between the two may be. To put the matter another way, given certain conditions, a particular event will invariably follow; and conversely, this event will never occur unless the right conditions previously exist. The "essential" factors in the prior situation are said to be the "cause" of the subsequent event; they are "essential" to the extent that if they were not there, the event in question would not follow. The event which necessarily follows them is said to be the "effect." This constant relationship between cause and effect may be expressed as a generalization, as we have seen, or natural law, as: heat causes gas to expand.

As we acquire more knowledge, we recognize more and more the order and consistency which exist in the sequence of many events. To the primitive mind the combination and arrangement of phenomena at a given moment seem quite haphazard and chaotic. Primitive-thinking people regard the phenomena they experience as independent entities, never as parts of a whole; relationships they regard as accidental. Existence for them is composed of separate units which can be arranged arbitrarily like a set of duckpins without altering the nature of the individual units. Such people see no inconsistency in placing a fish's tail on a woman's body or a man's head on a horse's body, not realizing that a fish's tail can exist only on a fish's body or that a man's head could not pass enough air to fill a horse's lungs. By the same token, thin-skinned hairless animals do not inhabit arctic zones; and emotionally stable people usually do not come from broken homes. Likewise, to the primitive mind, the sequence of facts, the course of events, the relationship between the facts of one moment and the facts of the next moment seem equally haphazard and erratic. A primitive thinker could imagine that almost anything might happen, in any circumstances, at any time: a stick could turn into a snake, the Nile could rise when the ibis came to its banks, the sun could stand still momentarily. The rational thinker, on the other hand, knows that when a certain phenomenon occurs, there must have been a cause. When the price of eggs goes up, he blames the increase on the fact that hens are not laying as many eggs or on some other relevant factor. Similarly, when something happens, he realizes that it will produce some other effect. When a bonus bill is passed, he predicts an increase in taxes.

In debate, causal reasoning often develops into a chain (actually the whole case is a causal chain) going back to causes and to the cause of causes or forward to effects and to the effects of effects (for all causes are effects of other causes and all effects in turn are causes of other effects). For example, one might encounter a causal chain like the following:

The UN cannot effectively cope with aggression by member nations and with other threats to peace.

It cannot do so because it cannot implement its policies.

It cannot implement its policies because it does not have an effective military force.

It does not have an effective military force because the member nations, particularly the major nations, insist upon retaining their full sovereignty.

And one could go on further.

4. DETECTING WEAKNESSES IN CAUSAL ARGUMENTS

Since the recognition of causal relationships is anything but easy or obvious, let us further consider the nature of such relationships and some guides for determining when they exist. Earlier it was noted that an effect must *regularly* and *necessarily* follow its cause. Regularity and necessity are therefore characteristics of a causal relationship. If we can show that fact A always precedes fact B, or that B never appears when A is absent, we have shown that there is a regular connection between facts A and B. In determining regularity, one must be careful not to mistake coincidence for regularity. Careless thinkers frequently do, and from such confusion have arisen many of our superstitions. Jones, after leaving his house one morning, is about to enter his car when a black cat crosses his path. On his way to the office he passes through a light just as it has turned red, and his car is hit by one coming from the other direction. Later that evening Jones blames his badly dented fender on the fact that a black cat had earlier crossed his path. Though it is quite apparent that fact A (a black cat crossing one's path) has no regular connection with fact B (a dented fender), such thinking is by no means uncommon and probably accounts for such superstitions as that it is bad luck to walk under a ladder, break a mirror, or spill salt.

True regularity, even when it exists, is by itself not proof of a causal relationship; for even when fact A regularly precedes fact B, it is possible that A is not the cause of B but that A and B are the effects of a common cause. For example, the ancient Egyptians worshipped the ibis because they believed that this bird in some way caused the River Nile to overflow its banks and irrigate the land. Their reasoning was based on the fact that the ibis regularly appeared just before this important event occurred. However, both occurrences were probably the effects of the same cause: the change of the season with its attendant change in the weather. There was no necessary connection between fact A (the appearance of the ibis) and fact B (the rise of the river), i.e., the nonoccurrence of fact A would not have prevented the occurrence of fact B. Conversely, there is a necessary connection between fact B (rise of the river) and fact C (change of season and increased rainfall); i.e., with the change of season and all the other circumstances being exactly what they were, the nonoccurrence of B (the river's rise) would have been inconsistent with some natural law, in this case, with the presumed forces of gravity.

In asserting causal relationships, one must be careful to distinguish between the cause of an event and the underlying circumstances or conditions of that event. This distinction, though not precise, is important. Most people—debaters included—tend to pick out one striking factor of a cause and to call it "the" cause. If a deer is felled by a shot from a gun, pulling the trigger of the gun is said to be the cause. All the other underlying and necessary conditions of the event are not mentioned; either they are unknown or are such constant factors that they are taken for granted. Thus, the term "cause," particularly in its common sense usage, is a vague term.

Picking out only one factor of a cause can lead to an oversimplification of the truth. Every day people speak loosely of "causes" that are not causes at all but are merely components of causes. World War I is said to have been "caused" by the assassination of Archduke Ferdinand at Sarajevo, or a cold is said to have been "caused" by a draft, whereas neither of these factors constitutes a sufficient cause of the event which followed. Under different circumstances, i.e., with different underlying conditions, a dozen assassinations would not have led to a war. The assassination of the Archduke was only one factor, a precipitating factor perhaps, but the true cause must be sought in all the essential factors of the prewar situation: the growth of the nation-state system and power politics, militarism, the system of rival alliances, secret diplomacy, economic imperialism, and the emotion of nationalism, to mention a few. Similarly, with the catching of a cold, a lowered bodily resistance and the presence of certain germs are only two of the factors that constituted the real cause of the cold.

For practical purposes, when dealing with cause, we may take the underlying conditions of an event for granted provided these conditions are normal, or not unusual; and we may then mention only part of the cause, namely, the special or unusual factors of it, as *the* cause. The rest can be understood. Thus I might say that I came late to the office this morning because I had to stop to fix a flat tire on my car. Actually, stopping to fix the tire was only one of many relevant factors—the time at which I left the house, the rate of speed at which I drove, and the route I took were others, but since these were normal or usual, I may cite the one extra fact, the flat tire, as the cause of my being late. This procedure would not do for a scientific explanation, which requires more precision, or for an explanation of a complex event like a war or an inflation. For as we have just seen, apropos the cause of World War I, there were many conditions besides the Duke's assassination which were by no means so usual that they could be taken for granted. Only when the factors of a cause are so well known that there is no danger of overlooking them may we take them for granted; otherwise, we must include all the essential factors of the cause. Failure to do so would leave one open to attack, as we shall see in a moment.

5. CONFUSION OF TERMS EXPRESSING CAUSAL RELATIONS

The degree of understanding which we possess about the world in which we live, about society, about ourselves, and about our ability to predict the future and control our environment depends largely upon our degree of knowledge of causes and effects. Many disputes, large and small, arise from differences of opinion as to what causes what. Some of these differences result from ignorance, some from confusion concerning what constitutes a cause-and-effect relationship. Whenever we express ourselves, even on the simplest subjects, we fall back on causal connections. As Beardsley says, the words we use for this purpose are among the trickiest in our language, among the most commonly misused: "affect" and "effect," "due to," "owing to," "because of." The term "cause" itself is, as we have seen, difficult to pin down. Beardsley discusses five common confusions concerning certain terms used in connection with causation,[1] which it would be well for all debaters to understand. These are:

1. Cause and Reason

(The distinction between these two concepts has already been explained. See p. 47.

[1] M. C. Beardsley, *Practical Logic* (Englewood Cliffs, N.J.: Prentice-Hall, Inc., 1950), pp. 463–466.

2. Cause and Factor

A cause, as we have seen, may be complex and involved; i.e., it may contain many components or factors, each of which is a necessary condition of the effect. The individual factors, however, are not causes; they are parts or elements of a single cause. Any given event or effect has but a single cause. Thus, it is confusing to say: "There are many causes of the present recession" or "There were several major causes of World War II." It is more accurate to say "There are many factors in the cause of the present recession" or "The cause of World War II was complex."

3. Necessary and Sufficient Condition

A condition or factor of a certain cause may be necessary before the effect occurs but by itself insufficient to bring about the effect; other factors must also prevail. Much futile argument often results from a confusion between a "necessary" factor and a "sufficient" factor. Take the statements:

To be healthy, one must have a well-balanced diet.
A well-balanced diet does not insure good health.

Both of these statements, as they apply to the average individual, are true and therefore consistent with one another, though at a cursory glance they seem to be contradictory. The first one says that a good diet is one of the necessary conditions for good health, which is true; the second says that good diet alone is not sufficient for good health, which is also true. Fresh air, exercise, etc., are also necessary conditions.

It is important to note that the distinction between "necessary" and "sufficient" is significant only when we wish to produce an effect, not eliminate one. In terms of eliminating an effect, a necessary condition is also a sufficient one. For example, if a cause, C, consists of factors x, y, and z, all three must be present, or are necessary, to produce an effect, E; neither one alone nor in combination with one other is sufficient to produce E. To eliminate E, however, the elimination of one necessary factor is sufficient. Thus, though the presence of a necessary factor is insufficient to produce E, the absence of a necessary factor is sufficient to eliminate E.[2]

This principle is important in debate, for failure to recognize its applicability can lead to weak cases. In the debate on compulsory unionism (the national college topic, 1957–1958), for example, many affirmative teams were reluctant to cite such evils as corruption and communism in

[2] A parallel may be drawn here with the relationship between the affirmative and negative positions. To prove the proposition the affirmative must prove several subpropositions, whereas to disprove the proposition the negative need disprove but one of these subpropositions.

unions presumably because of the problem involved in establishing a causal connection between these evils and compulsion. What they overlooked was the possibility that compulsion, though it could not be treated as a sufficient cause of such evils, might have been considered as a necessary condition; and thus they could have argued that eliminating this condition would eliminate the evils. A few affirmative teams did consider compulsion as a necessary condition and argued that it was a "major obstacle to the reform of such evils," in effect, the cause of their continued existence. This was an effective approach. Most affirmative teams, however, owing to their failure to understand the significance of necessary and sufficient conditions, treated "compulsion" per se as the major evil, that is, as an undesirable effect rather than as a causal factor, and thus constructed highly vulnerable cases, built mainly on the moral issue of compulsion.[3]

4. Cause and Effect

Frequently two characteristics or events are related causally, but it isn't always easy to determine which is the cause and which the effect. Does an addiction to drugs lead to crime or do criminal tendencies lead to drug addiction? Does gambling lead to dishonesty or does dishonesty lead to gambling, or do both stem from a third factor, such as a personality defect or neurosis? Where the cause and effect appear almost simultaneously or where the underlying factors are complex and difficult to detect, the relationship must be carefully examined before the cause or the effect can be inferred.

5. Action and Interaction

In a true causal relationship, the cause always precedes the effect; if A causes B, B doesn't cause A. This is readily seen when two events are causally connected: John studied diligently and made a high grade on the examination. Here we see the chronological sequence of cause and effect, diligent study preceding the high grade and not vice versa. However, not only is this sequence not always so clear cut, as we have seen, but frequently a so-called cause may be acted upon by the very effect which it has produced, so that the original relationship becomes in a sense reversed, with the original cause becoming the effect and vice versa. When cause and effect interact upon one another in this manner, we have action and interaction as well as cause and effect. For example, an environment may affect an individual, who may in turn affect that environment.

There are many instances where two things can mutually influence each

[3] The moral argument used by affirmative teams, namely, that it is immoral to force men to join unions, was, in this writer's opinion, at best a weak argument—hardly the kind upon which to base an entire case.

other, particularly where human beings are involved. In the economic cycle, for instance, interaction between certain forces is a potent factor in accelerating the cycle. At present, prices rise, workers demand and get more pay; the pay increases cause prices to rise even more, which in turn leads to more wage demands, and so on, until, unless the process is checked by the introduction of some new factor, we get what is known as a "galloping" inflation. In a depressed period, surpluses accumulate and men are laid off; unemployment reduces the amount of money in circulation; this in turn leads to less buying, which in turn leads to more surpluses, more unemployment, and so on. This action and interaction, occurring in all industries, leads to a "crash." These "circles" are not round or unbreakable, fortunately for our economy. By introducing new factors, one can slow down—and even stop—the process in either direction. The examples do show, however, that there is such a thing as mutual influence. It is important to remember that most complex causal relationships, such as those usually considered in debate, involve action and interaction. Thus, when the two sides argue over whether A caused B or B caused A, frequently both are wrong, with A and B actually influencing each other.

6. MILL'S EXPERIMENTAL METHODS APPLIED TO DEBATE

To provide a guide for determining and testing causal relations the English philosopher John Stuart Mill formulated certain principles, usually referred to as "Mill's experimental methods."[4] Of Mill's five canons, the most useful for the debater are the following:

1.a. Positive Method of Difference [5]

This method is formulated as follows: "If a case in which an effect occurs, and one in which it does not occur, are exactly alike except for the presence or absence of a single factor, the effect occurring when that factor is present, and not occurring when it is absent, then that factor is probably the cause" (or "an indispensable part of the cause"; this qualification prevails throughout). The method may be illustrated by the following data:

In North Carolina in 1954, the year that radar systems for clocking automobiles were instituted, there was a nineteen per cent reduction in the rate of automobile accidents and fatalities.[6]

[4] As Ruby says, " 'Experimental' here does not necessarily refer to laboratory experiments but to deliberate observations in testing hypotheses." Lionel Ruby, Logic: An Introduction (Philadelphia: J. B. Lippincott Company, 1950), p. 387.
[5] The terms as such are not important, rather the concepts they designate and the application of these concepts.
[6] The data concerning the use of radar in North Carolina have been freely adapted from an article which appeared in American City Magazine, July, 1955. They have been changed and other data invented wherever necessary to provide pertinent illustrations.

Since conditions in North Carolina in 1953 may be considered to have been the same as those in 1954 and since a new factor was introduced in 1954 (radar systems), that new factor may be presumed to be the cause of the effect (the 19 per cent reduction in accidents and fatalities), for this effect occurred when the new factor appeared (in 1954) and did not occur when that factor was absent (in 1953).

A slight variation of the same method is illustrated by the following data:

In 1953 North Carolina and Tennessee had approximately the same accident and fatality rate from automobiles. In 1954, with the introduction of radar systems in North Carolina, there was a 19 per cent reduction in accidents and fatalities in that state, while in Tennessee, where these systems were not introduced, the rate remained the same as that of the previous year.

Again, North Carolina and Tennessee may be considered to be alike in essential respects. A new factor, radar, was introduced in the former but not in the latter. Another new factor, reduction of accident rate, then appeared in the former but not in the latter. Thus, radar was probably the cause of the reduction.

The data used in the foregoing hypotheses, typical of those used in the social sciences or wherever the phenomena dealt with are extremely complex, show once more why such hypotheses must be regarded as extremely provisional and tentative and why they can be rated as no better than "probably true." For one thing, the situations being compared cannot be said to be *exactly* the same, even with regard to all relevant factors; time has elapsed and it is possible that new factors, though unknown, may have been introduced to change the picture. In the physical sciences, on the other hand, all relevant factors—such as speed, weight, temperature, pressure, etc.—can be carefully controlled and regulated; in other words, two situations can be exactly duplicated, or very nearly so. Thus, conclusions obtained under such conditions are much more reliable than those obtained otherwise.

1.b. Negative Method of Difference

This method is formulated as follows: "No factor can be the cause in whose presence the effect fails to appear." Thus, this method provides a guide for determining not what a cause is but what it is not. The method may be illustrated by the following data:

In 1954 North Carolina introduced radar systems to determine the speed of automobiles. The rate of traffic accidents and fatalities dropped 19 per cent. However, that same year Tennessee also introduced radar systems and the accident and fatality rate remained the same.

According to the negative method of difference, radar cannot be considered the cause of any reduction in traffic accidents since this effect did not appear in Tennessee when radar was introduced. If such an argument appeared in a debate the issue would now center on the question "But *why* did this effect (reduction) appear in North Carolina and not in Tennessee?" If a debater were intent upon proving that radar was truly a causal factor, he would have to show that some new factor in Tennessee, such as lowering the age requirement for drivers, was introduced which either obscured the effect (i.e., the rate of traffic accidents would have actually been higher than that of the previous year but was kept down by radar) or prevented the cause from operating (as, there weren't enough police to man these radar stations properly so that we didn't get a true test of their effectiveness). Needless to say, one may also use both types of answer.

If a debater were intent upon proving further that radar was not a causal factor, he would have to explain the 19 per cent reduction of traffic accidents in North Carolina by attributing this effect to some other new factor, such as, perhaps, the substantially increased number of patrols made by the state police that year.

2. Negative Method of Agreement

This method is formulated as follows: "No factor can be the cause in whose absence the effect occurs." This method also indicates what a cause is not rather than what it is. The method may be illustrated by the following data:

In North Carolina in 1954 a big radar drive on speeders was credited with a 19 per cent reduction in accidents and fatalities. But in South Carolina, with no radar and no antispeed drive, accidents and fatalities fell off by 28 per cent for that same period.

According to the negative method of agreement, radar cannot be a cause of reduction, for this effect occurred in the absence of radar.

Once again, if a debater were intent upon proving that radar was truly a causal factor, he would have to explain the effect (the 28 per cent reduction in South Carolina) by attributing it to some other cause, such as the increased number of police patrols, which was not operative in North Carolina, the only new factor operative in that state being radar. If a debater were intent on further proving that radar was not a causal factor, he might resort to the negative method of difference and perhaps to expert testimony, if available.

3. Method of Concomitant Variations

This method is formulated as follows: "If a certain factor varies in concomitance with variations in the effect, then that factor is probably the cause of the variations in the effect." This method may be illustrated by the following data:

To determine the effectiveness, if any, of radar installations, the North Carolina police in 1954 tried the following experiment: In April they found that with ten installations operating, the traffic accident rate was down 5 per cent from that of the previous April. In May they added ten more installations and found that the accident rate was 12 per cent less than that of the previous May. In June they added still another ten installations and found that the rate was down 19 per cent from that 'of June of the previous year.

According to the method of concomitant variations, radar was probably the cause of the reduction, for as the number of radar installations varied, the rate of reduction in the percentage of accidents varied accordingly. An argument of this type can be answered along the same lines as those used for the preceding examples, namely, by considering the question: are the situations comparable, have other relevant factors been overlooked?

7. HANDLING CAUSAL ARGUMENTS

To recapitulate, the debater should keep in mind the following tests and techniques in handling an argument presumed to be causal:

1. *Has coincidence, or an isolated example of sequence, been mistaken for regularity?*

Because one fact or event follows another, we cannot automatically conclude that the second event was caused by the first. As we have seen, coincidence is often mistaken for regularity, which itself is not sufficient proof of cause. Failure to consider this possibility may result in the fallacy known as *"post hoc, ergo propter hoc,"* a Latin phrase which means "after this, therefore because of this," which is merely an elliptical way of saying "that occurrence came after this occurrence; therefore, that occurrence came because of this occurrence." As many writers have pointed out, an unfortunately large number of politicians, doctors, and clergymen owe their reputation to the "post hoc" fallacy. The prophet prays for rain or for "peace in our time" and when, owing to other factors, these phenomena occur, it is all too often hastily concluded that the prayer was answered. By means of such "reasoning" one could take almost anything that one disapproved of (state-supported education, TVA, teaching of evolution, woman's suffrage, social security, etc.) and show that this fact was followed (maybe years later) by some unfortunate occurrence, such as the 1929 stock market crash or World War II. And, of course, one could do the same for things that one approved of.

In handling what appear to be "post hoc" arguments, the debater has, as always, many alternatives. For example, consider the argument:

"Right-to-work" laws weaken labor-management relations. In the right-to-work states of Florida and Tennessee, strikes have increased by as much as 15 per cent during the past year.

In preparing possible answers against such an argument, one should consider the following approaches:

Doubt: It might be pointed out that merely because one event precedes another, i.e., merely because right-to-work laws preceded a 15 per cent increase in strikes, one is not justified in concluding that the first event caused the second; there may have been other factors responsible for the increase. "We should like better proof that the events are causally connected."

Denial: Using Mill's canons, one may deny that the events are causally connected by using arguments like the following:

Virginia, Georgia, and Indiana are also right-to-work states, but there has been no increase in the number of strikes in these states. [Negative Method of Difference.]

In many states which do not have right-to-work laws—Michigan, Wisconsin, and Massachusetts—strikes have increased by as much as 17 per cent. [Negative Method of Agreement.]

Retort: On the contrary, right-to-work laws lead to better labor-management relations because, etc. [Give reasons.]

One may also retort by citing other causal factors, arguing in effect: *A* is not the cause of *B; C* is. Since this type of answer is very effective strategically—for it usually undermines the arguments of inherency and plan-meets-need—let us consider a few examples:

a. Argument: Neutralist countries in Asia resent the United States because we give them direct economic aid. Either they suspect us of imperialist motives, or we hurt their pride by unwittingly emphasizing the relationship between "have's" and "have not's." For as so-and-so says, etc.

Retort: Neutralist nations in Asia resent us for other reasons which have nothing to do with our giving them direct economic aid. Primarily, they are suspicious of our treatment of Negroes and other colored minorities, our past record in this respect being far from bright. They resent our policy of nonrecognition of Communist China, for they feel we are discriminating against the yellow race and not against a Communist government, since we recognize white Communist governments. As so-and-so, in his book such-and-such, has pointed out, etc.

b. Argument: These evils in unions cannot be eliminated because of compulsion, which makes possible the concentration of unbridled power in the hands of a few men As Raymond Moley wrote in *Newsweek*, September 23, 1957, "The root of the great power exercised by the leaders who control unions lies in the fact that the union makes captive the treasuries, the workers, and shop stewards." Thus, we see that the unchecked power of the union leaders is derived from the money and acquiescence of a captive membership of workers who must support the union or lose their jobs. Since these members are deprived of their only effective means of protest, the threat to leave the union and thus withdraw their support, union leaders do not have to be responsive to their wishes or best interests.

Retort: We are told that the present evils in unions cannot be eliminated because of compulsion. On the contrary, the evils are not being eliminated because of the indifference and unsophistication of the worker. The worker doesn't object to corrupt or communist officials so long as he is getting decent wages and working conditions. When the members of the West Coast ILA had an opportunity to quit and join a rival union, what did they do? They stuck with Bridges. They care nothing about Bridges' communist leanings so long as he works on their behalf. As John Cort, explaining the union members' views, wrote in *Commonweal*, December 13, 1957, "Hoffa has proven to the Teamsters that he can give them wages and working conditions. So what does it matter if he grabbed a little extra for himself? He produced for us, didn't he?"

2. *Has regularity been mistaken for cause?*

a. Are both components effects of a common cause? Even when regularity exists, i.e., when one component regularly follows another, it is possible that the two components are effects of the same cause. Consider the following example:

Careful research by the Human Engineering Laboratory shows that the most successful men have the largest vocabularies. This proves that an extensive vocabulary is a cause of success and should be diligently cultivated.

An effective answer to such an argument would be:

That an extensive vocabulary is very useful and should be cultivated will not be denied; but that an extensive vocabulary is a cause of success does not follow from the facts, since success and large vocabularies may both be the effects of a common cause, native intelligence. The fact that two phenomena regularly appear together is not proof that one causes the other. [It is even possible that there is action and interaction here, that a good vocabulary is a factor of success and that success in turn is a factor of a good vocabulary.]

b. Has cause been mistaken for effect and vice versa?

c. Have action and interaction or mutual influence been overlooked? Even when regularity exists, it isn't always easy to determine whether *A* causes *B* or *B* causes *A*. Also often overlooked is the possibility that both *A* and *B* mutually affect one another. Consider the argument:

An harmonious world community is a precondition of world government, and such a community doesn't exist at present. Instead, there is a lack of political, cultural, economic, and ideological unity, a lack of trust and understanding among the peoples of the world. A world federation is not possible until these conditions are eliminated.

Effective answers to such an argument would be:

Retort: This argument confuses cause and effect. We are told that only an harmonious world community can lead to world government. Actually, the reverse is true. A unified political system such as world government would lead to a better world community, for world government would minimize the differences now existing among peoples. As P. E. Corbett, Professor of International Law at McGill University, says in his book *Post-war Worlds:* "It is a familiar fact that by federal union highly individualized groups have achieved united strength, security against external aggression, and peaceful and prosperous mutual relations."

Denial: This argument oversimplifies the situation. Rather than harmony leading to good government or vice versa, what really happens is that the two mutually influence each other. World government would lead to greater harmony in the world community, which in turn would strengthen a world government.

3. Has a necessary factor been confused with a sufficient one, or is the alleged cause sufficient to have produced the alleged effect?

A causal factor, as we have seen, may be necessary but by itself insufficient to produce a given effect. Going back to a previous example, it would be inaccurate to say that World War I was caused primarily by the assassination of the Austrian Archduke Francis Ferdinand at Sarajevo. The Archduke's assassination may have been the immediate cause of hostilities but certainly not the primary or sufficient cause.

Consider also the argument:

The increased rate of juvenile delinquency during the war can be attributed mainly to the indifference of our public officials.

Here indifference is said to have been the main cause of juvenile delinquency. Indifference may have been a contributory or necessary factor but certainly not the only one. Fathers in the armed services, mothers working in factories, lack of adequate playground facilities, psychological and emotional maladjustments—these and others were also necessary factors that are overlooked in the argument and should not be, for they are not so usual that they can be taken for granted. When dealing with a complex effect, one must be particularly careful to diagnose the situation correctly and not single out one causal factor when others are also important. In attacking arguments of "insufficient cause" a debater need merely point out the sufficient one.

4. Have other relevant factors been overlooked which could obstruct or prevent the alleged cause from operating to produce the alleged effect?

Some years ago Soviet leaders predicted that when World War II ended, the unemployment which would result when factories stopped producing war goods would lead to an economic depression in the United States. This effect did not occur, as we know, because of a number of intervening factors—shortages of consumer goods created during the war, an expanding population, an increased demand for our goods by other countries, the Marshall Plan, Point Four, the war in Korea, etc. In debate,

all "impracticability" arguments—those which contend that the plan cannot be brought into operation or that there are obstacles which would
prevent it from operating—and many arguments concerning advantages
or disadvantages of the affirmative plan—those which contend that such-
and-such would happen—involve a consideration of possible "obstacles"
interfering with a cause-and-effect relationship. For example:

Argument: FEPC will give Negroes and other minorities a better break.

Reply: All evidence points to the fact that the South will resist bitterly and
prevent the FEPC law from operating or from being enforced. [In other words,
the plan won't work; and if it can't work, it can't meet the need.]

Argument: Federal aid to deserving high school students will give our
economy much needed scientists and teachers of science.

Reply: However, as our surveys have shown, very few students are interested
in science, so that even with this plan our economy would still be short of
scientists and science teachers by many thousands. [In other words, the plan
won't produce the desired effect, or the plan won't meet the need.]

Argument: A G.A.W. plan in the nonagricultural industries, by providing
purchasing power during a period of recession, would cushion the economy and
thus help pull it out of the decline.

Reply: On the contrary, a G.A.W. plan will siphon off much investment capital, since much of it will be going into a G.A.W. fund. Since it is investment
capital which is largely responsible for expansion and dynamic growth and since
in a period of decline such investment capital will be lacking, we would be
cemented in a depression. [In other words, the plan will produce a contrary
effect.]

Because of the importance of causal relations in debate, this chapter
should be carefully reread.

EXERCISES

1. Mill's methods may be summarized as follows:
   a^1. Positive Method of Difference:
   > When C is present, E occurs.
   > When C is absent, E does not occur.
   > Therefore, C is probably the cause of E.
   a^2. Negative Method of Difference:
   > When C is present, E does not occur.
   > Therefore, C is probably not the cause of E.
   b. Negative Method of Agreement:
   > When C is absent, E occurs.
   > Therefore, C is probably not the cause of E.
   c. Concomitant Variation:
   > When C varies, E varies accordingly.
   > Therefore, C is probably the cause of E.
In the following arguments, which of Mill's methods are used?

d^1. The most recent reports published in *Time* magazine show that the rate of lung cancer is much higher among heavy smokers (two packs or more a day) than among nonsmokers. Only one conclusion can be drawn from these data.

d^2. While it is true that many heavy smokers get lung cancer, many of them do not. Moreover, nonsmokers as well as heavy smokers get lung cancer.

d^1. Then how do you account for the fact that the incidence of lung cancer varies directly with smoking: the heavy smokers have the highest incidence; the moderate smokers have a lower incidence; and the nonsmokers have the lowest incidence.

e. It is doubtful if economic factors have much bearing on juvenile delinquency. The percentage of delinquents from underprivileged homes is practically the same as that from homes much better off economically.

f. If reading comic books leads to juvenile delinquency, as some educators claim, why don't all children who read such books become delinquents?

g. As the cost of living rises and real income diminishes, the number of manhours lost through strikes rises proportionately.

h. In May, 1946, the Chicago Crime Commission undertook a survey of conditions in the notorious Fifth Police District. It found sixteen families living in a dwelling built for three. It found a lodging house for single persons occupied by 200 families. In dozens of overcrowded tenements, bathroom and cooking facilities were being shared by several. Only 8 per cent of the people of Chicago live in the Fifth Police District, but this area produces 21 per cent of the city's murders, 12 per cent of its robberies, and 25 per cent of its rape cases.

i. In a certain textile plant in Philadelphia absenteeism and labor turnover in the mule-spinning department were excessive—250 per cent per year compared to 5 per cent for the other departments. Although wages were increased and bonuses offered, the excessive absenteeism and labor turnover continued. It was then decided on the basis of certain physical examinations to give the men regular rest periods throughout the day. After a year of this system there was no labor turnover at all.

j. In an unpublished study of Dr. George Marshall of the Brookings Institution, cited by Morris R. Cohen, it is revealed that variations in the membership of the International Association of Machinists from 1912 to 1920 are almost identical with those in the death rate of the state of Hyderabad, India, from 1911 to 1919. Also revealed is the fact that the rapid rise of college enrollments from 1920 to 1931 closely parallels the rise in the number of inmates in insane asylums during the same period.

k. "The Detroit Housing Commission reports that the pneumonia death rate is three times greater in the slum area than elsewhere; infant mortality six times that of normal neighborhoods; the tuberculosis death rate $10\frac{1}{2}$ times greater in the slums; and criminals in the blighted areas are fifteen times as numerous as in the better sections." [Senator Paul Douglas]

2. In general there are six ways of approaching a causal argument; i.e., by showing:

a. no cause, coincidence, or other cause

b. necessary but insufficient causal factor or causal factors overlooked *c.* cause confused with effect

d. action and interaction

e. inoperative cause due to obstacles

f. other effect(s) overlooked

Which approach is used in the following arguments?

g. American foreign policy had nothing to do with Chiang Kai-shek's defeat. His government fell because it was weak and corrupt.

h^1. A G.A.W. would provide the necessary financial incentives to industries to stabilize.

h^2. But these incentives already exist; they don't need a G.A.W.

h^3. If these incentives exist, why then don't the industries stabilize?

i. They tell us that a G.A.W. would lead to stabilization. However, since it would discourage industry from taking risks, it would really lead to stagnation.

j^1. Surveys indicate that most dope addicts are thin and undernourished. This seems to support the conclusion that a poor diet contributes to dope addiction.

j^2. Not so; both dope addiction and poor eating habits may be traced to a common factor: a disturbed and maladjusted personality.

k^1. Any student with the ability, initiative, and ambition can get a college education. Government aid is not needed.

k^2. On the contrary, the rising costs of tuition, fees, textbooks, and board and room have nullified, in the words of the President's Commission on Higher Education, "the comfortable idea that 'any boy can get a college education who has it in him.'"

l^1. Since United States forces could have taken Berlin unaided but waited for the Russian troops in the East to reach the city before moving in, the United States really conquered that territory and should have dominion over it now.

l^2. But United States forces were able to advance only because most of the German army was engaged in holding down over 100 Russian divisions on the Eastern Front. If that same German force had been turned against the thirty or so American divisions, the Americans would have been stymied and the Russians would have moved in. So the United States really had plenty of help from the Russian army in taking Berlin.

m. The five million rejections for physical unfitness during World War II were not due to inadequate medical care but to conditions which modern medicine as yet cannot prevent and to very rigid standards of physical fitness set by the Armed Forces.

n^1. Negroes in the South have poor schools because they don't pay as much taxes as the whites, and they don't pay as much taxes because they don't earn as much. Thus, if they were more ambitious, they would have better schools.

n^2. It is true that Negroes in the South have poorer schools than the whites and that they pay less taxes because they don't earn as much. But the first condition is not caused by the second. Both are manifestations of the same basic cause: the Negroes in the South are held down and exploited economically.

o^1. The Soviets not only started the cold war by refusing to demobilize their army right after World War II but have intensified it by many hostile acts, such as forcing the United States to undertake the Berlin airlift.

o^2. It's really not so simple as all that. Right after the war the United States announced her intention to continue the manufacture of atomic bombs and to hold the Japanese-mandated islands without giving the UN the right to inspect these islands. These policies, opposed by both Stimson and Hull incidentally, naturally made the Soviet Union suspicious of United States intentions, and from this mutual suspicion the cold war started. Thereafter, a hostile act by the Soviet Union provoked a hostile act by the United States, which in turn provoked another hostile act by the Soviets. And so it went, each retaliating against the other and intensifying the cold war.

p^1. A compulsory health insurance program would provide better medical care for the people.

p^2. But there would be so many malingerers that the doctors' time would be wasted ministering to nonexistent ailments, and the net result would be worse medical care.

q^1. Since atomic bombs have been tested regularly, storms seem to be more frequent and more violent. Apparently these explosions are affecting the atmosphere and producing bad weather.

q^2. However, every meteorologist who has studied the situation says there is no connection between storms and bomb tests. This seems to be a pretty clear case of *post hoc* reasoning.

r^1. All of the *summa cum laudes* who graduated during the past eight years were outstanding debaters. Debating undoubtedly produces great academic success.

r^2. While debating undoubtedly leads to the development of important academic skills and thus contributes to academic success, students could not be *summa cum laude* unless they had considerable capacity and industry to begin with.

s^1. Then there is seasonal unemployment due to seasonal fluctuations in manufacturing, as in the automobile industry.

s^2. However, seasonal fluctuations in manufacturing reflect fluctuations in demand. Production doesn't determine demand; demand determines production. How could a G.A.W. stabilize consumer demand?

t. How would you stabilize consumer demand? When the temperature is 100°, people don't burn coal. When there are six inches of snow on the ground, the building of houses stops. When there's a drought, the demand for agricultural implements falls off. When dacron and nylon become available, the people don't want cottons.

u^1. A G.A.W. would combat recessions that occur and are occurring now.

u^2. By a law passed in 1946 the government can do the same thing.

u^1. Why then are recessions still occurring?

v^1. Compulsory integration would not get at the cause of discrimination. Since the main cause is ignorance, we need a better educational system. Only when the people are better educated will there be better understanding between whites and Negroes and integration made possible.

v^2. Though increased education is unquestionably desirable, enforced integration leads to better education. Wherever enforced integration has occurred, as in the armed forces and in certain industries in the South, improved relations and better understanding between whites and Negroes have occurred. Being forced to work together leads to greater understanding of mutual differences, which in turn leads to more harmonious relations. More harmonious relations in turn lead to more tolerance and understanding. And so these two factors mutually influence each other.

CHAPTER 13

THE ANALOGICAL HYPOTHESIS

> The genius is one who, in De Quincey's phrase, possesses "an electric
> aptitude for seizing analogies."
>
> *Harold A. Larrabee*

1. REASONING BY ANALOGY

Related to the descriptive and causal hypotheses and often developed
from one or the other is the analogical hypothesis, which is a hypothesis,
to use Stebbing's words, "that what is true of one set of phenomena may
be true of another set owing to the fact that the two sets have in common
certain formal properties." Stebbing cites the example of the physicist
Maxwell "who recognized an analogy between certain problems in the
theory of gravitational attraction and certain problems in electrostatics."
That is, the law of the inverse square is the formula for both gravitational
"pull" and electrical attraction, although the nature of the electrical attraction is different. However, "there is between these two sets of phenomena
what might be called a structural identity." That is, there are the same
invariant relationships between the phenomena of one set as between the
phenomena of the other. As Stebbing says, "By developing this analogical
or structural hypothesis Maxwell was led to formulate his electromagnetic
theory of light." [1]

Reasoning by direct analogy involves a comparison between two sets
of data (actually, all inductive reasoning involves such a comparison,
though it is usually implicit). From the known structure of one set, knowledge concerning some unknown portion of the second set is inferred. The
basis for inference is that the structure of the second set is the same as
that of the first and that consequently invariant relationships, whether
descriptive or causal, which are manifested in the first set will be manifested in the second.

A few examples will illustrate the process. Dr. Jonas Salk reasons that
a serum prepared from dead polio virus will effectively combat polio

[1] L. S. Stebbing, *A Modern Introduction to Logic* (New York: Thomas Y. Crowell
Company, n.d.), p. 309.

because a serum prepared from dead diphtheria germs has effectively combatted diphtheria. The following is an analysis of his reasoning:

1st set of phenomena, known: diphtheria is a disease caused by a virus; once the virus was isolated a successful immunizing serum was made from dead virus.

2nd set of phenomena, known: polio is a disease caused by a virus, which has been isolated. *Inferred:* a successful immunizing serum can be made from the dead virus.

Or take this hypothetical argument, the kind that might be encountered in a debate:

In 1946, when Michigan had capital punishment, the number of homicides per one hundred thousand was 5.2. In 1947, with capital punishment abolished, the number of homicides per one hundred thousand was 4.8. In 1948, it was 5.5; in 1949, 4.9; in 1950, 5.1; and in 1951, 4.6. In other words, there was no appreciable change in the homicide rate when capital punishment was abolished. Thus, Wisconsin need have no fear about abolishing capital punishment.

In essence, the argument reduces to: Since Wisconsin resembles Michigan, what happened in Michigan may be expected to happen in Wisconsin. It is interesting to note that the various methods of testing a causal hypothesis involve analogy, with the reliability of the various tests depending upon how analogous or alike the two situations being compared are. In the previous example we have not only an analogical hypothesis—namely, that what happened in Michigan will happen in Wisconsin—but also a causal hypothesis based upon the negative method of agreement—namely, that removing capital punishment will not cause an increased homicide rate. This latter hypothesis in turn involves an analogy since it is based upon a comparison of what happened in Michigan from year to year, it being assumed that Michigan one year was the same as Michigan the next.

Thus, we see, inference by direct analogy is the inference that what is true of one set of circumstances is true of a similar set of circumstances, the inference being justified on the assumption that the two sets are homologous, or identical in their basic structure.

Writers often differentiate between two basic uses of analogy: analogy for explanation and analogy for inference (or argument). Others also differentiate between figurative and literal analogies. Such distinctions are not very significant and may even be misleading. Analogy for explanation, as we shall see in a moment, has the same structure as analogy for inference, the chief difference being that the former deals with noncontroversial data assumed to be true, whereas no such assumption can be made in analogy for argument. As for figurative and literal analogies, while it is true that things resembling one another in many ways are more likely to have in common certain structural relationships, it is also possible that things unlike in many ways may exhibit the same structural relationships. A map of a given territory, for example, and the territory itself are surely dissimilar in many ways; yet both have in common a certain structural relationship. And it is the structural relationship which is important in analogy, as in all reasoning.

2. ANALYZING ARGUMENTS BY ANALOGY

Analogy or comparison is the basis of all thinking. In formulating a hypothesis, whatever its nature—descriptive or causal—we are guided, consciously or unconsciously, by the knowledge that we are dealing with a situation or structure of fact identical or essentially similar to one encountered previously.[2] Without comparison or resemblances to guide him, man would be lost; he would have no way of seeing relationships, no way of thinking constructively. That man often goes astray in his thinking is due in large part to his seeing resemblances where none exist or to his hastily assuming that they exist, when careful analysis would reveal otherwise.

In debate, analogies are used both constructively and destructively, that is, for building and for attack. To facilitate the analysis of arguments by analogy, we shall designate the component of the analogy which involves the inference as the *primary component* and that which is known or which constitutes the reason for believing the inference, as the *secondary component*.

3. DETECTING WEAKNESSES IN ARGUMENTS BY ANALOGY

Since the force of analogical arguments depends upon the similarity of structure between two components, the basic attack on such arguments hinges on the question: are the components really analogous, do they exhibit the same structure? In some cases, the data concerning the primary component are so incomplete, sometimes only hinted at, that no comparison is even possible; or the data are assumed to be true when such assumptions are unwarranted. These "arguments" can be treated like all assertions. In other cases the components are just not analogous, i.e., they do not exhibit the same structure or illustrate the same principle, so that no inference is justified.

[2] This principle is especially apparent in the field of law, where direct analogy is the basis for deciding most law suits. That is, on the basis of a decision handed down in one set of circumstances, a structure or principle is abstracted, which is now applied to subsequent cases whose structure appears to be similar.

Analogies Containing Incomplete Data or Unwarranted Assumptions

To illustrate the fallacy of incomplete data or questionable assumptions we shall consider several typical analogical arguments that might be encountered in a debate.

For while it may be a sound policy not to invite the Soviet Union to enter into formal engagements—beyond her obligations under the UN charter—it cannot be sound policy not to be talking to the Soviet Union about the Middle East. That would be like deciding not to notice the elephant that has strolled into the dining room. [W. Lippmann, "Today and Tomorrow," Wilkes-Barre *Record*, Feb. 2, 1956]

Here the linking structure or generalization (that exhibited by both components of the argument) is presumably: One can't solve problems by pretending they don't exist or by refusing to acknowledge their existence. Ignoring the elephant in the dining room illustrates the principle, but does the United States attitude toward the Soviet Union on the Middle East illustrate it? Possibly, if it could be shown that the Soviet Union now plays a prominent role in that area and is creating a problem for the United States which is being ignored by our State Department. In other words, the data on the primary component are too incomplete to make any comparison. Or the data concerning this component are assumed, in which case the argument reduces to an assertion. If the situation which has been assumed could be proved,[3] the secondary component, being vivid and concrete, would be an effective illustration of the principle involved and would thereby make that principle clearer to the reader. Now while this type of comparison does not perhaps seek to prove anything, it does provide—like expert testimony, which also doesn't prove anything—an additional reason for *believing* something to be true and is thus persuasive in effect. It is this type of analogy that some writers call "explanatory," since it presumably seeks to clarify rather than prove. However, in debate the line between this type of explanation and argument is so thin as to be almost nonexistent; for the ultimate intent of both is the same: to gain acceptance of a given point of view. In this particular case, Lippmann is urging the reader to agree

[3] One may object here, since it is common knowledge that the Soviet Union has infiltrated the Middle East and is powerful enough to do immense damage, that this knowledge may be legitimately assumed and that, therefore, Lippmann demonstrates that something should be done to take its presence into account, just as something should be done to take into account the presence of an elephant which has wandered into one's dining room. However, even if these basic assumptions are warranted, Lippmann still does not demonstrate that the best way of noting the Soviet Union's presence is to sit down and talk.

with him in rejecting the present policy and in accepting his suggestion that the United States sit down and talk with the Soviet Union about the Middle East.

An argument similar in form to the preceding one, though perhaps a little more involved, is the following:

> Hanging over each European manufacturer who might be willing to try to sell us even in spite of our tariffs is the threat that if he is too successful he will have to climb a still higher wall which we will thereupon erect. [This is an allusion to the "escape" clause in the Reciprocal Trade Agreements Act which empowers the President to raise the tariff in any area that he sees fit.] It is like a pole vault where the bar is raised after each jump. (Clarence B. Randall, "Free Trade? Yes," *Saturday Review*, Jan. 23, 1954, p. 30.)

Here the escape clause is compared to a pole vault, the suggestion being that tariffs can be raised to a point where foreign manufacturers can't compete with their American counterparts just as a pole vault is raised until it reaches a point where a successful jump can't be made. There is the further suggestion that because of the threat of the escape clause foreign manufacturers are discouraged from making the effort to compete. Needless to add, it is only one short step from pointing out a serious defect of a given policy to urging its rejection.

In answering the foregoing argument, a debater would need to consider whether or not the escape clause is in fact a potentially insurmountable obstacle or whether the threat of it actually does deter European manufacturers. This might be considered an interesting hypothesis, but it has not been empirically established. Thus, one would have several choices in answering: How true is this hypothesis? Has the escape clause deterred European manufacturers? [Here one might show that many foreign manufacturers are successfully competing in American markets.] As for those who have not tried to compete, isn't it reasonable to assume that there may be other deterrent factors? [Here, one might cite other factors, such as inferior productivity, merchandising, etc.]

False Analogies

We come now to examples of analogical arguments whose two components are true (or hypothetically true) but differ in certain essential respects. In other words, they do not have the same structure so that what applies to one does not necessarily apply to the other. The basic attack on such arguments is to point out the false or misleading analogy. In the following examples an attempt is made to gain acceptance of a given principle; i.e., they may be considered "constructive" arguments.

> Advocate speaking on behalf of legalized horseracing: Gambling is part of living. A man gambles every time he takes a wife.

Here gambling on horses and taking a wife are clearly not analogous. According to the *Encyclopedia of Social Sciences*, gambling is defined as "the staking of valuable considerations upon factors which lie in the realm of pure chance." While there is a certain element of chance involved in taking a wife, in most marriages this element cannot be described as "pure chance"; the degree of chance involved is significantly less than that involved in betting on a horse. Thus, the fallacy here is also that of confusing contiguous categories, or the "fallacy of the beard."

This next example proves that even the best-intentioned and most highly regarded of men are not immune from using false analogies. This one was employed by Lincoln in a speech which he delivered during the Civil War period:

> Gentlemen, I want you to suppose a case for a moment. Suppose that all the property you were worth was in gold, and you had to put it in the hands of Blondin, the famous rope-walker, to carry across the Niagara Falls on a tight rope. Would you shake the rope while he was passing over it, or keep shouting to him, "Blondin, stoop a little more! Go a little faster!" No, I am sure you would not. You would hold your breath as well as your tongue, and keep your hands off until he was safely over. Now the government is in the same position. It is carrying an immense weight across a stormy ocean. Untold treasures are in its hands. It is doing the best it can. Don't badger it! Just keep still, and it will get you safely over.

Although both the government and Blondin are (hypothetically) in a precarious situation, with much depending upon the outcome, the two situations are not analogous. Blondin is faced with a problem whose solution depends upon individual physical skill and dexterity, and complete concentration. The government's problem—how to win the war—is entirely different. The solution depends upon intelligent planning and co-operative activity. Thus, where giving advice to Blondin—any kind of advice—might disturb his concentration and thus be hazardous, giving advice to the government would not necessarily have the same effect, as Lincoln suggests. On the contrary, if the advice were sound, it could do some good.

One may attack false analogies in another way, i.e., by accepting the analogy but attacking its underlying principle. For example, in an effort to justify the number of unemployed, approximately 5½ million at the time, Vice President Nixon stated:

> There will be no recession. . . . A normal economic system, like a normal human body, should not run at full speed all the time. There are times when it must slow down so that needed changes can be made and bad habits and faulty practices corrected. (Quoted in *Kiplinger Washington Letter*, April, 1958.)

Not only are the two cases, a normal human body running at full speed and a normal economic system with relatively full employment, not analogous (for when a normal body slows down, all parts of it continue to function normally whereas the unemployed in the "body economic" do not) but even if, for the sake of argument, they were considered analogous, one might point out that unemployment is a type of "slow down" which could seriously impair and possibly destroy the entire body economic, like a gangrenous limb which has ceased functioning and no longer receives sustenance from the rest of the body.

4. THE *REDUCTIO AD ABSURDUM* ARGUMENT

In the preceding examples, analogies (though faulty) were used for the purpose of winning approval for a given principle or policy. Often, however, analogies are used for the opposite purpose, to demonstrate the weakness, and by implication to urge rejection, of a given principle. The use of analogy for this purpose is called "*reductio ad absurdum.*" More specifically, the *reductio* argument consists of discrediting another argument by showing the falseness, or absurdity, of its underlying premise. The absurdity is shown by applying the premise, or principle, to a situation analogous to that dealt with in the argument being discredited. The following are *reductio* arguments:

The final blow falls, it seems to me, when it is admitted by the proponents of freer trade that to avoid undue disruption of the American economy it would be necessary to reduce import duties gradually over a period of years. This is somehow akin to offering a jobless man the promise of a good job if he will just wait around for five or ten years. (Leland I. Doan, "Free Trade? No," *Saturday Review*, Jan. 23, 1954, p. 31.)

Much of the revulsion against the use of atomic weapons arises because the very newness makes it seem more horrible. A careful cataloguing of the injuries resulting from the use of the automobile would also be impressive, but any proposal to outlaw the automobile would be considered ridiculous. (R. E. Lapp, *Must We Hide?* Reading, Massachusetts: Addison-Wesley Publishing Co., Inc., 1949, p. 18.)

Both arguments are faulty *reductio* arguments because the analogy in each case is questionable or false. In the first argument, the writer attempts to show that the policy of freer trade is bad (and should be rejected) because a gradual reduction in tariffs (gradual to avoid sudden and widespread unemployment) may be compared with promising a jobless man a job five or ten years hence. The fallacy lies in the writer's misinterpretation of the meaning and reason for gradualness in lowering trade barriers. By lowering duties slowly, the economy would have time to adjust, so that whatever temporary unemployment would occur would occur in small amount and would be quickly eliminated as the economy diverted production to areas where it has a comparative advantage. No one, presumably, would have to wait around five or ten years for a job—

and precisely because trade barriers would be lowered gradually. Actually, the argument exaggerates, without basis, the type of disruption which would occur with the gradual lowering of trade barriers. The fallacy is also that of the "argument of the beard," or the failure to recognize significant distinctions.

In the second argument, the writer attempts to prove that it would be unwise to outlaw atomic bombs (that we should reject this policy) because it would be unwise to outlaw automobiles, which also cause destruction. The argument overlooks the significant difference between atomic bombs and automobiles, namely that one is made solely for, and can only accomplish, destructive ends, while the other is made solely for, and does accomplish for the most part, useful constructive ends.[4]

5. SOUND ARGUMENTS BY ANALOGY

To this point we have considered a number of dubious analogical arguments and possible answers to them. However, such arguments, if used with caution, can be sound and quite helpful. Consider the following three:

The way to eliminate inflation is, first, to ascertain its cause and then to eliminate that. It is the same principle the doctor uses when he tells the patient to stop eating tomatoes after he has discovered that his patient is allergic to them.

A Senator from Georgia recently urged that the NAACP be declared a subversive organization because it advocates integration, a policy which is also advocated by the Soviet Union. The Senator's reasoning may be compared with that of the man who concludes that dogs are cats because both are mammals.

Efforts have been made to defend cheating on income tax by pointing out that it is done so often and so successfully. One might as well say that a driver who exceeds the speed limit isn't guilty because so many others do it and get away with it, or that a man who sells heroin to minors isn't guilty because so many others do it and get away with it.

In the first example, both components truly illustrate the principle of cause and effect. The secondary component, being more familiar than the primary, makes the primary better understood and thus more readily accepted or believed. Even though the two components are dissimilar in many respects, the relationship in each is the same.

[4] Another interpretation of Lapp's argument might be that atomic bombs, like anything new, will have to be got used to. Automobiles, like atomic bombs, cause fantastic numbers of deaths; since we have come to accept those deaths as a matter of course, we will come to accept the deaths from atomic bombs in a like manner. However, death by automobile is almost invariably death by accident, whereas death by atomic bombing is death by design. Thus, Lapp falsely compares the two; human beings may have got used to the former but have never quite got used to the latter (and, one hopes, never will).

In the second example, again the relationship between the facts in each component is identical; i.e., both components illustrate the structure: A is included in B, and C is included in B; therefore, A is included in C. This, as we shall see in a moment, is the structure of the deductive fallacy known as the "undistributed middle." Thus, the analogy, by illustrating the faulty reasoning manifested in the primary component, exemplifies a valid *reductio* argument.

The third argument is also a valid *reductio* argument, for the secondary components, speeding and dope peddling, truly illustrate the principle or relationship involved in the primary component, cheating on income tax, and the "absurdity" of thinking that such a principle is not wrong. One might object that the crimes are not analogous, that dope peddling is a much more serious violation of the law than cheating on income tax. However, the nature of the crime is irrelevant to the point made in the argument, which is that even if one gets away with breaking the law (as illustrated by both components of the analogy), it is still wrong and should not be condoned. How wrong is immaterial. Unfortunately the analogy may suggest that cheating on one's income tax is to be classed with crimes like dope peddling, but the hazard of conveying suggestions not intended exists in all arguments. Of course, if the speaker should subsequently develop this suggestion, he would be guilty of exaggeration and could be answered accordingly.

6. CAUSAL HYPOTHESIS FROM ANALOGY

Finally, there are those analogical arguments which are essentially causal, being developed from a causal hypothesis. These arguments are generally used in connection with the workability of the affirmative plan. For example:

A compulsory health insurance program has (or has not) worked in England; it therefore will (or will not) work in the United States.

Right-to-work laws have (or have not) worked in eighteen states; they therefore will (or will not) work in the rest of the country.

Possible answers to such arguments are similar to those illustrated for other causal arguments. Briefly, one should look for significant differences between the two components of the analogy, those which may affect the causal relationship. These differences may be obstacles or causal factors present in one component but absent in the other which may prevent the effect from occurring or produce an effect other than that predicted. Consider the argument

Surveys made in Germany and Britain show that after the compulsory health insurance program was put into effect the amount of sickness practically doubled and the average length of illness in those countries was twice as long as that in the United States.

This argument implies that the compulsory health insurance program caused or contributed to more and longer illnesses in Germany and Britain and may therefore be expected to do so in the United States. The argument overlooks some very significant factors: first, that the long and serious illnesses which came to light after the compulsory health insurance program went into effect might well have existed before this program but weren't recorded because many sick people just didn't have the money to get adequate treatment; second, that many may have died from neglect and that their illnesses, which might have been long and serious had they survived, just never came to light; and third, that the illnesses may have been due in large part to an inadequate postwar diet brought about by reduced living standards not prevailing in the United States. Thus, one might retort that a compulsory health insurance program, by making adequate medical care available to all, would lead to fewer serious illnesses and to fewer fatalities caused by the neglect of such illnesses.

In summary, arguments from analogy are generally not the strongest kind and therefore should be reinforced by other kinds.

EXERCISES

1. What is the relationship of reasoning by analogy to inductive and deductive reasoning?

2. Analyze the following analogical arguments, state the conclusion of each, and indicate possible weaknesses or lines of attack:

a. The Russians can hardly be criticized for killing the Hungarians. After all, under conditions of war soldiers kill their enemies and aren't criticized for performing an immoral act.

b. "No body can be healthful without exercise, neither natural body nor politic; and, certainly, to a kingdom, or estate, a just and honourable war is the true exercise. A civil war, indeed, is like the heat of a fever; but a foreign war is like the heat of exercise, and serveth to keep the body in health; for in a slothful peace, both courages will effeminate and manners corrupt." (Francis Bacon)

c. The government makes the regulations for private utility companies while simultaneously competing with those companies with projects like the TVA. The situation may be compared with a football game where the referee is playing for one of the teams.

d. We hear much criticism of colonialism, but no one complains when parents supervise their children until they become adults. When India grew up, didn't she receive her independence?

e. "If the proposal for our country to go Socialist were put up to our voters at the polls tomorrow, the proposal would be defeated by an overwhelming majority. Our danger is not that we accept Socialism deliberately. Our danger is that, step by step, we may be walking into it without knowing it. What we would not permit to enter by the front door we may permit to sneak in by the back door, if we are not more watchful." (Herman W. Steinkraus, "We Need a Fifth Freedom," *American Magazine*, CXLVIII, September, 1949, p. 125.)

f. Internal trade, on the other hand, is unproductive. It's like a dog who lives by eating its own tail.

g. "As Emerson wisely said: 'When you hitch a chain to a slave, you hitch the other end to yourself.' As certainly as government enters ever-broadening fields, so certainly government will assume increasing control of all the activities of our lives." (Senator Owen Brewster)

h. The brain may be compared with a sponge. It can take so much knowledge, just as a sponge can take so much water; once a saturation point is reached, no more can be absorbed.

i. With the government in charge of a health program we could expect much waste and inefficiency, for government employees are much less efficient than those in private industry. The Hoover Commission cites examples where individual output for identical jobs was four times greater in private industry than in government.

j. The sale of narcotics should be legalized in the United States, for legalization in Britain has reduced the number of addicts and the amount of crime connected with illegal sales.

k. "What we need to learn before all else, it seems to me, is that there are no short cuts in this world. Each must work and provide for his own salvation and his own security. To depend on others is a broken reed, for if Peter gets more, then Paul must get less. Depending on state security is like betting on a horse that will never leave the stable, or like a starving man who is expected to get satisfaction out of the promise of a future good dinner." (H. G. L. Strange, "There's No Short-cut to Security," *Northwestern Miller*, CCXL, Dec. 6, 1949, pp. 33–34.)

3. Construct *reductio ad absurdum* answers to the following arguments:

a. Since normal grade school pupils could learn foreign languages by the Army method, this method is not fit for college teaching.

b. This program should not be adopted, for the taxpayer would have to support it.

c. A compulsory health insurance program should be rejected, for it would subject the medical profession to political influence.

d. Legalizing lotteries would mean greater revenues for the state and therefore would be desirable.

e. Smith should not be elected to the city council, for he has never held any public office.

CHAPTER 14

MATERIAL IRRELEVANCIES

There is no expedient to which a man will not resort to avoid the real labor of thinking.

Sir Joshua Reynolds

1. RELEVANCY

Up to now we have considered the criteria of clarity, accuracy, reliability, and sufficiency for evaluating evidence. Still another criterion is relevancy, which, though indirectly considered, has not been systematically analyzed.

Relevancy is not always apparent or obvious and is difficult to define. The *American College Dictionary* defines "relevant" as "bearing upon or connected with the matter in hand; to the purpose; pertinent." Relevancy, then, means connection, but what is connection? Theoretically, all the facts of the universe are related or connected in some way. Relevancy, therefore, is not just any connection but a close connection and, more importantly, a connection that bears directly on the truth or falsity of the conclusion. In determining when a connection is of this nature, we can only rely on experience or previous knowledge. There are no simple tests for determining relevancy. To say that we shall employ logical criteria for determining it would be circular reasoning, for relevancy itself is a criterion of logic. Courts of law face this problem daily, and the way in which they solve it is instructive. During a trial no evidence may be admitted for consideration which, on the face of it, seems to the judge insignificant or far removed from the main issue. If a lawyer objects that a piece of evidence which has been ruled immaterial is really relevant, he may explain to the judge the connection he is trying to make; and if, in view of this explanation, the judge feels that the evidence may bear on the outcome, he will permit it to be entered for consideration.

Although experience is the best guide for determining relevancy, unfortunately, like the inductive procedures themselves, it is not infallible. Occasionally a fact which seems to be irrelevant to a conclusion is seen to be relevant when other facts are introduced. As Ruby points out, the building of the Great Wall of China appears to have nothing to do with the downfall of the Roman Empire. Yet investigation shows that the Great Wall kept the Huns out of China, who instead turned west and, in their travels for pillage and loot, finally came to the Roman Empire and contributed to its destruction.[1] In considering relevancy and its counterpart irrelevancy, however, we need not be disturbed by such apparent exceptions. As a rule, irrelevancy, though hard to define, is not very difficult to detect, as we shall see in a moment. Arguments whose evidence is irrelevant to the conclusion are called by some writers "evasions of the law of rationality" and by others "fallacies of counterfeit evidence." Although evidence may be irrelevant in an endless number of ways, typical irrelevancies may be classed as appeal to emotions, attacking the source, appeal to ignorance, and begging the question.

2. APPEAL TO EMOTIONS

How one feels about a proposition clearly does not affect its truth or falsity. One may like or dislike the idea, but one's feelings have no bearing on its truth or falsity, nor do they constitute a reason for believing or disbelieving it. The fallacy of "appeal to emotions" is substituting emotions for proof. Its basic form is: This proposition (inference, or conclusion) is true (or false). Why? Because I (or you) feel strongly that it is true (or false). Since emotions are complex and varied, the fallacy may take many forms, corresponding to the various emotions. Some of the commoner types are:

Appeal by the Confident Manner

This is usually an attempt to influence the hidden desires of the listener. Since most people are disturbed when they experience feelings of doubt, this appeal attempts to allay their doubts and help make up their minds. Debaters often use this technique by introducing such terms as "certainly," "obviously," "perfectly clear," and "surely"—terms which seem to resolve all doubt. Such expressions are unwarranted, even when proof is offered simultaneously, for proof in debate is, as we have seen, rarely conclusive. If one could prove a case "beyond a doubt," the subject would not be debatable. An example of this fallacy is the following statement made some years ago by Harold E. Stassen, who was then seeking the Republican presidential nomination: "I am certain that neither Taft nor Eisenhower will get the Republican nomination." The statement implies "Don't have any more doubts about whom to vote

[1] Lionel Ruby, *Logic: An Introduction* (Philadelphia: J. B. Lippincott Company, 1950), p. 127.

for; I don't ["I am certain"]; therefore, vote for me." The pertinent reason, Why? is not given.

Appeal to Fear, Pity, Pride, Flattery, Love, Laughter, Tradition, Sympathy, Force, etc. [2]

Most of these arguments are characterized by vivid imagery or word pictures, which appeal to the senses, or by highly emotive language, i.e., terms which connote feelings about the concepts they designate. There is no need to illustrate each type, for one type is very much like another. For example:

> There is no perfect security anywhere in the world. Life itself is uncertain. But we face the loss of all the accumulated gains of our civilization and the things our ancestors risked much to win, if we do not band together and stop this silly, Communist-encouraged socialistic idea of statism, or the welfare state that will care for all of us from the cradle to the grave—even as we care for chickens in brooder houses. I think I would rather be a wild bird—a duck, quail, or a dove—at the risk of being preyed upon by hawk or hunter. Life is more interesting outside the pen and besides the battery-reared chick is eaten in the end just the same.[3]

Aside from the dubious analogy (used here mainly for its imagery) between men living in a "welfare" state and chickens in brooder houses, the passage is filled with terms calculated to stir the emotions: "our civilization" and "the things our ancestors risked much to win" (appeal to pride and tradition, also called "glittering generalities"), "this silly Communist-encouraged socialistic idea of statism" (appeal to fear and hate, also called "name calling"); "cradle to grave . . . chickens in brooder houses" (appeal to ridicule), "wild bird—duck, quail, or a dove— . . . preyed upon by hawk or hunter" (appeal to courage and good sportsmanship), "battery-reared chick" (appeal to contempt), "is eaten in the end just the same" (appeal to fear).

Arguments of this type are really assertions, for implicit in all highly emotive language are unsupported judgments. That is, such language not only designates a concept but also passes judgment on it. Thus, "this silly Communist-encouraged socialistic idea of statism" not only refers to a particular government program but says in effect "I don't like it; it's no good" (and by implication, "therefore, you shouldn't like it"). The reasons why it is no good are not given; [4] they are merely assumed.

[2] Also known as *"argumentum ad populum," "argumentum ad vericundiam," "argumentum ad misericordiam," "argumentum ad baculum,"* etc.

[3] Representative Edward T. Miller, "Is the Administration's Move to Expand Social Security Sound?" *Congressional Digest,* XXVIII (December, 1949), p. 311.

[4] Unless one considers the underlying generalization that "security is incompatible with freedom," which is far from self-evident and, if anything, false.

Unfortunately, since most people are very suggestible, they are swayed by the suggestions contained in such "arguments." Aware of the fact that most people find it less trying to indulge their emotions than to think critically, professional propagandists—mass persuaders, high pressure salesmen, advertisers, and demagogues—rely heavily on such appeals. As Milburn Akers has pointed out: [5]

Overstatement, understatement, half-truths, distorted logic, innuendo, and sheer intellectual dishonesty characterize the utterances of far too many of our public men. They bandy opprobrious terms about, in describing each other. This juvenile penchant of many American public men serves, upon analysis, to demonstrate the contempt in which they hold the electorate. It is not sufficient, for their purposes, that the electorate be informed fully and correctly, and then permitted to draw its own conclusions . . . They seek to inflame rather than to inform. They seek to excite passion rather than reason. They appeal to fear instead of intelligence. And, in so doing, they evidence a contempt for the body politic and its ability to understand the issues of the day.

To use highly emotive language in a debate not only opens one to attack for being illogical but also creates doubt in the judge's mind concerning one's motives. Someone once expressed the point well when he said, "Keep your language cool by wrapping it in asbestos."

3. ATTACKING THE SOURCE INSTEAD OF THE ARGUMENT (GENETIC FALLACIES)

In considering reliability of evidence we saw that doubt concerning an argument may legitimately be created by showing that the source of the argument is unreliable as to its ability or willingness to tell the truth. To attack a source, however, for any other reason is irrelevant.

Argumentum ad Hominem

The commonest manifestation of this irrelevancy is known as "argumentum ad hominem" (attacking the man). Basically its form is: This proposition is true (or false). Why? Because its advocate has a certain characteristic (unrelated to his ability or willingness to tell the truth). To illustrate the difference between an irrelevant and a justifiable attack upon a source, let us consider an article which appeared in the New York Times. Written by a Frenchman, the article criticized American married women, the gist of the criticism being unimportant. As was to be expected, the Times was flooded with answers by the indignant ladies. Let us imagine that some of the answers were as follows (some of them actually were):

[5] Milburn P. Akers, Chicago Sun-Times, as quoted by Ruby, p. 74.

1. The author has probably never been outside France.
2. The author is probably an Americophobe, i.e., he hates all Americans.
3. The author is probably a frustrated divorcee. Now he hates all married women because his own marriage proved to be a failure.
4. The author is probably a sensation seeker, trying to make money by writing an article he knew would provoke American women.
5. The author probably had an unhappy childhood and developed a mother complex. Now he sees all married women in the image of his mother, whom he hated.
6. The author is probably a bachelor.
7. Latins are lousy lovers.
8. The French are immoral, i.e., sexually loose.

Answer 1, if true, would be a justifiable attack on the source, for it pertains to his ability to get the facts or know the truth. Answers 2, 3, 4, and 5 might also be considered valid if they could be substantiated, for they pertain to his willingness to tell the truth; in other words, they try to show that the source is prejudiced. Answers 6, 7, and 8, even if true, are irrelevant to the main issue and therefore *ad hominem*. Note that even if answers 1 through 5 could be substantiated, they would do no more than create doubt concerning the author's conclusions. To disprove them, facts and other evidence concerning American married women would have to be introduced.

Poisoning the Wells

A variation of the *ad hominem* argument is known as "poisoning the wells," i.e., discrediting the source before it is used. For example:

The basic argument for a third party always remains the same. It is a persuasive argument, especially for well-meaning people who have not had much first-hand experience in politics. It runs something like this: "Both of the traditional American parties are outrageous frauds . . . machines for grabbing power and distributing favors . . . special interest groups which have nothing in common except a lecherous craving for the public trough. . . ."

Many veteran third-party enthusiasts have been able to account for their failure only by assuming a perverse and rock-headed stupidity among the American electorate. This, in turn, sometimes leads to a secret conviction that the dopes don't know what is good for them—and that what this country needs is a Strong Leader or a small, tough party of the enlightened, which can herd the ignorant masses up the road to Utopia whether they like it or not. (John Fischer, "Unwritten Rules of American Politics," *Harper's Magazine*, November, 1948.)

Here the writer attempts to discredit the "third party argument" by discrediting its proponents, i.e., by suggesting they are naïve, inexperienced, illogical. He attributes immoderate language to them and, by distorting their position, suggests that many have Fascist or Communist leanings. Since this passage appeared at the beginning of his essay, Fischer is saying in effect, "The third party argument is a silly one because it is advanced by foolish or wicked people, but if you want to discuss it, all right." He not only attacks the source before considering it but also assumes beforehand what he is seeking to prove.

Miscellaneous Non Sequitur

Closely related to the *ad hominem* irrelevancy is the *non sequitur* (a general name for all irrelevancies) of the following type:

> Hart Crane was a poor poet; he drank too much.
> Jones would make a good mayor; he attends church regularly.

In both arguments the relationship between the conclusion and evidence is extremely remote.

A final example is the following, used in a debate:

> One important argument against the compulsory national health insurance plan is the fact that we are borrowing the idea from countries that don't have as good a system of health service or as fine a health record as the one we have in the United States.

This argument attempts to discredit a program by discrediting its source. A possible answer would be:

> What difference does it make what the source is? We are concerned only with the merit of the plan. If it is being suggested that we should never borrow an idea formulated by someone worse off than we, we might as well say that if a prison inmate discovers a cure for cancer or a cheap substitute for gasoline, we should ignore it because he is worse off than we.

[Note that in pointing out the irrelevancy, this answer uses the *reductio ad absurdum* technique.]

4. APPEAL TO IGNORANCE [6]

This irrelevancy is of the form: This proposition is true (or false). Why? Because it cannot be disproved (or proved). Inability to disprove a proposition is not the same as proving it. Only concrete evidence can constitute proof or disproof. An example of this fallacy is the following:

> Since the opposition cannot prove that the union shop has made workers more efficient, it follows that the union shop does not make them more efficient.

The inability to prove the proposition that the union shop makes workers more efficient does not disprove this proposition. The existence in

[6] Known also as *"argumentum ad ignoratiam."*

the universe of other solar systems containing human life cannot be disproved either, but this does not prove that they exist. Concrete evidence is needed to prove this proposition.

Negative teams commit this fallacy when they contend that the affirmative plan is unworkable because the affirmative can give no evidence that its plan *has* worked. Even if it can't, it can still prove by causal reasoning that its plan *would* work; and to disprove this contention a negative team cannot appeal to ignorance, or the lack of direct empirical knowledge of its workability, but must submit positive reasons why the plan would not work.

5. BEGGING THE QUESTION

Simple Circular Arguments

This irrelevancy is of the form: "This proposition is true (or false). Why? Because this proposition is true (or false)." In other words, the conclusion is used to prove itself, or that which is to be proved is assumed. Thus, the fallacy may also be attacked as an assertion or unwarranted assumption; e.g., "Capital punishment for murderers is justified because society has a right to put to death those who have committed murder." Here the reason is the same as the conclusion, only phrased differently. The absurdity of the argument is clearly seen when both are put into the same words: "Capital punishment for murderers is justified because capital punishment for murderers is justified."

Hidden Judgments

As already noted, arguments containing terms which themselves contain hidden assumptions or judgments commit the fallacy. Highly emotive terms ("socialistic," "bureaucratic," etc.) are such as well as terms signifying value judgments ("good," "efficient," "capable," etc.). For example, "This costly program would produce the following disadvantages. Etc." Even if the disadvantages were substantiated, the argument assumes that the program is costly, which is a value judgment that must first be substantiated.

Suggestive Questions

Another form of begging the question, especially common in debate though fortunately less common now than formerly, is posing suggestive questions that are really assertions. The negative is often guilty of this practice in dealing with objections to the affirmative plan; e.g.,

"But is it likely that the various nations will agree to such a plan?" [From the tone of the question, the implication is that it is not likely.]

"What guarantee do we have that we will be able to retain our air bases?" [Again, the implication is, we shall probably not be able to retain them.]

"What assurances are there that this plan can be enforced?" [Again, the suggestion, it is doubtful that the plan can be enforced.]

"How do we know that this program won't place a tremendous burden on the taxpayer?" [Again, the suggestion, the program *will* place such a burden on the taxpayer.]

If asking a series of such suggestive questions were valid, winning a debate would be a simple matter; for one could go on indefinitely with such "questions," which because of their tone are actually simple assertions. Unfortunately, some textbooks on debate not only condone but also encourage the use of such questions as good "strategy" to divert the opposition. Although the strategy works on inexperienced debaters, occasional success is no criterion of sound strategy; only sound logic is. And since the strategy in question is illogical, it is unsound. It succeeds only because many debaters are unaware of the fallacy or how to handle it. If handled properly, such strategy, like all illogical thinking, is self-defeating.

The best way to handle suggestive questions is to point out that they are conclusions without proof and then to ask for proof. A typical answer might go like this:

If our friends are suggesting that the various nations won't agree to such a plan or that the United States will not be able to retain its air bases [or whatever it is the questions suggest], we should like some evidence to support these contentions before dealing with them. As they stand now, they are mere assertions and unwarranted assumptions. We are not even sure they are entirely relevant to the discussion and should like some concrete proof on these matters.

In this way, the questions backfire and become a burden for the team asking them. Now it must spend much time supporting a series of assertions; if it does not, it places itself in a very unfavorable light.

Reasoning in a Circle

Another manifestation of begging the question is known as "reasoning in a circle." In this fallacy the conclusion which is used to prove itself is removed by two or three intermediary reasons. The form is: "This proposition P is true. Why? Because proposition Q is true. Why? Because proposition R is true. Why? Because proposition P is true." For example:

"We need more automobiles on the road because we would get more money from gasoline taxes. And we need more money from gasoline taxes in order to build more roads. We need more roads because we need more automobiles."

Thus, the proposition "we need more automobiles" is ultimately proved by the proposition "we need more automobiles." The more intervening propositions there are, the more difficult the error is to detect.

Assuming Relevance

Still another way to beg the question is to imply that an issue under consideration is true by considering another issue that is relevant only when the first issue has been proved. This was demonstrated earlier by the argument "First, let us consider why our present aid program is causing resentment in the neutral countries." To consider *why* a program is causing resentment assumes that it *is* causing resentment. The following arguments are of the same type: "When we recognize Communist China and lose Formosa, we will weaken our Pacific defenses." (Since the argument assumes that we will lose Formosa, one can answer, "Yes, but we will not lose Formosa"); "Now let us see what advantages would accrue from a policy of private investment in the underdeveloped countries." (The argument assumes that private investment will flow into the underdeveloped countries, a point which must first be proved.)

The Suppressed Major

An error resembling the foregoing is to assume the truth of an implied premise which is not a self-evident truth. For example, in the argument "The Soviet Union should be excluded from the UN because she is not a peace-loving nation," the truth of the implied premise that all non-peace-loving nations should be excluded from the UN is unjustifiably assumed. (This fallacy is also discussed on p. 135.)

Skipping Important Links

Another manifestation of begging the question is assuming that the proof of one argument proves or disproves a related argument when actually intermediary links must first be proved. In political campaigns, for example, one frequently hears arguments of this type: "The present administration is corrupt, or inefficient, etc. Vote for Jones." Such arguments unwarrantedly assume that Jones's party will not be corrupt, inefficient, etc.; the fact that one program is not working does not automatically prove that another will. Additional proof is needed. The affirmative frequently commits this error in developing its need; e.g., the argument "The status quo is evil and therefore should be completely changed" assumes that the status quo is inherently defective or that repairs would be impractical. Worse yet, the affirmative sometimes skips two steps in the reasoning process. The argument "The status quo is evil; therefore, we need government aid" assumes, first, that the status quo is inherently defective and, second, that government aid would solve the problem, both of which points cannot be asserted or assumed but must be proved.

All of the foregoing irrelevancies pertain to the relationship between the evidence and conclusion of an argument. In discussing the indirect attack we shall consider irrelevancies pertaining to the relationship of one argument to another.

EXERCISES

1. What type of irrelevancy, if any, is manifested in the following arguments?

a. Ezra Pound should not be tried for treason because, even if he weren't judged insane, his broadcasts for Mussolini during World War II did not induce any American soldier to surrender.

b. Thus, we have offered logical, irrefutable proof that we should not trade with Communist China.

c. The affirmative need is clear: we need national security.

d. Darwin's theory that only the fittest survive can be verified by simply looking around at the various species in existence today. These species are obviously the fittest because they have survived.

e. Since the government has not come up with conclusive proof that flying saucers don't exist, we must assume that there is a good likelihood that they do exist.

f. "We live in a fast-moving mechanized age in which men and women should have at least a minimum education to the high school level, in order to earn a comfortable living. I am certain Dr. Gould will agree to that." (Senator Scott Lucas)

g. As for being a great military strategist, Eisenhower wasn't even a first rate football player at West Point.

h. Ezra Pound broadcasting to Allied troops in Italy: "You are not going to win this war. None of our best minds ever thought you could win it. You never had a chance in this war."

i. Lawyer to jury: "If this man is permitted to go free, your daughter or your sister may be his next victim."

j[1]. Pound should not be convicted of treason because he is a great poet.

j[2]. But he is not a great poet; his influence on other poets has been, on the whole, degenerative.

j[1]. But look at the salutary influence he has had on poets like Eliot, Yeats, Williams, and Stevens.

. . *k.* A guaranteed annual wage would provide an unemployed worker with from 60 to 70 per cent of his take-home pay. Therefore, the unemployment compensation program should be eliminated.

l. Eighteen-year-olds can't serve on juries or hold property, for they are not considered mature enough. Therefore, they should not be permitted to vote.

m. Three different accounts of an audience addressed by Henry Wallace:

(1) Wallace's audience consisted mainly of the union rank and file, some

labor bosses, tired housewives, some assorted eggheads, and a bunch of school boys.

(2) Wallace's audience consisted mainly of enthusiastic ILGW workers, labor leaders, civic-minded mothers, and many intellectuals and college students.

(3) Wallace's audience consisted mainly of members and officers of the local ILGW Union, housewives, and many faculty members and students from the local college.

n. How can we take the word of a man who says he is against integration when he speaks in the South and for integration when he speaks in Harlem?

o. Since Hitler's remains were never found, one can't lightly dismiss the theory that he is living somewhere in South America.

p^1. Pound should not be released from St. Elizabeth's Hospital unless the psychiatrists who committed him declare him to be sane. And if he is declared sane, he should be released and made to stand trial for treason since, as an American citizen, he broadcast for Mussolini during World War II.

p^2. On the contrary, Pound should be released from St. Elizabeth's and set free because (1) there are few poets writing today who can say they have not been influenced directly or indirectly by his work; (2) he helped writers like Frost and Williams get their poetry published; and (3) T. S. Eliot is indebted to him for his revisions of *The Wasteland.*

q. One can't negotiate with the Communists, for you simply can't take their word for anything.

r. Public schools should have released time for religious instruction, for, despite their persecution by the Romans, the early Christians did not desert their religion, and, despite a long history of persecution, the Jews still cling to their faith.

s^1. All teachers should be required to take loyalty oaths. It is the only way to combat disloyalty among teachers.

s^2. But aren't you assuming that there are many disloyal teachers?

s^1. Not at all. The fact that certain states require loyalty oaths proves that there are disloyal teachers.

t. The simplest definition of "good" is Aristotle's, namely, "good is that which the good man approves."

u. We must rule out *X*'s views on American foreign policy since he's a well known pacifist, and we know how peculiar they are.

v. "If we pursue the lines of our own genius and resources, we can meet this—the greatest menace of a century. And being in the right the Almighty is on our side." (Herbert Hoover, radio address, Feb. 9, 1951)

w. There's nothing to be gained by having a summit conference. The Soviets want one only for propaganda purposes. However, if the people insist, we'll probably have one.

x. Ezra Pound broadcasting to American troops during World War II: "What are you doing in the war at all? What are you doing in Africa? Who amongst you has the nerve or the sense to do something that would conduce to getting you out of it before you are mortgaged up to the neck and over it? Every day of war is a dead day as well as a death day. More death, more future servitude, less and less of American liberty of any variety. . . ."

y. No wonder Professor X is opposed to loyalty oaths for teachers. In his course on comparative political systems he requires his students to study Communist theory.

z^1. Negroes should not be permitted in white schools because Negro students are on the whole inferior to white students of the same age.

z^2. But why are they inferior?

z^1. Because their training hasn't been equal to that of the whites.

z^2. And why has that been so?

z^1. They have been going to inferior schools for many years and have not had the same opportunities as the whites.

z^2. But why haven't they had these opportunities?

z^1. Because they are on the whole inferior to whites.

CHAPTER 15

DEDUCTIVE REASONING

> People untrained in logic can detect a formal fallacy in a syllogistic argument once the argument is set out. But a fallacious argument that would not mislead an intelligent child, provided that it is stated barely, in a few sentences, may mislead all of us . . . when wrapped up in much verbiage, or when combined with appeals to our passionate interests.
>
> *L. S. Stebbing*

1. THE SYLLOGISM

All reasoning, it will be recalled, was defined as a process of the mind which takes certain known or presumed truths and draws from them certain conclusions that go beyond these truths. If the truths or premises are accurate and the reasoning sound, or valid, the new conclusions will likely be true. It will also be recalled that underlying the process of reasoning are certain assumptions, the most important of which is that certain relationships between phenomena are invariant and recurrent throughout the universe.

We spoke of this assumption in terms of the uniformity and regularity of nature. Without this assumption there would be no basis for reasoning. Moreover, it is an assumption that is always implied rather than stated. For example, when a detective concludes on the basis of having observed certain footprints that the person making them was lame, his conclusion, or what we earlier called a causal hypothesis, is based upon several factors: previous knowledge that lame persons make a certain type of footprints, the assumption that certain phenomena are invariably related, the further assumption that a certain kind of footprints and lameness are invariably related; and finally, the knowledge that one component of this invariant relationship is visible; all of these enable him to infer the character of the other component. If his entire reasoning process were made explicit, the various steps would look something like this:

Observed: Footprints of a certain nature. (How to account for them sets the reasoning process in motion.)

Previous knowledge and study: Dozens of lame human beings have been known to make footprints of this nature.

Basic general assumption: Certain relationships are invariant and recurrent throughout the universe.

Specific assumption derived from steps 2 and 3: There is an invariant relationship between certain footprints and lameness; *or:* lame human beings will always make footprints of this nature; *or:* all human beings making footprints of this nature are lame.

Observed once more: One component of the relationship: footprints of a certain nature.

In conclusion, the nature of the other component of the relationship inferred: the human being making these footprints was lame.

If the detective were experienced, all of these thoughts would occur simultaneously to him. For purposes of study, if we were to take steps 4, 5, and 6 by themselves and consider them a unit of reasoning, we would be dealing with what logicians traditionally call syllogistic, or deductive, reasoning. (For our purposes here we shall consider the terms "syllogistic" and "deductive" to be synonymous, although some logicians regard syllogistic reasoning as one kind of deductive reasoning.)

Before analyzing this type of reasoning, let us look at its form a little more closely. First, let us reconstruct the last three steps of the previous example so that we may see just what a syllogism is.

All human beings making footprints of this nature are lame.
A certain unknown human being has made footprints of this nature.
Therefore, this certain unknown human being was lame.

We see first of all that a syllogism contains three propositions: a generalization, called the *major premise,* or major; a statement of fact related to the generalization, called the *minor premise,* or minor; and a *conclusion* drawn as a result of the particular relationship between the major and minor premises.

Secondly, we see that a syllogism has but three terms ("human beings making footprints of this nature," "lame human beings," "a certain unknown human being") each of which appears twice. These correspond to the three subjects and three predicate terms of the three propositions. Although each term is given a name, the only important one to remember is the *middle* term, which is identified as that term which does not appear in the conclusion, in this case "human beings making footprints of this nature."

As the student may have recognized, syllogistic reasoning is the form usually used in mathematics, in the various physical sciences, and even in the study of language. The application of formulas and principles to specific problems and instances constitutes syllogistic reasoning. For example, if one had to choose between "goes" and "go" as the proper verb for the subject "the men," he would apply the general rule that all verbs must agree with their subjects in number and accordingly choose "go." The syllogism in this case would be:

Major: All verbs must agree with their subjects in number to be grammatically correct.
Minor: The verb form "go" agrees in number with the subject "the men."
Conclusion: Therefore, the verb form "go" is grammatically correct.

2. THE VALUE OF THE SYLLOGISM

Logicians have long disputed whether or not the syllogism is a genuine form of inference, i.e., whether or not it actually results in new knowledge. The point at issue here is whether or not one must know the truth of the conclusion *before* knowing the truth of the major. If the conclusion is part of the evidence for the major, the reasoning is circular, and, of course, there is no genuine inference. To clarify this point, let us consider some hypothetical cases.

Suppose, for example, the proposition "Jones is a Democrat" were derived from the propositions "All elected officials of Louisiana are Democrats" and "Jones is an elected official of Louisiana." If the evidence for the major here consisted of an enumeration of instances that covered all of the elected officials of Louisiana, including Jones, i.e., if the major were empirically true, the reasoning would be circular; for the conclusion (Jones is a Democrat) would be proved by a proposition (all elected officials of Louisiana are Democrats) which in turn was partly proved by the conclusion (Jones, an elected official of Louisiana, is a Democrat). On the other hand, if the major were a generalization based on evidence which did not include the case of Jones, the reasoning would not be circular and the conclusion (Jones is a Democrat) would be a genuine inference (not necessarily a true inference but nevertheless an inference).

Thus, the way in which the major is arrived at determines whether syllogistic reasoning is circular or whether it leads to a genuine inference. To take another, and somewhat academic, example, if from the evidence A is mortal, B is mortal, C is mortal, D is mortal, one concludes that "all men are mortal," one may further conclude that X, a man not previously considered, is mortal. To repeat, the conclusion of a syllogism may represent a genuine inference but only when it is based upon a previous inference, or generalization. Whether, like John Stuart Mill, one considers that the reasoning in a syllogism "lies in the act of generalization, not in interpreting the record of that act," or, like others, one believes that the reasoning lies in the application of the generalization to a new circumstance is not important.[1] What is important is that in the syllogism, one has a powerful tool for testing both reasoning by causal hypothesis and reasoning by descriptive hypothesis because it draws attention to the implied major that underlies these forms of reasoning. As Mill pointed out, "the syllogistic form is an indispensable collateral security for the correctness of the generalization itself"[2] and thus provides a check for the correctness of the conclusion. Moreover, as we shall see in a moment, the syllogistic form also enables one to apply certain tests in the form of clear-cut rules for determining the soundness of the relationships between premises and conclusion.

Many errors in reasoning are due to the hasty conclusion that the presence of one factor of a known relationship assures the presence of the other. However, unless there is a one-to-one relationship between two factors (i.e., one never appears without the other), one is not justified in jumping to such a conclusion. Because of the imprecise, or abstract, way which we find useful for stating most relationships, it is possible for any one factor to be a part of many different relationships. For example, we say loss of appetite may be due to a high fever, to having just eaten a box of chocolates, or to being emotionally upset. Accordingly, if one doesn't feel like eating, he is hardly justified in concluding that he probably has a high fever. On the other hand, if one has a high fever, he is justified in concluding that this has probably caused his loss of appetite. In other words it is important, especially in causal relationships, to know which factor of the relationship is apparent. The rules of the syllogism provide tests for detecting errors which result from confusing the factors of a given relationship.

Because the syllogistic form provides various tests and safeguards, it appears in debate more as a means of detecting and exposing the weakness of opposition arguments than as a means of presenting constructive arguments. Actually, however, all constructive arguments could be phrased as syllogisms,[3] as, for example,

[1] This writer believes that the reasoning lies in both the act of generalization and in the application of the generalization, and therefore considers it a matter of crucial importance to consider the origin of the major when examining syllogistic arguments. Academic logicians, on the other hand, when they study the syllogism, are not concerned with how the premises are arrived at; that is, they are not concerned with the *truth* of a syllogistic argument but rather with its *structure*, or the relationships among the various propositions. Debaters, however, must be more practical and consider the origin of premises, since their ultimate concern is not merely with conclusions but with *true* conclusions.

[2] As quoted in L. S. Stebbing, *A Modern Introduction to Logic* (New York: Thomas Y. Crowell Company, n.d.), p. 220.

[3] Since in debating policy questions we begin with certain assumptions, or postulates, concerning desired ends, the entire case is actually a deduction from these postulates, or premises.

Any policy which is inherently defective should be changed.
This policy is inherently defective.
Therefore, this policy should be changed.

To save time, however, one usually omits the major and presents the argument elliptically as "This policy should be changed, for it is inherently defective."

3. VALIDITY AND TRUTH

Although the syllogistic form forces one to reconsider the truth of the major by making the major explicit, it in no way provides any tests for determining whether or not the major is true, or probably true. Such tests were discussed in connection with reasoning by descriptive generalization. However, the rules of the syllogism, which we are about to discuss, do provide tests for determining whether or not the relationships among its three propositions are valid. Thus, when we speak of validity, we have in mind the nature of relationships between propositions rather than the truth of such propositions. Reasoning is said to be valid when the conclusion is forced by the premises. Needless to say, a sound argument consists of both *true* propositions (or evidence) and *valid* relationships between the evidence and the conclusion.

4. TYPES OF SYLLOGISM

Because of certain linguistic variations, syllogisms are classed as four main types: the categorical, the hypothetical, the alternative, and the disjunctive. Since the basic difference among these types lies in their phrasing, any one type can be rephrased as any other type, although some awkward twisting of language may be required.

The Categorical Syllogism

The categorical syllogism is so designated because all three of its propositions are categorical statements, i.e., statements which mention two classes of ideas or things and state a relationship between the classes. Thus, the statement "any person making such footprints is lame" is categorical. Stating the same idea in the three other forms, we would get:

Hypothetical: If footprints are such, the person making them is lame.
Alternative: Either the situation is one where there are no such footprints or one where there is a lame person.
Disjunctive: There cannot be a situation where there are both such footprints and not a lame person.

To understand the rules of a categorical syllogism, we must first consider certain basic concepts, namely, those of "inclusion," "exclusion," "distributed term," and "undistributed term." Let us consider each briefly.

Inclusion

When it is asserted that an individual or group or class of things falls into another class of things, the former is said to be included in the latter. Thus, in the proposition "All dogs bark," "all dogs" is included in the class of "barking things." The sign for inclusion is <; thus, the proposition may be written: all dogs < barking things.

Exclusion

When it is asserted that an individual or a class of things is distinctly outside of or apart from another individual or class of things, the former is said to be excluded from the latter. Thus, in the proposition "Most dogs are not thoroughbreds," "most dogs" is excluded from "thoroughbreds." The sign for exclusion is ⋖; thus, the proposition may be written: most dogs ⋖ thoroughbreds.

"Distributed Term" and "Undistributed Term"

A term is said to be distributed if the pattern of the statement indicates that the term refers to all the members of the class designated by it; undistributed, if the pattern does not indicate that the term refers to all. For convenience we shall use the symbol (d) after a term if it is distributed, (u) if it is not. Such quantifying adjectives as "all," "no," "every," "some," "most" indicate whether the term which they modify is distributed or undistributed. "All dogs" is distributed, whereas "some dogs" is undistributed. However, problems of interpretation frequently arise when quantifiers are lacking for some reason or are expressed in ambiguous or unusual syntactical forms. Let us consider some of these problems.

1. Frequently the quantifier for the subject of the major is omitted; e.g., "Native-born Americans are citizens." In such cases the quantifier is assumed to be "all," i.e., the subject of the major (native-born Americans) is considered to be distributed.

2. Certain quantifiers and syntactical constructions are by their nature ambiguous or confusing. For example, take the proposition "All plane figures are not triangles" or "Not all plane figures are triangles." The "all-are-not" or "not-all-are" construction really means "some are not." Thus, the term "plane figures" in the preceding propositions is undistributed. Terms like "only," "none but," "none except," and "alone" also require some interpretation. If one says, "Only men are priests," one apparently means, "All priests are men." Thus, quantifiers of this nature indicate that the classes have been reversed, or transposed; and, in order to determine which terms are distributed and which undistributed, one must rephrase the proposition. Finally, there are quantifiers like "all but" and "all except," which, though they superficially resemble the preceding four, are

quite different. For example, the proposition "All but the extreme conservatives favor this legislation" means "All who are not extreme conservatives favor this legislation." This proposition in turn is ambiguous and may mean "All who are not extreme conservatives have already indicated that they favor the legislation. We don't know as yet how the extreme conservatives feel about it; they may or may not favor it." Or it may mean "No extreme conservatives favor the legislation, but all the others do." Needless to say, no conclusion could be drawn from an argument using such a proposition until the meaning of the latter was clarified.

3. For syntactical purposes, the quantifier is omitted from the predicate terms of most categorical propositions; e.g., "All native-born Americans are citizens." The problem here is, what is the proper quantifier for "citizens"? Although the proposition tells us the relationship between all native-born Americans and citizens, it does not tell us the relationship between all citizens and native-born Americans. Citizens can be naturalized without being native-born. Thus, the proper quantifier for "citizens" is "some," and the term is undistributed. In propositions of exclusion, however, the situation is different. For example, in the proposition "Some residents of the United States are not citizens" it is asserted that "some residents of the United States" are excluded from the entire class known as "citizens"; thus, in this proposition "citizens" means "all citizens." As a general rule, therefore, we may say that in propositions of inclusion the predicate terms are undistributed [4] and in propositions of exclusion the predicate terms are distributed.

Proper names, like John, are always distributed; for even though such names designate one individual, the one individual in this case represents an entire class.

Basic Rules of the Categorical Syllogism

The four basic rules which govern the validity of any categorical syllogism are as follows:

1. The syllogism must contain three and only three terms, each of which must appear twice.

2. The middle term, i.e., the term which does not appear in the conclusion, must be distributed at least once.

3. A syllogism may contain two and only two exclusions, one of which must appear in the conclusion.

---

[4] Propositions known as tautologies, that is, propositions whose subject and predicate terms are known to be equivalent, form an exception to this rule. Logical definitions are tautologies. For example, the proposition "All triangles are three-sided plane figures" may be written "All three-sided plane figures are triangles." Such propositions, however, cannot be made the basis of a genuine inference.

4. Any term that is distributed in the conclusion must be distributed at least once in the premises.

Violations of these rules result in the four fallacies known as the "four-term," "undistributed middle," "faulty exclusion," and "illicit distribution." In a moment we shall consider how a debater can express such fallacies in nontechnical terms which can be understood by most judges. For the present, let us illustrate each fallacy.

Four-term Fallacy

Strictly speaking, a four-term syllogism is not a syllogism at all since, by definition, a syllogism has but three terms. However, for practical purposes this type of argument is treated as a syllogism since its verbal form resembles that of the syllogism. An example of the four-term fallacy would be:

All voters should take part in primaries.
All qualified citizens should vote.
Therefore, all qualified citizens should take part in primaries.

The fallacy almost escapes detection because of the superficial resemblance between the term "voters," which means "those who do vote," and the term "should vote," which means "those who should vote." However, it must be conceded that there is a big difference between "those who do" and "those who should."

Occasionally, a fourth term creeps into a syllogism by way of equivocation, as:

No men who have faith are atheists.
All men have faith.
Therefore, no men are atheists.

The term "faith," of course, has a different meaning in the two premises.

Fallacy of the Undistributed Middle Term

All Communist sympathizers favor a sharp reduction in United States armaments.
All pacifists favor a sharp reduction in United States armaments.
Therefore, all pacifists are Communist sympathizers.

Here we see that the middle term, "those who favor a sharp reduction in United States armaments," is undistributed in both premises. In form, this reasoning is the same as that in

All dogs are mammals.
All cats are mammals.
Therefore, all cats are dogs.

Fallacy of Faulty Exclusion

Nothing exciting ever bores me.
But this book is not exciting.
That's why it bores me.

Although this syllogism has two exclusions, one of them is not in the conclusion. In form, this reasoning is the same as that in

No snakes are mammals.
This book is not a snake.
Therefore, this book is a mammal.

Other variations of this fallacy are syllogisms with one exclusion or with three exclusions.

Fallacy of Illicit Distribution

All sensational novels are popular.
Textbooks are not sensational novels.
Therefore, textbooks are not popular.

The term "popular (books)" is distributed in the conclusion but not in the major. In form, this reasoning is the same as that in

All dogs are mammals.
Cats are not dogs.
Therefore, cats are not mammals.

Rephrasing Categorical Propositions

Because of the way certain propositions are phrased, valid syllogisms sometimes appear to be fallacious. Therefore, in dealing with apparently invalid syllogisms one should consider whether rephrasing certain propositions will make such syllogisms valid. We have already seen some of the semantic problems involved in determining the proper quantifier of the various terms. If one did not properly interpret the word "only" in the proposition "Only those who studied hard did well on the examination," the following syllogism would appear to commit the fallacy of the undistributed middle term:

Only those who studied hard did well on the examination.
John did well on the examination.
Therefore, John studied hard.

By rephrasing the major, however, to "All who did well on the examination studied hard," we see that the syllogism is valid.

At this time we shall consider briefly some of the ways in which categorical propositions may be restated or turned into equivalent propositions. Restating a proposition not only enables one to test a syllogism but also reminds one that there is more than one way of stating the truth. The two important techniques for deriving an equivalent proposition from another are called conversion and obversion.

Conversion

To convert a categorical proposition consists of reversing its subject and predicate terms. However, one cannot convert all categorical propositions and get equivalent propositions. Since all categorical propositions take one of four forms (all X is Y; no X is Y; some X is Y; and some X is not Y), we shall consider the problem of conversion for each form.

A-form. This proposition has the form "All X is Y," or "All horses are mammals." Now, if all X is Y, can we say that all Y is X? If all horses are mammals, is it true that all mammals are horses? Obviously not. Therefore, we cannot convert A-form propositions and get equivalent propositions. However, if all horses are mammals, we may conclude that some mammals are horses, assuming that there are such things as "horses" and "mammals." Thus, A-form propositions may be partially converted, or converted by limitation. It is important to remember, however, that when we convert by limitation we get a new proposition that does not have the same meaning as the original one.

E-form. This proposition has the form "No X is Y," or "No horses are carnivorous." Now, if no X is Y, or if no horses are carnivorous, can we say that no carnivorous beings are horses? Yes, we can, since both classes are distributed and completely excluded from one another. In other words, "No X is Y" has exactly the same meaning as "No Y is X." Thus, E-form propositions can be converted to yield equivalent propositions.

I-form. This proposition has the form "Some X is Y," or "Some debaters are fast talkers." Now, if some debaters are fast talkers, can we say that some fast talkers are debaters? Yes, we can, since neither class is totally included in the other but each overlaps the other. This overlapping is more clearly seen when we draw two circles, one representing "debaters" and the other "fast talkers." Thus:

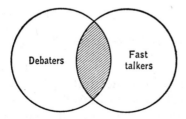

As we can see, the shaded area represents the group that is both "debater" and "fast talker." Thus, we get the same meaning whether we say

"Some debaters are fast talkers" or, "Some fast talkers are debaters."
That is, I-form propositions can be converted to yield equivalent propositions.

O-form. This proposition is of the form "Some X is not Y," or "Some
American citizens are not native-born Americans." Now, if true, may we
say that "Some native-born Americans are not American citizens"? No,
we cannot, for to say so would be to commit the error of illicit distribution. That is, the term "Some American citizens," which is undistributed,
becomes in the process of conversion "all American citizens," which is
distributed. Thus, the O-form cannot be legitimately converted.

Obversion

Obversion is another means of changing a given proposition into an
equivalent proposition. It consists of reversing the relationship (not the
position) between the subject and predicate terms and simultaneously
negating the predicate term. All categorical propositions may be legitimately obverted. The process is more clearly seen when we use symbols
for the terms and relationships. Thus, obverting $X < Y$, we get $X \not< -Y$,
or, in terms of an actual proposition, "All men are fallible" becomes
"No men are infallible (nonfallible)." The following table shows how
all four types of the categorical proposition are obverted:

Original A	$X(d) < Y(u)$	All X are Y	All wise people are in-telligent.
Obverse E	$X(d) \not< -Y(d)$	No X are $-Y$	No wise people are unin-telligent.
Original E	$X(d) \not< Y(d)$	No X are Y	No ambitious people are satisfied.
Obverse A	$X(d) < -Y(u)$	All X are $-Y$	All ambitious people are dissatisfied.
Original I	$X(u) < Y(u)$	Some X are Y	Some electrical conductors are metallic.
Obverse O	$X(u) \not< -Y(d)$	Some X are not $-Y$	Some electrical conductors are not nonmetallic.
Original O	$X(u) \not< Y(d)$	Some X are not Y	Some conductors are not metallic.
Obverse I	$X(u) < -Y(u)$	Some X are $-Y$	Some conductors are non-metallic.

We are now ready to consider further how apparently invalid syllogisms are occasionally seen to be valid after one either converts or
obverts certain propositions. Suppose it were argued that since all
convincing characters are realistic and that no unconvincing characters
are logically motivated, it follows that no logically motivated characters

are unrealistic. Reconstructed, we would get the following syllogism:

All convincing characters are realistic.
No unconvincing characters are logically motivated.
Therefore, no logically motivated characters are unrealistic.

A cursory look at this argument would reveal what appear to be five terms: "convincing characters," "realistic characters," "unconvincing characters," "logically motivated characters," and "unrealistic characters." However, by properly obverting and converting the various propositions, we get a valid syllogism. The process would be something like this:

$$
\begin{array}{cc}
A & B \\
\text{Convincing } (d) & < \text{realistic } (u) \\
-A & C \\
\text{Unconvincing } (d) & \not< \text{logically motivated } (d) \\
C & -B \\
\text{Logically motivated} & \not< \text{unrealistic } (d)
\end{array}
$$

Or, using symbols alone:

$$
\begin{array}{c}
A(d) < B(u) \\
-A(d) \not< C(d) \\
C(d) \not< -B(d)
\end{array}
$$

Converting the minor, we get $C(d) \not< -A(d)$; obverting the latter, we get $C(d) < A(u)$, or, "All logically motivated characters are convincing." Obverting the conclusion, we get $C(d) < B(u)$, or, "All logically motivated characters are realistic." Rewriting the syllogism with these changes made, we get:

$A(d) < B(u)$ All convincing characters are realistic.
$C(d) < A(u)$ All logically motivated characters are convincing.
$C(d) < B(u)$ All logically motivated characters are realistic.

This, as we can see, is a simple and valid syllogism. We see further that not only have the five terms become three but also the exclusions have disappeared.

We come now to the other linguistic forms of the syllogism, namely, the hypothetical, the alternative, and the disjunctive, forms which derive their names from the grammatical (syntactical) structure of the major. These forms are used instead of the categorical form whenever they facilitate expressing the relationship postulated in the major.

The Hypothetical Syllogism

The hypothetical, also called the "conditional," syllogism contains a major which expresses an "if-then," or conditional, relationship, as, "If the United States continues to stockpile nuclear bombs, she will be secure from aggression." The value of expressing the relationship between nuclear bombs and aggression hypothetically (conditionally) is seen when we translate this proposition into an equivalent categorical proposition: "All situations in which the United States continues to stockpile nuclear bombs will be situations in which the United States will be secure from aggression." Thus, for expressing certain relationships the hypothetical form is clearly more succinct than the categorical.

The minor of a hypothetical syllogism affirms or denies the existence of one factor, or condition, of the relationship ("The United States will continue, etc."; "The United States will not continue, etc."; "The United States will be secure, etc."; "The United States will not be secure, etc."); and the conclusion accordingly affirms or denies the existence of the other factor. Thus, there are four possible variations of the hypothetical syllogism. If we designate the first condition of the major as the *antecedent* and the second as the *consequent,* these four variations (taking their name from the minor) are called Affirming the Antecedent, Denying the Antecedent, Affirming the Consequent, and Denying the Consequent. Thus:

Affirming the Antecedent

If the United States continues to stockpile nuclear bombs, she will be secure from aggression.
The United States will continue to stockpile nuclear bombs.
Therefore, the United States will be secure from aggression.

Denying the Antecedent

If the United States continues to stockpile nuclear bombs, she will be secure from aggression.
The United States will not continue to stockpile nuclear bombs.
Therefore, the United States will not be secure from aggression.

Affirming the Consequent

If the United States continues to stockpile nuclear bombs, she will be secure from aggression.
The United States will be secure from aggression.
Therefore, the United States will continue to stockpile nuclear bombs.

Denying the Consequent

If the United States continues to stockpile nuclear bombs, she will be secure from aggression.
The United States will not be secure from aggression.
Therefore, the United States will not continue to stockpile nuclear bombs.

Of these four variations, the first and fourth are valid, and second and third are invalid. This could be shown by translating the various forms into corresponding categorical syllogisms. Thus, we would find that affirming the consequent corresponds to the fallacy of the undistributed middle and that denying the antecedent corresponds to the fallacy of illicit distribution.

Fallacies of the Hypothetical Syllogism

To enable the debater to express these fallacies in nontechnical terms, let us consider the underlying reasoning of each.

The Fallacy of Affirming the Consequent

To conclude that E has occurred because X has occurred (where X has been known to produce E) is to overlook the possibility that E might have occurred for some other reason. That is, the same general effect may be produced by several different causes. Loss of appetite may be the effect of just having eaten a heavy meal or of the presence of some virus in the body. Therefore, even if it is true that if one has a certain virus he will not be hungry, he may not conclude that because he is not hungry he has the virus. In the common-sense notion of cause and effect (which we shall explain in a moment) the inference goes only one way, from cause to effect.

The Fallacy of Denying the Antecedent

By the same process of analysis as that given above, to conclude that E will not occur because X (which has been known to produce E) has not occurred is to overlook the possibility that something else may have produced E. Thus, to conclude that because a tire has not run over a nail the tire is not flat is to overlook the possibility that the tire may be flat for other reasons.

If the relationship between the antecedent and consequent is such that *if and only if* the antecedent occurs the consequent will occur, then it makes no difference whether the minor affirms or denies the antecedent, or affirms or denies the consequent. The syllogism is valid in all four forms. This is so because the relationship between antecedent and consequent is one-to-one, i.e., one cannot appear without the other. Thus, it may be inferred that if one appears the other must be present and that if one doesn't appear, the other must be absent. For example, if there is a one-to-one relationship between, let us say, direct economic aid to Burma and resentment by the Burmese of that particular aid, then it is logical to say if no aid, then no resentment and, vice versa, if resentment against direct economic aid, then direct economic aid. In debate, because of imprecise phrasing or an equivocal interpretation of the consequent, confusion frequently arises as to whether or not a team has committed the fallacy of denying the antecedent. This point is important enough to be pursued further.

It will be recalled that in analyzing the cause of existing evils, the affirmative attempts (or should attempt) to pinpoint both the evil and its cause; it tries to show a one-to-one relationship between the evil effects it cites and the cause of those effects; in sum, it tries to establish a *particular* cause of a *particular* effect. Failure to do so would leave the affirmative open to a subsequent charge of having denied the antecedent, a fallacy which, in effect, guards against the pitfall that results from the common-sense usage of the term "effect." When the average person speaks of the "effect" of a particular cause, the effect he has in mind is actually an abstraction. That is, from a complex set of conditions he abstracts certain properties. When he speaks of death by drowning, death by poisoning, death by shooting, etc., he means by "death" that the heart has stopped beating and that breathing has ceased. From the practical point of view "death" is regarded as a *single* occurrence. But, as Stebbing points out: [5]

Such occurrences, taken as *single*, are of varying degrees of abstractness. Thus *death* is an abstraction requiring analysis. Such analysis takes us away from the standpoint of common sense. It involves looking at the whole situation retrospectively, not prospectively. The former attitude is that of the coroner's court and the scientific investigator, the latter is that of the practical agent; the one is concerned with *knowing*, the other with *doing*. Both are concerned with uniformities, i.e., regular connections. The practical agent, however, is content with a relation that is determinate only in the direction *from* cause *to* effect: *wherever X occurs, E occurs.* Such a relation may be many-one: given the cause, then the effect is determined, but not conversely. But the scientific investigator wants to find a relation that is equally determinate in either direction, that is, he seeks a one-one relation: *wherever X occurs, E occurs, and E does not occur unless X has occurred.* He has accordingly to analyze the conditions into their constituent factors so that he may ascertain whether any are irrelevant, and whether any, though necessary, are not sufficient to the occurrence of the result. The appearance of a plurality of causes, for example, that death may sometimes be caused by pneumonia, sometimes by drowning, etc., or that thirst may be quenched by water or by cider, rises from the neglect of certain factors in the total situation that constitutes the effect-occurrence.

The point is this: in their analysis of a problem or of particular effects and in their attempts to ascertain a particular cause, debaters may be compared with the scientific investigator. Although their analysis may be inaccurate, their reasoning that the elimination of a given cause will eliminate a given effect is perfectly valid. Thus, the fallacy of denying

[5] Stebbing, *A Modern Introduction to Logic*, p. 264.

the antecedent, which is predicated on the common sense notion of cause-and-effect, is not applicable to many of the causal arguments encountered in debate. Suppose, for example, an affirmative team were to argue that if the nations of the world continued testing nuclear weapons, the people throughout the world would be exposed to much harmful radiation and that, consequently, if the various nations agreed to prohibit tests, this hazard would be eliminated. Putting the argument into the form of a hypothetical syllogism, we get:

If the various nations continue to test nuclear weapons, people will be exposed to much harmful radiation.
(Under the affirmative plan) the various nations will not continue to test nuclear weapons.
(Under the affirmative plan) people will not be exposed to much harmful radiation.

On the surface this looks like the fallacy of denying the antecedent. In fact, in an actual debate judged by this writer, the negative replied that even if nations stopped testing, people would still be exposed to much harmful radiation—from natural causes. In effect, the negative answer was an attempt to show that the affirmative had committed the fallacy of denying the antecedent: "No antecedent, no consequent, the affirmative says; but the consequent may still occur because of a different antecedent." However, though the affirmative here may be charged with faulty knowledge or with being remiss in its phrasing, it cannot be charged with being illogical; for it is quite clear that the consequent it was talking about was a *particular kind* of harmful radiation, that produced by testing nuclear weapons.

In other words, in this instance the relationship between antecedent and consequent is one-to-one. For the opposition to interpret "radiation" in the broad and abstract sense of "all harmful radiation" is to equivocate on the affirmative's meaning of the term; clearly, "radiation from bomb tests," the affirmative meaning, is not the same as "all radiation." A proper answer by the affirmative to this type of equivocation would be: "We never contended that eliminating bomb tests would eliminate *all* radiation—but *only that* caused by bomb tests." To forestall this type of negative attack—for it is a common one—the affirmative should take special pains to identify the consequent it has in mind and thus to show a one-to-one relationship between antecedent and consequent. If in arguing against the present United States tariff policy, for example, an affirmative team contended that this policy was causing resentment in Argentina, the affirmative should make clear at the outset that if this policy were changed, *all* resentment against the United States in Argentina would not disappear but *only* that portion of it which is directly caused by the present United States tariff policy.

To sum up, the fallacies of affirming the consequent and denying the antecedent are fallacies only because in common-sense usage the relationship between antecedents and consequents is not precisely defined. Essentially, these fallacies guard against semantic, rather than logical, pitfalls.

The Alternative Syllogism

The alternative syllogism, like the other types, is distinguished by its major premise. This premise offers two alternatives, or a choice between two propositions, at least one of which is presumably true, though both may be true. In a valid alternative syllogism the minor denies one alternative, and the conclusion affirms the other. In an invalid alternative syllogism the minor affirms one alternative; since the other alternative may also be true, no conclusion is possible. To illustrate:

Valid

Either she is rich or very resourceful.

She may be both, but at least one alternative is presumably true.

She is not rich.

Therefore, she is very resourceful.

Since one alternative is false and since one has to be true, by the process of elimination this one is true.

Invalid

Either she is rich or very resourceful.

She is rich.

? . . . .

Since both alternatives may be true, she may or may not be resourceful; no conclusion is possible.

This type of syllogism has little practical application in debate.

The Disjunctive Syllogism

In a disjunctive syllogism the major offers two disjuncts, or mutually exclusive choices, at least one of which is presumably false, though both may be false. In a valid disjunctive syllogism the minor affirms one disjunct and the conclusion denies the other. In an invalid disjunctive syllogism the minor denies one disjunct; since the other disjunct may also be false, no conclusion is possible. To illustrate:

Valid

One cannot become both a teacher and wealthy.

Both disjuncts may be false, but at least one is false.

He is a teacher.

He cannot become wealthy.   *Since we know that one disjunct is true, by the process of elimination this disjunct must be false.*

Invalid

One cannot become both a teacher and wealthy.

He is not a teacher.   *Since both disjuncts may be false, no*
? . . . .   *conclusion is possible.*

This type of syllogism also has little practical application in debate. A type which is fairly common, however, is one that combines the alternative and disjunctive forms. In this type the major offers a choice between two contrary or contradictory propositions, one of which is presumably true and one presumably false; e.g., "Hitler is either living or dead" (two contradictories), or "Eisenhower is either in Washington or in Valley Forge" (two contraries). A syllogism with this type of premise is valid in all forms. If the minor affirms one proposition, the conclusion denies the other, and vice versa. To illustrate:

Hitler is either living or dead.
He is dead.
Therefore, he is not living.

Eisenhower is either in Washington or in Valley Forge.
He is not in Washington at present.
Therefore, he is in Valley Forge.

The weakness of this particular type of syllogism lies not in its form but in its major premise when that premise offers a pair of contrary propositions. The resulting error is frequently one of "false alternatives" (discussed earlier). Example:

The United States can provide dollars to foreign countries either by trading with them or by giving them outright gifts.
Giving outright gifts is not desirable.
Therefore, trading is the only answer.

Although the form of the argument is correct, the truth of the major premise is questionable because the two alternatives do not exhaust all possibilities. The United States, for example, might lend money to foreign countries or encourage private investors to invest there. Actually, the two proposed choices are not even contrary, for the United States could pursue both courses simultaneously.

5. THE ENTHYMEME

In considering the various syllogistic arguments up to now, we have been concerned mostly with relationships or validity rather than with truth. To a debater, however, both validity *and* truth are important, for a sound conclusion depends on both. Like the builder desirous of constructing a good house, he must have both the knowledge and the proper materials. One is not much good without the other. In this respect, one should remember that only syllogisms whose major consists of a generalization can yield a genuine inference. As was noted earlier, generalizations are propositions that cannot be said to be absolutely or certainly true; their degree of probable truth ranges along a continuum from "almost certainly true" to "certainly false." In using the syllogistic forms of argument, a debater must consider this fact by qualifying the major and thus, the conclusion. Consider the argument:

Whenever a company puts in automatic machinery, it lays off workers.
X Company has just installed many automatic machines.
X Company will soon lay off a number of its workers.

Since the major is a generalization, one should not imply that the immediate effect of automation is *always* unemployment but should qualify this statement by such terms as "usually" or "very probably." Accordingly, one should also qualify the conclusion in the same manner; thus: "X Company will very probably lay off a number of workers soon."

Another type of probability must be considered in connection with "partial generalizations," those covering not all but a fairly definite proportion of all cases involved. Thus, "Most homes in the United States have bathtubs," "75 per cent of all automobiles are insured," "Slum environments tend to produce juvenile delinquents." Such "proportional" or "partial" generalizations are common in debate and may be used as a major in syllogistic arguments. Needless to say, when such arguments are used, the conclusion must be qualified roughly to the same degree of tentativeness expressed in the major. Consider the argument:

Most second graders can write their names.
Mary is a second grader.
Therefore, Mary can probably write her name.

Actually, arguments of this type commit the fallacy of the undistributed middle. (In this case, the middle term, "second grader," is not distributed in either premise. "Most second graders" is clearly not "all second graders.") Nevertheless, such arguments are legitimate, a fact recognized by Aristotle, the father of syllogistic reasoning, who called such arguments *enthymemes*, by which he meant syllogisms based upon probabilities.[6] In passing, one should note that no inference can be drawn from a major which refers to a vague quantity such as "some" or "many."

6. FURTHER ANALYSIS OF THE FALLACY OF THE UNDISTRIBUTED MIDDLE

As we have just seen, when partial generalizations are involved, an argument which appears to commit the fallacy of the undistributed middle may be a legitimate argument. Actually, the fallacy of the undistributed middle, like all general concepts, is an abstraction which derives its meaning from a particular relationship between propositions, the truth of the propositions being disregarded. In debate, however, since we are ultimately interested in the truth or probable truth of the conclusions reached, further analysis of this fallacy is called for; that is, we must consider not only the form but also the substance of an argument. Considering the latter leads one to the realization that all fallacies of the undistributed middle are not fallacious to the same degree and that some, by conversion of the major, yield conclusions that actually possess a high degree of probable truth. Consider the following three syllogisms:

All card-bearing Communists are mortal.
John is mortal.
Therefore, John is a card-bearing Communist.

All card-bearing Communists are collectivists.
John is a collectivist.
Therefore, John is a card-bearing Communist.

All card-bearing Communists follow the Communist Party line.
John follows the Communist Party line.
Therefore, John is a card-bearing Communist.

Although all three syllogisms commit the fallacy of the undistributed middle, the third does not appear to be as fallacious as the first; in fact, the third even appears somewhat reasonable. Why this is so can be seen when we convert the major of each by limitation and simultaneously use some outside knowledge. For the first syllogism we would get the following premises:

Some mortal beings are card-bearing Communists.
John is mortal.

Since the proportion of card-bearing Communists to the total number of mortal beings is known to be quite small, the only conclusion that could

---

[6] Today logicians use the term *enthymeme* (which literally means "in the mind") in an entirely different sense, applying it to syllogisms which are incompletely stated, i.e., syllogisms in which one of the three propositions is implied. In the argument "Like all newly formed countries, Ghana has many adjustments to make," the minor premise, "Ghana is a newly formed country," is implied. Actually, all arguments by causal or by descriptive hypothesis are incompletely stated syl-

be drawn from these premises is that there is little likelihood that John is a card-bearing Communist, or that the proposition "John is a card-bearing Communist" is probably false. In other words, the conclusion has a probability close to zero.

For the second syllogism we would get the following premises:

Some collectivists are card-bearing Communists.
John is a collectivist.

Since the proportion of collectivists to Communists is known to be quite large, it may be concluded from these premises that there is a higher degree of probability that John is a Communist than that he is a socialist or anything else. Although one may not conclude conclusively that John is a card-bearing Communist, one may conclude that there is a fairly good likelihood that he is, or that the proposition "John is a card-bearing Communist" is more likely to be true than false.[7]

For the third syllogism we would get the following premises:

Some who follow the Communist Party line are card-bearing Communists.
John follows the Communist Party line.

Since practically all who follow the Communist Party line are known to be card-bearing Communists, one may conclude from these premises that John is very probably a card-bearing Communist, or that the proposition "John is a card-bearing Communist" is very probably true, even though not conclusive. Thus, as Ruby says, "many invalid arguments may be transformed into valid arguments containing conclusions which are probable when we know that the major premise may be converted into a proposition which states a probability."[8] In other words, certain fallacies of the undistributed middle may be converted into sound enthymemes, as the third example clearly shows. Restated as an enthymeme, this argument would appear thus:

Practically all who follow the Communist Party line are card-bearing Communists.
John follows the Communist Party line.
John is very probably a card-bearing Communist.

In short, when speaking of the fallacy of the undistributed middle—or even of the fallacy of illicit distribution—we are speaking of an abstrac-

---

logisms with the major implied. Thus, the argument "He will probably make a good lawyer since he's an excellent debater" suppresses the major "All excellent debaters usually make good lawyers."

[7] It is quite conceivable that even this conclusion is not warranted and that the conclusion "John is a card-bearing Communist" should be rated as "uncertain" or "inconclusive," even though it has a much higher degree of probability than that of the first syllogism.

[8] Lionel Ruby, *Logic: An Introduction* (Philadelphia: J. B. Lippincott Company, 1950), pp. 325–326.

tion which, like all abstractions, overlooks many individual differences, some of which can be quite relevant in determining just how sound or unsound an argument really is.

7. COMPOUND SYLLOGISTIC ARGUMENTS: THE DILEMMA

Certain complex arguments are more clearly conveyed by means of compound syllogisms, i.e., by a combination of two or more different types of syllogism. The most interesting and useful type of compound syllogistic argument is the dilemma, an argument which combines the hypothetical syllogism with the alternative-disjunctive syllogism. In the dilemma form of argument, the major consists of two hypothetical premises ("If *P*, then *R*" and "If *Q*, then *S*"); the minor consists of an alternative-disjunct ("Either *P* or *Q*"); and the conclusion consists of the other alternative-disjunct ("Therefore, either *R* or *S*").

Elected public officials are often confronted with a dilemma when the time comes to vote on a proposed bill. If they vote for the bill, they risk antagonizing one segment of their supporters; and if they vote against the bill, they risk antagonizing another segment. In either case, the choice is not a pleasant one. Because dilemmas frequently offer two unpleasant choices, the term "dilemma" has acquired the connotation of being "an unpleasant choice." From the standpoint of logic, however, it doesn't make any difference whether the choices are pleasant or unpleasant. Actually the term "dilemma" designates a form of syllogistic reasoning.

In debate the dilemma may be used for both constructive purposes and for attack, whereas the categorical syllogism is usually used for exposing the weakness of an opposition argument. Several years ago negative teams used the following dilemma quite effectively in developing an objection to the affirmative plan of Federal grants to the various states for the purpose of equalizing educational opportunities:

Major: If the Federal Government grants aid to the educational systems of the Southern States, it will, in effect, be supporting an undemocratic (or inefficient) dual system of education in those states. And if the Federal Government refuses aid to the educational systems of the Southern States, it will, in effect, be permitting educational inequalities to continue.

Minor: The Federal Government must either grant aid or refuse aid to the educational systems of the Southern States.

Conclusion: Therefore, the Federal Government must either support undemocratic (or inefficient) educational systems or permit educational inequalities to continue.

In effect, the negative argued that the affirmative plan either would be disadvantageous or would not meet the need. Reduced to symbols, the argument is:

Major: If *P*, then *R;* If not-*P*, then *S*.
Minor: Either *P* or not-*P*.
Conclusion: Therefore, either *R* or *S*.

Sometimes two or more dilemmas are combined and stated elliptically, the result being an argument somewhat difficult to analyze. Consider the following argument that a student might use to rationalize an imprudent action:

"If I study late, I'll be tired in the morning and probably fail the exam; and if I don't study late, I'll be unprepared and probably fail. So I might as well go to the movies."

Reconstructing this argument and supplying all implicit premises, we get the following two dilemmas and hypothetical syllogism:

1. *Major:*

    If I study late, I'll be tired.

    If I don't study late, I'll be unprepared.

    Minor:
    (implicit)

    Either I must study late or not study late.

    Conclusion:
    (implicit)

    I'll be either tired or ⟶ unprepared.

2. *Major:*

    If I'm tired, I'll probably fail.

    If I'm unprepared, I'll probably fail.

    Minor:

    I'll be either tired or un- prepared.

    Conclusion:
    (implicit)

    In either case, I'll prob- ⟶ ably fail.

3. *Major:*
    (implicit)

    If I'm going to fail, I might as well go to the movies.

    Minor:

    I'll probably fail.

    Conclusion:

    I might as well go to the movies.

The weakness of the argument lies in the assumptions it makes and not in its form, which is to say, its form is valid but its premises are untrue. Incidentally, the second dilemma presents a variation of the standard form. Thus:

If *P*, then *R*.
If *Q*, then *R*.
Either *P* or *Q*.

Therefore, *R*.

Although the dilemma is a dramatic and seemingly devastating form of argument, most dilemmas one encounters in debate or in political speeches are unsound because they are predicated upon certain false assumptions, usually unstated and obscured because of this fact as well as the complexity of the form. Consider the following argument:

If prices are set so that the larger firms can make a fair profit, these prices will force the smaller firms out of business and the ultimate effect will be the creation of large monopolies. If, on the other hand, prices are set so that the smaller business can make a fair profit, the large firms will make excessive profits. Thus, price-fixing would create either monopolies or excessive profits, neither of which would be desirable.

Before analyzing the argument, we must know what is meant by the terms "larger firms" and "smaller firms." Let us assume that by "larger firms" is meant "giant" corporations like du Pont, United States Steel, General Motors, and General Electric, and by "smaller firms" all other firms not considered to be "giants." With these meanings in mind, we may now proceed with the analysis.

Major: If prices are fixed at a point where giant corporations can make a fair profit, other types of firms will be forced out of business; i.e., monopolies will result. And if prices are fixed at a point where other than giant corporations can make a fair profit, the giant corporation will make excessive profits.
Minor (unstated): Prices must be fixed at a point where one or the other must make a fair profit.
Conclusion: Therefore, price-fixing will create either monopolies or excessive profits.

In symbolic form the argument reduces to:

If *P*, then *R*.
If *Q*, then *S*.

Either *P* or *Q*.

Therefore, *R* or *S*.

Thus we see that the form is valid. The conclusion is dubious, however, because the major contains certain hidden assumptions that are doubtful. The first such assumption is that giant corporations are generally more efficient than other types, that since they produce more goods, they can sell them more cheaply. According to the available evidence, however, giant corporations are only sometimes more efficient; in most industries, to quote D. C. Doyle, noted engineer and economist, "the middle-sized plant works better than either the small or the big." Although only one dubious assumption is enough to undermine an argument, this argument contains still another; that is, even if large corporations were more efficient than other types, it would not necessarily follow that they would earn excessive profits; for this assumes that an excess profits tax is nonexistent or could not be instituted. Thus, what appears to be at first glance a convincing argument—convincing perhaps because of its valid form—turns out to be a weak one when all of its hidden assumptions are brought to light.

8. ANSWERING A DILEMMA

Since the form of dilemma arguments is usually sound, the weakness of such arguments must be sought in the premises. Thus, the two important ways of answering a dilemma consist of attacking the truth of the premises. The attack on the major is called "Taking the dilemma by the horns" and that on the minor, "Slipping between the horns." Let us consider each briefly.

Taking the Dilemma by the Horns

The term "horns of a dilemma" is merely a figurative way of designating the two consequents contained in the two hypotheticals of the major (horns, from the horns of a bull, suggesting the nature of these consequents). Thus, to take a dilemma by the horns is to show that one or both of the consequents do not regularly or necessarily follow from the antecedents. In pointing out the weakness of the preceding dilemma, for example, both horns, or consequents, were attacked; i.e., it was argued that smaller corporations would not necessarily be forced out of business and that giant corporations would not necessarily earn excessive profits. Let us take one more example:

Major: If a planned economy controls all segments of the economy, it will be dangerously centralized.
If a planned economy does not control all segments of the economy, it will be ineffectual.
Minor: A planned economy either will or will not control all segments of the economy.
Conclusion: Therefore, it will be either dangerously centralized or ineffectual.

To take this dilemma by the horns would be to point out that controlling all segments of the economy would not necessarily result in dangerous centralization or that not controlling all segments would not necessarily be ineffectual.

Slipping between the Horns

Like faulty alternative syllogisms, dilemmas are often faulty because the minor offers two choices which are not mutually exclusive; often overlooked are other choices. To slip between the horns of a dilemma is to point out that the minor is false because a third choice exists. In the dilemma concerning the student faced with the problem of preparing for a test, for example, it could be pointed out that one could stay up late to prepare for the test without staying up too late and being tired the next morning. To take one more example:

Major: If the United States is ahead of the Soviet Union in nuclear weapons development, the Soviet Union would not join any ban on nuclear weapons testing.
If the Soviet Union is ahead of the United States, the United States would not join.
Minor: Either the Soviet Union is ahead of the United States or the United States is ahead of the Soviet Union.
Conclusion: Therefore, one or the other would not join.

The weakness in the argument lies in the minor since it overlooks an important alternative, namely, that the United States and the Soviet Union are on a par in nuclear weapons development. In pointing out this third alternative, one is said to slip between the horns of the dilemma.

At the outset of a debate negative teams sometimes resort to the clumsy strategy of asking the affirmative team a question containing two alternatives, such as "Who do you think is ahead in the nuclear weapons race, the Soviet Union or the United States?" the purpose of the question being to trap the affirmative into making a damaging admission; for, as we can see here, either alternative chosen by the affirmative can be turned into a damaging argument. If the affirmative answers "the United States," the negative will argue that the Soviet Union won't join a test ban; and if the affirmative answers "the Soviet Union," the negative will argue that the United States won't join. The affirmative in this case can slip between the horns by answering "neither." However, such questions are unwarranted in the first place since they do not elicit information concerning a point made by the opposition, the only legitimate purpose for asking questions. As a rule, only novice debaters use questions as stratagems.

The Counterdilemma

Logicians frequently speak of a third way of answering a dilemma, namely, by posing a counterdilemma. Although the counterdilemma appears to be a very dramatic and persuasive answer, it is really not an answer at all to a dilemma but merely a restatement of it. Take the dilemma of the elected public official; suppose he stated it in these terms:

Major: If I vote for this bill, I will alienate the farmer.
  If I vote against this bill, I will alienate the manufacturer.
Minor: I must vote either for or against this bill.
Conclusion: Therefore, I will alienate either the farmer or the manufacturer.

Now the counterdilemma doesn't deny or contradict anything; it merely brings to light certain aspects contained, but not emphasized, in the original argument. And it accomplishes this feat by switching and simultaneously negating the two consequents of the major. Thus:

Major: If I vote for this bill, I will not alienate the manufacturer.
  If I vote against this bill, I will not alienate the farmer.
Minor: I must vote either for or against this bill.
Conclusion: Therefore, I will not alienate either the manufacturer or the farmer.

Admittedly, this conclusion looks like the contradictory of the original, but it is entirely compatible with it. The illusion is a semantic one. If we were to combine both conclusions and be perfectly precise, we would get: "Either I will not alienate the farmer while alienating the manufacturer or I will not alienate the manufacturer while alienating the farmer." Thus, since the counterdilemma is not really an answer to a dilemma, it should not be used as such. On the other hand, when a counterdilemma is used by the opposition, one should point out that such an answer in no way denies or contradicts the consequents of the original dilemma.

9. SOME PRACTICAL APPLICATIONS OF THE SYLLOGISM IN DEBATE

As indicated earlier, most syllogistic arguments encountered in debate and elsewhere do not appear as formal syllogisms. What we have called reasoning by analogy, reasoning by causal hypothesis, and reasoning by descriptive hypothesis can be dealt with as abbreviated syllogistic arguments with the major omitted. Frequently, the weakness of such arguments is revealed when the major is supplied; either it is seen to be probably false, or, if probably true, the relationship between premises and conclusion is seen to be invalid. Consider the argument:

Pacifists are probably Communist sympathizers since X organization, known to be sympathetic to the Communist cause, recently went on record as favoring a radical reduction in United States armaments.

If we treat the argument as argument by analogy, the implication is that there is an invariant one-to-one relationship between the characteristic of "being a Communist sympathizer" and that of "favoring a radical reduction in United States armaments." In other words, all who favor a radical reduction in United States armaments are Communist sympathizers. But this generalization, which is needed to link the components of the analogy, is patently false and thus the analogy falls flat. On the other hand, if we considered the major to be "All Communist sympathizers favor a radical reduction in United States armaments," we could, from previous knowledge, accept this as being a rather sound generalization. However, constructing a syllogism with such a generalization gives us the fallacy of the undistributed middle. Converting the major by limitation we would get "Some who favor a radical reduction in United States armaments are Communist sympathizers." Since "some" in this instance does not stand for any well known determinate proportion of the whole, the proposition is too inconclusive to admit any conclusion.

10. EXPRESSING SYLLOGISTIC FALLACIES IN NONTECHNICAL TERMS

Frequently, the question arises, how does one express syllogistic fallacies in everyday language? After all, a debater can't very well use such terms as "the fallacy of illicit distribution" and expect to be understood. Actually, the problem is not very serious, for, as we have already seen in many instances, syllogistic fallacies can be either simply explained or expressed in terms of corresponding inductive fallacies. To sum up, let us consider briefly how each of the four fallacies of the categorical syllogism might be handled in a debate:

Four-term

As we have already seen, this fallacy may be handled in much the same way as fallacies of equivocation or "ground-shifting." For example, "First, our friends speak of 'voters' as those who vote, and then they speak of them as those who should vote, implying that these two meanings are the same. However, there is an important difference between those who *do* and those who *should* vote."

Undistributed Middle

This fallacy may be handled like any questionable analogy; e.g., "Our friends tell us that pacifists are probably Communist sympathizers because both groups favor a sharp reduction in armaments. However, the fact that two groups have one characteristic in common doesn't mean that they share other characteristics. Mushrooms and toadstools also look alike, but one would hardly be justified in concluding that because one is edible the other is."

Faulty Exclusions

There is no set pattern for dealing with this type of fallacy; however, in its commonest form it can be turned into the fallacy of the undistributed middle and treated accordingly. For example, "Our friends admit that no retrogressive tax is desirable, but claim that since their tax is not retrogressive it is desirable. However, they overlook the fact that it has other features which make it undesirable, namely, etc." Set forth in syllogistic form, the argument being answered here is:

Major: No retrogressive tax is desirable.
Minor: But this tax is not retrogressive.
Conclusion: Therefore, this tax is desirable.

As it stands, this is a fallacy of faulty exclusions (two in the premises). However, it can also be made into the fallacy of the undistributed middle. Thus, by converting and obverting the major and obverting the minor, we get:

Major: All desirable taxes are non-retrogressive.
Minor: This tax is non-retrogressive.
Conclusion: Therefore, this tax is desirable.

Illicit Distribution

The best way, perhaps, to handle this fallacy is to explain its underlying reasoning in terms of the particular argument. For example, "Our friends imply that since clean bombs are needed, unclean bombs aren't needed. But this is not so. For although clean bombs may be needed for certain tactical uses, unclean bombs are also needed for other tactical uses, as, for example, etc." Set forth in syllogistic form, the argument being answered here is:

Major: Clean bombs are needed.
Minor: The bombs in question are not clean.
Conclusion: Therefore, the bombs in question are not needed.

This, as we can see, is the fallacy of illicit distribution, for the term "needed" is distributed in the conclusion but not in the premise.

Since we have already considered how to deal with the fallacies of the other syllogistic types, there is no need to consider them further.

EXERCISES

1. What is the distinction between validity and truth?
2. How is deductive reasoning related to reasoning by descriptive hypothesis, reasoning by causal hypothesis, and reasoning by analogy?
3. Identify the fallacy, if any, in the following syllogisms:
   a. All syllogisms are arguments.
   Some arguments are fallacious.
   Therefore, some syllogisms are fallacious.

b. All illegal votes were challenged.
His vote was not illegal.
Therefore, his vote was not challenged.

c. All professors need exercise.
No athletes need exercise.
Therefore, no professors are athletes.

d. No president may be under forty years of age.
Smith is not under forty years of age.
Therefore, Smith is eligible to be president.

e. All underdeveloped nations deserve our aid.
England is not an underdeveloped nation.
Therefore, England does not deserve our aid.

f. According to the laws of physics, whatever goes up must eventually come down.
Prices have been going up steadily during the past twenty years.
Therefore, prices must eventually come down.

g. All who profess to believe in the Constitution should have no qualms about taking an oath to that effect.
Teachers profess to believe in the Constitution.
Therefore, teachers should have no qualms about taking an oath that they believe in the Constitution.

h. All good debaters are conscientious students.
Most conscientious students make good marks.
Therefore, some good debaters make good marks.

i. Great works of art are scarce.
Hamlet is a great work of art.
Therefore, *Hamlet* is scarce.

j. No protective tariffs are fair to the consumer.
A sales tax is not a protective tariff.
Therefore, a sales tax is fair to the consumer.

4. If the proposition "Some dishonest people are intelligent" is true, which of the following propositions are true, false, or undetermined?

a. All dishonest people are unintelligent.
b. Most dishonest people are unintelligent.
c. Some intelligent people are not honest.
d. No intelligent people are dishonest.
e. Some unintelligent people are honest.
f. Some intelligent people are dishonest.
g. All dishonest people are intelligent.
h. All intelligent people are honest.
i. Some dishonest people are not unintelligent.
j. Some dishonest people are unintelligent.
k. No dishonest people are intelligent.

5. If the proposition "All competent workers are industrious" is true, which of the following propositions are true, false, or undetermined?

a. Only industrious workers are competent.
b. None who are industrious are incompetent.

c. Some competent workers are not industrious.

d. All nonindustrious workers are incompetent.

e. No industrious workers are incompetent.

f. None but industrious workers are competent.

g. Some industrious workers are competent.

h. No incompetent workers are industrious.

i. No unindustrious workers are competent.

j. Some who are not industrious are incompetent.

k. No competent workers are unindustrious.

l. None but competent workers are industrious.

m. Some competent workers are industrious.

n. Some incompetent workers are not industrious.

o. All who are not industrious are incompetent.

6. What conclusions may be drawn from the following premises?

a. Americans are always in a hurry but don't know where they are going most of the time.

b. Automobile manufacturers favor lowering the tariff, but watch manufacturers want to keep it high.

c. Debating is a highly specialized activity, but some debating is pretty poor.

d. People who think clearly can usually write clearly, though some clear thinkers don't bother to write anything.

e. Extenuating circumstances make certain crimes understandable, but there were no extenuating circumstances in this case.

7. Analyze the following syllogistic arguments and indicate how they might be answered if encountered in a debate.

Categorical

1. No one favoring right-to-work laws is a friend of labor. Since many representatives of management are friendly to labor, they favor the union shop (i.e., they oppose right-to-work laws).

2 No one who has studied the problem of fallout can have any doubt about the serious consequences to the human race. Many scientists have indicated the dangers from leukemia and bone cancer, so it is clear that they have studied the problem of fallout.

3. Only proposals having the support of the Soviet Union and the United States will be discussed at the next summit conference. Since a nuclear weapons test ban is supported by both countries, we may conclude that this problem will be discussed.

4. People who invoke the Fifth Amendment are usually guilty of something, but at no time has the witness done so; so he must be considered innocent.

5. Since coal is plentiful in the United States, anthracite coal must be plentiful.

6. The dean said that only those with exceptional records will not be tested, but since I was tested, I guess my record wasn't exceptional.

7. Hedonists may be defined as those who regard pleasure as the supreme

good. Therefore, the Greek philosophers who regarded pleasure as the supreme good were hedonists.

8. Whoever obeys laws submits to the will of a governing body. All matter obeys laws; therefore, all matter submits to the will of a governing body.

9. That which is empirically proved is true. That there is life on Mars is unproved and thus false.

Hypothetical

1. If capital punishment is justified, then it follows that punishment is not intended to rehabilitate the criminal—for how can someone who has been put to death be rehabilitated? However, punishment, according to the American penal code, is supposed to rehabilitate the criminal. Therefore, capital punishment is not justified.

2. If the measure had been defeated, we might suspect that some pressure had been brought to bear on Congress. But since the measure passed, it seems clear that no such pressure was exerted.

3. Assuming that people are motivated solely by self-interest, we should expect to find that whenever they do something, they do it mainly for their own benefit. Since this is what we do find, our initial assumption must be correct.

4. If companies overexpand and extend their credit to a point where they have trouble meeting their bills, they soon go bankrupt and a depression results. However, since most companies are very careful these days about their credit, a depression seems unlikely.

5. If we can show the status quo to be inherently defective, then we have shown a need for changing it. The evils we have cited—their nature and cause—indicate that the present program is defective beyond practical repair. This, therefore, constitutes a need.

6. If a hypothesis is to be considered a fact, it must be empirically verified. Einstein's hypothesis that energy has mass has been empirically verified and may therefore be considered a fact.

7. If the United States would repel an attack by some foreign force on Cuba, Communist China is justified in trying to take the Pescadores. Under the Monroe Doctrine the United States would repel such an attack on Cuba; so Communist China can hardly be blamed for trying to take over islands which are situated right off the mainland and occupied by an enemy force.

Alternative, Disjunctive, and Alternative-disjunctive

1. Either Congress must get information from the executive branch, or the people will not be well informed. Under the present administration much information is being needlessly withheld from Congress, and the people, therefore, hardly know what is going on.

2. You can't have a welfare state and at the same time expect complete protection of individual liberties. But since we don't have a welfare state, our liberties are protected.

3. A plan for suspending nuclear weapons tests would either work or not work. Since most scientists seem to think it will work, we should rule out the thought of failure.

4. You can't be critical of the present economic system and still support it. Since you have pointed out several defects of this system, you apparently don't support it.

5. Either the country must have a good educational system or democracy will suffer. We have seen the growth of antidemocratic ideologies in recent years, so we must conclude that we don't have a very good educational system.

6. Since the defendant couldn't have been in both places at the same time and since he was not in his office when the shooting occurred, he must have been at home.

7. The unidentified flying object recently reported must be either an airplane, a weather balloon, a flying saucer from some extraterrestrial planet, or an illusion produced by some atmospheric phenomenon. Since the first two have been ruled out by the Army and the third by common sense, it must have been the latter.

Dilemma

1. If the conclusion of a syllogism is merely a statement of something contained in the premises, then it is not a genuine inference and is quite useless. If the conclusion, on the other hand, goes beyond what is contained in the premises, then it is false and the syllogism is invalid. Now the conclusion either goes beyond the premises or does not; so a syllogism is either useless or invalid.

2. When Omar the Caliph ordered the famous library at Alexandria destroyed, he reasoned thus: If the books contain the same ideas that are in the Koran, they are unnecessary; if they contain contradictory ideas, they are evil. In either case, therefore, they should be burned.

3. If we don't continue price supports, many farmers will go bankrupt and much unemployment will result. If we do continue them, food prices will continue to rise and inflation will result. Therefore, whether we continue them or don't, we can look forward to either a recession or an inflation.

4. If we send most of our aid to the Far East, Europe's economy will suffer and become a target for Communism. If we send most of our aid to Europe, the nations in the Far East will become a prey to Communism. In either case, the outlook isn't too bright.

5. In awarding Ezra Pound the Bollingen Award, the Library of Congress Committee honored either a madman or a traitor as the best American poet of 1949. If he is really insane, as the psychiatrists claim, then the award reflects the sad state to which American poetry has fallen. And if he is not insane, then he is a traitor and a committee representing the American government honored a man who betrayed that government. In either case, the committee showed bad judgment.

6. Protagoras agreed to teach Euathalus how to practice law. Half of Protagoras' fee was to be paid him when Euathalus won his first case.

Euathalus, however, decided not to practice, whereupon Protagoras sued him for the balance of his fee and presented his case to the court thus: If Euathalus loses this case, then by the order of the court he must pay me. And if Euathalus wins this case, then by the terms of our agreement he must pay me. Euathalus must either lose or win and therefore must pay me.

Euathalus, who had been taught well by Protagoras, countered: If I lose this case, then by the terms of our agreement I need not pay Protagoras. And if I win this case, then by the order of the court I need not pay Protagoras. So whether I lose or win I need not pay Protagoras.

CHAPTER 16

THE INDIRECT ATTACK

It may be good tactics, if your aim is to win an argument at all costs, to insist that your opponent is saying nothing but "blab-blab," but it may be a very irresponsible type of argument. . . .

R. T. Harris and J. L. Jarrett

1. THE INDIRECT ATTACK

Earlier we considered two basic types of attack, direct and indirect, the direct being an attack upon the evidence and reasoning of an argument, the indirect upon the relationship of one argument to another. In the indirect attack one does not question, deny, or retort to the conclusion of an argument; rather one tries to undermine the conclusion by showing it to be insignificant, irrelevant, or inconsistent with the conclusion of another argument. In effect, the indirect attack says, "Your conclusion may be true, but what have you proved?" Skillful debaters often combine both types of attack, trying to establish, first, that the conclusion of an argument is untrue and, second, that even if true, it proves little with respect to a presumably related argument.[1]

When one uses the indirect attack exclusively, the opposition can claim that he has not denied the truth of their argument. Thus, in countering the indirect attack, a debater may answer in this vein: "It is interesting to note that our friends never deny that a problem exists; they tell us instead that the problem is not significant. Well, let us see just how insignificant it really is. Etc." One should not conclude, however, that the indirect attack is any weaker than the direct attack. On the contrary, the indirect attack is used to undermine the structure of the opposing case and to defend one's own. And proficiency in these areas usually has an important bearing on the decision.

Although relationships between arguments may be handled in many ways, we shall consider three general criteria: significance, relevancy, and consistency. The failure of a relationship between two arguments to

[1] Although this dual approach is frowned on in a court of law as being "argumentative," this writer considers it effective in debate.

measure up to these criteria results in the following fallacies, which may be exposed by the indirect attack.

2. INSIGNIFICANCE

Weak Conclusion

The relationship between two arguments is weak or insignificant when the conclusion of one is not strong enough to prove or to disprove the conclusion of the other. The error is the same as insufficient evidence. When a debater argues, for example, that there is a problem and that this problem warrants a complete change of the present system, he must first prove that the problem is significant, or big, before a drastic change can be considered. Otherwise, the negative may answer, "Yes, there is a problem, but it is minor and thus does not justify such a change." This type of attack should always be considered when one is confronted with empirical evidence that cannot be attacked directly, particularly by the negative when dealing with the affirmative need. One may show that a conclusion is insignificant by introducing evidence which supports a contrary conclusion, i.e., by placing the opposition's conclusion into a context which makes it seems insignificant or as representing only a small part of the whole. Although we have already considered this approach in connection with "ambiguity of significance," let us take one more example:

A. (Argument): The problem of corruption in unions is seen in the fact that 35 million dollars have been siphoned off union welfare funds by corrupt union officials and in that four million workers belong to corrupt unions.

B. (Answer): This problem is minimal when you consider that such welfare funds run to a total of 35 billion dollars and that 13 million workers belong to clean unions. Thus, the problem is not significant enough to warrant right-to-work legislation.

In effect B answers, your facts may be true but the conclusion which may be drawn from them does not constitute adequate proof that we have a serious enough problem to merit the drastic change you are proposing.

Stressing a Minor Point

A common manifestation of the insignificant argument is the attack upon or defense of a minor point. By emphasizing a minor point, i.e., by attaching to it more importance than it merits, debaters are often guilty of diverting attention from the main issue and thus of being irrelevant. Making a to-do over an unintentional or unimportant slip by the opposition would be such a diversion. Examples:

A. (Argument): In his work *Theory of the Leisure Class*, published in 1900, Thorstein Veblen said, "Etc."

B. (Answer): But Veblen's book was published in 1899, not in 1900.

A. (Argument): In discussing mature economies Hansen has said, "Etc."

B. (Answer): But Hansen isn't the outstanding authority on mature economies; John Maynard Keynes is.

In the first example *B* makes an issue over the year Veblen's book was published—a most insignificant objection—rather than over what Veblen said, the important issue. In the second example, *B* makes an issue over who is the outstanding authority on mature economies—irrelevant in this instance since Hansen and Keynes say substantially the same thing—rather than over whether such economies function as described, the real issue. Oddly enough, some debate textbooks advise the student to open his speech by first attacking some minor point of the preceding speech and then launching into his own case. This suggestion is deplorable since it is illogical.

Sometimes debaters commit the error under discussion by playing up a minor point of their own case which they think cannot be handled by the opposition, e.g.,

And we have still heard no answer to our argument concerning picketing rights, which is perhaps the most crucial objection to the affirmative plan.

What may have started out as a minor objection becomes "most crucial" because of the opposition's inability to counter it. Aside from its dishonesty, this tactic can backfire; for if the opposition should come up with a good answer, an admittedly "important" part of one's case will have been undermined.

3. IRRELEVANCY, OR "SLIPPING AWAY FROM THE POINT"

In discussing relevancy of evidence, we saw that relevancy is difficult to define. In considering relevancy in connection with the relationship between arguments, however, the term has a fairly specific meaning, namely, the same point must be discussed in both arguments. If not, then one argument, whether used in defense or attack, is irrelevant to the other. Because of the multiplicity and complexity of arguments used in a typical debate, this type of irrelevancy, though common, is often overlooked. The error may be committed either in defense of or attack upon another proposition. In defending, when one feels hard pressed by an effective attack, one often shifts ground to a more defensible position which may resemble but differs from the original position. This is known as "ground shifting." In attacking, when one is confronted with a strong position, one often distorts, misrepresents, or subtly diverts from that position and answers a different propositions; i.e., one builds a "straw man" argument and answers it instead of the real argument. All of the following irrelevancies may be characterized as failures to stick to the point.

Answer by Independent Proposition

In attacking an opposing argument, a debater, as we have seen, may try to prove either a contradictory or contrary proposition. However, if he proves a proposition compatible or consistent with the proposition answered, his answer is irrelevant. On the other hand, if in supporting one of his own propositions, he establishes a contradictory or contrary proposition, he is inconsistent. Thus, inconsistency, which will be considered in a moment, is also a form of irrelevancy, since in both fallacies what is presumed to have been done has not been done.

An answer by independent proposition—independent since it has no bearing on the truth or falsity of the proposition answered [2]—is usually a simple diversion from the point at issue, e.g.,

A. (Argument): Coeducation is harmful academically, for it creates distractions which in turn lead to poorer study habits and grades. According to a survey conducted by, etc.

B. (Answer): But tests show that there are no basic differences in intelligence between men and women students. So-and-so reports, etc.

Although presumably answering A, B completely ignores A's point and establishes an independent proposition. A's defense against this type of diversion is simply to point out the original proposition and the fact that B's answer is unrelated to it: "We contended that coeducation is harmful. Our friends never deny this. They tell us instead that men and women have the same mental capacity. Frankly, we fail to see what bearing this has on the point we have made [or, we fail to see any relevancy in this answer]."

Another example, taken from an actual debate, is the following:

A. (Argument): United States prestige in Asia is low. [Cites proof.] Asians fear American imperialism. [Cites proof.]

B. (Answer): Communist China's prestige in Asia is low. [Cites proof.] Asians fear Chinese imperialism. [Cites proof.]

Here B's proposition is independent of A's since its truth or falsity does not affect the truth or falsity of A's.

Answer by Equivalent Proposition

Though one would hardly expect a debater to establish the very same conclusion he is answering, he sometimes does so in the heat of a debate, e.g.,

[2] Symbolically, the relationship of independence is shown by the following table:

$$P \text{ true} \ldots Q? \qquad Q \text{ true} \ldots P?$$
$$P \text{ false} \ldots Q? \qquad Q \text{ false} \ldots P?$$

The question mark means "undetermined."

A. (Argument): Indirect negotiation with Communist China is unsatisfactory; direct negotiation is avoided by the United States lest it imply recognition.

B. (Answer): But according to Hackworth's *Digest of International Law,* indirect negotiation with unrecognized countries is possible.

Here B's answer that indirect negotiation is possible is the same point made by A. A's further point, however, that such negotiation is unsatisfactory (which implies that it is possible), is ignored by B.

Shift to a Moderate Position

Whether attacking or defending, debaters frequently shift ground and, like an army in an exposed position, retreat to a more defensible, more moderate, position. Thus, they slip away from the original point, e.g.,

A: American prestige in Asia is high. [A cites a piece of evidence.]
B: American prestige in Asia is low. [B effectively attacks A's point by citing several pieces of evidence.]
A: But American policies are slowly but surely being understood and American prestige is increasing. [Evidence.]

From his original point that "American prestige is high," A retreats to the point that "American prestige is increasing." Needless to say, American prestige may be increasing and still be low.

All relative terms lend themselves to this type of ground shifting and thus should be carefully watched. When they appear in the debate resolution itself, debaters occasionally define them one way at the outset and another in the subsequent argument, particularly to counter an attack. This type of equivocation, by means of shifting or elusive definitions, has already been considered in Chapter 3.

Ground Shifting by Impromptu Definition

Frequently debaters will counter an attack by merely redefining the terms used in the original argument. Thus, they shift from a vulnerable position without directly meeting the attack upon it, e.g.,

A: Francis C. Lowell built the first cotton mills in New England and thus may be credited with making New England an industrial area.
B: But Sam Slater built a cotton mill in New England in 1790, twenty-four years before Lowell built his mill.
A: Although Slater's mill was the first to have spinning machinery, it still used hand looms. Lowell's mill was the first to use power looms.

Here A diverts from the original proposition that Lowell's mill was the first cotton mill in New England to the proposition that Lowell's mill was the first to use power looms. If B could now show that mills using power looms were built in New England before Lowell's mill, A might now contend that Lowell's mill was the first, however, to be run by water-power. And so on. In other words, A might continue to counter attacks merely by redefining his position. If A had meant "power looms" in his first argument and wasn't merely shifting ground when attacked, he should have made his point clear in the first place. As presented, how-ever, his original argument is now subject to considerable doubt as a result of his arguing by impromptu definition.

Ground Shifting by Diversion

Occasionally debaters shift to a more defensible position by simply diverting to an issue that may be associated with, but is not directly re-lated to, the original issue, e.g.,

A: Direct aid enables us to get valuable air bases, as in Saudi Arabia.
B: But Saudi Arabia is an isolated instance. It doesn't prove that aid gen-erally works in this way.
A: Well, there's Spain, Iceland, Taiwan, Korea, Turkey, etc.
B: But air bases are no longer vital to our defense.

Here B, when answered, shifts from the proposition that direct aid doesn't secure air bases to the proposition that such bases are unimportant. A's answer should now be to point out this diversion and to claim that the initial point, that direct aid secures air bases, has been carried, that B has apparently abandoned this issue and now wishes to argue on another point, whether or not such bases are important.

The foregoing shifts and diversions usually occur when an original point has been effectively answered. Another group of irrelevancies, which may be classed as misrepresentation, frequently appear in answer to an original point effectively made by the opposition. Misrepresenta-tion may take many forms, the following being fairly typical:

Misquoting the Opposition

This error is self-explanatory and is illustrated by the following:

A. (Argument): Books which are immoral are very often lacking in literary value. For example, etc.
B. (Answer): To quote A "Books which are immoral are lacking in literary value." However, etc.

Here B misrepresents A by misquoting him. By failing to consider the qualifying phrase "very often," B extends A's position to a point where it will be easier to attack. This error is akin to quoting out of context. A's defense would be: "But I did not make any such categorical statement as B claims. You will recall I said 'very often,' which B has overlooked in quoting me. Thus, *B*'s answer is irrelevant to my original point, which still stands." *A* should not be sarcastic in his reply but should consider *B*'s error unintentional.

Misstating the Opposition's Evidence

This error, also self-explanatory, resembles the previous one, e.g.,

A. (Argument): The present policy of nonrecognition is a source of disagreement between the United States and her allies. "In Asia," according to the *New York Times,* "the Allies have sharp differences over how to deal with Peiping. Nonrecognition produces a visible strain on our alliance with Great Britain, who recognizes Communist China. Other allies, such as Canada, Australia, and Japan, have indicated a desire to recognize this government but have refrained from doing so only because of strong political pressures exerted by the United States." On a visit to the United States last fall French Premier Mendes-France urged that we recognize this government.

B. (Answer): *A* tells us that the effects of our present policy are all wrong, first because it leads to disagreement with our allies. What allies, we don't know. They didn't mention any of the allies. Perhaps they assume Great Britain, since that is the only European ally concerned with the problems in Asia.

Although this type of answer clearly misstates the opposing evidence, a debater should not impute dishonest motives to it or become indignant and reply sarcastically as inexperienced debaters would do, "Apparently *B* wasn't listening when I made the point that, etc." or "If *B* had been paying closer attention, he would know that I cited, etc." or "In answer to *B*'s gross misrepresentation of my original point that, etc." The best reply to this type of misrepresentation is to point out the inaccuracies dispassionately thus: "*B* tells us that we didn't cite any allies, but you will recall that we cited Great Britain, Canada, Australia, Japan, and France. We indicated that these countries want to recognize Communist China and why they do not, a point never alluded to by the gentleman. We cited evidence to the effect that, etc., never considered by *B*."

Oversimplification

This error resembles the previous two, for the answer overlooks many pertinent aspects of the original argument or ignores much of its context, e.g.,

A. (Argument): As we have shown, direct negotiation is not possible and indirect negotiation is unsatisfactory. Thus, unsolved problems between the two countries, since they cannot be satisfactorily negotiated, may lead to open conflict.

B. (Answer): *A* claims that we can't negotiate at present and that the only alternative is war. Well, let us examine this argument. Etc.

In attacking A's argument, B oversimplifies it. Actually, A did not say "we can't negotiate at present"; he qualified his position by considering both direct and indirect negotiation and contended that indirect negotiation though possible was unsatisfactory. B's second oversimplification—more an extension of A's position—is that war is the only alternative. Actually, A indicated that unsolved problems might lead to war but did not indicate that war was the "only alternative."

Negative debaters often oversimplify the affirmative need by implying that one point constituted the entire need, after the affirmative presented four or five points. Once again, the best defense is to point out the opposition's omissions before considering anything else. Since the first negative speaker usually neglects some portions of the first affirmative speech, the second affirmative speaker should open his constructive speech by emphasizing the negative speaker's omissions.

Distortion

This error is often difficult to detect, for the diversion usually touches on some minor aspect of the original argument, e.g.,

A. (Argument): India disagrees with the United States over its policy of nonrecognition of Communist China. Mr. Nehru, Indian Prime Minister, has characterized American policy as "the root cause of all international troubles during the past four years."

B. (Answer): But Communist China was the main cause of the difficulties in the Far East, not the United States—intervention in Indochina, invasion of Tibet, tension in the Formosa Straits, invasion of Korea. Yet A claims that these troubles have been caused by the United States. We fail to understand this reasoning.

Here A's proposition that India disagrees with the United States over the policy of nonrecognition of Communist China is answered by the proposition that Communist China has caused certain difficulties in the Far East, two independent propositions. If A had claimed that the United States had caused the troubles in question, B's answer would be relevant. But A did not make this claim; Nehru did. Thus, B has answered Nehru and not A's argument that India regards United States policy as being wrong. Whether Nehru's reasoning is right or wrong is immaterial, the point being that Nehru's reasoning proves that Nehru disagrees with United States policy. Since B had nothing to say on this point, while presuming to do so, his answer is a diversion.

A similar diversion, or distortion, is seen in the following example:

A: Most Asians believe that the United States is discriminating against the yellow race in not recognizing Communist China. They point to other Communist states which we have recognized—all white—and say, therefore, that we do not recognize China not because it is Communist but because it is yellow.

B: But we don't discriminate against the yellow race. We recognize other countries whose population is predominantly yellow—Japan, Philippines, Burma, etc.

A: Whether we discriminate or not is beside the point. The point is, most Asians *think* we do. And this is the point we made—still unanswered—and this is the sentiment which Communist propaganda is successfully capitalizing on in the Far East.

Equivocation

Although this error has been touched on, let us consider one more example:

A. (Argument): We cannot negotiate satisfactorily at present. We refuse direct negotiation lest it imply recognition, and Communist China balks at indirect negotiation. [The implication is that recognition would lead to satisfactory negotiation, i.e., to a friendly discussion of mutual grievances.]

B. (Answer): But Communist China is intransigent. In view of her past record, there is little likelihood that even after recognition she would be willing to make concessions to the United States.

Here *B* interprets "negotiate satisfactorily" as "willing to make concessions." Although negotiation sometimes leads to concessions by just one party, it usually involves concessions by both parties. By equivocating on the term "negotiate satisfactorily," *B* in effect extends *A*'s position to "China will yield to the United States" and answers this proposition rather than *A*'s original one, namely, that after recognition China and the United States would be willing to discuss their mutual grievances.

Extension or Exaggeration

This error consists of exaggerating an opponent's claim or extending it to a point where it can be more readily attacked than the original, and then attacking the misrepresentation of the original. This is also known as tearing down a "straw man." The defense against this fallacy, as against all irrelevancies, is to reaffirm the original argument and to point out that the answer to it is unrelated, e.g.,

A: If we recognize Communist China, there will be greater opportunities for the United States and Communist China to reconcile their differences by peaceful negotiation. Of course, we realize that after recognition there will still be differences between the two countries, but at present we cannot even discuss those differences. With recognition, direct and continuous negotiation is possible and this in turn is the best means for the peaceful settlement of disputes.

B: A tells us that if we recognize Communist China, all at once they will become a peace-loving nation. But I should like to point out, etc.

A: We never contended that "all at once" Communist China would become a peace-loving nation. We indicated that there might still be differences after recognition but that direct and continuous negotiation was the best means for resolving them. To this contention we have as yet heard no answer; we have heard, instead, an answer to a point which we never presented.

By reaffirming his original position A refuses to be diverted by B's misrepresentation.

In conclusion, the point to remember concerning all of the foregoing irrelevancies is: what is the issue being discussed, and how does the opposition's answer relate to it? [3]

4. INCONSISTENCY

Inconsistency may be defined as using contradictory or contrary evidence or arguments in support of the same case. In pointing out inconsistencies—also called contradictions—in the opposing case, one does not necessarily disprove the two points or arguments involved but one does cast considerable doubt on their truthfulness since, being inconsistent with one another, both cannot be true. Also, since consistency is one of the ideals of logic, inconsistency marks one as illogical, and the doubt created by one inconsistency may permeate the entire case. Inconsistency also connotes sophistry, or arguing for the sake of arguing rather than for determining the truth. Because of these connotations, inconsistency is a most damaging error, and pointing it out a most effective attack.

Detecting Inconsistencies

A simple illustration of inconsistency is the following: "Citation easily outdistanced the field, though he managed to win by only a nose over Stymie." In debate, however, inconsistencies are often difficult to detect because they rest upon hidden assumptions. Consider, for example, the following pair of arguments:

Negative attacking the affirmative's definition of terms: "If you stop testing, you don't necessarily stop nuclear weapons development."
Negative citing a disadvantage of the affirmative plan: "If you stop testing, the United States will be unable to develop the small tactical nuclear weapons that she needs."

In the first argument the underlying assumption is that testing is not a necessary condition of development, and in the second, that testing is a

[3] Though it does not involve misrepresentation, another type of irrelevancy is defending a point never answered by the opposition. Defending an argument presumes that it has been answered; therefore, defending it when it has not been is irrelevant and a waste of time. One must bear in mind here the distinction between defending an argument and elaborating upon it, the latter being legitimate even when the argument has not been answered.

necessary condition of development. In debates on the prohibition of nuclear weapons development (the 1958–1959 national college debate topic), many negative teams also argued thus:

Attacking affirmative need: "Radiation from nuclear weapons tests is not a serious hazard. Etc." [Underlying assumption: fallout, whether from clean or dirty bombs, is not hazardous.]

Citing disadvantage of affirmative plan: "The United States must continue tests to develop small clean nuclear weapons. Etc." [Underlying assumption: fallout from dirty bombs is hazardous.]

The best way to become familiar with potential contradictions is to engage in long preliminary discussions and practice sessions. Generally, the negative position is more vulnerable to contradictions than the affirmative.

Another reason why contradictions are not readily apparent is that they usually appear in different parts of the case, either in different parts of the same issue or in entirely different issues. Let us consider some examples.

Affirmative arguing against compulsory unionism, in one part of the need issue: Unions don't really cause wage increases and better working conditions; they only take credit for them.

In another part of the need issue: Strong unions are detrimental to the economy. For one thing, they contribute to inflation by their insistent wage demands. By steadily forcing wages up, they also force prices up. Etc.

Thus it is argued that unions simultaneously do not and do cause higher wages, a contradiction from which there could be no escape if the opposition pointed it out.

A similar error—typical of the negative—is the following:

Negative arguing against United States economic aid going through the UN,

Objection 1: If the United States channeled its economic aid through the UN, it would gain much control over that organization. Eventually, the UN would lose its character as an international organization.

Objection 2: If the United States gave its economic aid through the UN, it would lose control over this aid. It would have no assurance that aid would go where it served the best interests of the United States, as to Guatemala when that country was in danger of being taken over by a Communist *coup d'état.*

Here, the negative argues, first, that United States influence in the UN would be increased and, second, that it would be diminished simultaneously, two contrary propositions. One may use contrary objections only as alternatives, as in a dilemma, arguing that either one effect or the other would occur but not both simultaneously.

Inconsistencies often appear in arguments used to support different issues. The following examples should help one both to avoid and to capitalize on such inconsistencies.

Negative arguing against voluntary unionism: *1:* No need; in elections held by the NLRB 5½ million workers, or 91 per cent of those voting, favored the union shop. *2:* Disadvantage; under "right-to-work" laws there would be many "free riders" [those who leave a union and still get all the benefits of collective bargaining] and thus much friction.

In the first argument the negative contends that most workers, when given the choice, want the union shop and, by implication, want to stay in unions. In the second argument the negative contends that many workers, if given the choice as under voluntary unionism, would leave the union. These are contrary propositions. (Since the first is empirically established, the second is probably false.)

Countering the Charge of Inconsistency

Occasionally one may counter a charge of inconsistency by demonstrating that an apparent inconsistency is due either to a lack of precise phrasing or explanation, or to some misinterpretation by the opposition, e.g.,

Negative arguing against voluntary unionism (right-to-work laws),

Objection 1: On impracticability; right-to-work laws are difficult to enforce; they are actually ignored in many states which have passed them. [Cites evidence of what has happened in six right-to-work states.]

Objection 2: Disadvantage; serious consequences have resulted from the passage of right-to-work laws in the South—labor unrest, strikes, etc.

On the surface there seems to be a contradiction here. First, the negative argues that right-to-work laws have not been successfully enforced and presumably couldn't be, if passed on a national scale. Then the negative argues that serious consequences have resulted from the passage of such laws, the implication being that the laws were enforced, for how else could there have been any consequences? There are two ways in which the negative might clear up this apparent inconsistency: first, he might point out that although the laws are on the whole difficult to enforce, they have been enforced in a few areas with serious consequences; or, second, he might clarify his objection by pointing out that the serious consequences were the results of unsuccessful *attempts* to enforce the law.

Real and Apparent Inconsistencies

In his zeal to pick out inconsistencies, a debater must be careful not to confuse a seeming inconsistency with a true one. In the previous example there was considerable doubt as to whether the two arguments were consistent, for they had not been accurately or precisely worded. However, the reader may recall that in the discussion of the truth relations among propositions we saw that certain types of compatible propositions seem on the surface to be contradictory or contrary, as,

Some labor leaders are corrupt.
Some labor leaders are honest.

Some labor leaders are corrupt.
Some labor leaders are not corrupt.

Both pairs contain compatible statements, i.e., both may be true simultaneously, and it is with such propositions that one must be careful in his search for inconsistencies. Consider the following arguments:

Negative arguing against voluntary unionism,
Objection 1: No need (existing evils can be eliminated under the status quo); workers in corrupt unions can ask for decertification elections; in fact, in the latest quarter 38 of these elections were held and the unions lost their bargaining rights in 28 cases, or 74 per cent.
Objection 2: Plan won't meet need; the great majority of workers, even if given a choice, are too indifferent or too unsophisticated to withdraw from corrupt unions.

The seeming inconsistency is that, on the one hand, workers are not indifferent to corruption as evidenced by their asking for decertification elections and that, on the other, they are indifferent and wouldn't leave corrupt unions. However, the inconsistency disappears when the appropriate quantifier is placed before the term "workers" in each argument. Thus, in the first argument we get "*some* workers are not indifferent" and in the second, "*most* workers are indifferent," two compatible propositions. If one were charged with inconsistency here, he could answer that the opposition has missed the point, namely, that despite the indifference of most workers, the means are available to them under the status quo as evidenced by the fact that *some* workers have successfully employed them.

Special Pleading, or the Self-defeating Principle

Another type of inconsistency frequently encountered in debate is the fallacy of special pleading, or the self-defeating principle. It consists of attacking an opposing argument by applying a general principle that is damaging to one's own position or of defending a position compatible with the opposition's. The contradiction consists in implying that a principle is true for the opposition but not for oneself, or vice versa. However, if a principle is true for one, it is true for another, and it is inconsistent to presume otherwise. In committing this fallacy, one usually fails to realize that a generalization is involved for it is usually implied. Also, because of emotional involvement, one recognizes the fallacy more readily in others than in himself.

In debate the self-defeating argument may take many forms, e.g.,

Negative debater arguing on the desirability of the affirmative plan: You are merely speculating or theorizing that your plan will work. [Or "Your plan is merely theoretical" or "All we have heard is mere theory."]

In effect, the speaker here questions the validity of causal reasoning by calling it "mere" theory or speculation. He fails to realize, however, that he himself is also theorizing, for the very denial of a causal theory is a causal theory; more important, any citation of disadvantages of the affirmative plan must also be considered invalid or "mere speculation," for they, too, are based on causal reasoning. Thus, in rejecting the principle to attack the affirmative he damages his own case even more, or, as the French would say, he is "hoist by his own petard."

The same may be said of the argument "... and furthermore the point is based on only one man's word." If the underlying assumption here is true, any argument based on one man's word is invalid; and since in debate there are usually many such arguments advanced by *both* sides, the objection becomes a two-edged sword cutting in both directions.

Less apparent is the fallacy in the following argument which many affirmative teams used in debating compulsory unionism (to save time only the conclusion of the argument is given, as in many of the preceding examples):

On evils of the status quo: Many workers at present are intimidated and afraid to testify concerning union irregularities.

One might retort: "If true, workers would also be intimidated under the affirmative plan. In fact, with the unions insecure, workers might conceivably be intimidated even more, to get them to remain in unions." If the first speaker could show that the power to intimidate was derived from the compulsory aspect of unionism and that this power would be eliminated by the affirmative plan, his original argument would not be self-defeating.

Self-defeating arguments are quite common in the area of inherency. In debating the question "Congress Should Nationalize the Basic Nonagricultural Industries," an affirmative team tried to prove that the evils of the status quo were caused largely by the self-interest of congressmen. Thus, in establishing its need, the affirmative defeated itself on practicability.

An affirmative team is often guilty of special pleading when it cites evils not caused by the status quo and, therefore, unrelated to the affirmative plan. The error, more common than it should be, results from failure to consider the cause of evils, e.g.,

Affirmative arguing against the electoral college system (and for direct vote for the President), on the evils of the status quo: As matters now stand, all the electoral votes of one state go to one candidate; the minority vote, though it might be 49 per cent of the total vote, is discounted. The minority might just as well have not voted.

This argument is self-defeating, for the so-called evil is not the result of the electoral college system but of the democratic process itself and thus would exist under the affirmative program unless the democratic process (under which the majority wins, or in effect "gets all the votes") were eliminated along with the electoral college system. If the affirmative in this case meant that a candidate who gets 51 per cent of the vote sometimes loses the election, then his argument would be pertinent. As presented, however, it is not.

A similar example on the same question is the following:

On evils of the status quo: Under the present system candidates concentrate on the large states and neglect the small ones.

This argument is also self-defeating unless it can be shown that under the affirmative plan large states would lose their significance in an election. If the affirmative meant that under the present system candidates concentrate on large states where the vote is likely to be close and that they therefore spend much time and money to influence a relatively small number of votes in those states and little time and money to influence a much larger number of votes in a state not considered important, then the argument would not be self-defeating. This, however, was not the affirmative point.

The effect of such inconsistencies is that the affirmative plan cannot meet its own need. All well-trained negative teams try to undermine the affirmative case by attacking the causal relationship between the affirmative evils and the status quo. When the affirmative disregards this relationship and introduces evils unrelated to the status quo, the negative task is considerably easier. One very common manifestation of this affirmative error is the claim that the present program is wasteful because of poor administration or insufficient administrative personnel. Since such shortcomings are usually not inherent defects of any system; they can be eliminated without altering the essential character of the system.

A similar inconsistency is for the affirmative to introduce as part of its plan provisions unrelated to evils caused by the status quo but related to evils caused by some other policy. If in arguing against compulsory unionism, for example, an affirmative team were to present a plan containing such provisions as public audits of union finances, supervised elections, instituting labor courts to handle labor-management disputes, and giving men on strike the right to vote in decertification elections, it would imply that the evils it had previously cited were caused by something other than compulsory unionism. For if compulsory unionism were the cause, such provisions would not be needed; one could simply eliminate compulsory unionism, the cause, to eliminate the evil effects. Such provisions, therefore, imply that the evils are not caused by compulsory unionism. In reply the negative may point this out and then endorse the same provisions, e.g.,

These recommended changes have nothing to do with the main issue, compulsory unionism. We think they are fine and would incorporate them into the status quo [i.e., adopt the changes and retain compulsory unionism].

Occasionally, answers presumably to the fallacy of special pleading are themselves fallacious. Take the argument:

If, as you claim, we couldn't enforce a national right-to-work law, why then should we suppose that the Mitchell Plan, also national in scope, would be enforceable?

Since the national character of the affirmative plan (right-to-work law) had nothing to do with the original negative objection, this answer misconstrues the opposing argument. In other words, the speaker knocks down a "straw man."

In conclusion, a debater is like a military strategist: sometimes he attacks directly, sometimes indirectly, and sometimes he does both simultaneously.

EXERCISES

What fallacy, if any, is committed in the following arguments?

a^1. In the past twenty years the Soviet Union has broken forty out of forty-two of its agreements.

a^2. Yes, but these violations occurred under Stalin's regime. Show us where the present regime has broken any of its agreements.

a^1. Well, here's a report from the New York Times that says that recently the Soviet Union has rejected eighteen out of twenty United States proposals.

b^1. Many 18-year-olds have little knowledge of current issues and would therefore make poor voters.

b^2. Many 21-year-olds also have little knowledge of current issues but are still permitted to vote.

b^1. That may be true, but no system is perfect; we have to take the bad along with the good.

c^1. Being considerate of others will make others considerate of you.

c^2. On the contrary, humbling oneself before others only encourages them to take advantage of you.

d^1. According to the Joint Chiefs of Staff, the United States will not have time to train an army should another war break out.

d^2. But war is very costly. The cost of one heavy bomber would build a first-rate school.

e^1. Poetry written by women usually lacks masculine vigor.

e^2. How about Amy Lowell's poetry? It seems pretty vigorous.

e^1. But Amy Lowell acted and thought like a man.

f^1. Increased automation will lead to increased worker productivity and ultimately to a higher standard of living for all.

f^2. As for the contention that automation will make us all rich, the opposite seems true. If unchecked, it will lead to severe unemployment and ultimately to a depression.

g^1. The American Communist Party should be outlawed, for it is controlled by a foreign power. Thus, a bill like the Mundt-Nixon Bill, which in effect outlaws the Communist Party, should be passed.

g^2. But the Mundt-Nixon Bill doesn't outlaw the Communist Party. Mundt himself says so. The bill merely says it is a crime to try to overthrow the government of the United States and establish a dictatorship under the control of a foreign government. It says nothing about outlawing the Communist Party.

h^1. Communist China entered the Korean conflict only when her vital interests in Manchuria were being menaced.

h^2. If Truman had not interfered with MacArthur, the war would have ended much sooner.

i^1. Despite recent increases in many states, unemployment compensation benefits are still too low.

i^2. But the unemployment compensation program is flexible. States can change the program. In 1955 every state did; thirty-two increased benefits.

j^1. Low-cost attractive housing units would improve the over-all health of the community.

j^2. Such units have been built in sections of New York and the health of the people living there is by no means perfect.

k^1. Unemployment compensation programs and other give-away benefits only encourage indolence and discourage initiative.

k^2. But didn't you go through college on a free scholarship? Was your initiative dampened?

k^1. I was a special case. I was very ambitious and the scholarship only made it easier for me to realize my ambitions.

l^1. A Guaranteed Annual Wage would discourage many companies from taking risks in manufacturing new products; for if the products didn't sell, the companies would have to continue paying their workers.

l^2. This is a mere assertion and according to the rules of debate need not be answered. The opposition might have introduced some evidence on this point, but since they did not, we simply deny it.

m^1. Low seniority workers are laid off first. As for those in seasonal industries, they receive more wages in proportion to the seasonal nature of the industry.

m^2. The negative team admits that the low seniority workers are laid off first and therefore get less than the average wage. If so, these workers do not benefit from the proportionately higher wage paid in seasonal industries. In short, the negative is now faced with its own objection. If you're going to argue about unemployed workers, then don't quote the average wage in seasonal industries because the unemployed workers are not receiving that wage. Therefore, the point as advanced by the negative contains the contradiction which they say is in the affirmative case and is a self-defeating point.

n^1. All contemporary educational theorists have been strongly influenced by Dewey's doctrines.

n^2. How about Professor X? He disagrees vigorously with Dewey.

n^1. That may be true, but X also shows the strength of Dewey's influence by rebelling against it. So my point still stands.

o^1. Outlawing the American Communist Party would be unconstitutional.

o^2. But Communism is a menace to world peace. As General G has said, "We must maintain our armed forces at full strength against the threat of international communism."

p^1. A new international noncommunist organization would be able to implement its decisions by having a joint military force.

p^2. But just what could the smaller nations contribute to this force? Only recently the Minister from Iceland declared, "We have no planes, no tanks, no men, and no money." I tank I go home. [Laughter.]

q^1. Nuclear weapons, according to General MacArthur, have effectively outlawed war as an instrument of policy.

q^2. But nuclear weapons have not brought much understanding between the Soviet Union and the United States.

r^1. How can the demand for cotton products, for example, be stabilized when substitute products are developed which the people prefer? Cottons sold well until rayon came along; then came dacron and after that nylon.

r^2. As for dacron and your other "crons," it was perfected long after nylon was; so your facts are simply inaccurate.

s^1. To sum up, unemployment compensation benefits are low, there is chronic misadministration of the program, states vie with each other in keeping benefits low, and agricultural interests, which have no stake in the program, control most state legislatures.

s^2. They tell us that there is chronic misadministration of the unemployment compensation program. Is this a reason for a change? Why not go in with a broom and simply clean it up? Moreover, what guarantee do we have that the affirmative program would be immune to misadministration? What assurances have they given us?

t^1. Show us where this so-called resentment has resulted in any adverse effects to the United States.

t^2. They challenge us to show some of the adverse effects of resentment, but we challenge them to show where this program has actually made friends for the United States.

CHAPTER 17

ORGANIZING THE ANSWER
TO AN ARGUMENT

True eloquence consists in saying all that is necessary and nothing but what is necessary.

La Rochefoucauld

1. GENERAL ORGANIZATION

In answering an opposing argument, one should do the following:

1. State briefly and accurately the argument in question, indicating when feasible the issue to which it is related and its relative importance to that issue.

2. State one's stand on or reaction to the argument, or in general terms how one proposes to answer it.

3. Support step 2 with evidence and reasoning.

4. Summarize briefly the effect of the answer.

Now let us consider each step in greater detail.

Designating the Argument to Be Answered

To repeat, one should begin his answer by stating briefly and accurately the argument in question, indicating when feasible the issue to which it is related and its relative importance to that issue. If the argument is one of the main supports of the issue, this fact should be indicated; for then, if the attack is effective, the judge will know that a main prop of the opposing case has been undermined. For example,

Our friends tell us that the affirmative plan is impracticable because management would oppose it. Since this is their only point concerning impracticability, we may assume that if management would not oppose it, the plan would be practicable. Well, let us see just how management really feels, etc.

Another way of indicating the significance attached to an opposing argument is seen in the following introduction:

256

Now the last speaker spent almost half of his speech trying to prove that the cost of the affirmative plan would be prohibitive.

Finally, consider this example:

Now our friends have based almost all of their objections on the supposition that recognition [the affirmative plan] would result in the loss of Formosa.

Here, in one short sentence the speaker effectively does three things:
1. Points up the argument to be attacked, namely, the loss of Formosa;
2. Relates this argument to a main issue, namely, negative disadvantages of the affirmative plan; and
3. Points up the significance which the opposition has attached to the argument by the phrase "have based almost all of their objections." Thus, if the argument is effectively answered, an entire issue is undermined.

In rebuilding an argument, one should state both the original argument and the attack on it, e.g.,

You will recall that my colleague pointed out that industry can stabilize its production but lacks the sufficient financial incentive to do so. In answer to this, our friends tell us, "Well, you can't control weather and consumer buying habits, the main causes of instability."

As a debate progresses it often becomes necessary to present a summary of several exchanges on an issue before answering the opposition's last point; in effect, one finds himself saying "We said ... they said ... we said ... they said ... and now we say ..."

Stating General Reaction

After designating the argument to be answered, one usually states his general reaction to it or indicates what the nature of his answer will be. As we have seen, one may attack directly by expressing doubt, denying, or retorting, or attack indirectly by questioning the significance, relevancy, or consistency of the argument. One may be fairly specific in indicating the nature of the answer: the facts are incomplete or inaccurate, the conclusion does not follow, the cause is other than that claimed, the point distorts the original one, etc. Typical remarks are:

"Now we should like to clash directly on this point."
"But would this necessarily occur?"
"But does their evidence warrant this conclusion?"
"However, this is not true."
"This seems to be a contradiction of their point that ..."

When one is pressed for time and wishes to cover several points rapidly, this step is frequently omitted. In one sense, this step is unnecessary, for the next step executes the intention stated in this one. However, stating an intention before executing it makes for greater clarity and emphasis.

Supporting the Answer

Having stated a point, one now supports it with evidence and reasoning. The previous two steps are merely the introduction to this one, which contains the body of the answer.

Summarizing the Effect

In concluding the answer, one summarizes briefly its effect and/or restates its main point. One may also relate the answer to a main issue, e.g.,

So we see, contrary to the negative contention, purchasing power is an influential factor in our economy and the affirmative plan, by maintaining a high level of purchasing power, would maintain prices and production and help to prevent a recession, as in 1953.

2. SAMPLE ANSWERS

Basically, the foregoing organization amounts to saying what one is going to say, saying it, and then saying what one has said. In actual practice, a debater doesn't always have the time to present each step distinctly and often telescopes three into two and even into one.

At this time we shall consider several typical answers from an actual debate:

[1] Then they tell us that defense expenditures are not being appreciably decreased. [2] Not so, [3] for as they tell us this, the money spent for defense this year has been decreased by 11 billion dollars. Furthermore, we still have 65 cents out of every tax dollar going into defense expenditures. [4] We ask, what will happen when this figure is appreciably reduced in the future and consumer demand fails to take up the slack?

This answer consists of:

1. A statement of the argument to be answered.
2. An indication of the type of answer to be given or the speaker's reaction to the argument. Specifically, "Not so" indicates denial.
3. Answer supported by evidence.
4. Summary of effect. Though presented as a question, the conclusion in effect is a statement suggesting that the preceding argument is significant, or rather, that the problem involved is significant. This is an example of the "suggestive question," earlier referred to, but its use here is legitimate since it doesn't pretend to be an argument in itself but merely the conclusion of one. In the fallacious suggestive question, no supporting evidence is given.

Consider another example:

[1] Then the negative tells us, as for automation [the question of unemployment as caused by automation], ours is only an isolated instance [of an industry in which substantial unemployment did occur]. [2] But rather than quibble over separate industries, the facts are that at the end of last year the Bureau of Labor Statistics indicated that all manufacturing industries in the United States were producing as much as they had a year earlier, even though the number of factory workers had dropped by nearly a million. [3] This, gentlemen, is no accident—it's automation.

This answer consists of:

1. A statement of the argument to be answered. Since the argument is an attack upon a previous argument, both the original argument (automation is creating serious unemployment, as in the automobile industry) and the attack upon it (the automobile industry is only an isolated instance) have to be mentioned. Note, however, that the speaker alludes to both elliptically, i.e., he merely mentions the terms "automation" and "isolated instance," expecting his listeners to fill in the missing parts.

2. The answer supported by evidence. Here the speaker does not say what his answer will be but instead gives it. He might have said, "We deny this contention" or "On the contrary, the problem is industrywide" or both.

3. Summary or conclusion. The speaker points up the significance of the previous data by means of suggestion, the suggestion being that there is a cause-and-effect relationship between increased automation in industry and decreased employment. Note the terse, dramatic quality of this particular conclusion.

The next example shows how a series of points may be dealt with in one answer:

[1] Moving on, the negative has contended that a Guaranteed Annual Wage is impracticable for three reasons. [2] They tell us there would be a problem of integration [the problem of integrating a Guaranteed Annual Wage Plan with the Unemployment Compensation Program] because there was one in Ohio. [3] But may I point out here that Ohio refused the Unemployment Compensation increase and supplementary payments because it was a political question. New York accepted the payments. [4] So here again we see that the states will go along with an integrated program. [5] They tell us that management will not accept the pooling of risks [required by a Guaranteed Annual Wage Plan], [6] but under Unemployment Compensation we have the pooling of risks. [7] They tell us that we can only get the plan through unions [the argument being answered here was that Guaranteed Annual Wage plans can only be brought about by collective bargaining since management wouldn't voluntarily initiate them because such plans would be disadvantageous to management], [8] but we are presenting a plan that deals with the causes and effects of unemployment, besides having additional advantages for management; [9] and for this reason we think that management will accept it. [10] So

we see that the three points advanced by the negative with regard to impracticability do not stand up under the light of the affirmative analysis. In a word, we see that the affirmative plan is practicable.

An analysis of this answer reveals:

1. A reference to the main issue to be dealt with, namely, impracticability.

2. A reference to the first subpoint under this issue advanced by the opposition.

3. The answer to this point; specifically, a denial that there would be a problem of integration, supported by evidence.

4. A restatement of the conclusion of the first answer in affirmative terms: "The states will go along, etc."

5. A reference to the second subpoint under this issue.

6. The answer to the second subpoint, supported by evidence and reasoning though the nature of the reasoning (by means of analogy) is implied. Note the speed with which this argument is introduced and answered. Such speed is often necessary in the final rebuttal speeches, where the entire case is usually summarized and reviewed. In the constructive speeches one has more time to spend on individual answers.

7. A reference to the third subpoint.

8. The answer to the third subpoint, supported by reasoning. Again, since this is a final rebuttal speech, the answer constitutes a review and summary.

9. A restatement of the conclusion drawn from the preceding answer.

10. A restatement of the significance of the entire answer, in effect, "We deny the opposition claim; we affirm our own."

EXERCISE

1. Examine a rebuttal speech of a debate appearing in the *University Debaters' Annual* or a similar volume and consider each answer from the standpoint of the outline discussed in this chapter. Were any departures from the outline justified? Would any answers not adhering to the outline have been more effective had they adhered to it? Fill in the parts that are missing in any of the answers.

PART FOUR

PRESENTATION

CHAPTER 18

LANGUAGE

Language is but the instrument conveying to us things useful to be known.

Milton

Presenting the debate speech, like presenting any speech, involves many factors. These may be put into two main categories, language and delivery. We shall consider each from the standpoint of the debater. For further information the student may consult textbooks on these subjects.

1. SIMPLICITY AND DIRECTNESS

Language is primarily a medium of communication. It is not an end in itself but a means to an end, the end being to communicate ideas clearly and concisely. Language which calls attention to itself not only detracts from but usually obscures the meaning it is supposed to convey. In speaking as in writing, one should avoid flowery, stilted, or pedantic diction; and choose words that are simple, direct, and as specific as possible. As an example of how simple meanings can become obscured by the use of circumlocutions, pseudotechnical terms, pompous phrasing, and similar excesses prevalent in much writing today, consider this passage:

Then there is the allegation by the members of the negation that under the stipulations of the present program 80 per cent of all workers not gainfully employed and involuntarily so, may receive gratuities commensurate with their prior earnings and that under the stipulations of the program advanced by the affirmation only ten million workers may receive such gratuities. This allegation, however, is at variance with the facts. For in accordance with the stipulations of the plan adumbrated by my colleague, a plan which would operate concomitantly with the existing program of unemployment compensation benefits, not only would 80 per cent receive grants proportionate to prior earnings, but all workers not gainfully employed in agricultural pursuits would receive a more adequate compensation than that which is possible under legislation now operative.

And now consider how it might have been said for maximum clarity:

Then our friends tell us that 80 per cent of the unemployed can be covered under their plan and only ten million under ours. This is false. For under our plan, which retains the unemployment compensation program, not only will 80 per cent be covered but all nonagricultural workers will be covered more adequately.

Unfortunately, many debaters in trying to impress the judge use the jargon of the first version and succeed only in beclouding their arguments and in befuddling everyone present.

2. THE CONVERSATIONAL STYLE

The best debate style is conversational in quality, i.e., "direct, spontaneous, unaffected, unpretentious, simple, uncomplicated, informal" as opposed to "stilted, bookish, ponderous, complex, pedantic, obscure, affected, studied, remote." [1] The chief characteristics of a conversational style have been summarized as follows:

1. The use of repetition and restatement—much more than in written composition.

2. The choice of common, nonacademic words, without at the same time sacrificing accuracy.

3. Looser sentence structure, with fewer dependent clauses and qualifying phrases than in most writing.

4. A large number of short, simple sentences.

5. A freer use of personal pronouns, contractions, colloquial or slang terms, and exclamations than in writing.

6. A relaxation of strict grammatical principles to obtain a more informal sentence pattern, especially the use of parenthetical remarks and asides, the shifting of syntax in the middle of a sentence, and more flexibility in word order.

7. The tendency to use more direct discourse or dialogue than in most writing.

To get a better idea of what constitutes an effective debate style, the student should study tapes or printed versions of actual debates. Discussion and practice debate sessions which precede the opening of the debate season provide a good opportunity for developing an appropriate debate style, particularly if such sessions are supervised by an experienced teacher.

[1] W. Charles Redding, *Argumentation and Debate*, ed. David Potter (New York: The Dryden Press, Inc., 1954), pp. 205–206.

3. USEFUL RHETORICAL CONSTRUCTIONS

There are several useful rhetorical or grammatical constructions which may be used periodically to heighten or emphasize a point. Although such constructions are not persuasive per se, by focusing attention on important points they contribute to persuasion. Among the most useful rhetorical devices are the rhetorical question, repetition, and parallelism.

The Rhetorical Question

A rhetorical question is one which is asked and then immediately answered by the person asking it. It is not a question in the sense that an answer is expected from the opposition. For example,

1. And why do we of the affirmative advocate recognition? Because we believe that only by recognition can the best interests of the United States be served.
2. What, then, is the law of comparative advantage? It is an economic principle, etc.
3. But, you may ask, can't we eliminate these evils without eliminating direct economic aid? The answer is no, for direct economic aid is the very cause of these evils, and an effect can be truly eliminated only by eliminating its cause.

Effective Repetition

Like the rhetorical question, effective repetition serves to focus attention on an important idea or issue. This is undoubtedly why Lincoln chose to conclude the "Gettysburg Address" with the words "of the people, by the people, for the people shall not perish from this earth" instead of with its verbal equivalent "of, by, and for the people, etc." Note in the following example how effectively repetition is used:

Who shot down an American plane and held eighteen Americans incommunicado? The Chinese Communists. Who aggressed in Korea? The Chinese Communists. Who invaded Tibet and sent troops to Indochina? The Chinese Communists. And who is now stirring up trouble in the offshore islands of Quemoy and Matsu? The very same Chinese Communists.

Note that here we have repetition both of structure and phrasing.

Parallelism

Parallelism is a form of effective repetition, i.e., the repetition of certain grammatical forms such as phrases and clauses. Parallelism or "balance," as it is sometimes called, is an ingredient of rhythm as well as a means of emphasis. As the critic John Livingston Lowes has pointed out, one of the distinguishing characteristics of the King James Bible is the matching of phrase against phrase and clause against clause. Effective parallelism is seen in a passage like the following (from Thomas Paine's attack on monarchy): [2]

> An office that may be filled by a person without talent or experience, an office that does not require virtue or wisdom for its due exercise, an office which is the reward of birth and which may consequently devolve on a madman, an imbecile, or a tyrant, is, in the very nature of things, an absurdity and, whatever its ostentation, has no real utility.

4. DEBATE TERMINOLOGY

Preparation, as we have said repeatedly, is the key to successful debating. This means preparation not only of arguments but also of the means for tying these arguments together. As we have seen, except for the first affirmative speech, all other speeches must be adapted to some previous speech or speeches. This means that most of the material that goes into them must be selected while the preceding speaker is still speaking. Thus, the problem is, how to adapt and yet avoid the impression of giving a choppy, fragmentary speech. The problem is solved in part by sticking fairly close to a prearranged schedule, by tying the various arguments to the main issues, and by using judiciously placed summaries. Also helpful are the terms which express transitions and relationships, terms which we shall now consider.

In debate, as in all specialized activities, there is a specialized vocabulary or language pattern; and the sooner the debater learns it, the more readily he can integrate his ideas. Most debaters acquire facility in using the language of debate through constant practice and actual debating. At first they learn much by listening to experienced debaters or to recordings of actual debates and even by reading sample debates. However, their learning can be speeded up if they also study the language forms directly as a distinct project.[3] Although teachers and judges of debate may tire of hearing certain debate phrases repeated year after year, such phrases are indispensable to effective debating. As a start, the following list [4] should prove helpful to the novice:

[2] Philip Foner, ed., *The Complete Writings of Thomas Paine* (New York: The Citadel Press, 1945), p. 518. Paine, incidentally, was no mean debater, and a reading of his works would well repay the student of debate.

[3] Though some coaches may feel that this practice may result in an excessive use of debate jargon, this writer has found that such fears are unwarranted.

[4] A. N. Kruger, "Debate Terminology," *The Pennsylvania Speech Annual*, XI and XII (June, 1955), pp. 18ff.

Opening the Case

Defining Terms

1. The terms of the question are self-explanatory, with the exception of ...

2. A simpler way of stating the resolution might be ...

3. Another way of stating this question is to say ...

4. Now in order that we may clearly understand (the issues of this debate) (what is to follow), let us (inquire into) (examine) the meaning of ...

Some Useful Opening Remarks

1. Now let us (inquire into) (examine) the affirmative case as it has been presented thus far. You will recall that the first major affirmative contention in this debate was.... The affirmative went on to say....We of the negative should like to clash directly on these points. We contend, first....

2. As first rebuttal speaker for the affirmative, I should now like to consider the entire affirmative case in relation to the negative objections, in so far as time will allow. You will recall that (in my opening remarks I pointed out...) (the affirmative predicated its case for...on three major contentions. First.... Second.... Third....) Now what (did we hear) (have we heard) from the negative on (these points?) (this point?)

3. Friends, from the vantage point of the first rebuttal speaker, let us review the entire constructive case of the affirmative team and see how it holds up against the (objections) (challenges) brought against it by my colleague and myself. First of all, the affirmative contended....

4. As final (negative speaker) (speaker in this debate) it will be my (duty) (pleasure) to tie up the various issues which have been presented and to

... see how the two cases stand in relation to one another

... see how the constructive arguments of the affirmative stand in relation to the negative (objections) (attack upon them)

... tie up the various loose strings of the debate and to give you a coherent picture of what has (transpired) (occurred)

... bring into focus the main issues of the controversy and to see (wherein) (exactly where) the two teams have clashed and the results of that clash

Building and Developing the Case

Useful Verbs

advanced the point
advocated
answered
asked
asserted
believe
cited
concluded
considered
contended

dealt with
do feel
feel
have shown
heard
indicated
maintained
neglected to
omitted
pointed out

questioned
quoted
reasoned
referred to
refuted
reiterated
repeated
stated
submitted
substantiated

Connective and Transitional Terms

after all
again
also
and
and so
and thus
another
as a result
as has been stated
as I have said
as you see
at any rate
at first glance
at least
at the same time
because
besides
but
by contrast
consequently
contrary to
finally
first
for
for example
for instance

for this reason
further
furthermore
hence
however
in addition
in any event
inasmuch as
incidentally
in contrast
indeed
in fact
in other words
I repeat
in short
instead
in sum
in the meantime
in the next instance
in the same manner
in this regard
in this respect
lastly
likewise
meanwhile

moreover
namely
nevertheless
next
notwithstanding
now
of course
once again
on the contrary
on the other hand
second
since
so that
still
that is (to say)
then
therefore
third
thus
to begin with
to continue
to go back
to go further
we repeat
yet

Direct Questions (followed by explanation)

1. (Now) just what is ... ?
2. (Now) what does this mean?
3. (Now) what is the significance of this fact? Simply this. ...
4. (Now) what does this all add up to?
5. And what would happen if ... ?
6. (To this point) (At this juncture) what have we seen?

General Terms

1. (We) (The gentlemen) (The members) (Our friends) of the (affirmative) (negative) (opposition)
2. Our (affirmative) (negative) friends
3. Our friends from (name of institution)
4. (We) (The affirmative) (The negative) have predicated (our) (its) (their) case on (two) (three) (four) major contentions
5. The (first) (second) (third) major contention of the (affirmative) (negative) (is) (was)
6. In the (first) (second) (third) place
7. Let us now (I should like to) consider (take up) (the first contention) (this last point) (the argument advanced by...) with you ...
8. This brings us to the (next point) (first) (affirmative) (negative) contention, (which is) (namely)
9. The (question) (issue) resolves itself to this:
10. For further clarification of (To further clarify) this point (our thinking) in this discussion
11. Let us (consider) (review) briefly for a moment
12. Turning to (Considering) (Let us turn to) (Let us consider) additional (more) (other) authorities (statistics) (proof) (examples)
13. We (They) have introduced (introduced) (shall introduce) evidence to (the effect that) (support) (substantiate)
14. To (support) (substantiate) this (that) point (contention) (issue)
15. In furtherance (support) (view) of this (that) issue (point) (argument) (contention) (fact) (opinion) (quotation)
16. Permit me (I should like) to quote
17. We (I) (They) refer (you) (us) to
18. You (may) (will) recall
19. We believe (feel) (do feel) that
20. For (this) (that) reason (we) (they) (the affirmative) (the negative) (our friends)
21. Now the reason for ... is (clear) (apparent) (not hard to find) (determine) (ascertain)
22. In the light (In view) (On the basis) of (this) (that) (those) (these) empirical evidence (fact(s)) (point(s)) (reason(s)) (reasoning) we (the affirmative) (the negative) reaffirm (take our stand) (contend) (believe) (submit)
23. At this stage of the debate (Thus to this point) (Thus up to now) (Thus at this point) (To review the progress up to this point) (Thus far we have shown) (we have seen)

Attack and Defense

Opening the Attack

1. Before (I) (we) proceed, let us (consider) (see what)

2. Now let us (consider) (examine) (turn our attention) to the arguments (points) (contentions) (reasoning) of the (preceding speaker) (negative) (affirmative)

3. Before (considering) (taking up) the (contentions) (arguments) as they have been presented

4. It will be my (pleasure) (pleasant duty) to...

5. Perhaps (I feel that) the best service I can perform at this time (juncture of the debate) is

6. ... to tie up the loose ends and see (where) (how) (the affirmative) (the negative) stands in relation to the (arguments) (objections) (presented against it) (which it has presented against the) (affirmative) (negative)

7. ... to review

8. ... to clear the air of any misconceptions

9. ... to integrate

10. The (first) (second) (affirmative) (negative) speaker stepped to the floor and (told us that) (introduced evidence) (to support) (to the effect that) which (clearly) (revealed that) (indicated that)

11. Now let us consider the (first) (second) (third) objection (contention) of the (affirmative) (negative) namely...

General Terms

1. We (They) might (say) (add) (point out)

2. The next (affirmative) (negative) argument which has been advanced is that...

3. Now with these (negative) (affirmative) contentions in mind, let us (examine) (reexamine) the (negative) (affirmative) arguments (reasoning) (position)

4. Now let (me) (us) review (consider) briefly this (first) (second) (third) (affirmative) (negative) argument (contention) (point)

5. We would like to (clash) (take issue) directly with the (affirmative) (negative) on (this) (that) point (issue) (score)

6. We are (pleased) (happy) (glad) that the (affirmative) (negative) has raised (brought up) (introduced) this point (the point that...)

7. We must (Let us) consider (not forget)

8. The (affirmative) (negative) have failed to consider (have not considered) (the fact that...) (in its proper historical perspective) (the background of...) (the history of...) (the underlying circum-

stances which have led . . .) (the underlying cause of . . .) (the causal factors which have brought about . . .)

9. We (They) (The affirmative) (The negative) countered (attacked this argument) (objected to this point) (answered this objection) (voiced their objection) (attempted to refute this point) (pointed out the weaknesses of this argument) (pointed out the fallacy in this reasoning)

10. (They) (The affirmative) (The negative) neither denied (refuted) (contested) (attacked) nor questioned (challenged) (attempted to refute) (dealt with) this (point) (argument) (contention)

11. The only (refutation of) (evidence to support) this (point) (argument) that we heard . . .

12. On this (issue) (point) we (the affirmative) (the negative) have heard (nothing as yet) (little or nothing) (very little . . .) (only . . .) from (the opposition) (the affirmative) (our negative) friends

13. And so (As of now) (At this late stage of the debate) this objection (point) (contention) (argument) still stands

14. Another point (that stands unchallenged) (that was not refuted) (not questioned) (not challenged) (not denied)

15. We would remind you (our friends) (the affirmative) (the negative)

16. We (The affirmative) went on to say (continued by saying) (pointing out) that . . .

17. The (affirmative) (negative), in addition, (went on to say) (cited) (pointed out) (submitted)

18. We should like to point out (consider) two aspects (facets) of that argument

19. We note however (moreover) that . . .

20. It should not (must not) be forgotten that . . . certain areas of (reasonable doubt) (agreement) (contention)

21. It would appear, (It appears,) therefore, that the evidence (plan) of the (affirmative) (negative) is (was) adequate (sufficient) (complete to warrant the conclusion that) (to justify our believing)

22. The (affirmative) (negative) inference (conclusion) that . . . is (is not) justified (supported) (warranted)

23. The (affirmative) (negative) conclusion (contention) that . . . is (not reasonable) (a mere assumption) (an unwarranted assumption) (not supported by the facts) (by the realities of)

24. The (affirmative) (negative) argument is (based) (predicated) upon mere assertion

25. This is not a matter for generalizing

26. Our (Their) reasoning (argument) here is based upon (the assumption that . . .) (fact) (authoritative views) (mere opinion)

27. We have given you facts to support

28. Can we (We cannot) afford to ignore (the facts which have been presented) (the realities of the present situation)

29. We admit (concede) that the (affirmative plan) (affirmative proposal) (negative counterplan) (status quo) is not perfect, but...

30. We agree, but we contend (maintain) (feel) (believe) (think) (are of the opinion) that...

Rhetorical Questions (repetition often effective)

1. But is there not a reasonable doubt that...?

2. Does this show (prove)..., as our affirmative (negative) friends claim,

3. But has this point been proved (substantiated?)

4. But have our friends (the affirmative) (the negative) once denied that...? (offered evidence to support...?) (proved to us...?) (shown us how...?) (introduced any evidence to lead us to believe that...?) (told us how) (when) (where)...?

5. Do not our friends (the affirmative) (the negative) realize that...?

6. Would our friends (the affirmative) (the negative) call this...?

7. But is it (not) true that...?

8. Are we therefore to conclude (assume) (believe) (advocate) (abolish) (reject) (get rid of) (act hastily)...?

Concluding the Case

1. (In summary, then...) (In a brief review) (To review briefly) (To sum up) (To summarize) (To reiterate briefly)

2. In a brief (summary) (recapitulation) (reiteration) of the (affirmative) (negative) points (case) (issues) (arguments) (main contentions)

3. In a brief review, we of the (affirmative) (negative) take this stand (find ourselves contending)

4. (Let me once again state) (Here again let me reiterate) the (affirmative) (negative) position (stand)

5. (For these reasons) (Therefore) on the basis of (logic and evidence) (empirical fact) (hard, cold realities) we conclude (feel) (believe) (say) (advocate) that

6. The affirmative plan (program) (policy) is needed (sound) (practicable) (desirable) (workable) (advantageous) (unwise) (dangerous) (ill-advised) (long overdue)

7. We feel (urge) (believe) that we (the United States) should (must) enact (adopt) (recognize) (pass) (bill) (program) (policy) (law)

8. We ask that you concur in accepting (rejecting) the affirmative resolution

9. We ask your acceptance (rejection) (concurrence)

10. We move for the acceptance (rejection) of the affirmative resolution

11. Therefore, we resolve (are resolved) that [state resolution affirmatively or negatively]

12. On this (these points) the affirmative (negative) stands (takes its stand)

5. SUMMARY

The foregoing terms will enable the debater (and in many instances the discussant) to make transitions easily from one argument to another, to clarify the relationship between main points and subpoints, to show the interrelationships between one debate speech and another, in sum, to tie up the many facets of a full-fledged debate into a coherent whole. A judge may easily become lost in a multitude of fragments; he appreciates and responds to a cohesive, unified presentation, and the foregoing terms are one means to that end.

In conclusion, the student is reminded of the other factors of effective expression briefly considered here: concreteness, conciseness, variety, clarity, euphony, simplicity, and emphasis. Unfortunately, there is no short cut to an effective prose style; skill in the use of language is the product of long training and constant practice. However, one can hasten the learning process by reading widely and frequently, by writing and speaking frequently under the guidance of an experienced teacher, and possibly by planning a systematic word study with the aid of a good dictionary.

EXERCISE

1. Analyze a debate speech or a speech on a controversial subject from the standpoint of the language used. Comment on the following factors:
   a. Simplicity and concreteness
   b. Conversational qualities
   c. Introductory, summarizing, and transitional terms
   d. Rhetorical devices: repetition, balance or parallelism, and legitimate rhetorical questions
   e. Specialized debate terms

CHAPTER 19

DELIVERY

> You will have carried over into your public delivery the most desirable qualities of conversational speaking when you fully realize the content of your words as you utter them.
>
> *Adapted from James A. Winans*

Although much may be written about delivery, we shall consider only those aspects particularly significant to the debater. More detailed information may be obtained from a textbook on speech.

1. CULTIVATING THE PROPER ATTITUDES

Attitudes are important for they influence behavior. Thus, how a debater behaves on and off the platform is determined in large part by his attitudes toward the subject debated, the opposition, and the judge.

Attitude toward Subject Debated

If academic debate is considered to be primarily an exercise in logical thinking, an application of the scientific method to social, political, economic, and cultural problems, an effective medium for seeking out the truth, the debater will realize that his primary task is to develop and to present the most logical case of which he is capable. His situation resembles the lawyer's, whose task it is to present the best possible case for his client. At times the student may find himself defending a position he doesn't personally believe in, and at times he may be required to uphold first one side of the question and then the other. There are critics of academic debate—one such critic was Theodore Roosevelt—who believe that debating both sides of a question, and thus presumably defending a position one doesn't believe in, is either unrealistic or insincere. However, such critics fail to realize that the objectives of academic debate are not the same as those of legislative or political debate. As indicated earlier, academic debate provides a laboratory for the student wherein he may learn such skills as thinking critically and logically, organizing counterarguments swiftly, and extemporizing persuasively. Stu-

274

dents do not go out for debate to promote their own personal beliefs. Most of them have no convictions one way or another about the subject. The subject is and should be considered merely a vehicle through which important skills may be learned. This view is in keeping with the long tradition of debate as an educational tool or process, with the Roman *declamatio* of Seneca and with the "syllogistic disputations" required of students in the universities of medieval Europe and in the colleges of Colonial America. That the subjects debated today deal with real national and international problems should not obscure the fact that they are primarily a medium for training the student. Since they deal with important problems, they may enhance the value of that training, but they are still used for training. Thus, in academic debate the question of sincerity or deep conviction is immaterial.

In legislative or political debate the situation is admittedly different. Here, one has presumably reached a conclusion after a long period of analysis and study and then attempts to win others over to his point of view. In other words, in this type of debate to convince others is the primary goal. In academic debate the student is first given the conclusion and is then expected to support it with logical arguments. His primary goal is not to convince but to construct and to present a more logical case than the opposition's. How well he accomplishes this should determine his success as an academic debater. The situation differs from that in real life, for academic debate is primarily an educational exercise with emphasis on training the mind, on developing logical thought processes. In debates before a public audience, however, where attitudes may be influenced, student debaters should not be made to advocate a position they don't personally believe in.

One further point should be made about alternately debating both sides of the same question. Not only is it better training for the academic debater, as most debaters themselves who have had the experience will attest, but it also inculcates a deep-seated attitude of tolerance toward differing points of view. To be forced to debate only one side leads to an ego-identification with that side, which is understandable since only that side has been analyzed and researched with a view to constructing a case for it. The other side in contrast is seen only as something to be discredited. Arguing as persuasively as one can for completely opposing views is one way of giving recognition to the idea that a strong case can generally be made for the views of earnest and intelligent men, however such views may clash with one's own. No sincere and intelligent person's opinion can be written off as being on its face absurd; it always deserves at least a hearing. Promoting this kind of tolerance is perhaps one of the greatest benefits debating both sides has to offer.

With these distinctions between academic and nonacademic debating in mind, the student's attitude toward his case should be clinical and objective; he should not let his personal feelings interfere with the task of constructing the most logical case possible.

Attitude toward Opposition

If, as we have said, academic debate is an intellectual contest, with the emphasis primarily on evidence and logical reasoning, then the opposition must be regarded as representing merely a different point of view, one which must be analyzed objectively and answered logically and dispassionately. The opposition must not be regarded as an enemy or as an obstacle to victory that must be overcome at any cost. They are merely a vehicle for presenting certain arguments which must be considered in the over-all search for truth; the members of the opposition are not to be regarded as personalities about to be engaged in personal combat. Moved by a strong desire to win at any cost, debaters frequently take the wrong attitude toward the opposition and become, as critics are quick to point out, overly intense or overly aggressive, sarcastic, bombastic, arrogant, hostile, overbearing, truculent, dogmatic, combative, unfriendly, and conceited. Such attitudes and such behavior succeed not in winning over the judge but in antagonizing him. There is no excuse for ungentlemanly conduct. Although academic debate is primarily training in argumentation and logic, like all educational processes it is also training in human values. A debater must be good natured and sportsmanlike, ready if necessary to compliment the opposition speakers. Good manners indicate a regard for the feelings of others, and a good debater always has good manners.

Attitude toward Judge

In line with the foregoing remarks, the judge should be regarded as an expert in argumentation, as a person to be won over by reason—by sound analysis, logical development, and good evidence—not by cajolery or by various appeals to emotion. Some debaters feel that they can win by "conning" or "snowing" the judge.[1] Such tactics, however, fail far more often than they succeed; usually they succeed only in alienating the judge.

2. SPEAKING AND PLATFORM MANNER

Voice, Movement, Eye Contact, Gestures, and Posture

Like good clothes, good speaking is unobtrusive; it does not call attention to itself; it is a means to an end, the end being to communicate

[1] "Con" is a slang term for "confidence." Used as a verb, it connotes "deceive" or "swindle." "Snow" is a slang term for "greatly impress," usually by fraudulent or irrelevant means.

ideas to and with people. In all speaking situations the ideas are of primary concern, delivery secondary. However, an effective delivery, though not an element of persuasion per se, contributes indirectly to persuasion by enhancing the clarity of the ideas communicated. A poor delivery, on the other hand, may make it difficult for the judge to grasp what is being communicated and thus to evaluate it properly.

The principles of effective delivery and platform manner are the same for the debate speech as for any other type. To begin with, the speaker should at all times be poised and gentlemanly. He should know his short-comings as a speaker and try to overcome them as much as possible and to adapt the speaking situation to them. As a rule, a friendly, sincere, conversational tone creates the best effect. Variations in pitch, force, and rate, combined with meaningful pauses, are desirable as an aid to clarity and emphasis. It must be remembered that there are important differ-ences between spoken and written discourse. In written discourse a reader is guided by punctuation, he may pause and go back over a difficult pas-sage, he may look up unfamiliar words in a dictionary, and he may mull over an idea for as long as he chooses. In spoken discourse, however, the listener can do none of these things. Therefore, a speaker must take special pains to make his meaning clear. By using his voice properly he can indicate fine distinctions between ideas, he can emphasize certain points. In other words, he can do what punctuation and syntax accom-plish in written discourse. Needless to say, if he is to use meaningful in-flections, meaningful pauses, and meaningful variations in rate and force, he must thoroughly understand and fully appreciate or feel the signif-icance of the ideas he is trying to convey. Incidentally, one doesn't al-ways have to shout to emphasize important points. Oftentimes a sup-pressed intensity—an actual lowering of volume—gets better results.

In approaching the platform, the speaker should be calm, erect, and purposeful in his movements. He should not begin speaking until he has his bearings. The best practice is to stand still momentarily, look around at the audience for a few moments so as to establish some contact with them, and then begin to speak.

When speaking, the speaker should look at his audience—see them and speak to them as individuals. He should resist looking out the window, at the ceiling or floor, or at his notes too often. By using good "eye contact," i.e., by looking into the eyes of first one member of the audience and then another and another, the speaker can gauge the effect of his remarks; he can determine whether or not he is being understood, which points are registering and which are not. If he detects signs of flagging interest or lack of comprehension, he should change the speaking mood at once— either by stepping up or stepping down the pace, raising his voice or lowering it, rephrasing the point or adding more supporting data, asking a rhetorical question or summarizing his previous remarks—in other words, by making some distinct change appropriate to the situation.

An effective debater controls his hands. He should resist the temptation to fiddle with his pencil, notes, or chalk; to stroke the lectern; rub his chin; take off and put on his glasses repeatedly; or twist his hair. Instead, he should use his hands meaningfully, in integrated uninhibited descriptive, suggestive, and emphatic gestures. Like voice inflections and changes in force, meaningful gestures—including meaningful facial expressions —are an aid to clarity and understanding, which in turn are an aid to persuasion. When not used in gesturing, the hands should hang naturally at the sides, the fingers slightly curled.

The speaker should stand on both feet, neither slouching nor leaning. He should stand comfortably and naturally, neither stiffly "at attention" nor at the "parade rest" position. His feet should be about six inches apart, one foot slightly in front of the other, with the weight of his body evenly distributed on both feet. All movements should be free and easy but meaningful and not random. The speaker should avoid aimless shifting, swaying, or tottering. When making a point he considers especially significant, he should take a step forward and indicate by his tone and gestures the importance of the point. Other meaningful movements are stepping back or walking to one side; such movements correspond to paragraphing in written discourse and prepare the audience for a shift of subject.

Before leaving the platform, the speaker should be sure to complete his final sentence. He should stand for a second or so after he has uttered the final word of his speech and should then walk off in a manner consistent with the mood of the speech. If time is called when one is in the middle of a sentence, one should complete the sentence, i.e., one may speak overtime for a few seconds but no more. Experienced debaters usually watch the time cards carefully and if for some reason they do not have time to give a long summary, they are always ready with a short one. One should never end a speech without some kind of a summary, regardless how short. Even short summaries, if carefully thought out beforehand, can be quite effective, like one which this writer once heard: "Three negative questions, three affirmative answers. We ask your concurrence."

Sitting at Table

When sitting at a table while someone else is speaking, a debater should try to conceal signs of nervousness or discomfort. Concentrating on the work at hand helps. One should not talk so loudly with his partner that he can be heard. One may pass notes or whisper occasionally to him but always as unobtrusively as possible. One should not grimace in response to certain remarks, but should maintain a calm, objective expression. One should sit naturally without slouching. One should not drum on the table with a pencil, clasp and unclasp his hands, or do anything that might distract the speaker or call attention to himself.

Using Notes

For notes, one should use either 3-inch by 5-inch or 4-inch by 6-inch note cards, preferably the latter for debate. One should not use large sheets of paper; they are unwieldly and too conspicuous. Occasionally, one may choose to read directly from a book or periodical, particularly when the opposition has used the same source or when the source is especially important. Since the use of notes in debate is practically mandatory, one should not try to hide the fact that he is using them. When quoting a piece of evidence—an opinion or some statistics—one should read directly from the card, looking up periodically to make contact with the audience. The point is, one should not talk to the notes but to the audience. Where practicable, one should number the cards; and, as each one is used, should place it upon the lectern or table or carefully on the bottom of the stack. One should not use note cards as a crutch, hanging onto them with both hands, and one should not play with them or juggle them. Such movements not only distract but also prevent one from using his hands in meaningful gestures.

Using Visual Aids

In using charts, diagrams, maps, drawings on the board, or other visual aids, one should stand aside and talk to the audience, not to the aids. As with notes, one should not use them as crutches or let them become hindrances instead of aids. One should not display an aid until it is time to use it. When finished with it, one should put it away; if it is a drawing on the board, one should erase it. When writing on the board, one should use large firm strokes; drawings should be ample and vigorous so that they may be readily seen and understood. This is also true of prepared charts. Above all, visual aids should be used to clarify a point, not to impress the judge or to befuddle the opposition. Generally, visual aids are used very little in debate.

3. PRONUNCIATION

This subject is important enough to merit special attention. Most debaters, like most people, are extremely careless about their pronunciation. Correct pronunciation requires real effort and concentration; one must expend energy to move the lip, chin, and tongue muscles so as to pronounce certain sounds properly. Characteristic faults of American pronunciation are slurring, swallowing parts of words, bumping syllables, failing to differentiate between certain sounds, and stressing the wrong syllable. Such faults are a barrier to understanding. If a debater is not to defeat his purpose at the outset, he should take pains to pronounce his words correctly. If his pronunciation tends to be poor, he should practice reading aloud, preferably in the presence of a speech teacher. As a start, debaters should pay particular attention to the following list of commonly mispronounced words:

actually - - - akshally
American - - - 'mer'can
and - - - an'
accuracy - - - acc'racy
agriculture - - - ag'iculture
approximately - - - approximadely
argument - - - argiment
appreciate - - - appriciate
athlete - - - athalete
arctic - - - ar'tic
attitude - - - atteetood, attitood
authority - - - authoridy
because - - - 'cuz, becuz, b'cuz
behind - - - behin'
can - - - kin
candidate - - - can'idate
catch - - - ketch
center - - - cen'er
company - - - comp'ny
column - - - coll'lum
couldn't - - - kou'n't
consists - - - consis'
decide - - - dee'cide
defy - - - dee'fy
definitely - - - definaly
designs - - - dee'signs
dictionary - - - diction'ry
disastrous - - - disasterous
didn't - - - dint
divide - - - dee'vide
different - - - dif'runt
dissolve - - - dee'zolve
defense - - - dee'fense
disease - - - dee'sease
do you - - - d'ya, d'y'

doing - - - doin'
doubt - - - doud
education - - - ejacation
engineer - - - ingineer
emphasize - - - imphasize
escape - - - excape
every - - - ev'y
eventually - - - evenchally,
                eevenchally
fact - - - fack
fifty - - - fi'ty
first - - - firs'
finance - - - fineance
film - - - fillum
fellow - - - fella
for - - - fer, f'
for instance - - - f'rinstance
forward - - - fo'ward
from - - - f'om
gets - - - gits
general - - - gen'ril
gesture - - - guesture
genuine - - - genuwine
gives - - - gi's
government - - - govament,
                gov'ment
grievous - - - grievious
going to - - - gonna
figures - - - figgers
figurative - - - figgerative, fig'rative
have to - - - hafta
here - - - ear
him - - - 'im
hindrance - - - hinderance
history - - - hist'ry

hundred – – – hunerd
hungry – – – hungary
idea – – – idee
immediately – – – immed'ately,
              immejately
important – – – impordan',
              import'tant
inquiry – – – in'quiry
integral – – – indegral
individual – – – indivijal,
              indeevidjal
into – – – intuh, in'a
irrelevant – – – irrevalent
just – – – jist, jus', jest, jes', jis'
laboratory – – – labatory
least – – – leas'
length – – – lengt'
lest – – – les'
library – – – lib'ary
literature – – – litachur
little – – – liddle, li'l
lot of – – – lotta
medicine – – – med'cine
maybe – – – mebbe
mental – – – men'al, menttil
mathematics – – – math'matics
mixture – – – mickshure
most – – – mos'
must – – – mus'
naturally – – – nacherly, nach'ly
new – – – noo
ninety – – – nine'y
nothing – – – nuthin'
numerous – – – noomerous
objects – – – objecks
of – – – a
officer – – – off'cer
often – – – offten
only – – – on'y
opening – – – op'ning
or – – – er
particularly – – – patikally
personally – – – person'ly

precedence – – – precedents
perhaps – – – p'raps
pamphlet – – – pamflit
picture – – – pitcher
performed – – – preformed
physical – – – phys'gal
practical – – – pragdigal
propaganda – – – propagan'a
professor – – – p'fessa
probably – – – prob'ly, proba'ly
preferably – – – prefer'bly
properties – – – prop'ties
pretty – – – purty, priddy
quantity – – – quan'idy
question – – – ques'ion
recently – – – recendly
recognize – – – recanize
regulation – – – regalation
resists – – – resis'
representative – – – represendadive
research – – – ree'search
running – – – runnin'
Saturday – – – Sattidy, Sattiday
second – – – secon'
sentence – – – sendence
separate – – – sep'rit
shouldn't – – – shunt
soldiers – – – sojers
sophomore – – – soph'more
something – – – somp'n
students – – – stoodents
structure – – – struckshure
statistics – – – stadisdigs
suggest – – – sujjest
supposed – – – s'posed
surprise – – – su'prise
terrible – – – turrible
toward – – – toeward
temperature – – – tempachur,
              temprachur,
              temperchur
the – – – da
this – – – dis

them – – – dem

twenty – – – twen'y

those – – – dose

these – – – dese

unfortunately – – – unforchunaly

united – – – unidad

used to – – – uster, usta

usually – – – us'ly, usaly

vacuum – – – vacum, vacyum

various – – – var'ous

was – – – wuz

want to – – – wanna

with – – – wit', wid

wouldn't – – – wunt

yesterday – – – yestiddy

yes – – – yeh, ya

you – – – ya

your – – – yer

4. A SUMMARY OF "DO'S" AND "DON'T'S"

The following "do's" and "don't's" cover points on delivery and platform manner for which debaters are frequently criticized:

1. Attack an argument, never a speaker.

2. Control your hands. Don't put them in and out of your pockets, on your hips, or behind your back; don't hold them clasped in front of you, and don't clench and unclench your fingers.

3. Stand up when you speak. Don't lean back against the blackboard or forward on the desk or podium.

4. Don't use the podium or speaker's stand as a crutch; stand in back of or slightly to one side of it; don't pull it toward you or curl one arm over it.

5. Control your bodily movements. Don't continually take off and put on your glasses or use them as a pointer. Don't clean or continually adjust them while speaking. Don't play with your tie, hoist your trousers, or keep buttoning and unbuttoning your coat. Don't fiddle with your watch chain, coins, or other objects on your person.

6. When speaking, make eye contact with your audience. Don't look abstractedly out of the window, at the ceiling or floor, or over the heads of those present. Don't talk to the opposition all the time, for to do so is to suggest a personal encounter; consider them as part of the audience.

7. Don't bounce or sway or constantly shift your weight. Don't pace up and down.

8. Don't speak too fast. Rapid fire delivery is an occupational hazard of academic debate. Normally, one's rate should vary between 125 and 150 words a minute. It is better to develop fewer points effectively than many points hurriedly. Rate of speaking, like pitch and force, should vary in accordance with the nature of the ideas being expressed. Go more slowly on difficult or complicated points.

9. Speak up. Use plenty of force, but don't shout.

10. The most effective speakers are animated. They seem to understand fully and to feel the significance of their ideas. Accordingly, they vary

their facial expressions, their gestures, their inflections, their force, and their rate of speaking. Don't be wooden or stiff in your movements, sluggish in your articulation, monotonous in your vocal range, or "deadpan" in your expression. Don't smile constantly, or frown, or look bored or supercilious.

Above all, be natural, friendly, and sincere in what you say and do and in how you say and do it.

EXERCISES

1. Suggestion to instructor: Get a tape recording of an actual debate and play excerpts from the speeches of the four speakers. After each excerpt have the students criticize the speaker on the basis of voice quality, pitch, force, rate, articulation, and pronunciation.

2. Suggestion to instructor: Have each student give a 4- to 6-minute speech on some phase of a debate topic (use the current national topic if practical) and have the rest of the class record anonymous written comments on the speaker's delivery. Give these to the speaker along with your own written comments. Later on consult with each student and suggest means of improving his delivery.

Suggestion to the student: Use the following check list in commenting on the delivery of your classmates:

1. *Attitude*
   Friendly
   Pleasant
   Impersonal
   Overfriendly
   Hostile
   Overbearing
   Indifferent
2. *Quality of voice*
   Pleasant
   Resonant
   Too high
   Too low
   Guttural
   Nasal
   Rasping
   Flat
3. *Pitch*
   Limited range
   Good range, meaningful inflections
   Monotone
   Inappropriate stress (failure to go up or down at the right time)

4. *Force (volume)*
   Adequate
   Meaningful variations
   Too loud
   Too soft
   Inappropriate stress
5. *Rate*
   Meaningful variations
   Too fast
   Too slow
   Meaningful pauses
   Inappropriate pauses
6. *Pronunciation and articulation*
   Clear, distinct
   Sluggish or lazy
   Slurring
   Word endings blurred or dropped
   Syllables dropped or bumped
   Improper accent
   (List words mispronounced)
7. *Posture*
   Natural, relaxed
   Too stiff, "at attention," or "parade rest"

Overrelaxed, slouching
Feet too far apart
Feet too close together
Leaning or resting on lectern, desk, or against blackboard

8. *Movement*
Meaningful (stepping forward or backward or to the side for emphasis or change of topic)
Random, meaningless
Insufficient or no movement

9. *Gestures of hands and arms*
Integrated
Poorly timed
Natural, easy
Inhibited or stiff
Varied
Stereotyped

Too few
Too many
Appropriate number
Meaningful
Random or meaningless

10. *Facial expressions*
Meaningfully varied
No expression ("deadpan")
Fixed expression
Nervous manifestations (unnatural smile, twitching, etc.)
Good eye contact
Spasmodic eye contact
Poor eye contact (looking at notes, ceiling, etc.)

11. *Miscellaneous*
Too many "uh's," "well's," "so's," and "and's."

THE CASE IN ACTION

PART FIVE

THE CASE IN ACTION

CHAPTER 20

A SAMPLE DEBATE

Be calm in arguing; for fierceness makes
Error a fault, and truth discourtesy.

Herbert

The following is an actual debate which occurred in 1955 on the national collegiate debate topic. Since the debate is analyzed in considerable detail in the next chapter, the names of the participants have been withheld so that any adverse comments made by the writer will not embarrass anyone. The decision has also been withheld to avoid influencing the reader while he studies the analysis. Editorial changes of phrasing have been kept to a minimum so that the reader may get an idea of how debaters actually express themselves during the heat of a debate.

"RESOLVED, THAT THE UNITED STATES SHOULD EXTEND DIPLOMATIC RECOGNITION TO THE COMMUNIST GOVERNMENT OF CHINA"

First Affirmative

Thank you very much, ... Needless to say, it's a very distinct pleasure for . . . and me to represent . . . in the . . . Tournament.

But now to the question itself, "Resolved, That the United States Should Extend Diplomatic Recognition to the Communist Government of China." My partner and I feel that the terms of this question are self-explanatory, with the possible exception of "extend," by which we mean "offer," and "diplomatic recognition," by which we mean the "acknowledgment of a new political regime and its right to represent the state of China in the family of nations." This would, of course, include the exchange of diplomatic agents with that government.

To clarify the issues of this debate, let us consider what any affirmative team must consider, namely, how can the best interests of the United States be served? What are the best interests of the United States? We feel—and I'm sure the negative agrees—that we, the United States, are seeking conditions that are conducive to the establishment and maintenance of a state of honorable peace in the world. This, it is clear, serves our own best interests.

The next question is: Does our present policy of nonrecognition of Communist China further this goal? Is it promoting the best interests of our country? We of the affirmative contend that it is not; and in support of this contention, we shall prove three major issues:

First, that our present policy weakens the position of the United States

Second, that only by recognizing Communist China can these evils be mitigated, and

Third, that recognizing Communist China will result in additional advantages to the United States

I shall discuss the first two issues, my colleague, Mr. . . . , the third.

Since the first two issues are so closely related, I should like to discuss them with you concurrently. In furtherance of these issues, namely, that our present policy weakens the United States and that only by recognizing Communist China can these evils be mitigated, I should like to consider the effects of our policy of nonrecognition in three spheres: the political, the military, and the ideological.

Now let us examine the political. We point out that nonrecognition is politically detrimental to the United States in two ways: First, it is a source of disagreement between us and our allies in Europe, and between us and the millions of Asia. In support of this contention, I quote from the *New York Times* of January 9 of this year [1955]: "In Asia the allies have sharp differences over how to deal with Peiping. The chief difference between American and British policy is this question of recognition, which produces a visible strain on our alliance. Britain recognizes and we do not. Other allies, such as Canada, Australia, and Japan, have indicated a desire to recognize this government and have refrained only because of strong political pressures exerted by the United States." On a visit to the United States last fall Mendes-France urged that we recognize this government.

Mr. Nehru, leader of India's millions and certainly a confirmed anti-Communist, has characterized American policy as "the *root cause* of all international troubles during the past four years." And Norman Palmer, writing in the January issue of *Current History,* had this to say: "American refusal to recognize the Communist government of China is regarded as shortsighted and even stupid, as a refusal to face the facts of life, and almost as an insult to the people of Asia."

And so we see there is a direct cause-and-effect relationship between nonrecognition and the evil we have cited; friction between us and Europe and friction between us and the millions in Asia.

Now the second political disadvantage of our present policy is that it weakens the United Nations. We call to your attention the present cumbersome and unsatisfactory methods which must be used to even contact this government of the world's most populous nation. The UN, dedicated to the peaceful settlement of international disputes, is weakened by our policy of nonrecognition. For since the United States wishes the UN to conform to its policy of nonrecognition, it has exerted tremendous pressure to achieve that goal. I call to your attention the fact that the United States has threatened to withdraw financial aid and even to withdraw membership from this body if Red China is given a seat. Once again, a direct relationship between our policy of nonrecognition and the weakening of the UN. For as John Foster Dulles himself said in 1950, and I quote: "If the Communist government in fact proves its ability to govern China without serious domestic resistance, then it too should be admitted to the UN. . . . If we want to have a world organization, then it should be representative of the world as it is." Unquote. And let us not forget that when the UN is weakened, so too is the United States.

The second sphere of disadvantage under the present policy is military. We of the affirmative contend that nonrecognition is detrimental to our avowed policy of coexistence. In support of this contention I quote from the *New York Times* of November 19, 1954: "There is profound doubt here that Southeast Asia can be salvaged or a real settlement in Korea achieved in the absence of improved relations between the United States and Communist China."

The *New York Times* of February 15 of this year [1955] points out that the UN Security Council has ceased its efforts to ease the tension in the Formosa Straits, and that traditional, secret, nation-to-nation diplomacy will now be tried. But, under the policy of nonrecognition, we are unable to negotiate with this government except through the UN. Now what does this mean? Since disputes between nations can be settled only by war or negotiation, and since our present policy makes negotiation unfeasible, war is the only alternative. Surely this conflicts with our avowed policy of coexistence. And finally, a UN commission currently meeting to consider world disarmament is unable even to consult this government which has vowed to raise and maintain the world's largest army. The military situation is deteriorating as a result of our present policy.

And how does this second area of disadvantage, that is, the military, result from nonrecognition? I point out that, although the United States and Communist China might still disagree on many points after we recognize them, direct and continuous negotiation is a better means of solving these disputes than sporadic indirect negotiation. For as C. P. Fitzgerald pointed out in *Pacific Affairs:* "One cannot really negotiate peace with an unrecognized government. The fact of negotiation implies recognition." Once again, a direct relationship: recognition—negotiation—the means to prevent war.

As for disarmament, we can't even begin to consider it with China excluded from the discussions and thus free to arm as she pleases. Again, the relationship is clear: the failure of the UN Disarmament Commission to make any progress in London—a fact admitted only this week by Harold Stassen—and nonrecognition of the government with the world's largest army.

The third sphere in which the present policy is disadvantageous is ideological. The peoples of China and Asia view the American position as a denial of the right of self-determination. The good will of the uncommitted peoples of the world—including Burma, Pakistan, Ceylon, India, and Indonesia, all of whom have recognized this government—is crucial in the ideological struggle. Under the status quo, the democracy which denies self-determination is merely a mask for traditional western imperialism. When we point out that it is communism to which we object, they answer that, since we recognize other Communist governments, our policy is anti-Asian or anti-yellow, for which the past record of the Western powers is certainly not too bright. In further support of this contention, I quote Hallett Abend, who said: "As a country, the United States certainly does not dare to stand forth as the champion of liberty and democracy against the tyranny of communism, and at the same time attempt to stand as the helper of the corrupt and detested Chiang Kai-shek regime in China which has been notably reactionary and predatory. Such a policy would not only repel the Chinese people but would earn us the cynical distrust of other hundreds of millions native to the Asian continent." End quote. Abend said this in 1950 and yet this is our present policy.

And what is the direct relationship between nonrecognition and this ideological evil of the status quo? In 1952, H. J. Van Mook, former Lieut. Governor General of Indonesia, said: "The Asiatic nations may come to resent a long-drawn nonrecognition by the West of the altered situation in China. In their opinion—and they may well be right—the change is the result of a popular upheaval. Continued support to a government which the people have rejected is but another instance of Western highhandedness." Once again, a direct relationship between the evils and nonrecognition.

Now what has the affirmative done? We have shown you that three related aspects of the status quo are weakening the United States. These aspects are evils because they weaken the United States. These evils result directly from our policy of nonrecognition. The elimination of these political, military, and ideological evils would mean three areas of advantage to the United States. We ask you to agree with us in eliminating the evil effects by eliminating their cause, namely, the present policy of nonrecognition. My colleague, Mr. . . . , will discuss additional advantages to the United States of a policy of recognition.

In closing, I would like to leave with you a thought conveyed to the House of Lords by Winston Churchill: "One has to recognize lots of things and people in this world of sin and woe that one does not like. The reason for having diplomatic relations is not to confer a compliment but to secure a convenience."

First Negative

Mr. Chairman, ladies and gentlemen, we of the negative do not believe the United States should extend diplomatic recognition to the Communist government of China. Before we present the various reasons why we think such action would be wrong, let us examine the affirmative case as it has so far been presented in the debate and let us see if they have proved what they said they were going to prove. You will find that basically the first affirmative contention has been that the effects of our policy are all wrong, first that it leads to disagreement with our allies. What allies? We don't know. They did not mention any of the allies, except possibly we consider they assumed Great Britain because Great Britain is the only European ally which is concerned with the problems in Asia. Let us see if Great Britain disagrees with our policy of nonrecognition. You will find from the House of Commons, July 4, 1954, Sir Winston Churchill pointing out that at this time it is not conceivable or it is not wise for the United States to recognize the Communist government of China. You will find him in the same House of Commons in the same month, only two days later, stating again that it is not wise at this time for the Communist government of China to be seated in the UN. We find, too, from an Associated Press dispatch, February 7 of this year [1955], Foreign Minister Mr. Anthony Eden—now Prime Minister—defended President Eisenhower's proposed defense of Formosa and the Pescadores. You will find from *Time* magazine in February 14 of this year that Anthony Eden recognized that, if the United States should get into a large-scale war with Communist China over Formosa, Great Britain would considerably and decidedly come in alongside the United States. So we see that the assumption that our allies are being split over the policy of nonrecognition certainly has not been proved by the affirmative.

To the second part they said that our policy is misunderstood in Asia and as a reason for showing that our policy is misunderstood we find a quotation from Nehru, who claims that American policy is the root cause of all international problems for the last four years. It wasn't Communist China who invaded North Korea; the invasion was the fault of the United States. It wasn't Communist China who intervened in Indochina—it was the United States. It wasn't Communist China who invaded Tibet. No, the reason for this invasion was the United States. It's not Communist China today who is causing tension in the Formosa Straits. No, the tension is the fault of the United States. This is the reasoning of the affirmative team.

But let us look at Asia. Let us see if Communist prestige is so high and United States prestige is so low. We find from Jim Lucas, foreign writer in the Scripps-Howard newspapers, December 13, 1954, that originally Communist Chinese were welcomed as fellow Asian nationalists; gradually smaller nations are awakening to the fact that Communist China is the new imperialist and that her expansionist ambitions apparently know no bounds. A growing awareness of the true nature of Chinese Communism is forcing the neutralists to reevaluate their position. We find from the *U.S. News & World Report*—this week's issue as a matter of fact—that Communist China at Bandung has no aid to offer to the Asians and is in fact regarded with suspicion and fear by the Asian nations within its range. We see that the Communist prestige is declining and we see that the American prestige is increasing in Asia. We find from *Newsweek*, February 14 of this year [1955], that now the prospect of stopping Communist expansion in Asia has improved. The Manila Pact was a step toward improving it. The reiteration of our determination to defend Formosa and the Pescadores was a second step. The understanding with which our allies in Asia accepted the Formosa resolution must be recorded in the plus column. It showed that our alliances and diplomacy in Asia were in good working order.

So as to the question of Asia, we deny the fact that United States prestige is definitely on the decline. We say that our prestige or policy is today slowly but surely being understood and that Communist policy is being seen for what it actually is.

The third affirmative contention has been that the UN is weakened. Obviously they wish that the UN should have to seat the Communist Chinese in that organization. They quoted John Foster Dulles in 1950 as saying Communist China should be there, but John Foster Dulles in 1954 and 1955 has more than one time stated, as for instance from *Newsweek* magazine of March 30 of this year: "It would be folly if the UN would seat the Communist Chinese at this time, especially at a time when the Communist Chinese waged war against the UN and violated the truce against the UN forty times." This is Dulles now—not five years ago.

We look at the other affirmative contentions. We find that our policy today is the complete opposite to coexistence. Coexistence is a two-way street. We're willing to coexist with Communist China, but, ladies and gentlemen, is Communist China willing to coexist with this country? Her insistent demands that this country is an imperialist and a warmongering nation certainly does not sound as if they want to coexist with the United States. The gentlemen have maintained that we cannot negotiate with Communist China unless we negotiate through the UN. And yet we find that that is false. We see that it frequently happens, from Green Hackworth's *Digest of International Law*, Department of State, Volume I, page 327—that it frequently happens that the establishment or maintenance of informal relations is important and most desirable with unrecognized governments. Such necessary intercourse may be maintained in a number of ways with unrecognized states and governments. The assertion that we can't negotiate with Communist China because we don't recognize her is completely false. The gentleman has said, "One can't negotiate peace without recognition." Why? Why can't we negotiate peace with the Communist Chinese without recognition? Is it because they are claiming we are not going to negotiate peace with you unless you recognize Communist China —unless you recognize it? Is it the political blackmail that Communist China is offering us? One, give us recognition and we'll give you peace. And yet they violated the peace agreement and the truce agreement in Korea forty times.

As to the ideologies in Asia, we have already proved that our position in Asia is slowly but surely being understood and that our present policy of non-recognition is reaping rewards.

Now, my colleague and I believe that there are many reasons why this country should not recognize the Communist government of China. Time will allow the presentation of only five. I shall prove the first three, my colleague shall prove the last two.

We contend, first, that recognition of Communist China would force the United States to sever its relations with the island of Formosa. Why? Simply because the island of Formosa belongs to the state of China. To prove this, we recall a statement that President Harry Truman sent to the Eighty-second Congress on January 5, 1950. He pointed out that according to the Cairo and Potsdam Declarations Formosa was supposed to be returned to the state of China immediately following World War II. And in keeping with these agreements Formosa was returned to the state of China. As a matter of fact, in December of 1945, it was returned to the state of China. The fact then is that we cannot recognize one country, cannot recognize two governments of the same country—you can't recognize the Communists as the government of China and continue to recognize the Nationalists as a government of China. That is impossible. So we contend that recognition of Communist China would force this country to sever its relations with the forces on the island of Formosa.

We contend, secondly, that this abandonment of the isle of Formosa would weaken the United States militarily in the Pacific and in Southeast Asia. I am sure that all of us in this room understand the position of this country, as Formosa is considered to be vital to the defense perimeter in Southeast Asia and in the Pacific, that Formosa in the hands of the Communists would pierce the island arc of defense that we have made there over the last five years.

We contend, thirdly, that recognition of Communist China would harm our relations in Asia, not improve them, simply because we will once more be retreating in the face of Communist bluff. We have said, "We're going to defend Formosa against Communist Chinese attack"; and now for us to abandon the island of Formosa, the effect on the Asians, I am sure, would be quite startling. But more important than that is the premise that for the past five years we have maintained that the United States will not recognize Communist China so long as Communist China violates international law and refuses to accept her international obligations. At this time Communist China is holding prisoners of war as spies—one of the grossest violations of international law you can find in the books. Would it be wise for this country, at this time especially, to recognize this government when they're continuing to violate international law? We consider then that our effect on the Asians would be to decrease our prestige in Asia.

Because the affirmative team has not been able to prove a split or even major disagreement between Great Britain, our strongest ally in Asia, and the United States; because they cannot contend that our policy is diminishing our prestige in Asia simply because we have been able to prove through late sources of evidence our prestige is increasing and Communist prestige is going down; because the UN would not be strengthened, with having the only aggressor in this organization; because of the fact that you can negotiate without recognition; because the ideology argument concerning Asia we have disproved; and because the negative contentions—three of them so far—have been proved, we contend that the United States should not recognize the Communist government of China.

Second Affirmative

Now let's move in to what has been said by our friends of the negative about the affirmative presentation so far in this debate. If you will recall, my colleague told you that the affirmative would present three major issues, two of which he would deal with: first, that the present policy is weakening the United States in three areas—political, military, and ideological; and second, that because these weaknesses were caused by nonrecognition, the evils of the present policy could be mitigated only by a policy of recognition. And he told you that I was going to deal with certain additional advantages, as I plan to do.

Before I discuss with you what our friends of the negative have said about the affirmative case, let me recall briefly to your minds what they have not said. As to the political disadvantage of the status quo, J . . . told you that it was a source of friction between the United States and its allies, and he mentioned England. And he also pointed out that other countries, such as France, Japan, Australia, and Canada, had indicated a desire to recognize this government. And our friends of the negative told us, they supposed England was the only ally we had reference to. Then J . . . went on to the military and he told you there were difficulties as to the ability to negotiate with these people; and he told you we were drifting closer toward war. And our friends didn't deny this, but they merely said we cannot coexist with these people because they do not want to coexist. And it seems to me, they leave us a rather grim alternative, war under negative proposal. But J . . . , as to the military, also told you that the UN Disarmament Commission cannot even consult the nation which has vowed to raise and maintain the world's largest army. This was entirely overlooked by our friends of the negative. And we can see that this is certainly a disadvantage of the status quo. And finally, as to the ideological evil of the status quo, our friend merely told us that our present policy is being understood in Asia, after J . . . pointed out four separate arguments: the denial of self-determination, the fact that this policy is anti-Asian and anti-yellow, traditional Western imperialism, and Asians' resentment of our support of Chiang as the government of China. So we see much of the affirmative case still untouched by the negative and still standing.

Now I would like to go back to deal with what our friends have said. They have said, what's all wrong? Our allies are not really against us—there's no basic split with Great Britain. And even if there are disagreements, they have very little to do with the policy of nonrecognition. But is this so? Allow me to quote from Britain's largest newspaper, the *Daily Mirror*, with a circulation of four million five hundred thousand. This ran an editorial: "America's present policy on China is wrong and perilous; and if America involves herself in a major war because of this policy, such a war would not command the sympathy of the British people. The present crisis is the direct result of an historical blunder. The blunder was America's refusal to recognize the Communist government of China." End quote.

And then our friends told us—when they didn't discuss the other nations—they told us, well, the Asians don't really feel this way. And I call to your attention that the Asians are in empirical disagreement with the United States because all but 12 per cent of the population of Asia has recognized the Communist government of China and invited a Chinese government to Bandung—which one? the Chinese Communist government. This is empirical disagreement. As the *Current History* of January, 1955, points out: "Thailand finds itself in a precarious position; as the only nation in Southeast Asia, excepting the new states of Vietnam, Laos, and Cambodia, which does not recognize Red China, Thailand occupies a rather lonely position." And so we see this disadvantage of the status quo stands.

We discussed with you the UN. And our friends told us, well, it won't help to have them in the UN because they have been a trouble maker. They pointed out that the Dulles quote from 1950 merely means that Mr. Dulles has changed his mind since then. Nevertheless, they did not deny that the UN is being weakened. For as Trygve Lie has said: "The conduct of certain governments both inside and outside the UN may be condemned from time to time by the organization; but the latter's influence, both for world peace and upon the conduct of governments in relation to the obligations and objectives of the Charter, would undoubtedly be greater if all such governments were in the organization." End quote. And so we can see, recognizing this government and bringing it in to the UN would strengthen not only the UN but the hope for peace.

As to negotiation, they tell us, we can negotiate under the status quo—look at Geneva, look at Panmunjom. I call to your attention, we didn't negotiate at Panmunjom—the UN did. I call to your attention that at Geneva Mr. Dulles was not even allowed to speak to Chou En-lai. I call to your attention that under the status quo U Nu, at the request of Chou En-lai, invited the United States to negotiate. Is this unwillingness on their part? No. Chou En-lai through U Nu invited us to negotiate over the tense situation in Formosa, and Mr. Dulles turned down negotiation because it would imply recognition to the Asians. Is this a satisfactory policy in view of the grim alternative our friends have offered us—war? We think not.

As to the ideological, they tell us that the Asians are understanding our policy a little better every day. Well, this doesn't just seem to hold true, for just today—the *New York Times* of today, Saturday, April 23—says, "The issue that links the Bandung powers psychologically is to a large degree the ugly one of color." It goes on to say, Communist propaganda emphasizes the fact that "the United States has assumed the mantle of colonialism and encourages racial discrimination." Unfortunately, this kind of propaganda has considerable success. "New nations seek recognition of their pride and self-respect." And so we can see this disadvantage of the status quo still standing.

Now before I go on to discuss with you additional advantages which would accrue from a policy of recognition, I should like to discuss with you the so-called disadvantages very briefly. The negative has told us that we would have to give up Formosa under a policy of recognition. We contend that this is just not the case. And we point out, as H. G. Woodhead did, Great Britain formally recognized the Communist regime in January, 1950, though Sir Winston Churchill had made it plain that his government does not advocate turning Formosa over to the Reds. The *Foreign Policy Bulletin* of January 15 of this year says, "Formosa never formed an essential part of the Chinese empire and was never under the control of the Republic." The affirmative point here, which I wish to make absolutely clear in your minds, is that under the status quo Formosa is indeed a tinder box; and it is only after a policy of recognition, when we can negotiate with this government over the status of Formosa, that there is to be hope for a constructive policy for the United States. And we have seen there is no need, no reason to believe that Formosa would have to be turned over to the Communist Chinese.

Our friends then told us another disadvantage would be that communism would spread in Asia, that recognition would represent a retreat from communism. Woodrow Wyatt had this to say about this objection: "Once China has been accorded all the trappings of nationhood and treated with as much consideration and respect as any reasonable person could demand, then the attitude of the rest of Asia will harden toward any hint of Chinese aggression." End quote. And so we can see, the second negative objection just does not hold true in the light of logical analysis.

And the third, that it would be a violation of international law, Mr. Dulles has told us there are two criteria: national self-interest and effective control. Who can deny that this government has effective control, and of course we are debating the question as to national self-interest. And we feel it would be in the national self-interest of the United States to recognize this government. So we see the disadvantages of the status quo stemming from nonrecognition standing, and we see the negative objections falling.

But let me consider with you now certain additional advantages which would accrue to the United States. Sir Alexander Grantham, Governor and Commander-in-Chief of Hong Kong, speaking to the Detroit Economic Club last October, pointed out three major areas of advantage which Britain has obtained from a policy of recognition. They are, first, the protection of British subjects in China. This advantage was seen last November when Communist China agreed to pay Britain over one million dollars in damages for an accidentally downed British airliner. When an American plane is shot down, thirteen prisoners are held incommunicado. The difference? Britain recognizes.

Second, the presence of a British chargé d'affaires in Peking. Of this advantage Grantham said: "This has paid off. He has been able to garner a great deal of useful information, and he has, as it were, had his finger on the pulse of what was going on in China."

A third advantage, the weakening of the present Sino-Soviet alliance. Let me make clear that we do not contend that a policy of recognition will, *ipso facto,* split China from Russia. We do contend that the present policy of nonrecognition intensifies the alliance and precludes our taking advantage of any disagreement which may exist between these governments. China's dependence on Russia is furthered by nonrecognition since she is without UN representation and without contact with our government except through Russia. But are there any friction points in this alliance on which we might capitalize after recognition? Authorities such as Harry Schwartz, Arthur Dean, and Sir Alexander Grantham have pointed out five soft spots or friction points in the alliance: one, strong nationalism in both countries; two, the Chinese view of "Asia for the Asiatics"; three, Russia's drive to industrialize limits the amount of economic aid she can give to China; four, Russian resentment of a potential rival on her border; and five, the question of who will lead world communism. We reiterate that nonrecognition intensifies this alliance; while recognition, making contact with the West available to China, would create conditions making it possible for us to take advantage of the friction points in this alliance.

And now, as I close out the affirmative constructive presentation, I would like to lay before you briefly our major contentions: the evils inherent in the status quo—political, military, and ideological—result directly from our present policy of nonrecognition. Logically, these evils can be mitigated only by eliminating their cause and adopting a policy of recognition. In addition to these three areas of advantage—political, military, and ideological—additional advantages which I have explained to you would accrue from recognition. For these compelling reasons we ask your concurrence. Thank you very much.

Second Negative

Mr. Chairman and friends, my colleague and I believe that the United States should not extend diplomatic recognition to the Communist government of

China. We believe this at the present time for many reasons, but this afternoon we are going to give for your consideration five reasons as to why we think we should not recognize Communist China.

Before we go into these reasons, however, let's examine the case which the members of the affirmative team have presented to us and see just how it stands up in this debate. First of all, they tell us that the present policy of the United States weakens the international position of the United States. They say this is true because of three reasons: it hurts us politically, it hurts us militarily, and it hurts us ideologically in Southeast Asia. Well, I'd like to point out to you one thing in this place in the debate. In the first place, the political and ideological views of Southeast Asia would be precisely the same; so we see, these can be handled under the same point.

Let's look at these views and see just how they stand up. The members of the opposition have told us that Great Britain has recognized Communist China; so the United States should do the same thing. We should follow their policy because they say that it's advantageous and that, because we do not recognize Communist China today, the United States, Great Britain, and all her other allies are differing widely on their policies. Well, let's examine this matter a bit closer. We find in a dispatch from Manila of November, 1954, the United States, Great Britain, and France have come to quick agreement on some problems in the Pacific. The support Great Britain and France gave the pacts of United States shows the uniform allied unity in this sphere of the world. The members of the opposition quoted us a British newspaper, which, I would like to point out to you, does not express the views of the British government. However, we find in an Associated Press dispatch from John Hightower, February 18, that Sir Anthony Eden has said, with British support the United States has established a firm line in the defense of Formosa. That's Eden speaking at the present time. We find, further, that he pointed out in January 28, 1955, that neither now nor in the future could there be any question of abandoning Formosa itself and the neighboring Pescadores. Whatever their significance in the island chain of America's defense, they would clearly have to be defended against Communist China by the United States and Great Britain. So we see, the divergencies in policy in Southeast Asia today clearly do not exist.

Let's turn to the other sphere which the members of the opposition have mentioned, that of Asia. They say that, because so many of the nations of Southeast Asia have recognized Communist China, then the United States should do so if she is going to be effective. Let's look at their ideological argument. What did they say? They said that the Asian people today fear Western imperialism, Western aggression. Let's look at the situation logically, ladies and gentlemen. Who invaded North Korea? Who is the imperialistic power in this area of the world? Who took Tibet? It's not the United States who is imperialistic at the present time—it's Communist China. We find that these nations which have recognized Communist China are today realizing that fact. As we find from the *New York Times* of January 26, despite the professed friendship between Indonesia and Communist China, at the same time the Indonesians are expressing more and more their fears of an expansionistic China. We find Prime Minister Nehru of India pointing out that his country is uneasy about Communist China's intentions in Southeast Asia. These are the very nations which the members of the opposition brought up. They mentioned the Afro-Asian Conference. What's happening at the Afro-Asian Conference? We find that Ceylon, one of the nations which recognize Communist China, points out that they do not go along with her policies in Southeast Asia, those of aggression and imperialism. This is Asian opinion speaking at the United States at the present time.

What would the members of the opposition have us do? Reverse a position that we've supported for five years? We said we will not withdraw in the eyes of communism again, we will not reverse our position. And so we see, for us to do so would be detrimental in this sphere of the world at the present time. We are pursuing the ideology that is advantageous for the United States at the present time.

The members of the opposition have said that our present position is anti-Asian. Obviously, we see that this is not the truth with our relations with Japan and other nations of Southeast Asia. We find also that they said there are basic differences between the United States and Communist China. Obviously, we see these same differences exist between Russia and China, and still we see the situation there. So we see the situation in Asia today is not as the members of the opposition would have you believe. But to the contrary, our policies are being understood in this area of the world.

And, secondly, the members of the opposition have said that our policy is disadvantageous in the military spheres of the world because we can't negotiate; and if we can't negotiate with the Communists, then we have no alternative but to go to war. The members of the opposition are assuming a very large thing. They are saying, if we extend diplomatic recognition, the Communists will negotiate with us. Recently, the UN urged Communist China to negotiate over the matter of Formosa. Even Russia herself asked them to negotiate. What was the answer? An abrupt refusal. This is the type of negotiation Communist China carries on at the present time.

Let's look at Korea. We negotiated there—the UN negotiated. What happened? They violated this truce some forty times. Is this the type of international organization—do they live up to their international obligations at the present time? We see obviously this does not follow. The members of the opposition certainly cannot say that if we extend recognition, we're going to avoid all possibilities of war at the present time.

Something else is very interesting, too. They said that we cannot negotiate unless we recognize them. My colleague has pointed out to you previously that in Hackworth's *Digest of International Law* the recognized and unrecognized nations certainly can negotiate. The members of the opposition further proved this by stating that direct negotiation is more emphatic than sporadic negotiation. We have had sporadic negotiation, you might say, in Korea, where they violated the truce, where they ignored international law, where they flagrantly violate their international obligations. We have negotiation at the present time if the need arises, and you certainly see the outcome at the present time.

So we see, the members of the opposition have failed in the debate thus far to present a real need for recognition. They have not proved that had these evils existed they could correct them under a policy of diplomatic recognition.

Let's look at the third point which they brought up in the debate. They said that there are three areas of advantage for the United States if we should recognize Communist China. And they are basing this theory on the British idea. Well, let's look at the situation. We find that the British recognized Communist China and for quite a while—for five years, to be exact—the Communists refused to exchange diplomats with them. And the members of the opposition have said, well, look, Great Britain had a plane shot down and got them to pay for it. The fact is that it didn't stop them from shooting down the plane. So we see that obviously this advantage does not follow.

Further, they told us that we were going to send an American chargé d'affaires to Communist China. Have they given us an indication that Communist China is willing to go along with this exchange—that they would allow an American diplomat there? You saw what happened to Great Britain. They, too, were eager to recognize Communist China, and Communist China completely ignored her for five years. That's the situation that Britain wound up in.

Now, as to their third advantage, they imply that at the present time we have no alternative but to force Communist China into the Moscow regime, that if we recognize Communist China, all at once they're going to turn around and lean toward the United States. I'd like to point out that Great Britain recognized Communist China and she's still in the sphere with the Russians at the present time. And further, from the *Department of State Bulletin* of April, 1954, we found that at the very outset the Mao regime declared that it was by choice in the Soviet camp, announcing that it would pursue a lean-to-one-side policy in foreign affairs, one of the greatest understatements of the ages. So we see that the affirmative contentions do not necessarily follow in the debate.

Now, let's look at the five disadvantages my colleague and I believe would accrue if we recognized the Communist government of China. First of all we would have to sever our relations with the island of Formosa. Secondly, we feel this would weaken our military protection in Southeast Asia. And third, we feel that it would weaken our relations with borderline nations. Now I'd like, at this point in the debate, to bring up our fourth point and to draw a very interesting analogy here. We believe that if we recognize Communist China the United States would have to reverse its position and vote for the admission of Communist China to the UN. Now the members of the opposition are advocating this. They said that it would be advantageous for Communist China to be seated in the UN. One thing they obviously don't realize: the state of China is today a permanent member of the UN. If we withdraw our recognition from the Nationalist government on the island of Formosa and extend it to the Communists, then we will have no alternative but to vote for the admission of Communist China to the UN, knocking Nationalist China out of the UN. And we, sir, obviously do not go along with the policy which the members of the opposition are supporting, to seat Communist China in the UN. We feel that it would be disadvantageous for several reasons to have Communist China in the UN. In the first place, it would allow the very power which aggressed against the UN to be seated among it as one of its members. Communist China is today the only nation which has been declared an aggressor by the UN. We certainly don't feel it would benefit this organization to have Communist China seated in it as one of its members. Secondly, the seating of Communist China in the UN would raise the prestige and power of that government in Asia more than any other single instrument. And thirdly, we feel it would actually be offering a reward for the aggression which Communist China has committed against the UN. We find from a *Foreign Policy Bulletin* of July 15, 1954: "UN membership is an obligation assumed willingly by states that proclaim they are willing to abide by the Charter." Communist China by acts of aggression not only in Korea has shown no sensitivity to the Charter of the UN. They have shown that they have no intentions of abiding by it at the present time. So we see that it would be detrimental to have Communist China seated in the UN. The members of the opposition feel that by recognition they could certainly seat China in the UN, that it would be to our advantage, and yet they have certainly pointed out no advantages at the present time.

Fifthly, we state that recognition would be against the stated foreign policy of the United States. It's more than a mere stated foreign policy. Since 1949 we've consistently recognized the Nationalists on the island of Formosa. We've recently completed a defense pact with them. To reverse ourselves in Southeast Asia would certainly be detrimental after Communist China has violated international law, refuses to uphold her international obligations. Certainly for us to reverse our position on our allies would be detrimental. For these reasons, my colleague and I believe that we should not extend recognition to the Communist government of China. Thank you.

First Negative Rebuttal

At this time, at the beginning of the rebuttals in the debate, I would like to examine both cases as presented by the affirmative and by the negative to see how they stand in this debate.

If you recall, one of the basic contentions of the negative team has been that to recognize the Communist Chinese would force this country to sever its relations with the island of Formosa. We pointed out to you that two past agreements said that the island should be returned to the state of China. We pointed out to you also that the island was returned to the state of China. And what did the gentlemen of the opposition say to this? They read from a couple of men who said that, no, the issue has not been decided. Well, hasn't it been decided? If Formosa were returned to the state of China in 1945, why wouldn't it still belong to the state of China? Simply because of the change of governments? Certainly not. But to top it all off, we quote and we find that in the mutual defense treaty which was signed by this government and the Nationalist government of China in January, it was pointed out that there is a provision in the pact which formally recognizes Formosa and the Pescadores as territories of the Republic of China. But even more important than that is that both the Communist government and the Nationalist government legally regard Formosa as Chinese territory. We find this in the *Legislative Reference Service* of April, 1955—the Chinese governments themselves recognize the fact that Formosa is part of the state of China. Can you make Formosa an independent state? Only if it has the tacit approval of both the Nationalist and Communist governments. And yet we find from Wellington Koo, the Nationalist ambassador to the United States, that under no circumstances will Nationalist China decide to be recognized as an independent state. We find from Mao Tse-tung, the Communist leader in China, in February of this year, that he has said that under no consideration at all will the Communists regard Formosa as an independent state. So we see that the island of Formosa is part of the state of China, from past agreements and from an agreement signed just three months ago. We find that to recognize the Communist government at this time would force this country to sever its relations with Formosa. We'd have to abandon the island, and it would weaken us militarily in Asia and in the Pacific. This is the contention of the negative and we feel it certainly has been proved.

Now upon examining the affirmative case, we find some very interesting things. They first argue that there is a split between Great Britain and the United States over recognition of Communist China. We have shown you, one, that Churchill, the Prime Minister—the late Prime Minister—did not feel that this was the time for the United States to recognize Communist China. We pointed out that Great Britain did not feel it was wise at this time to seat Communist China in the UN. We pointed out that the present Prime Minister, Sir Anthony Eden, stands with the United States on Formosa. And what did the affirmative do? They quoted a British newspaper to show the official stand of the British government. Certainly, this we deny as quite logical.

Now we examine the second contention of the affirmative case. It has been that our policies in Asia are wrong. We have been able to show you with evidence that Communist prestige is declining. They have not denied this. We have shown you that American prestige is increasing. And what did they say? All but 12 per cent have recognized Communist China. But does that mean anything? One of the countries which recognize Communist China is the very country called Ceylon. And yet we find from yesterday's *New York Review* that the Ceylon Premier, Sir John Kotawala, bitterly attacked the Communists as the new imperialists. We find that Pakistan is a country which recognized Communist China. And yet the day before, Mr. Aly of Pakistan again bitterly attacked the Communists as being the new aggressors. We find that Indonesia has recognized Communist China. And if you will recall, my colleague brought up to you and proved that the Indonesians are beginning to see that the Communist Chinese are the new imperialists. Does this look as if our policy is wrong? Does it look as if Communist China is marching through Asia with increasing prestige? Certainly not.

They say that the UN should seat the Communist Chinese and in the very same breath they say that the main purpose of the UN is to promote the peace. Just what signs, we ask you, have the Communist Chinese given to lead us to believe they want peace? Just where? Just why does it seem that the Communist Chinese want to promote peace?

The gentlemen have said, "Well, we've got to negotiate with Communist China." Let us examine a country which has recognized the Communist Chinese. Have they negotiated? Recognition does not mean negotiation by any manner of means. We find from *Newsweek* of April 4 of this year that perhaps even more important are the private accounts of efforts by India and the British to persuade Peking to accept some compromise course. Towards these approaches the Chinese Reds have adopted a policy of uncompromising belligerency. They have rejected all Indian attempts to mediate. Similar British representations have been met with what is described as "studied tactics of contempt and insult."

Because the affirmative case—the major contentions of the affirmative case have not been proved and because my colleague and I have proved our case, we contend that the United States should not recognize the Communist government of China. Thank you very much.

First Affirmative Rebuttal

As a rebuttal speaker I should like to consider with you the entire affirmative case and see just how it has stood up under the brunt of the negative attack. But before doing so, I should like to consider two of the disadvantages which our negative friends have presented in this debate.

I should like to consider them concurrently since they are so closely related. They told us that in Asia the United States would be retreating from the flow of communism and that we would therefore lose our prestige in Asia when we recognized this government. And they also told us by an analogy that the United States would have to admit Communist China to the UN and that Asians do not like this, and that our prestige would be even further lowered. I think the proper place to go for Asian opinion is to Asia itself. What do the Asians really think? Typical is this observation from the Pakistan *Civil and Military Gazette*, January 18, 1954: "Why is it that America whose sentimentality has a hard core of the starkest realism is still withholding recognition? Commitments to Chiang Kai-shek, the inadvisability of making the slightest concession to the enemy in the interbloc cold war, and other similar arguments of the antirecognitionists are pure sentimentality." End quote. And, further, I should like to quote John Layton Stuart, who was born and raised in China and spent fifty years of his life there—he wrote a book entitled *Fifty Years in China*—he had this to say: "Among those who have transferred recognition to Communist China are several of China's most influential neighbors. That is to say, a great many Asians opposed to communism do not appear to believe that refusal to recognize China is the best way to fight communism." And so we see, contrary to what our negative friends would have us believe, the Asian nations think that if they are to fight communism, we must recognize that government; and that the United States would not lose prestige in Asia but would, on the contrary, gain prestige in Asia, for the Asiatic nations want us to recognize this government.

With regard to the UN, again I quote from the *Civil and Military Gazette* of Pakistan, January 24, 1952: Dr. Mohammed Roehm, Indonesian Foreign Minister, urged that China be admitted to the UN because such membership would, quote, "entitle her not only to rights but also to certain essential obligations." End quote. And our negative friends have pointed repeatedly in this debate to the violations of international agreements by the Red Chinese —at Geneva and at Panmunjom, for example. But we point out that unless you recognize this government, unless you recognize them as a legal entity, unless you give them certain responsibilities in the UN, it is sort of ridiculous for the United States to brand them as an aggressor. For only when they are treated as equals, only when they are treated as a government which has responsibilities, only when we recognize this government, can we consider them as being responsible for their international acts—as was pointed out again in the Pakistan *Civil and Military Gazette.*

But let's get back to the political, military, and ideological evils of the status quo. You may recall that we pointed out that there is a good deal of disagreement between the United States and her allies in Europe, as well as in Asia. We mentioned Canada, Japan, Australia, and other nations which our negative friends have chosen not to deal with in this debate. However, they did choose to discuss Great Britain at some length, and they told us that, well, Anthony Eden has told us that they would join us in a fight over Formosa, but this does not belie the fact that they do disagree violently with our policy of nonrecognition. In furtherance of this contention, I quote from *Harper's Magazine,* February, 1955. Alistair Buchan, Washington correspondent of the *London Observer,* had this to say: "There is a basic difference in the attitude of Great Britain and the United States toward Communist China. Not the least disturbing event of 1954 was the almost complete breakdown of understanding and good will between the people of the governments of the two great English-speaking nations. In Britain the name 'Dulles' became something to frighten one's children with." End quote. From this we can see, then, that the split certainly does exist in Europe.

But with regard to Asia, our negative friends never denied that the split exists. They merely chose to combine our political and ideological arguments. I shall consider this point in a moment.

Now let's move to the military argument of the affirmative. We pointed out that our present policy is contrary to our avowed policy of coexistence. But our negative friends told us that we are assuming that the Chinese will negotiate with us. And they point to the UN and they say, we invited them to negotiate and they refused. But why did they refuse, gentlemen? It was because they were to appear before the UN as a defendant; and as Sir James Barrington, Burma's Ambassador to the United States, has told us, the only way you can negotiate successfully with this government is to recognize them as equals, to negotiate with them at the conference table as equals. The only way you can solve world problems is by treating this government as a government and as an equal. And so we can see that the military contention of the affirmative still stands in this debate.

With regard to disarmament, we have yet to hear anything from our negative friends.

And now with regard to the ideological. They told us that we are not misunderstood in Asia and they told us that we know we're not imperialistic—

it's merely Chinese Communist propaganda. They told us that we know we are not discriminating against the Asians because we recognize Japan and we have relations with India and so on. However, the fact is that the Asians regard our policy as imperialistic, the Asians think we are discriminating against the yellow race, the Asians think we are opposed to self-determination. Whether it is propaganda or not, whether it is the truth or not, is not a point in this debate. The point is, the only way we can erase these convictions which the Asians have about the United States is to recognize the Communist government of China.

And so we see that the political, military, and ideological contentions of the affirmative in this debate still stand. And we think, again, that we should recognize the Communist government of China. Thank you very much. It's been a fine debate.

Second Negative Rebuttal

We believe that we should not extend diplomatic recognition to the Communist government of China. In the words of the members of the opposition, only when you recognize Communist China can you hold her to international obligations, only when you recognize her. It's all right for her to violate international law today, it's all right for her to invade Korea today, it's all right for her to hold UN prisoners. If this were true, why should she want recognition, I ask you, when she can do anything possible under the sun and it's perfectly all right for her at the present time? We see that the members of the opposition are largely debating assumptions this afternoon. I would like to point out further that the member of the opposition in his last stand in the debate did not mention the first one of the disadvantages which we have pointed out would accrue from a policy of recognition. Before I reemphasize these disadvantages once again for you, though, let's look at the basic things which they're considering.

They say, first of all, that we have political, military, and ideological differences. Ideological and political differences are necessarily the same. If the Asians would disagree with us in one sphere, necessarily it would be in two. But is that the true situation? The members of the opposition have said all Asia is against our present policy and whom did they use as a source? Themselves. We pointed out in this debate today that though these nations have recognized Communist China, that is today no criterion for the United States to do the same thing. The members of the opposition have quoted John Layton Stuart. We find that he says further that "it would dishearten and demoralize those of the peoples of Asia who are resisting the Communist advance at the present time and others to doubt the reliability of United States support if we recognize Communist China. It would diminish the capacity and weaken the will of many nations to persevere in their present fight against Communist China." That's John Layton Stuart.

India's Nehru has stated at the present time, he's looking with a wary eye to Communist China's expansionistic policies. I pointed out, Indonesia, Ceylon —all the nations that have recognized Communist China in Southeast Asia— this is Asian opinion today; this is why the present policy of the United States is effective, because Asians today realize that it's Communist China that's the imperialistic nation in this area of the world and not the United States. So we see that the ideological argument and this political argument which the members of the opposition have presented does not stand.

And, secondly, they tell us there are splits with Great Britain, and yet Eden has stated that he is with the United States on the island of Formosa. We have the SEATO agreements in Southeast Asia. Do these look like splits? I ask you. Obviously, by a policy of recognition, which the members of the opposition are advocating, nothing could be accomplished.

Now let's look at their third point. They say that, first of all, if we recognize Communist China, all these goods will accrue. They are assuming another thing in this debate, that Communist China will return the negotiation with us, that they will send reciprocal ambassadors for our ambassadors that are sent to China—which is a complete assumption at the present time. We pointed out that we can negotiate if it's necessary. We negotiated in Korea. What happened? They violated this truce. That is the present situation of the Communists.

And the members of the opposition are saying that our present policy is leading to war, and either we negotiate, either we disarm, or we will certainly go to war if we don't recognize Communist China. But how have they proved to you that if we do recognize Communist China, they will prevent any war? They speak of disarming. I ask you, does Communist China look like a nation that is disarming today? Who aggressed? Who has been charged by the UN? Who violated these treaties? We see that until or at the time that Communist China lives up to some sense of international obligations, this is a complete assumption on the part of the members of the opposition.

Let's go into our case. We said that if we recognized Communist China we would have to sever our relations with Formosa. The last speaker at the platform said nothing. Since this is our last stand at the platform, I want to emphasize this point for you. In the past three months the United States recently completed the defense treaty with Formosa in which it was explicitly stated that Formosa and the mainland of China are of the same sovereignty. You cannot recognize two governments within one state as the government of that state. If we recognize the Communists, of necessity we will have to withdraw our recognition from the Nationalists. We have no alternative. Though it's a nice theory that you can make an independent state of Formosa, Chou and Chiang both say no. Though it's a nice theory that you can place her under a UN protectorate, it's impossible under the UN Charter today. Though the British might say it's a nice idea, it is not legally possible because Formosa is legally a part of China by our own defense treaty. You cannot split the two; they are inseparable; you cannot recognize two governments within one state.

Secondly, we pointed out that if we recognize the Communists, it will weaken our military protection in Southeast Asia. The joint chiefs of staff—all the major generals of the United States—have pointed out that Formosa is strategically important to the United States.

Thirdly, it will weaken our position if we reverse our present opinion in Southeast Asia. We have stated a stand. We've stuck by this stand since 1949. The Communists consistently call us paper tigers in Southeast Asia. If we back down again after we've said we were going to support our allies in the Nationalist government, if we break this treaty which we have, obviously it would be psychologically against the United States.

Fourthly, it would not be to the advantage of the UN to have this aggressor nation seated in that organization. How would recognition lead to her seating other than as a legal government?

Fifthly, it is against our stated policy which would be detrimental to the United States.

We've given you concrete reasons as to why we should not recognize Communist China. The needs which the members of the opposition have outlined in their debate do not exist at the present time. They are adequately handled under the present situation, and we find that recognition would not eliminate these problems. For these reasons my colleague and I believe that we should not extend diplomatic recognition to the Communist government of China. Thank you.

Second Affirmative Rebuttal

As final speaker in this debate, I'd like to say briefly, thank you, gentlemen, we owe a great deal to you and we're very grateful. But let's get on to what our friends of the negative have said. And I would like to consider with you the disadvantages which would accrue from a policy of recognition as proposed by the negative and then move on to show a positive constructive policy designed to accomplish certain ends, a policy of recognition.

Our friends have told us, first, that this policy would look bad to the Asians and that this would weaken the Asian will to resist communism. I pointed out that Woodrow Wyatt told us exactly the opposite would happen. But would we be like a paper tiger to the Asians after recognition? John Carter Vincent has said: "It is interesting to note that the Times report of the Dulles radio speech of March 8 of this year opened with the Secretary's statement that the United States is no paper tiger. He's right and Asians do not so regard us. One does not earn the title of paper tiger in the eyes of Asians or of others by withdrawing from an exposed position which no longer serves its original purpose." End quote.

But let me reason this out with you a little further. Our friends have told us that a policy of recognition will aid in the spread of communism. Our friends have told us the Asians want to resist the spread of communism. Then I ask you, why, if nonrecognition will check the spread of communism and recognition will aid its spread, have our friends of Asia recognized this Communist government? Obviously, they do not feel that it spreads communism in Asia.

Then our friends have gone on to tell us that there is another disadvantage —it is contrary to the present United States foreign policy. This seems to be begging the question because the present United States foreign policy is what we're debating today.

Then they tell us that we're going to have to give up Formosa. And I pointed out to you that there is no reason why we will have to give up Formosa. I didn't quote a couple of men. I quoted Winston Churchill, who was at the Cairo Conference and said it had become an international problem. I quoted the *Foreign Policy Bulletin.* I quoted the *New York Times.* And I call to your attention, by the admission of the negative, Britain will stand by us on the policy of Formosa and yet British recognition of Communist China has neither been repudiated by China nor has Britain found this policy—that is, a separate Formosa, a recognition of the mainland—to be incompatible with recognition. It is not we who are debating assumptions; it is the negative. We give you facts.

And, finally, our friends have told us that it would be a violation of international law—which would look bad to the Asians. I pointed out that Mr. Dulles has told us, there are only two criteria for recognition, national self-interest and effective control. This has not been touched again in the debate, and we see the objections—the purely negative objections just don't seem to stand.

But let's see how the affirmative has made out in this debate and what has been done to the affirmative case. We told you, there were disagreements in the world, between us and our allies. And we cited many nations. Of those many nations we cited in the Western world and our allies, our friends have yet to deal with other than Great Britain. But I point out to you the empirical fact that the United States policy is intrinsically different from the British policy. And Joan Robinson in the *London Economist*—the British economist —said to us: "If the United States pushes Great Britain too hard on this policy she will eventually have to choose between a dependent position within the Anglo-American alliance and an independent position outside of the Anglo-American alliance." This is a basic fissure in our alliance which is growing day by day as America pursues this policy.

As to the Asians, our friends have told us, oh, there really isn't any problem here because our prestige is rising in Asia. And they have tried to lump the political and the ideological together. But they are not the same because in the political sphere it is a policy disagreement; in the ideological, it is the contention of the Asians that this policy disagreement is based on discrimination, is based on colonialism. And we have seen by today's *New York Times* this problem still exists.

But is there disagreement between the United States and Asia? Our ambassador to India said—this is from yesterday's *Washington Star*—United States Ambassador to India George Allen said yesterday that "the major problems in United States–Indian relations were the recognition of Communist China, fear of the atom bomb, and United States military assistance to Pakistan. Ambassador Allen said that when he went to India he felt the question of recognition of Red China was merely a debating issue. He now finds that it is something much more fundamental than that." End quote. And so we can see, this disadvantage still exists.

Our friends have told us the UN would be weakened, but I pointed out to you that Trygve Lie felt the organization's influence for world peace would undoubtedly be greater. And our friends have not denied that we are at loggerheads with the Chinese Communists. They have left you with the alternative that this can be settled only by war. They have told us the Chinese Communists are unwilling to negotiate and will not negotiate and therefore the military disadvantage of the affirmative does not stand. But I quote from the

Geneva dispatch to the *New York Times,* May 28, of 1954. "A Communist Chinese spokesman at the Geneva Conference on Far Eastern Affairs stated yesterday that the best way for the United States to get release of Americans held in China would be through direct negotiations between Chinese and American officials." End quote. And I pointed out to you that Mr. Dulles turned down the invitation to negotiate under the status quo lest negotiation imply recognition. And so we can see that this disadvantage under the status quo still exists.

Our friends say, "Well, will they disarm if we recognize? How can recognition guarantee this?" The affirmative claimed—and we pointed out to you —that disarmament cannot even be considered at present. Certainly, there is some hope in a policy of something rather than a policy of nothing.

As to the ideological evil, I have shown you why it cannot be linked with the political. And we have seen that it has not been validly attacked just because it has been linked with the political; it still stands in this debate because of the Asian feeling concerning our policy, never denied by the negative.

As to the additional advantages, the protection of our nationals, they merely said, "Well, they shot down the plane." But I point out to you, the indemnity was over one million dollars. This is certainly a greater benefit than the United States is receiving under its present policy.

As to the pulse on China, they said, "Well, would China reciprocate?" As a matter of fact, is there any reason to believe that our chargé d'affaires could go to Peking? We think there is, and we point to the present policy of Great Britain and say, this has occurred.

As to the "Titoism" argument, they told us Britain's recognition hasn't broken her from Russia. But I pointed out to you, we never contended that the split would occur "all at once." In my constructive speech I indicated that nonrecognition was driving Russia and China into a closer alliance and that this was disadvantageous to the United States. I cited five friction points in this alliance upon which we might capitalize by a policy of recognition. Our friends of the negative did not deny the effect of the present policy nor did they deny that it is disadvantageous to us. They chose merely to assert that a split is unlikely and has not been brought about by British recognition. We of the affirmative feel that a positive policy designed to eliminate one of the causes of this alliance is better than the purely negative approach of our friends. And I believe that in conclusion I may use this issue to generalize on the entire debate this afternoon. We have cited evils inherent in the status quo. These evils have not been denied. Our friends have merely stated that recognition is not the solution. They have offered no solution, and yet it is obvious that such pressing problems demand a solution. We give you one: positive, constructive, peaceful recognition. The choice is yours.

EXERCISE

1. Which side do you think did the more effective debating? Why? Consider such factors as analysis, evidence, adaptation and strategy, reasoning, attack and defense, and expression.

CHAPTER 21

THE ANATOMY OF A DEBATE

Much might be said on both sides.
Addison

To bring to a focus many of the principles which have been discussed throughout this book, we shall now analyze issue by issue the debate which appears in the preceding pages. In this debate the following issues were involved:

"RESOLVED, THAT THE UNITED STATES SHOULD EXTEND DIPLOMATIC RECOGNITION TO THE COMMUNIST GOVERNMENT OF CHINA"

I. Is there a need for changing the status quo?
  A. Is nonrecognition politically detrimental to the United States?
    1. Is nonrecognition a source of friction between the United States and other nations?
      a. Is there serious disagreement between the United States and her allies?
      b. Is there serious disagreement between the United States and the governments of Asia?
    2. Does nonrecognition weaken the UN?
      Contrary: Would recognition be harmful to the UN?
  B. Is nonrecognition militarily detrimental to the United States?
    1. Is nonrecognition contrary to a policy of coexistence?
      a. Can the United States and Communist China effectively negotiate at present?
      b. Is nonrecognition an obstacle to disarmament?
  C. Is nonrecognition ideologically detrimental to the United States?
    1. Is the policy of nonrecognition misunderstood and resented by the people of Asia?
II. Would the affirmative plan meet the need?
  A. Would recognition be disadvantageous to the United States?
    1. Would recognition lead to the loss of Formosa and the weakening of United States defenses in the Pacific?

2. Would recognition lower United States prestige in Asia by being considered a "retreat from communism"?
B. Would recognition secure additional advantages for the United States?
   1. Would it result in better treatment of Americans by Communist China?
   2. Would it result in giving the United States more information on Communist Chinese affairs?
   3. Would it be an opening wedge in the Sino-Soviet alliance?

Issue I.A.1.a.

Is there serious disagreement between the United States and her Allies?

First Affirmative Constructive

Now let us examine the political [effects of nonrecognition]. We point out that nonrecognition is politically detrimental to the United States in two ways: first, it is a source of disagreement between us and our allies in Europe and between us and the millions of Asia. In support of this contention, I quote from the New York Times of January 9 of this year [1955]: "In Asia the allies have sharp differences over how to deal with Peiping. The chief difference between American and British policy *is* this question of recognition, which produces a visible strain on our alliance. Britain recognizes and we do not. Other allies, such as Canada, Australia, and Japan, have indicated a desire to recognize this government and have refrained from doing so only because of strong political pressures exerted by the United States." On a visit to the United States last fall Mendès-France urged that we recognize this government.

Comment. To avoid confusing the political with the ideological disadvantage later claimed by the affirmative, the speaker should not have used the phrase "the millions of Asia" but should have said instead "the governments of Asia."

First Negative Constructive

. . . You will find that, basically, the first affirmative contention has been that the effects of our policy are all wrong, first, because it leads to disagreement with our allies. What allies? We don't know. They did not mention any of the allies, except possibly we consider they assumed Great Britain because Great Britain is the only European ally which is concerned with the problems in Asia. Let us see if Great Britain disagrees with our policy of nonrecognition. You will find, from the House of Commons, July 4, 1954, Sir Winston Churchill, pointing out that at this time it is not conceivable or wise for the United States to recognize the Communist government of China. You will find him, in the same House of Commons, in the same month, only two days later, stating again that it is not wise at this time for the Communist government of China to be seated in the United Nations. We find, too, from an Associated Press dispatch, February 7 of this year [1955], Foreign Minister Anthony Eden—now Prime Minister—defended President Eisenhower's proposed defense of Formosa and the Pescadores. You will find, from *Time* magazine, in February 14 of this year, that Anthony Eden recognized that, if the United States should get into a large-scale war with Communist China over Formosa, Great Britain would considerably and decidedly come in alongside the United States. So we see that the assumption that our allies are being split over the policy of nonrecognition certainly has not been proved by the affirmative.

Comment. The speaker begins by misrepresenting the affirmative argument, asserting "we don't know" what allies the affirmative had reference to. "They did not mention any." The affirmative, however, mentioned five: Great Britain, Canada, Australia, Japan, and France. The misrepresentation continues with the statement, "We consider they assumed Great Britain." The affirmative not only mentioned Great Britain but pointed out that Great Britain was in empirical disagreement with the United States: Great Britain recognizes Communist China and the United States does not. Misrepresenting these affirmative points evades them. In effect, the negative attack to this point consists of questioning the clarity of, and the evidence for, the affirmative conclusion. The negative speaker might have asked for more evidence concerning the countries other than Great Britain, but he should not have ignored these countries.

The negative speaker then proceeds to deny the affirmative conclusion concerning Great Britain. His reasoning here is: there is no friction or disagreement between the United States and Great Britain because there is harmony or agreement between them. These two propositions, however, are not contradictory since there could simultaneously be some agreement *and* some disagreement. A more logical approach to this affirmative argument would be the indirect attack, that is, to question the significance of the affirmative conclusion: how serious can this disagreement be if there is so much harmony between the two nations? How serious are the consequences of this disagreement if Britain is willing to support the United States in a war against Communist China? Outright denial of the affirmative conclusion is much too rigid an approach, especially in view of the empirical disagreement between the two countries.

In passing, it is interesting to note the negative speaker's effective use of rhetoric as a means of emphasis, the repetition of the "you will find" construction. His use of the term "certainly," however, in the summarizing sentence is an attempt to persuade by the confident manner. In debate very few arguments are ever "certainly" proved or disproved; debating, as we have pointed out repeatedly, is concerned with probabilities, not certainties.

Second Affirmative Constructive

Before I discuss with you what our friends of the negative have said about the affirmative case, let me recall briefly to your minds what they have not said. As to the political disadvantage of the status quo, J . . . told you that it was a source of friction between the United States and her allies, and he mentioned England. And he also pointed out that other countries, such as France, Japan, Australia, and Canada, had indicated a desire to recognize this government. And our friends of the negative told us, they supposed England was the only ally we had reference to. . . . Now I would like to go back to deal with what our friends have said. They have said, what's all wrong? Our allies aren't really against us—there's no basic split with Great Britain. And even if there are disagreements, they have very little to do with the policy of nonrecognition. But is this so? Allow me to quote from Britain's largest newspaper, *The Daily Mirror*, with a circulation of four million five hundred thousand. This paper ran an editorial, quote: "America's present policy on China is wrong and perilous; and if America involves herself in a major war because of this policy, such a war would not command the sympathy of the British people. The present crisis is the direct result of an historical blunder. The blunder was America's refusal to recognize the Communist government of China." End quote.

Comment. The affirmative begins effectively by alluding to the negative's misrepresentation concerning the other allies and to the negative's failure to deal with this affirmative argument. He then supports his partner's conclusion regarding friction with Britain, quoting an editorial from Britain's largest newspaper. However, he does not consider the negative point that there is some harmony between the two countries. Actually, he could have accepted this conclusion and pointed out that "some harmony" is not incompatible with "some friction." He might have replied, further, that the empirical fact of disagreement was not denied (as it could not be) and that this fact further showed that "some agreement" does not prove that there is no disagreement. Where the previous speaker's errors were those of "commission," the errors here are those of "omission."

Second Negative Constructive

. . . The members of the opposition have told us that Great Britain has recognized Communist China; so the United States should do the same thing. We should follow their policy because they said that it's advantageous and that because we do not recognize Communist China today, the United States, Great Britain, and all her other allies are differing widely on their policies. Well, let's examine this matter a bit more closely. We find in a dispatch from Manila of November, 1954, the United States, Great Britain, and France have come to quick agreement on some problems in the Pacific. The support Great Britain and France gave the pacts of the United States shows the uniform allied unity in this sphere of the world. The members of the opposition quoted us a British newspaper, which, I would like to point out to you, does not express the views of the British government. However, we find in an Associated Press dispatch from John Hightower, February 18, that Sir Anthony Eden has said, with British support the United States has established a firm line in the defense of Formosa. That's Eden speaking at the present time. We find, further, that he pointed out in January 28, 1955, that neither now nor in the future could there be any question of abandoning Formosa itself and the neighboring Pescadores. Whatever their significance in the island chain of America's defense, they would clearly have to be defended against Communist China by the United States and Great Britain. So we see, the divergencies in policy in Southeast Asia today clearly do not exist.

Comment. The opening remark which represents the affirmative argument as being that the United States should recognize Communist China because Britain recognizes this government is misleading; for it suggests that the affirmative advanced only one reason for advocating such a course. This suggestion is thus an oversimplification. The negative then continues to deny the affirmative contention by showing agreement between the United States, Britain, and France "on some problems in the Pacific." "Some problems" is rather vague (it probably refers to problems in Indochina); at least one cannot tell whether these problems concern Communist China, the country at issue. Also, it is doubtful if the all-inclusive conclusion that the allies are in agreement on all problems in Asia ("the uniform allied unity in this sphere of the world") is warranted by the evidence that there is agreement on some problems.

The attack on one of the affirmative's sources, the British newspaper, is effective since, as the negative speaker correctly points out, there is no necessary connection between disapproval by a newspaper and disapproval by the government; disapproval by one does not prove disapproval by the other. In making his next point, concerning Britain's support of Formosa, however, the speaker makes the same type of error by suggesting that since there is no divergency in the British and United States policies concerning the defense of Formosa, there is no divergency in the British and United States policies concerning the recognition of Communist China. Again, proving one does not necessarily prove the other.

In passing, the repeated reference to the affirmative team as "the members of the opposition" should be avoided since this phrase does not suggest a very friendly attitude. By contrast, the affirmative refers to the negative as "our friends of the negative" and "our friends." Of course, being too friendly may give the impression of trying to persuade by the friendly manner. Using first names, for example, as the affirmative is inclined to do, is suspect for this reason. The most honest approach is to be pleasant but impersonal.

First Negative Rebuttal

Now upon examining the affirmative case, we find some very interesting things. They first argue that there is a split between Great Britain and the

United States over recognition of Communist China. We have shown you, one, that Churchill, the Prime Minister—the late Prime Minister—did not feel that this was the time for the United States to recognize Communist China. We pointed out that Great Britain did not feel it was wise at this time to seat Communist China in the UN. We pointed out that the present Prime Minister, Sir Anthony Eden, stands with the United States on Formosa. And what did the affirmative do? They quoted a British newspaper to show the official stand of the British government. Certainly, this we deny as quite logical.

Comment. Since the affirmative team has not yet had the opportunity to consider the points introduced by his partner, the speaker properly chooses to summarize the course of the issue to this point. However, he continues to ignore the affirmative point concerning "the other allies" and somewhat oversimplifies the affirmative's position regarding Great Britain: "What did the affirmative do? They quoted a British newspaper." This is not entirely accurate since the affirmative also pointed up the empirical disagreement between the two countries, a point not mentioned in the summary. The speaker might have mentioned it and attacked it as being insignificant. Emphasizing the weakness of the affirmative's evidence is effective, but the over-all summary does not accurately represent the affirmative's treatment of the whole issue.

First Affirmative Rebuttal

. . . You may recall that we pointed out that there is a good deal of disagreement between the United States and her allies in Europe, as well as in Asia. We mentioned Canada, Japan, Australia, and other nations which our negative friends have chosen not to deal with in this debate. However, they did choose to discuss Great Britain at some length, and they told us that, well, Anthony Eden has told us that they would join us in a fight over Formosa; but this does not belie the fact that they do disagree violently with our policy of nonrecognition. In furtherance of this contention, I quote from *Harper's Magazine,* February, 1955. Alistair Buchan, Washington correspondent of the *London Observer,* had this to say: "There is a basic difference in the attitude of Great Britain and the United States toward Communist China. Not the least disturbing event of 1954 was the almost complete breakdown of understanding and good will between the people of the governments of the two great English-speaking nations. In Britain the name 'Dulles' became something to frighten one's children with." End quote. From this we can see, then, that the split certainly does exist in Europe.

Comment. After alluding once more to the negative omissions—an effective procedure—the affirmative exposes the basic weakness of one negative argument by pointing out that agreement over Formosa does not necessarily prove agreement over nonrecognition, or, from the affirmative point of view, that it does not disprove disagreement over nonrecognition. In effect, the affirmative shows that this negative argument is not entirely relevant. The speaker then introduces further evidence to support his original point, that there is disagreement between Great Britain and the United States, but ignores the negative evidence of the Churchill quotations. The affirmative should have tried to weaken the effect of such quotations by pointing out that official pronouncements of this type are often made in the interest of diplomacy, that is to say, in the interest of presenting a "united front" to the rest of the world, particularly to the Communist bloc, and that the true situation is more likely to be reported by a newspaper or by a reliable journalist like Buchan. The use of "certainly" in the summarizing sentence should be avoided for reasons already given.

Second Negative Rebuttal

. . . they tell us there are splits with Great Britain, and yet Eden has stated that he is with the United States on the island of Formosa.

Comment. To the end the negative refuses to consider the "other nations." As to Britain, the speaker reasserts what Britain's stand on Formosa is but overlooks the attack on this argument by the preceding affirmative speaker.

One can only speculate as to why the negative did not accept the affirmative challenge concerning "the other nations." Possibly the negative did not consider these countries to be very important; they might have considered that since Great Britain was the most important United States ally, they could carry the whole issue by carrying a major portion of it. If this was their reasoning, they should have clarified their position at the outset. Another possibility is that they were not prepared to discuss these countries. Whatever the reason, their refusal to consider other United States allies without saying why was a noticeable omission (repeatedly pointed up by affirmative) and thus ineffective strategy.

Second Affirmative Rebuttal

. . . We told you, there were disagreements in the world, between us and our allies. And we cited many nations. Of those many nations we cited in the Western world and our allies, our friends have yet to deal with other than Great Britain. But I point out to you the empirical fact that the United States policy is intrinsically different from the British policy. And Joan Robinson, in the *London Economist*—the British economist—said to us: "If the United States pushes Great Britain too hard on this policy she will eventually have to choose between a dependent position within the Anglo-American alliance or an independent position outside of the Anglo-American alliance." This is a basic fissure in our alliance, which is growing day by day as America pursues this policy.

Comment. Again, the affirmative points out the negative failure to deal with the entire affirmative argument. Then in considering Great Britain, the country contested by the negative, the affirmative speaker reaffirms what is perhaps the strongest facet of this argument, a facet not directly contested by the negative, namely, the empirical disagreement between the United States and Great Britain. As a final thrust he introduces further support of the affirmative position by quoting a British economist. However, he should have tried also to undermine the effectiveness of the Churchill quotation in the manner previously suggested.

Summary of Issue

Both sides, as we have seen, were guilty of certain lapses, the affirmative in failing to deal directly with the Churchill quotation and the negative attack on the affirmative source of information; and the negative in failing to deal with the other countries mentioned by the affirmative, in tending to oversimplify the affirmative position, and in not considering the two facets of the affirmative argument regarding Great Britain, namely, the empirical disagreement between the two countries and the affirmative attack on the negative's "Formosa accord" argument.

Issue I.A.1.b.

Is there serious disagreement between the United States and the governments of Asia?

First Affirmative Constructive

Mr. Nehru, leader of India's millions and certainly a confirmed anti-Communist, has characterized American policy as "the *root cause* of all international troubles during the past four years." And Norman Palmer, writing in the January issue of *Current History*, had this to say: "American refusal to recognize the Communist government of China is regarded as short-sighted and even stupid, as a refusal to face the facts of life, and almost as an insult to the people of Asia." And so we see, there is a direct cause-and-effect relationship between nonrecognition and the evil we have cited: friction between us and Europe and friction between us and the millions in Asia.

Comment. To save time, perhaps, the affirmative in this first treatment of the issue concentrates on the most significant country of Southeast Asia, India, and then introduces a quotation to prove general disapprobation of United States policy by "the people of Asia." To avoid any subsequent misunderstanding, the speaker should have included another sentence to emphasize that the point concerning Nehru's sharp criticism of American policy is not whether or not that criticism is justified but that it exists.

First Negative Constructive

To the second part they said that our policy is misunderstood in Asia and as a reason for showing that our policy is misunderstood we find a quotation from Nehru, who claims that American policy is the root cause of all international problems for the last four years. . . It wasn't Communist China who invaded North Korea; the invasion was the fault of the United States. It wasn't Communist China who intervened in Indochina—it was the United States. It wasn't Communist China who invaded Tibet. No, the reason for this invasion was the United States. It's not Communist China today who is causing tension in the Formosa Straits. No, the tension is the fault of the United States. This is the reasoning of the affirmative team.

But let us look at Asia. Let us see if Communist prestige is so high and United States prestige is so low. We find from Jim Lucas, foreign writer in the Scripps-Howard newspapers, December 13, 1954, that originally Communist Chinese were welcomed as fellow Asian nationalists; gradually, smaller nations are awakening to the fact that Communist China is the new imperialist and that her expansionist ambitions apparently know no bounds. A growing awareness of the true nature of Chinese Communism is forcing the neutralists to reevaluate their position. We find from the *U.S. News and World Report* —this week's issue as a matter of fact—that Communist China at Bandung has no aid to offer to the Asians and is in fact regarded with suspicion and fear by the Asian nations within its range. We see that the Communist prestige is declining and we see that the American prestige is increasing in Asia. We find from *Newsweek*, February 14 of this year [1955], that now the prospect of stopping Communist expansion in Asia has improved. The Manila Pact was a step toward improving it. The reiteration of our determination to defend Formosa and the Pescadores was a second step. The understanding with which our allies in Asia accepted the Formosa resolution must be recorded in the plus column. It showed that our alliances and diplomacy were in good working order.

So as to the question of Asia, we deny the fact that United States prestige is definitely on the decline. We say that our prestige or policy is today slowly but surely being understood and that Communist policy is being seen for what it actually is.

Comment. The first portion of the negative argument is that friction in Asia is not due to United States policy but to Communist China's aggression. However, this is an answer to Nehru's belief concerning the "root cause" of international troubles. It is not an answer to the affirmative argument that Nehru regards United States policy as being wrong. Thus, the negative argument is a diversion. Because of the emphasis which the negative now places on this argument, it becomes a "straw man" argument. As such, it is developed with much emotional appeal, both through the use of rhetorical flourishes (the repetition of the ironical expression "It wasn't China; oh no, it was the United States.") and through the elaborate citation of Communist China's military operations. The concluding sentence of this particular argument—"This is the reasoning of the affirmative team"—misrepresents the affirmative point, for Nehru's reasoning was not the affirmative's reasoning. As previously pointed out

—and as the affirmative perhaps should have pointed out more emphatically at the outset—the quotation by Nehru was used to show how India felt about United States policy; the affirmative did not endorse Nehru's reasoning but cited it as a manifestation of the disagreement between the United States and India. The irrelevancy of the negative argument can be seen when it is juxtaposed with the affirmative:

Affirmative: There is friction between the United States and India as indicated by Nehru's sharp criticism of United States policy.

Negative: Communist China's aggression has been the source of friction in Asia.

The second portion of the negative argument, comparing Communist Chinese and United States prestige in Asia, is relevant only if one accepts the underlying assumption that if United States prestige is high and Communist Chinese prestige low, there cannot be any significant friction between the United States and other Asian nations over the United States policy of nonrecognition. If this was the negative's assumption, as it probably was, the negative should have stated it and attempted to support it since it is not a self-evident truth; United States prestige might be high and there still might be friction over the policy of nonrecognition. Also, it should be noted that the speaker is not very clear as to whether he is denying the affirmative's conclusion, saying, in effect, "There is no friction," or whether he is saying, "Yes, there is some friction but it is insignificant." The latter approach would be more reasonable in this case. To avoid confusion and to guard against the pitfall of ground-shifting, the speaker should have been more explicit.

As for the speaker's conclusion that American prestige is high, it does not seem to be warranted by the proof offered. The weakness of the argument appears when it is stripped to its essentials:

American prestige is high, for
    1. There is a good prospect of stopping Communism in Asia, and
    2. United States policies are slowly but surely being understood, for
       a. The Asians accepted the United States resolution to defend Formosa

The first reason, though backed by evidence, does not appear to be relevant; and the second reason, that United States policies are slowly but surely being understood, dubiously supported by the assertion concerning the Formosa resolution, does not necessarily prove that United States prestige is high. United States prestige could still be low even though United States policies were gradually being understood. Finally, the point that Communist China's prestige is low is also irrelevant—another straw-man argument—for it does not contradict the proposition that America's prestige is low; the prestige of both countries could be low.

Second Affirmative Constructive

And then our friends told us—when they didn't discuss the other nations —they told us, well, the Asians don't really feel this way. And I call to your attention that the Asians are in empirical disagreement with the United States because all but 12 per cent of the population of Asia *has* recognized the Communist government of China and invited a Chinese government to Bandung— which one? the Chinese Communist government. This is empirical disagreement. As the *Current History* of January, 1955, points out: "Thailand finds itself in a precarious position; as the only nation in Southeast Asia, excepting the new states of Vietnam, Laos, and Cambodia, which does not recognize Red China, Thailand occupies a rather lonely position." And so we see, this disadvantage of the status quo stands.

Comment. Here the speaker cites empirical evidence that there is disagreement between the policy of the United States and the policies of most Southeast Asian nations with regard to recognition. Although such evidence cannot be denied, the negative's implication has been that this disagreement is not very significant since it has not produced friction. Disagreement per se over a given policy does not necessarily mean that there is friction. The speaker, however, does not meet this negative attack. Also, by disregarding the previous speaker's arguments, he passes up the opportunities available to him for exposing the various diversions and irrelevancies introduced in the previous speech.

Second Negative Constructive

Let's turn to the other sphere which the members of the opposition have mentioned, that of Asia. They say that, because so many of the nations of Southeast Asia have recognized Communist China, then the United States should do so if she is going to be effective. Let's look at their ideological argument. What did they say? They said that the Asian people today fear Western imperialism, Western aggression. Let's look at the situation logically, ladies and gentlemen. Who invaded North Korea? Who is the imperialistic power in this area of the world? Who took Tibet? It's not the United States who is imperialistic at the present time—it's Communist China. We find that these very nations which have recognized Communist China are today realizing that fact. As we find from the *New York Times* of January 26, despite the professed friendship between Indonesia and Communist China, at the same time the Indonesians are expressing more and more their fears of an expansionistic China. We find Prime Minister Nehru of India pointing out that his country is uneasy about Communist China's intentions in Southeast Asia. These are the nations which the members of the opposition brought up. They mentioned the Afro-Asian Conference. What's happening at the Afro-Asian Conference? We find that Ceylon, one of the nations which recognizes Communist China, points out that they do not go along with her policies in Southeast Asia, those of aggression and imperialism. This is Asian opinion speaking at the United States at the present time.

Comment. To be accurate, the speaker should have qualified his opening comment concerning the affirmative's reasons for recognizing Communist China by indicating that the difference between United States policy and that of many Asian nations was one of the main reasons, and not the only reason, as he suggests. (His designation of this affirmative argument as "their ideological argument" had been preceded by the assertion that the negative considered the political and ideological arguments of the affirmative as one and the same, a point which we shall discuss shortly.) Then, instead of considering the issue in question, whether or not there is a serious disagreement between the United States and the Asian nations over nonrecognition, the speaker takes up another point brought up by the affirmative, namely, that Asians fear Western imperialism.

To disprove this point he argues that China is the aggressor in this area of the world (and, by implication, should be feared). In effect, he does the same thing that his partner did earlier, setting up a "straw man" argument containing much emotional appeal. The argument is irrelevant; for, even if many Asian nations do fear Chinese imperialism, this conclusion does not contradict the conclusion that they fear American imperialism; they could fear both. As for the argument at issue—that many Asian nations differ widely with the United States on their policy concerning Communist China—the negative argument here is a diversion.

The phrase "They mentioned the Afro-Asian Conference" suggests that the affirmative first mentioned this Conference and that the speaker is now "turning the tables," always an effective procedure. The negative team first mentioned this Conference, however, and it was the affirmative which had turned the tables. Such misrepresentation, usually unintentional in the heat of a debate, should be avoided because it only alienates an alert judge.

First Negative Rebuttal

Now we examine the second contention of the affirmative case. It has been that our policies in Asia are wrong. We have been able to show you with evidence that Communist prestige is declining. They have not denied this. We have shown you that American prestige is increasing. And what did they say? All but 12 per cent have recognized Communist China. But does that mean anything? One of the countries which recognize Communist China is the very country called Ceylon. And yet we find from yesterday's *New York Review* that the Ceylon Premier, Sir John Kotawala, bitterly attacked the Communists as the new imperialists. We find that Pakistan is a country which recognized Communist China. And yet the day before, Mr. Aly of Pakistan again bitterly attacked the Communists as being the new aggressors. We find that Indonesia has recognized Communist China. And if you will recall, my colleague brought up to you and proved that the Indonesians are beginning to see that the Communist Chinese are the new imperialists. Does this look as if our policy is wrong? Does it look as if Communist China is marching through Asia with increasing prestige? Certainly not.

Comment. In summarizing the issue in question, the speaker points out that the affirmative has not denied the negative contention that Communist prestige is declining. The relevancy of this negative contention, however, is still doubtful; for, as previously explained, both United States and Communist prestige could be declining, a point which the affirmative team should have made but did not. The statement "We have shown you that American prestige is increasing" represents a shift in emphasis from the original negative point that American prestige is high; American prestige could be increasing and still not be high. The speaker then questions the significance of the fact that all but 12 per cent of the Asian nations have recognized China, pointing out that some of these nations— Ceylon, Pakistan, and Indonesia—are still highly critical of China. This is an effective parry, but still the relationship between the propositions that United States policy is therefore not wrong and that China's prestige is diminishing needs to be clarified. The evidence might indicate that United States policy is not helping China at the expense of the United States, a conclusion which, for effectiveness, might have been made explicit. The implication, however, that China's prestige is diminishing *because* of United States refusal to recognize her is not supported by, but is actually inconsistent with, the negative evidence that China's prestige is diminishing because of her expansionist policies.

At no time does the negative show any clear connection between United States policy and the diminishing prestige of Communist China, a connection which the negative should have tried to establish. Merely proving that Chinese prestige is diminishing does not disprove the affirmative contention that there is friction between the United States and many Asian nations over nonrecognition.

A more effective approach by the negative would have been: There may be some disagreement, but how significant is it? It has not caused any Asian nations to side with Communist China against the United States. (At this point, if it could be shown that United States policy has actually emboldened certain Asian nations to take a firmer stand against China, the attack would be appreciably stronger.) Many Asian nations are still far more critical of China than of the United States. What are the harmful consequences of this disagreement? Even good friends have occasional disagreements. Has United States policy led to any breakdown in the relations between United States and any Asian nations? Has it hurt the United States militarily in Asia—politically? Are any Asian nations leaning more than they were towards Communism because of United States policy?

This type of attack would put a burden on the affirmative to show a causal relationship between disagreement and some significant evil. On the other hand, the actual negative argument appears only vaguely related to the affirmative contention; a judge has to fill in too many gaps to grasp the significance of the former or to see the relationship between the affirmative point and the negative answer to it.

First Affirmative Rebuttal

But with regard to Asia, our negative friends never denied that the split exists. They merely chose to combine our political and ideological arguments. I shall consider this point in a moment.

Comment. Although it is true that the negative team did not deny that "the split exists," it did try to show that the United States isn't being hurt by the disagreement, that her prestige in Asia is high or rising, and that Communist Chinese prestige is low. The speaker should have dealt with this negative line of attack, pointing up the failure of the negative team to show a clear relationship between its argument and the affirmative point.

Since the second negative speaker considered the affirmative's political and ideological arguments together, the speaker here, to preserve the original order of the affirmative case, considers the "Western imperialism" argument later in his speech. Originally, the affirmative introduced the latter argument under what it termed the ideological disadvantage of the status quo.

Second Negative Rebuttal

... Ideological and political differences are necessarily the same. If the Asians would disagree with us in one sphere, necessarily it would be in two. But is that the true situation? The members of the opposition have said all Asia is against our present policy and whom did they use as a source? Themselves. We pointed out in this debate today that though these nations have recognized Communist China, that is today no criterion for the United States to do the same thing. ... India's Nehru has stated at the present time, he's looking with a wary eye to Communist China's expansionistic policies. I pointed out, Indonesia, Ceylon—all the nations that have recognized Communist China in Southeast Asia—this is Asian opinion today; this is why the present policy of the United States is effective, because Asians today realize that it's Communist China that's the imperialistic nation in this area of the world and not the United States. So we see that the ideological argument and this political argument which the members of the opposition have presented does not stand. ... We have the SEATO agreements in Southeast Asia. Do these look like splits? I ask you. Obviously, by a policy of recognition, which the members of the opposition are advocating, nothing could be accomplished.

Comment. Relating several opposition arguments and treating them as one is often necessary and effective. In this instance, however, the two affirmative arguments, though related, were different and for the sake of clarity should have been treated separately, as are subpoints under the same general heading. The affirmative might have forestalled the confusion by emphasizing in its very first speech the distinction between the two arguments which were:

1. There are serious political differences between the government of the United States and certain governments of Southeast Asia over the policy of nonrecognition.

2. The people of Asia resent the United States policy of nonrecognition as being imperialistic and anti-yellow.

The distinction between these two arguments might have been emphasized thus: "On the one hand, we are speaking of governments and on the other, of people; the one concerns official governmental policy, the other, the thoughts and feelings of the people."

The speaker's initial suggestion that integrating the two affirmative arguments is in itself an attack upon them is misleading, for integrating only saves time or promotes clarity. The speaker then misrepresents the affirmative argument in several ways: "all Asia" is a questionable extension of the affirmative argument, and there is a distinction, though subtle, between the speaker's phrase "against our policy" and the affirmative phrase "disagree with us on our policy." The statement that the affirmative used themselves as sources is equivalent to saying that they gave no proof, that their arguments were assertions. In the heat of battle a debater is sometimes tempted to say, "They haven't offered a shred of evidence." As previously pointed out, extreme statements of this type should be avoided because they are usually untrue, as in this case, and smack of poor sportsmanship. The use of extreme language and persistent misrepresentations only succeeds in creating the impression that one is contentious and unfriendly and desires to win at any cost. Such attitudes and impressions should be studiously avoided, and they can be if one uses a moderate, conciliatory, and friendly approach.

The statement that recognition by other Asian nations is no criterion for United States recognition of China tends to oversimplify the affirmative position since it suggests that this criterion has been the sole or key affirmative criterion for recognition. However, the affirmative criterion, as stated in the introductory remarks of the first affirmative constructive speech, was the establishment and maintenance of a state of honorable peace in the world, to be achieved by strengthening the position of the United States with her allies and with the Asian nations, by strengthening the UN, etc. That is, all of the affirmative's main arguments must be taken as the affirmative's criteria, or reasons, for recognition.

The argument that the Asian nations which have recognized—the speaker says "all," an unwarranted extension since he deals with only three—are opposed to Chinese imperialism does not prove, as previously pointed out, that they are opposed to recognition. Opposition to the one policy does not necessarily entail opposition to the other; these nations may simultaneously oppose both Chinese and American policies. If opposition to Chinese policies does in some way show approval of America's policy of nonrecognition, the speaker should have tried to establish this connection rather than hint at it, especially in the face of empirical evidence to the contrary.

The point of "the SEATO agreements," though proving "some agreement," is not incompatible with the affirmative stand that there is "some disagreement." The real issue is, how significant is the disagreement? This should have been clarified and dealt with more directly by both teams. In passing, it is noted that such terms as "obviously" and "nothing" are out of place and rarely justified in debate.

Second Affirmative Rebuttal

But is there disagreement between the United States and Asia? Our Ambassador to India said—this is from yesterday's *Washington Star*—United States Ambassador to India George Allen said yesterday that "the major problems in United States–Indian relations were the recognition of Communist China, fear of the atom bomb, and United States military assistance to Pakistan. Ambassador Allen said that when he went to India, he felt the question of recognition of Red China was merely a debating issue. He now finds that it is something much more fundamental than that." End quote. And so we can see, this disadvantage still exists.

Comment. For the sake of organization, the speaker's comments concerning the preceding speaker's integration of the political and ideological arguments have been put under issue I, *C*, the ideological issue. In this argument, which follows these comments, the speaker returns to the affirmative's original point, that there is disagreement between the government of the United States and the governments of Asia, and resupports the example of India. Since this is a rebuttal speech in which many arguments must be crystallized, the speaker cannot be too detailed. However, he should have pointed up the basic weakness of the negative attack (as revealed here) and dealt directly with the implication that disagreement has not led to significantly harmful consequences for the United States. Doing these things would have been much more effective than quoting a piece of evidence.

Summary of Issue

In general, the treatment of this issue by both sides parallels that of the preceding issue, the affirmative being guilty predominantly of errors of omission and the negative, of commission. Specifically, the affirmative should have dealt more directly with the negative attack, pointing up such negative shortcomings as misrepresentation, ground-shifting, extension, and emotional appeals; and it should have dealt more directly with the negative implication that disagreement per se is not significant. The negative, on the other hand, should have been more flexible and more moderate in its approach; it should have tried to clarify the relationship between its line of argument and the affirmative's, and it should not have distorted or oversimplified the affirmative position.

Issue 1.A.2.

Does nonrecognition weaken the United Nations?
Contrary: Would recognition be harmful to the United Nations?

First Affirmative Constructive

Now the second political disadvantage of our present policy is that it weakens the United Nations. We call to your attention the present cumbersome and unsatisfactory methods which must be used to even contact this government of the world's most populous nation. The UN, dedicated to the peaceful settlement of international disputes, is weakened by our policy of nonrecognition. For, since the United States wishes the UN to conform to its policy of nonrecognition, it has exerted tremendous pressure to achieve that goal. I call to your attention the fact that the United States has threatened to withdraw financial aid and even to withdraw membership from this body if Red China is given a seat. Once again, a direct relationship between our policy of nonrecognition and the weakening of the UN. As John Foster Dulles himself said in 1950, and I quote: "If the Communist government in fact proves its ability to govern China without serious domestic resistance, then it too should be admitted to the UN. . . . If we want to have a world organization, then it should be representative of the world as it is." Unquote. And let us not forget that when the UN is weakened, so too is the United States.

Comment. Basically, the argument boils down to this: the UN is weakened, first, because China, being unable to enter into its deliberations, cannot be influenced by such deliberations, whose major aim is peace; and, second, the United States, in order to keep China out of the UN, has brought various pressures to bear on the UN, such pressures presumably weakening the independence of the UN. In effect, nonrecognition undermines the influence and prestige of the UN. The Dulles quotation supports the principle that any world organization, to be effective, must have as members all of the world's leading nations. In presenting his points, the speaker should have specified the name, source, and date of the evidence concerning United States pressure on the UN. To be completely effective, evidence must always be clearly identified.

First Negative Constructive

The third affirmative contention has been that the UN is weakened. Obviously they wish that the UN should have to seat the Communist Chinese in that organization. They quoted John Foster Dulles in 1950 as saying Communist China should be there, but John Foster Dulles in 1954 and 1955 has more than one time stated, as for instance from *Newsweek* magazine of March 30 of this year: "It would be folly if the UN would seat the Communist Chinese at this time, especially at a time when the Communist Chinese waged war against the UN and violated the truce against the UN forty times." This is Dulles now—not five years ago.

Comment. The speaker's reference to "the third affirmative contention" is understandable since this was the third important argument of the affirmative. However, the affirmative considered it the second subpoint under its political argument. (See outline.) The speaker overlooks both facets of the affirmative argument, pressure on the UN and incomplete representation, and argues that China should not be seated in the UN because Dulles says so. The remark "This is Dulles now—not five years ago" implies that Dulles has either reversed himself or been quoted out of context. However, the affirmative used the Dulles quotation to support a principle by showing that even Dulles supported it at one time. (Since, as Secretary of State, he was one of the major architects of foreign policy, it is evident, in view of that policy, that he did not abide by that principle at the time.) As to the soundness of the principle, the real point at issue, who enunciated it or when it was enunciated is immaterial; Aristotle could have enunciated it over two thousand years ago and it could still be sound. The speaker does not attack the principle itself, however, but shows only that Dulles apparently no longer subscribes to it (a fact evident from the debate itself). Since the soundness of the principle does not depend upon what Dulles says, his subsequent disavowal of the principle does not necessarily invalidate it or the affirmative argument. In effect, the speaker's argument on this point is practically a tautology, a form of begging the question: China should not be seated in the UN because the United States (according to the official pronouncement of Dulles) does not want China seated in the UN. However, the main issue of the debate is, is present United States policy wise?

Later in the debate one of the negative team's constructive arguments (objections) was that recognition would weaken the UN. Since this is a retort to the affirmative's conclusion, it should have been introduced at this point and not held in abeyance (as planned before the debate) until the second negative constructive speech.

Second Affirmative Constructive

We discussed with you the UN. And our friends told us, well, it won't help to have them in the UN because they have been a trouble maker. They pointed out that the Dulles quote from 1950 merely means that Mr. Dulles has changed his mind since then. Nevertheless, they did not deny that the UN is being weakened. For as Trygve Lie has said: "The conduct of certain governments, both inside and outside the UN, may be condemned from time to time by the organization; but the latter's influence, both for world peace and upon the conduct of governments in relation to the obligations and objectives of the Charter, *would undoubtedly be greater* [emphasis supplied by speaker] if all such governments were in the organization." End quote. And so we can see, recognizing this government and bringing it in to the UN would strengthen not only the UN but the hope for peace.

Comment. The speaker implies that Dulles is not the issue and correctly indicates that the preceding speaker did not deal with the affirmative's contention that the UN was being weakened ("They did not deny it"). Since the error involved in the preceding speaker's treatment of the Dulles quotation is not clearly evident without some analysis and explanation, the present speaker should have used the time to pinpoint the fallacy instead of quoting Lie. Reading the Lie quotation undoubtedly required much less mental effort than analyzing the opposition's reasoning. The speaker, however, missed a good opportunity.

Second Negative Constructive

... Now I'd like, at this point in the debate, to bring up our fourth point and to draw a very interesting analogy here. We believe that if we recognize Communist China, the United States would have to reverse its position and vote for the admission of Communist China to the UN. Now the members of the opposition are advocating this. They said that it would be advantageous for Communist China to be seated in the UN. One thing they obviously don't realize: the state of China is today a permanent member of the UN. If we withdraw our recognition from the Nationalist government on the island of Formosa and extend it to the Communists, then we will have no alternative but to vote for the admission of Communist China to the UN, knocking Nationalist China out of the UN. And we, sir, obviously do not go along with the policy which the members of the opposition are supporting, to seat Communist China in the UN. We feel that it would be disadvantageous for several reasons to have Communist China in the UN. In the first place, it would allow the very power which aggressed against the UN to be seated among it as one of its members. Communist China is today the only nation which has been declared an aggressor by the UN. We certainly don't feel it would benefit this organization to have Communist China seated in it as one of its members.

Secondly, the seating of Communist China in the UN would raise the prestige and power of that government in Asia more than any other single instrument. And thirdly, we feel it would actually be offering a reward for the aggression which Communist China has committed against the UN. We find from a *Foreign Policy Bulletin* of July 15, 1954: "UN membership is an obligation assumed willingly by states that proclaim they are willing to abide by the Charter." Communist China, by acts of aggression not only in Korea, has shown no sensitivity to the Charter of the UN. They have shown that they have no intentions of abiding by it at the present time. So we see that it would be detrimental to have Communist China seated in the UN. The members of the opposition feel that by recognition they could certainly seat China in the UN, that it would be to our advantage, and yet they have certainly pointed out no advantages at the present time.

Comment. The speaker evidently does not mean to say "draw an analogy," for he does not draw any; what he means is that both sides happen to have chosen this issue as part of their constructive case. A more accurate phrasing would be: "Now we should like to clash directly on this point. We believe that not only is the UN not weakened at present but that it would be weakened by recognition." As previously explained, the argument should have been introduced in the first negative constructive speech.

The argument itself does not clash with the affirmative's reasons why the UN is being weakened but clashes rather with the affirmative's conclusion. That is, it consists of presumed disadvantages to offset the affirmative's presumed advantages. A more effective attack would have been, first, to counter the affirmative's reasons and then to develop the disadvantages, i.e., to deny first and then to retort.

Taking the disadvantages singly, the first (though it is not labeled), forcing Nationalist China out of the UN, is based on the assumption that recognition will be withdrawn from that government if it is extended to Communist China, an assumption contested by the affirmative in connection with another issue. As previously pointed out in the discussion of "direct" and "indirect" disadvantages, a conclusion based on another controversial conclusion is generally vulnerable since the former can be attacked indirectly; if the latter falls, the former falls. The second disadvantage (though labeled the first), that recognition would allow membership to a nation which had committed aggression against the UN, should have been substantiated somewhat. Why would membership to such a nation defeat the purposes of the UN? Merely saying that it will, or implying that the reason is obvious, is not very convincing.

The third disadvantage (called the second), that membership would increase the prestige and power of Communist China, is also an assertion; some proof should have been given. The fourth disadvantage (called the third), that granting membership in the UN would be equivalent to offering a reward for aggression, is also an unsupported assertion and (as will be seen later) conflicts with a previous negative suggestion that China does not want diplomatic recognition. If the latter were true, China would be indifferent to the consequences of recognition and would not consider that she was being rewarded. To avoid this inconsistency, the speaker might have pointed out that other Southeast Asian countries would perhaps consider that China was being rewarded and that, for this reason, the effect on them would be bad. The point, however, would have to be supported by evidence.

Implicit is a fifth disadvantage, that China would not abide by the UN Charter, a point which might have been integrated with the second disadvantage. Finally, the remark that the affirmative has "certainly" pointed out no advantages in having Communist China in the UN is inaccurate because the affirmative speakers pointed out several, although indirectly: pressure on the UN by the United States would be lessened; the UN would be able to exert more influence upon Communist China and thus promote more effectively the objectives of the Charter.

Many judges might consider this rapid and sketchy development of several points as a "shotgun" attack, which succeeds only against inexperienced teams and which alienates many judges. But soundness of argument rather than fairness should be the paramount consideration here. Sketchy or superficial arguments can be disposed of by an alert debater as quickly as they are introduced. Instead of being put at a disadvantage by such arguments or having to depend on a judge's sympathy, a skillful debater can turn them to his own advantage.

First Negative Rebuttal

They say that the UN should seat the Communist Chinese and in the very same breath they say that the main purpose of the UN is to promote the peace. Just what signs, we ask you, have the Communist Chinese given to lead us to believe they want peace? Just where? Just why does it seem that the Communist Chinese want to promote peace?

Comment. This argument assumes that only peaceful nations should be seated in the UN. With this assumption as the major, we get the following syllogism:

Major: All nations which are seated in UN should be peaceful.
Minor: Communist China is not peaceful.
Conclusion: Therefore, Communist China should not be seated. Although the form is valid, there is some doubt about the truth of the major. Some of the nations now seated are not always peaceful or inclined to be so. Many would contend that membership in the UN is a more effective check on their aggressiveness than nonmembership would be. Thus, although the major is a controversial proposition, the speaker treats it as a self-

evident truth and offers little proof to support it. Debaters frequently do this. It remains then for the opposition to question the truth of the implied major and to support a contradictory proposition.

First Affirmative Rebuttal

With regard to the UN, again I quote from the *Civil and Military Gazette* of Pakistan, January 24, 1952: Dr. Mohammed Roehm, Indonesian Foreign Minister, urged that China be admitted to the UN because such membership would, quote, "entitle her not only to rights but also to certain obligations." End quote. And our negative friends have pointed repeatedly in this debate to the violations of international agreements by the Red Chinese—at Geneva and at Panmunjom, for example. But we point out that unless you recognize this government, unless you recognize them as a legal entity, unless you give them certain responsibilities in the UN, it is rather ridiculous for the United States to brand them as an aggressor. For only when they are treated as equals, only when they are treated as a government which has responsibilities, only when we recognize this government, can we consider them as being responsible for their international acts—as was pointed out again in the Pakistan *Civil and Military Gazette*.

Comment. In effect, the speaker attacks the underlying assumption of the previous argument (though it would have been more effective had he pointed this out), contending that membership in the UN should not necessarily be limited to peaceful nations because the obligations entailed by membership will make a nation less intransigent and more responsible. In mentioning Indonesia, the speaker might have pointed out that this was one of the countries cited by the opposition as being suspicious of China but that nevertheless it felt that membership in the UN would curb China. In passing, attention is called to the speaker's effective use of rhetoric for emphasis, his repetition of the "unless you" and "only when" constructions. As pointed out earlier, oral discourse is much more difficult to follow than written discourse, and it is by means of such rhetorical devices that a speaker can get his points across effectively to an audience.

Second Negative Rebuttal

We believe that we should not extend diplomatic recognition to the Communist government of China. In the words of the members of the opposition, only when you recognize Communist China can you hold her to international obligations, only when you recognize her. It's all right for her to violate international law today, it's all right for her to invade Korea today, it's all right for her to hold UN prisoners. If this were true, why should she want recognition, I ask you, when she can do anything possible under the sun and it's perfectly all right for her at the present time? We see that the members of the opposition are largely debating assumptions this afternoon . . . it would not be to the advantage of the UN to have this aggressor nation seated in that organization. How would recognition lead to her seating other than as a legal government?

Comment. Essentially, the speaker argues that if Communist China can do as she pleases now and that if recognition (or membership in the UN) would restrain her, as the opposition claims, why should Communist China desire recognition (or membership)? Reconstructed as a syllogism, the argument takes the form:

If recognition (or membership) would restrain Communist China, she would not want recognition (or membership).
Recognition (or membership) would restrain Communist China.
Therefore, Communist China would not want recognition (or membership).

Or it is possible that the speaker may be arguing:

If recognition (or membership) would restrain Communist China, she would not want recognition (or membership).
But Communist China does want recognition (or membership).
Therefore, recognition (or membership) would not restrain her.

In the first syllogism the suggestion is that even if the affirmative's conclusion (that Communist China would be restrained by recognition) is accepted, then the affirmative proposal (recognition) is not practicable. This is a form of the indirect attack, showing a conclusion to be self-defeating ("True, China might be restrained, but then she would not accept recognition"), and would be effective here except that the speaker cannot accept the affirmative's conclusion without contradicting the premise of his partner's argument.

In the second syllogism, the suggestion is that the affirmative's conclusion is incorrect, but the affirmative's reasoning why Communist China would be restrained is not dealt with here.

In his final summary, the speaker reiterates the negative's stand, denial ("It would not be to the advantage of the UN" to have China seated), but does not deal with the preceding speaker's reasoning. The meaning of the speaker's last sentence ("How would recognition lead, etc.") is not clear.

A more reasonable approach, perhaps, would have been to argue that though membership might exert a certain restraining influence on Communist China, this influence would not be very significant, as in the case of Soviet Russia, and that the disadvantages of membership (several could be cited) would far outweigh any advantage. Outright denial, the approach taken most often by the negative team, is not the only form of answer. In fact, owing to the nature of debate questions, it is the most inflexible and usually the least reasonable type of answer. As a rule, the opposition isn't always *entirely* wrong. It is usually more reasonable, then, to concede that there may be some truth in what they say but simply not enough to warrant belief in their position.

Second Affirmative Rebuttal

Our friends have told us the UN would be weakened, but I pointed out to you that Trygve Lie felt the organization's influence for world peace would undoubtedly be greater.

Comment. In summarizing the affirmative's stand, the speaker should have mentioned that the preceding speaker did not consider the affirmative's reasons why membership would exert a restraining influence on Communist China.

Summary of Issue

The basis of the affirmative argument was that recognition and the subsequent seating of China in the UN would lessen the pressure currently being brought to bear on the UN by the United States, would give the UN a more complete representation as a world organization, and for this reason as well as for the reason that certain restraints, or obligations, would be imposed on Communist China, would increase its effectiveness as a promoter of world peace. On the whole, the negative team did not deal directly with these contentions but argued, basically, that Communist China is an aggressor nation and, therefore, does not deserve recognition or membership in the UN. Both teams would have been more effective had they clashed more directly and capitalized more on the opposition's omissions and errors.

Issue I.B.1.a.

Can the United States and Communist China effectively negotiate their differences at present?

First Affirmative Constructive

The second sphere of disadvantage under the present policy is military. We of the affirmative contend that nonrecognition is detrimental to our avowed policy of coexistence. In support of this contention I quote from the *New York Times* of November 19, 1954: "There is profound doubt here that Southeast Asia can be salvaged or a real settlement in Korea achieved in the absence of improved relations between the United States and Communist China."

The *New York Times* of February 15 of this year [1955] points out that the UN Security Council has ceased its efforts to ease the tension in the Formosa Straits and that traditional, secret, nation-to-nation diplomacy will now be tried. But, under the policy of nonrecognition, we are unable to negotiate with this government except through the UN. Now what does this mean? Since disputes between nations can be settled only by war or negotiation, and since our present policy makes negotiation unfeasible, war is the only alternative. Surely this conflicts with our avowed policy of coexistence. . . .

And how does this second area of disadvantage, that is, the military, result from nonrecognition? I point out that, although the United States and Communist China might still disagree on many points after we recognize them, direct and continuous negotiation is a better means for solving these disputes than sporadic indirect negotiation. For, as C. P. Fitzgerald pointed out in *Pacific Affairs:* "One cannot really negotiate peace with an unrecognized government. The fact of negotiation implies recognition." Once again, a direct relationship: recognition—negotiation—the means to prevent war.

Comment. The argument presented here is quite complex, involving several syllogisms. Without reconstructing these in their entirety, the main points of the argument are as follows:

1. There are at present disputes between the United States and Communist China.
2. It is desirable that these disputes be resolved. [A permissible assumption.]
3. Disputes may be resolved peacefully (i.e., by negotiation) or nonpeacefully (i.e., by war). [Disputes, of course, may also remain unresolved as at present.]
4. Negotiation is unlikely at present, for, of the two types
   a. Direct (and continuous) negotiation is ruled out by the present United States policy of nonrecognition.
   b. Indirect (and sporadic) negotiation has been temporarily abandoned.
5. Therefore, war is left as the only alternative at present for resolving the aforementioned disputes. Proposition 5 does not mean that war is inevitable since there is the alternative that the disputes in question can remain unresolved, as at present. However, since this proposition tends to be ambiguous, the speaker should have taken the time to mention this other alternative. Actually the key point of the argument is presented last: that "direct and continuous negotiation is a better means for solving these disputes than sporadic indirect negotiation." For clearness, the speaker should have begun with this point and built the rest of the argument around it.

First Negative Constructive

We look at the other affirmative contentions. We find that our policy today is the complete opposite of coexistence. Coexistence is a two-way street. We're willing to coexist with Communist China, but, ladies and gentlemen, is Communist China willing to coexist with this country? Her insistent demands that this country is an imperialist and a war-mongering nation certainly does not sound as if they want to coexist with the United States. The gentlemen have maintained that we cannot negotiate with Communist China unless we negotiate through the UN. And yet we find that that is false. We see that it frequently happens—from Green Hackworth's *Digest of International Law,* Department of State, Volume I, page 327—that it frequently happens that the establishment or maintenance of informal relations is important and most desirable with unrecognized governments. Such necessary intercourse may be maintained in a number of ways with unrecognized states and governments. The assertion that we can't negotiate with Communist China because we don't recognize her is completely false. The gentleman has said, "One can't negotiate peace without recognition." Why? Why can't we negotiate peace with the Communist Chinese without recognition? Is it because they are claiming we are not going to negotiate peace with you unless you recognize Communist China—unless you recognize it? Is it the political blackmail that Communist China is offering us? One, give us recognition and we'll give you peace. And yet they violated the peace agreement and the truce agreement in Korea forty times.

Comment. The phrase "the complete opposite of" represents an extension of the affirmative position "contrary to." The point that the United States wants peace but that China does not is not proved by the evidence that China has called the United States a warmonger. The evidence may prove that China is unfriendly to the United States but not that China wants war; it is possible for China to think that the United States does not want peace and for China to want it herself.

Because the affirmative point on the matter of negotiation was that indirect negotiation was not as satisfactory as direct negotiation—the former being exemplified by negotiation through the UN and temporarily abandoned, according to the previous speaker—the present speaker's point that indirect negotiation is possible (according to Hackworth) amounts to an answer by an equivalent proposition. Juxtaposed, the two arguments are:

Affirmative: Indirect negotiation is possible but not satisfactory.

Negative: The affirmative is wrong; indirect negotiation is possible.

Whether or not such negotiation is satisfactory, the real point at issue, is overlooked by the speaker.

In dealing with the Fitzgerald point, that direct negotiation implies recognition, the speaker bypasses Fitzgerald's reasoning (if one speaks directly to another, the former implies that he recognizes the other's existence) and suggests that if peaceful negotiation is not possible at present, it is only because the Chinese are blackmailing the United States, an effective retort.

Second Affirmative Constructive

... Then my partner went on to the military, and he told you there were difficulties as to the ability to negotiate with these people; and he told you we were drifting closer toward war. And our friends didn't deny this, but they merely said we cannot coexist with these people because they do not want to coexist. And it seems to me, they leave us a rather grim alternative, war under the negative proposal. . . .

As to negotiation, they tell us, we can negotiate under the status quo—look at Geneva, look at Panmunjom. I call to your attention, we didn't negotiate at Panmunjom—the UN did. I call to your attention that at Geneva Mr. Dulles was not even allowed to speak to Chou En-lai. I call to your attention that under the status quo U Nu, at the request of Chou En-lai, invited the United States to negotiate. Is this unwillingness on their part? No. Chou En-lai through U Nu invited us to negotiate over the tense situation in Formosa, and Mr. Dulles turned down the negotiation because it would imply recognition to the Asians. Is this a satisfactory policy in view of the grim alternative our friends have offered us—war? We think not.

Comment. The speaker first considers the omissions, or implicit admissions, of the negative, always an effective procedure. In doing so, he should have clarified the "drift toward war" argument by specifying rather than by implying the alternatives under the status quo, namely, either ignore the present disputes or try to resolve them by indirect negotiation, neither course being very desirable. Also, to forestall further confusion concerning negotiation, the speaker should have emphasized the difference between indirect and direct negotiation and then indicated that the various examples which he cited were examples of indirect negotiation.

The phrase "we didn't negotiate at Panmunjom—the UN did" is misleading, for it suggests that no United States negotiation with the Chinese Communists is possible under the status quo, whereas the speaker is actually arguing that no *direct* negotiation is possible, a point amplified by the next example, Dulles' having to speak to a third party in order to communicate with Chou En-lai at Geneva. In a word, the speaker should have dealt directly with the preceding speaker's argument that indirect negotiation is possible by saying something like "We never denied that indirect negotiation was possible; my partner, in fact, indicated that it was possible. The point we make is, indirect negotiation is not as satisfactory as direct negotiation, which is not possible under the status quo but which would be possible if China were recognized. In sum, the issue here is indirect versus direct negotiation." A point to remember is that, before introducing evidence, a debater should indicate clearly the general point he is about to make and his position concerning that point.

Second Negative Constructive

And, secondly, the members of the opposition have said that our policy is disadvantageous in the military spheres of the world because we can't negotiate; and if we can't negotiate with the Communists, then we have no alternative but to go to war. The members of the opposition are assuming a very large thing. They are saying, if we extend diplomatic recognition, the Communists will negotiate with us. Recently the UN urged Communist China to negotiate over the matter of Formosa. Even Russia herself asked them to negotiate. What was the answer? An abrupt refusal. This is the type of negotiation Communist China carries on at the present time.

Let's look at Korea. We negotiated there—the UN negotiated. What happened? They violated this truce some forty times. Is this the type of international organization—do they live up to their international obligations at the present time? We see obviously this does not follow. The members of the opposition certainly cannot say that if we extend recognition, we're going to avoid all possibilities of war at the present time.

Something else is very interesting, too. They said that we cannot negotiate unless we recognize them. My colleague has pointed out to you previously that in Hackworth's *Digest of International Law* the recognized and unrecognized nations certainly can negotiate. The members of the opposition further proved this by stating that direct negotiation is more emphatic [effective] than sporadic negotiation. We have had sporadic negotiation, you might say, in Korea, where they violated the truce, where they ignored international law, where they flagrantly violate their international obligations. We have negotiation at the present time if the need arises, and you certainly see the outcome at the present time.

Comment. The phrase "if we can't negotiate . . . , then we have no alternative but war" oversimplifies and extends the affirmative position, which was: we can't negotiate directly, indirect negotiation is unsatisfactory, and unsolved problems, since they cannot be satisfactorily negotiated, may lead to war. Thus, the phrase "assuming a big thing" is more applicable to the present speaker than to the preceding one. The point that China at present refuses to negotiate indirectly with the United States through the UN over the problem of Formosa does not contradict but is compatible with, and almost equivalent to, the opposition's point that China rejects indirect negotiation at present, which the United States might accept, but would accept direct negotiation, which the United States rejects lest direct negotiation imply recognition. The speaker's point actually supports the opposition's point that indirect negotiation at present is unsatisfactory, not even being available in this instance.

The speaker's next point that negotiation—presumably direct negotiation—would not be satisfactory in any event, or that the affirmative plan would not meet the need, because China has violated international agreements in the past and therefore could be expected to do so in the future is a good one. However, the speaker does not consider the affirmative contention that altered circumstances due to recognition and membership in the UN would make China more sensitive to her international obligations. The phrase "we're going to avoid all possibilities of war" is, as previously pointed out, an extension of the affirmative position; actually, the first affirmative speaker carefully qualified the affirmative position by stating in effect, "We admit there might still be differences after recognition but these could be better resolved by improved relations and direct negotiation between the two countries."

The speaker's final point that indirect negotiation is possible at present has already been commented upon. The blame for the confusion here must be shared by both teams—the affirmative's neglect to state explicitly the distinction between direct and indirect negotiation and the negative's inability to recognize that the distinction was implicitly made by the affirmative.

First Negative Rebuttal

The gentlemen have said, "Well, we've got to negotiate with Communist China." Let us examine a country which has recognized the Communist Chinese. Have they negotiated? Recognition does not mean negotiation by any manner of means. We find from *Newsweek* of April 4 of this year [1955], that perhaps even more important are the private accounts of efforts by India and the British to persuade Peking to accept some compromise course. Toward these approaches the Chinese Reds have adopted a policy of uncompromising belligerency. They have rejected all Indian attempts to mediate. Similar British representations have been met with what is described as "studied tactics of contempt and insult."

Comment. The attack here is basically that the affirmative plan would not meet the need, that United States recognition of Communist China would not result in any conciliation of disputes between the United States and China as evidenced by the examples of India and Great Britain, two countries which recognize Communist China. However, the argument is quite muddled for two reasons. First, the speaker equivocates on the term "negotiation" by departing from the accepted meaning "to confer regarding a basis of agreement" and using the meaning "compromise," or "to reach agreement by mutual concessions." Although negotiation may result in compromise, or mutual concessions, it does not necessarily have to. Second, the evidence concerning India and Britain is ambiguous; it is not clear whether or not these countries attempted "to persuade Peking to accept some compromise course" with regard to the problem of Formosa itself or with regard to the problem of negotiating the problem of Formosa. If their efforts at persuasion were directed to the latter, as seems likely, then the speaker's point would coincide with the affirmative point that China insists on negotiating directly at present.

Whether China is right in her insistence on this point and the United States wrong in her refusal to acquiesce is the very issue of the debate, in which case the evidence would beg the question. On the other hand, if the efforts of India and Britain were directed to the former course, there would be some doubt that the generalization that China, after recognition, would compromise on *no* issues is warranted by the evidence that China at present will not compromise on certain issues, in view of the affirmative's point that United States recognition would make China less intransigent and also make direct continuous negotiation possible, points not directly considered by the negative.

First Affirmative Rebuttal

Now let's move to the military argument of the affirmative. We pointed out that our present policy is contrary to our avowed policy of coexistence. But our negative friends told us that we are assuming that the Chinese will negotiate with us. And they point to the UN and they say, we invited them to negotiate and they refused. But why did they refuse, gentlemen? It was because they were to appear before the UN as a defendant. And, as Sir James Barrington, Burma's Ambassador to the United States, has told us, the only way you can negotiate successfully with this government is to recognize them as equals, to negotiate with them at the conference table as equals. The only way you can solve world problems is by treating this government as a government and as an equal. And so we see that the military contention of the affirmative still stands in this debate.

Comment. Tacitly accepting the preceding speaker's extension of the meaning of "negotiate" to "compromise," the speaker explains why the Communist Chinese rejected indirect negotiation through the UN and why tensions between the two countries remain unresolved. Although the speaker could not take the time at this stage of the debate to unravel the negative's argument, he should have clarified the apparent confusion between direct and indirect negotiation, especially in view of the obfuscation by the negative team and the importance of the distinction to the affirmative case.

Second Negative Rebuttal

Now let's look at their third point. They say that, first of all, if we recognize Communist China, all these goods will accrue. They are assuming another thing in this debate, that Communist China will return the negotiation with us, that they will send reciprocal ambassadors for our ambassadors that are sent to China—which is a complete assumption at the present time. We pointed out that we can negotiate if it's necessary. We negotiated in Korea. What happened? They violated this truce. That is the present situation of the Communists.

And the members of the opposition are saying that our present policy is leading to war, and either we negotiate . . . or we will certainly go to war if we don't recognize Communist China. But how have they proved to you that if we do recognize Communist China, they will prevent any war?

Comment. The suggestion that Communist China would reject diplomatic recognition and direct negotiation is the impracticability argument that the affirmative plan could not be put into effect. Since this is a new issue, it should not have been introduced in a rebuttal speech. As presented, the argument itself is an assertion and is also vulnerable because it conflicts with the negative team's previous arguments that China is blackmailing the United States for diplomatic recognition ("Give us recognition and we'll give you peace.") and that diplomatic recognition would increase China's prestige, both of which, if true, would indicate that China desires diplomatic recognition.

The points that negotiation is possible at present and that negotiation would be futile after recognition and the extension of the opposition's point ("we will certainly go to war if we don't recognize Communist China") have already been discussed. In each case the speaker simply reiterates his own stand without considering what the opposition arguments have been.

Second Affirmative Rebuttal

... And our friends have not denied that we are at loggerheads with the Chinese Communists. They have left you with the alternative that these disputes can be settled only by war. They have told us the Chinese Communists are unwilling to negotiate and will not negotiate and therefore the military disadvantage of the affirmative does not stand. But I quote from the Geneva Dispatch to the *New York Times*, May 28, 1954. "A Communist Chinese spokesman at the Geneva Conference on Far Eastern Affairs stated yesterday that the best way to get release of Americans held in China would be through direct negotiation between Chinese and American officials." End quote. And I pointed out to you that Mr. Dulles turned down the invitation to negotiate under the status quo lest negotiation imply recognition. And so we can see that this disadvantage under the status quo still exists.

Comment. The point that war is the only alternative for settling disputes with the Communist Chinese at present tends to be ambiguous. It is not clear whether the speaker is suggesting that war is inevitable unless the United States recognizes Communist China and thereby accepting the negative team's extension of the original affirmative point or whether he means that war is the only alternative for settling the disputes at present unless one is content with leaving them unsettled. The time spent on the quotation from the *New York Times* could have been more effectively spent on pointing out just how the opposition has failed to come to grips with the affirmative arguments, either by ignoring them or by misrepresenting them.

Summary of Issue

The issue got off to a bad start because the affirmative team did not make its position absolutely clear at the outset. Later, when it saw how the issue was being misinterpreted by the negative team, it should have taken the time to emphasize the distinction between direct and indirect negotiation instead of letting examples carry the burden. Also, the affirmative team was remiss in pointing up weaknesses and omissions in the negative team's line of attack.

The negative team either did not understand the point at issue or deliberately obscured it. It repeatedly misrepresented the affirmative position or ignored many of the affirmative team's arguments, being content with reiterating its own position without regard to its relevance.

Issue I.B.1.b.

Is nonrecognition an obstacle to disarmament?

First Affirmative Constructive

... And finally, a UN commission currently meeting to consider world disarmament is unable even to consult this government which has vowed to raise and maintain the world's largest army. The military situation is deteriorating as a result of our present policy. . . .

As for disarmament, we can't even begin to consider it, with China excluded from the discussions and free to arm as she pleases. Again, the relationship is clear; the failure of the UN Disarmament Commission to make any progress in London—a fact admitted only this week by Harold Stassen—and nonrecognition of the government with the world's largest army.

Comment. Since this issue was integrated with the previous one, the concluding sentence of the first paragraph was used to summarize the entire "military" issue. The attempt to show a direct causal relationship between the evil cited and the present policy is in effect a plan-meets-need argument; for if nonrecognition is causing the evil, recognition would eliminate it by eliminating the cause.

First Negative Constructive

(No reference was made to this issue.)

Comment. Perhaps the speaker did not consider the disarmament argument important enough to answer at this time, especially since there were more important issues to cover. However, he should have made some passing reference to the point, for, by ignoring it, he might have created the impression that he had no answer for it.

Second Affirmative Constructive

... But J ... as to the military, also told you that the UN Disarmament Commission cannot even consult the nation which has avowed to raise and maintain the world's largest army. This was entirely overlooked by our friends of the negative. And we can see that this is certainly a disadvantage of the status quo.

Comment. The speaker not only points to the omission but reminds the judge of its significance. If several omissions have been pointed out, one should emphasize the fact that a significant portion of his case still remains intact. Again, the term "certainly" should not be used in debate.

Second Negative Constructive

(No reference was made to this issue.)

Comment. In view of the preceding speaker's remarks, failure to mention the issue would seem to confirm the suspicion that the negative team was at a loss to cope with it. The speaker might have tried to attack the argument indirectly on the question of significance.

First Negative Rebuttal

(No reference was made to this issue.)

Comment. Silence to this point is practically a concession.

First Affirmative Rebuttal

With regard to disarmament, we have yet to hear anything from our negative friends.

Comment. The speaker might have added, "Thus, we may consider the point conceded."

Second Negative Rebuttal

... the members of the opposition are saying ... either we disarm, or we will certainly go to war. ... They speak of disarming. I ask you, does Communist China look like a nation that is disarming today? Who aggressed? Who has been charged by the UN? Who violated these treaties? We see that until or at the time that Communist China lives up to some sense of international obligations, this is a complete assumption on the part of the members of the opposition.

Comment. Attributing to the affirmative the argument "either we disarm or we will certainly go to war" both extends and distorts the actual affirmative argument. In discussing the military disadvantage of the status quo, the affirmative contended that the present policy is leading to war— "certainly" represents an extension of this position. Also, the affirmative did not present the alternative of either disarming or going to war; their claim was that disarmament is another channel to peace and that this channel is blocked at present.

The point that China is an aggressor and is not disarming today is of questionable relevance since the affirmative did not contend that China is disarming today or would disarm in the future. The affirmative point was simply that the problem of disarmament could be discussed with

China if she were a member of the UN, whereas at present this problem cannot be discussed with China. The speaker is probably arguing plan-won't-meet-need—that disarmament is unlikely in any event—but the point is somewhat lost in a welter of emotional appeals.

Second Affirmative Rebuttal

Our friends say, "Well, will they disarm if we recognize? How can recognition guarantee this?" The affirmative claimed—and we pointed out to you—that disarmament cannot even be considered at present. Certainly, there is some hope in a policy of something rather than in a policy of nothing.

Comment. The speaker corrects the previous speaker's extension by restating the affirmative's original position, namely, that disarmament cannot be considered at present. An additional sentence or two explaining the opposition's misinterpretation of the issue or its failure to deal directly with it might have been included.

Summary of Issue

Despite the affirmative team's prodding, the negative team failed to deal with the issue until its final speech and then, in haste perhaps, misrepresented the issue.

The student is now invited to try his hand at analyzing the remaining issues of the debate in the same way that the preceding issues have been analyzed. To aid him, suggestive questions are listed after each rejoinder.

Issue I.C.1.

Is the policy of nonrecognition misunderstood and resented by the people of Asia?

First Affirmative Constructive

The third sphere in which the present policy is disadvantageous is ideological. The peoples of China and Asia view the American position as a denial of the right of self-determination. The good will of the uncommitted peoples of the world—including Burma, Pakistan, Ceylon, India, and Indonesia, all of whom have recognized this government—is crucial in the ideological struggle. Under the status quo, the democracy which denies self-determination is merely a mask for traditional western imperialism. When we point out that it is communism to which we object, they answer that, since we recognize other communist governments, our policy is anti-Asian or anti-yellow, for which the past record of the Western powers is certainly not too bright. In further support of this contention, I quote Hallett Abend, who said: "As a country the United States certainly does not dare to stand forth as the champion of liberty and democracy against the tyranny of communism, and at the same time attempt to stand as the helper of the corrupt and detested Chiang Kai-shek regime in China which has been notably reactionary and predatory. Such a policy would not only repel the Chinese people but would earn us the cynical distrust of other hundreds of millions native to the Asian continent." End quote. Abend said this in 1950 and yet this is our present policy.

And what is the direct relationship between nonrecognition and this ideological evil of the status quo? In 1952, H. J. Van Mook, former Lieut. Governor General of Indonesia, said: "The Asiatic nations may come to resent a long-drawn nonrecognition by the West of the altered situation in China. In their opinion—and they may well be right—the change is the result of a popular upheaval. Continued support to a government which the people have rejected is but another instance of Western highhandedness." Once again, a direct relationship between the evils and nonrecognition.

Questions

1. Is the argument clearly conveyed? Are there any portions of it that could be clearer? Is the distinction between the political and ideological evils clear?

2. Why does the speaker say, "Abend said this in 1950 and yet this is our present policy"? Is this effective?

3. Why is the speaker concerned with showing a "direct relationship between nonrecognition and this ideological evil of the status quo"?

First Negative Constructive

As to the ideologies in Asia, we have already proved that our position in Asia is slowly but surely being understood and that our present policy of nonrecognition is reaping rewards.

Questions

1. Has the speaker confused the opposition's political and ideological arguments, or is he justified in combining the two?

2. Has the speaker dealt adequately with the preceding argument?

3. May a policy be "slowly but surely" understood and reap rewards, and simultaneously be resented by the people?

Second Affirmative Constructive

. . . And, finally, as to the ideological evil of the status quo, our friends merely told us that our present policy is being understood in Asia, after J . . . pointed out four separate arguments: the denial of self-determination, the fact that this policy is anti-Asian and anti-yellow, traditional Western imperialism, and the Asians' resentment of our support of Chiang as the government of China. So we see much of the affirmative case still untouched by the negative and still standing. . . .

As to the ideological, they tell us that the Asians are understanding our policy a little better every day. Well, this just doesn't seem to hold true, for just today—the *New York Times* of today, Saturday, April 23—says, "The issue that links the Bandung powers psychologically is to a large degree the ugly one of color." It goes on to say, Communist propaganda emphasizes the fact that "the United States has assumed the mantle of colonialism and encourages racial discrimination." Unfortunately, this kind of propaganda has considerable success. "New nations seek recognition of their pride and self-respect." And so we can see this disadvantage of the status quo still standing.

Questions

1. How effective is it to point up omissions at the outset?

2. Was the opposition guilty of the omissions attributed to it by the speaker?

3. In quoting the *New York Times,* why does the speaker emphasize the date? What is the effect of quoting a newspaper published on the same date as that of the debate?

4. How effective is the whole argument as an answer to the preceding one? Is there anything else the speaker might have done?

Second Negative Constructive

... Well, I'd like to point out to you one thing in this place in the debate. In the first place, the political and ideological views of Southeast Asia would be precisely the same; so we see, these can be handled under the same point. Let's look at these views and see just how they stand up. . . .

The members of the opposition have said that our present position is anti-Asian. Obviously, we see that this is not the truth in view of our relations with Japan and other nations of Southeast Asia. We find also that they said there are basic differences between the United States and Communist China. Obviously, we see these same differences exist between Russia and China, and still we see the situation there. So we see the situation in Asia today is not as the members of the opposition would have you believe. But to the contrary, our policies are being understood in this area of the world.

Questions

1. Are the political and ideological views of Southeast Asia "precisely the same"? Should the speaker have given a reason for this interpretation?

2. Did the opposition say that the United States position is anti-Asian, or did the opposition say that the people of Southeast Asia regard the United States position as anti-Asian? Is there a distinction here? If so, is the speaker's evidence concerning United States relations with Japan relevant?

3. Is the point concerning "basic differences between United States and Communist China" or the point concerning differences between Russia and China clear? What is the speaker trying to prove? Is the argument expressed coherently? Is the speaker's conclusion warranted?

First Negative Rebuttal

(No reference was made to this issue.)

First Affirmative Rebuttal

And now with regard to the ideological. They told us that we are not misunderstood in Asia, and they told us that we know we're not imperialistic—it's merely Chinese Communist propaganda. They told us that we know we are not discriminating against the Asians because we recognize Japan and we have relations with India and so on. However, the fact is that the Asians regard our policy as imperialistic, the Asians think we are discriminating against the yellow race, the Asians think we are opposed to self-determination. Whether it is propaganda or not, whether it is the truth or not, is not a point in this debate. The point is, the only way we can erase these convictions which the Asians have about the United States is to recognize the Communist government of China.

Questions

1. How effective is the speaker's answer to the preceding argument? Does he clearly point out the error made by the preceding speaker?

2. What is his reason for emphasizing "Asians" by repeating it several times? Is there anything else he might have said? Has he communicated his point effectively?

Second Negative Rebuttal

... The members of the opposition have quoted John Layton Stuart. We find that he says further that "it would dishearten and demoralize those of the peoples of Asia who are resisting the Communist advance at the present time and others to doubt the reliability of United States support if we recognize Communist China. It would diminish the capacity and weaken the will of many nations to persevere in their present fight against Communist China." That's John Layton Stuart.

[*Note:* the affirmative quoted J. L. Stuart in connection with its political evil.]

Questions

1. Does this argument clash with the preceding one? If so, how? If not, why not?

2. What type of attack is involved? Could it be strengthened? How?

Second Affirmative Rebuttal

As to the Asians, our friends have told us, "Oh, there really isn't any problem here because our prestige is rising in Asia." And they have tried to lump the political and ideological together. But they are not the same because in the

political sphere it is a policy disagreement; in the ideological it is the contention of the Asians that this policy disagreement is based on discrimination, is
based on colonialism. And we have seen by today's *New York Times* this problem still exists. . . .

As to the ideological evil, I have shown you why it cannot be linked with
the political. And we have seen that it has not been validly attacked just because it has been linked with the political; it still stands in this debate because
of the Asian feeling concerning our policy, never denied by the negative.

Questions

1. Is the distinction between the political and ideological evils made
clear?

2. Is it true that the negative "never denied" the affirmative contention
concerning "Asian feeling"?

3. Is the speaker's summary of the issue effective?

Issue II.A.1.

Would recognition lead to the loss of Formosa and the weakening of
United States defenses in the Pacific?

First Affirmative Constructive

(This issue was initiated by the negative.)

First Negative Constructive

We contend, first, that recognition of Communist China would force the
United States to sever its relations with the island of Formosa. Why? Simply
because the island of Formosa belongs to the state of China. To prove this, we
recall a statement that President Harry Truman sent to the Eighty-second Congress on January 5, 1950. He pointed out that according to the Cairo and Potsdam Declarations, Formosa was supposed to be returned to the state of China
immediately following World War II. And in keeping with these agreements
Formosa was returned to the state of China. As a matter of fact, in December
of 1945, it was returned to the state of China. The fact then is that we cannot
recognize one country, cannot recognize two governments of the same country
—you can't recognize the Communists as the government of China and continue to recognize the Nationalists as a government of China. That is impossible.
So we contend that recognition of Communist China would force this country
to sever its relations with the forces on the island of Formosa.

We contend, secondly, that this abandonment of the isle of Formosa would
weaken the United States militarily in the Pacific and in Southeast Asia. I am
sure that all of us in this room understand the position of this country, as Formosa is considered to be vital to the defense perimeter in Southeast Asia and in
the Pacific, that Formosa in the hands of the Communists would pierce the
island arc of defense that we have made there over the last five years.

Questions

1. What is the structure of this argument? Is it valid?

2. Is the contention warranted here that it is "impossible" for the United States to recognize both the Communist and Nationalist governments, that the United States must recognize one or the other?

3. Does the conclusion that recognition would force the United States to sever its relations with the government on Formosa follow from the evidence? On the basis of the evidence given, is this conclusion "probably true"?

4. Is the conclusion warranted here that United States recognition would mean the "abandonment" of Formosa to the Communist Chinese? On the basis of the speaker's reasoning, is this conclusion "probably true"?

5. Is the argument that the United States would be weakened militarily a "direct" or "indirect" disadvantage? Which type of disadvantage is better? Why?

Second Affirmative Constructive

Now before I go on to discuss with you additional advantages which would accrue from a policy of recognition, I should like to discuss with you the so-called disadvantages very briefly. The negative has told us that we would have to give up Formosa under a policy of recognition. We contend that this is just not the case. And we point out, as H. G. Woodhead did, Great Britain formally recognized the Communist regime in January, 1950, though Sir Winston Churchill made it plain that his government does not advocate turning Formosa over to the Reds. The *Foreign Policy Bulletin* of January 15 of this year says, "Formosa never formed an essential part of the Chinese empire and was never under the control of the Republic." The affirmative point here, which I wish to make absolutely clear in your minds, is that under the status quo Formosa is indeed a tinder box; and it is only after a policy of recognition, when we can negotiate with this government over the status of Formosa, that there is to be hope for a constructive policy for the United States. And we have seen, there is no need, no reason to believe that Formosa would have to be turned over to the Communist Chinese.

Questions

1. What is the structure of this argument? Is it sound?

2. In view of the evidence, how should the contention that recognition would not mean the loss of Formosa be rated as to "probable truth"?

3. What is the speaker's purpose in arguing that recognition would be a "constructive policy"?

4. Was it necessary for the speaker to consider the second disadvantage, that the loss of Formosa would weaken the United States militarily?

Second Negative Constructive

(No mention was made of this issue.)

First Negative Rebuttal

If you recall, one of the basic contentions of the negative team has been that to recognize the Communist Chinese would force this country to sever its relations with the island of Formosa. We pointed out to you that two past agreements said that the island should be returned to the state of China. We pointed out to you also that the island was returned to the state of China. And what did the gentlemen of the opposition say to this? They read from a couple of men who said that, no, the issue has not been decided. Well, hasn't it been decided? If Formosa were returned to the state of China in 1945, why shouldn't it still belong to the state of China? Simply because of the change of governments? Certainly not. But to top it all off, we quote and we find that in the mutual defense treaty which was signed by this government and the Nationalist government of China in January, it was pointed out that there is a provision in the pact which formally recognizes Formosa and the Pescadores as territories of the Republic of China. But even more important than that is that both the Communist government and the Nationalist government legally regard Formosa as Chinese territory. We find this in the *Legislative Reference Service* of April, 1955—the Chinese governments themselves recognize the fact that Formosa is part of the state of China. Can you make Formosa an independent state? Only if it has the tacit approval of both the Nationalist and Communist governments. And yet we find from Wellington Koo, the Nationalist Ambassador to the United States, that under no circumstances will Nationalist China decide to be recognized as an independent state. We find from Mao Tse-tung, the Communist leader in China, in February of this year, that he has said that under no consideration at all will the Communists regard Formosa as an independent state. So we see that the island of Formosa is part of the State of China, from past agreements and from an agreement signed just three months ago. We find that to recognize the Communist government at this time would force this country to sever its relations with Formosa. We'd have to abandon the island, and it would weaken us militarily in Asia and in the Pacific. This is the contention of the negative and, we feel, it certainly has been proved.

Questions

1. What is the significance of the phrase "the opposition read from a couple of men"? Whom did the opposition quote?

2. From the evidence that both Nationalist China and Communist China oppose the formation of Formosa as an independent state, does it follow that recognition of Communist China would force the United States "to sever its relations with Formosa," and, further, "to abandon the island"?

3. Has the speaker "certainly" proved his major contention? Considering all of the arguments to this point, how should his contention be rated as to "probable truth"?

First Affirmative Rebuttal

(No mention was made of this issue.)

Question

1. Was it good strategy for the speaker to occupy himself with other issues and leave this issue to his partner?

Second Negative Rebuttal

... I would like to point out further that the member of the opposition in his last stand in the debate did not mention the first one of the disadvantages which we have pointed out would accrue from a policy of recognition. ...

Let's go into our case. We said that if we recognize Communist China we would have to sever our relations with Formosa. The last speaker at the platform said nothing. Since this is our last stand at the platform, I want to emphasize this point for you. In the past three months the United States recently completed the defense treaty with Formosa in which it was explicitly stated that Formosa and the mainland of China are of the same sovereignty. You cannot recognize two governments within one state as the government of that state. If we recognize the Communists, of necessity we will have to withdraw our recognition from the Nationalists. We have no alternative. Though it's a nice theory that you can make an independent state of Formosa, Chou and Chiang both say no. Though it's a nice theory that you can place her under a UN protectorate, it's impossible under the UN Charter today. Though the British might say it's a nice idea, it is not legally possible because Formosa is legally a part of China by our own defense treaty. You cannot split the two; they are inseparable; you cannot recognize two governments within one state. Secondly, we pointed out that if we recognize the Communists, it will weaken our military protection in Southeast Asia. The joint chiefs of staff—all the major generals of the United States—have pointed out that Formosa is strategically important to the United States.

Questions

1. What is the purpose of the speaker's opening remarks? Are such remarks effective?
2. What syllogisms are involved here? Are they valid? Are their premises sound?
3. Does the argument contain any assertions which should be supported, or may the assertions be classed as "self-evident" truths?
4. How effective is the speaker's summary of the issue?

Second Affirmative Rebuttal

Then they tell us that we're going to have to give up Formosa. And I pointed out to you that there is no reason why we will have to give up Formosa. I didn't quote "a couple of men." I quoted Winston Churchill, who was at the Cairo Conference and said it had become an international problem. I quoted the *Foreign Policy Bulletin*. I quoted the *New York Times*. And I call to your attention, by the admission of the negative, Britain will stand by us on the policy of Formosa; and yet British recognition of Communist China has neither been repudiated by China nor has Britain found this policy—that is, a separate Formosa, a recognition of the mainland—to be incompatible with recognition. It is not we who are debating assumptions; it is the negative. We give you facts.

Questions

1. How effective is the refutation here?

2. Considering all of the arguments pro and con, how should the proposition "Recognition would mean the loss of Formosa" be rated— "probably true," "inconclusive," or "probably false"? Why?

Issue II.A.2.

Would recognition lower United States prestige in Asia by being considered a "retreat from communism"?

First Affirmative Constructive

(This issue was initiated by the negative team.)

First Negative Constructive

We contend, thirdly, that recognition of Communist China would harm our relations in Asia, not improve them, simply because we will once more be retreating in the face of Communist bluff. We have said, "We're going to defend Formosa against Communist Chinese attack"; and now for us to abandon the island of Formosa, the effect on the Asians, I am sure, would be quite startling. But more important than that is the premise that for the past five years we have maintained that the United States will not recognize Communist China so long as Communist China violates international law and refuses to accept her international obligations. At this time Communist China is holding prisoners of war as spies—one of the grossest violations of international law you can find in the books. Would it be wise for this country, at this time especially, to recognize this government when they're continuing to violate international law? We consider then that our effect on the Asians would be to decrease our prestige in Asia.

Questions

1. Is the disadvantage introduced here "direct," "indirect," or a combination of the two? Is the disadvantage weakened or strengthened by being tied to the loss of Formosa argument?

2. What is the over-all effect of the argument? Would it be considered a prima facie argument?

Second Affirmative Constructive

Our friends then told us another disadvantage would be that communism would spread in Asia, that recognition would represent a retreat from communism. Woodrow Wyatt had this to say about this objection: "Once China has been accorded all the trappings of nationhood and treated with as much consideration and respect as any reasonable person could demand, then the attitude of the rest of Asia will harden toward any hint of Chinese aggression." End quote. And so we can see, the second negative objection just does not hold true in the light of logical analysis.

And the third, that it would be a violation of international law, Mr. Dulles has told us there are two criteria: national self-interest and effective control. Who can deny that this government has effective control, and of course we're debating the question as to national self-interest. And we feel it would be in the national self-interest of the United States to recognize this government. So we see the disadvantages of the status quo stemming from nonrecognition standing, and we see the negative objections falling.

Questions

1. Should the speaker have identified Woodrow Wyatt? Does the effectiveness of the quotation from Wyatt depend on the prestige of the authority, on his reasoning, or both?

2. Did the opposition contend that recognition would constitute a violation of international law or that Communist China was violating international law? Is there a distinction here? If so, are the speaker's remarks on international law relevant?

Second Negative Constructive

What would the members of the opposition have us do? Reverse a position that we've supported for five years? We said we will not withdraw in the eyes of communism again, we will not reverse our position. And so we see, for us to do so would be detrimental in this sphere of the world at the present time. We are pursuing the ideology that it is advantageous for the United States at the present time. . . .

Fifthly, we state that recognition would be against the stated foreign policy of the United States. It's more than a mere stated foreign policy. Since 1949 we've consistently recognized the Nationalists on the island of Formosa. We've recently completed a defense pact with them. To reverse ourselves in Southeast Asia would certainly be detrimental after Communist China has violated international law, refuses to uphold her international obligations. Certainly for us to reverse our position on our allies would be detrimental.

Questions

1. Has the speaker refuted the preceding argument? Does he add to what his partner has said?

2. Would United States recognition of Communist China violate the United States defense pact with Nationalist China?

3. What could the speaker have done to increase the effectiveness of his answer?

First Negative Rebuttal

(No mention was made of this issue.)

First Affirmative Rebuttal

.... I should like to consider two of the disadvantages which our negative friends have presented in this debate.

I should like to consider them concurrently since they are so closely related. They told us that in Asia the United States would be retreating from the flow of communism and that we would therefore lose our prestige in Asia when we recognized this government. And they also told us . . . that the United States would have to admit Communist China to the UN and that Asians do not like this, and that our prestige would be even further lowered. I think the proper place to go for Asian opinion is to Asia itself. What do the Asians really think? Typical is this observation from the Pakistan *Civil and Military Gazette*, January 18, 1954: "Why is it that America whose sentimentality has a hard core of the starkest realism is still withholding recognition? Commitments to Chiang Kai-shek, the inadvisability of making the slightest concession to the enemy in the interbloc cold war, and other similar arguments of the antirecognitionists are pure sentimentality." End quote. And, further, I should like to quote John Layton Stuart, who was born and raised in China and spent fifty years of his life there—he wrote a book entitled *Fifty Years in China*—he had this to say: "Among those who have transferred recognition to Communist China are several of China's most influential neighbors. That is to say, a great many Asians opposed to communism do not appear to believe that refusal to recognize China is the best way to fight communism." And so we see, contrary to what our negative friends would have us believe, the Asian nations think that if they are to fight communism, we must recognize that government; and that the United States would not lose prestige in Asia but would, on the contrary, gain prestige in Asia, for the Asiatic nations want us to recognize this government.

Questions

1. Was the speaker justified in considering two of the negative's points concurrently?

2. How effective is the *Pakistan Civil and Military Gazette* as a source of Asian opinion? Where would a debater get such information?

3. What is the general nature of the attack here (doubt, denial, retort, etc.)? Is it effective?

Second Negative Rebuttal

Thirdly, it will weaken our position if we reverse our present opinion in Southeast Asia. We have stated a stand. We've stuck by this stand since 1949. The Communists consistently call us paper tigers in Southeast Asia. If we back down again after we've said we were going to support our allies in the Nationalist government, if we break this treaty which we have, obviously it would be psychologically against the United States. . . . Fifthly, it is against our stated policy which would be detrimental to the United States.

Question

1. Is this an answer or a summary? Is it effective?

Second Affirmative Rebuttal

Our friends have told us, first, that this policy would look bad to the Asians and that this would weaken the Asian will to resist communism. I pointed out that Woodrow Wyatt told us exactly the opposite would happen. But would we be like a paper tiger to the Asians after recognition? John Carter Vincent has said: "It is interesting to note that the *Times* report of the Dulles radio speech of March 8 of this year opened with the Secretary's statement that the United States is no paper tiger. He's right and the Asians do not so regard us. One does not earn the title of paper tiger in the eyes of Asians or of others by withdrawing from an exposed position which no longer serves its original purpose." End quote.

But let me reason this out with you a little further. Our friends have told us that a policy of recognition will aid in the spread of communism. Our friends have told us the Asians want to resist the spread of communism. Then I ask you, why, if nonrecognition will check the spread of communism and recognition will aid its spread, have our friends of Asia recognized this Communist government? Obviously, they do not feel that it spreads communism in Asia.

Then our friends have gone on to tell us that there is another disadvantage— it is contrary to the present United States foreign policy. This seems to be begging the question because the present United States foreign policy is what we're debating today. . . .

And finally, our friends have told us that it would be a violation of international law—which would look bad to the Asians. I pointed out that Mr. Dulles has told us, there are only two criteria for recognition, national self-interest and effective control. This has not been touched again in the debate, and we see the objections—the purely negative objections—just don't seem to stand.

Questions

1. Is the "paper tiger" argument handled effectively?
2. What is the structure of the argument pertaining to the spread of communism and recognition by Asian countries of Communist China? What are the implications of this argument?
3. Is the opposition argument that recognition should be withheld because it is the present United States foreign policy an example of begging the question, as the speaker claims?
4. What is the significance of the phrase "the purely negative objections"?
5. Is international law an issue in the debate? In what way?

Issue II.B.1.

Would recognition result in better treatment of Americans by Communist China?

(This issue was initiated by the second affirmative constructive speaker.)

Second Affirmative Constructive

But let me consider with you now certain additional advantages which would accrue to the United States. Sir Alexander Grantham, Governor and Commander-in-chief of Hong Kong, speaking to the Detroit Economic Club last October, pointed out three major areas of advantage which Britain has obtained from a policy of recognition. They are, first, the protection of British subjects in China. This advantage was seen last November when Communist China agreed to pay Britain over one million dollars in damages for an accidentally downed British airliner. When an American plane is shot down, thirteen prisoners are held incommunicado. The difference? Britain recognizes.

Question

1. Does the evidence indicate that British subjects receive better treatment than American subjects?

Second Negative Constructive

Let's look at the third point which they brought up in the debate. They said that there are three areas of advantage for the United States if we should recognize Communist China. And they're basing this theory on the British idea. Well, let's look at the situation. We find that the British recognized Communist China and for quite a while—for five years, to be exact—the Communists refused to exchange diplomats with them. And the members of the opposition have said, well, look, Great Britain had a plane shot down and got them to pay for it. The fact is that it didn't stop them from shooting down the plane. So we see that obviously this advantage does not follow.

Questions

1. What is the point of the argument that Communist China didn't exchange diplomats with Great Britain until five years after recognition? How is this argument related to the next one?
2. Would the argument concerning the shooting down of the plane be considered "turning the tables"? How effective is this argument? Does it answer the opposition argument?

Second Affirmative Rebuttal

As to the additional advantages, the protection of our nationals, they merely said, "Well, they shot down the plane." But I point out to you, the indemnity was over one million dollars. This is certainly a greater benefit than the United States is receiving under its present policy.

Question

1. Has the speaker proved his point? Would recognition afford more protection to American nationals in China?

Issue II.B.2.

Would recognition result in giving the United States more information on Communist Chinese affairs?

(This issue was initiated by the second affirmative constructive speaker.)

Second Affirmative Constructive

Second, the presence of a British chargé d'affaires in Peking. Of this advantage Grantham said: "This has paid off. He has been able to garner a great deal of useful information, and he has, as it were, had his finger on the pulse of what was going on in China."

Second Negative Constructive

Further, they told us that we were going to send an American chargé d'affaires to Communist China. Have they given us an indication that Communist China is willing to go along with this exchange—that they would allow an American diplomat there? You saw what happened to Great Britain. They too were eager to recognize Communist China, and Communist China completely ignored her for five years. That's the situation that Britain wound up in.

Questions

1. How does the speaker attack the causal relationship of the opposition argument?
2. Is the attack here consistent with the negative team's contention that Communist China is trying to blackmail the United States into officially recognizing her?
3. Would an indirect attack here have been more effective?

Second Affirmative Rebuttal

As to the pulse on China, they said, "Well, would China reciprocate?" As a matter of fact, is there any reason to believe that our chargé d'affaires could go to Peking? We think there is, and we point to the present policy of Great Britain and say, this has occurred.

Questions

1. Has the speaker proved his initial point that Communist China would accept diplomatic representatives on her soil?
2. Could the attack have been amplified? Should it have been?

Issue II.B.3.

Would recognition be an opening wedge in the Sino-Soviet alliance?

(This issue was initiated by the second affirmative constructive speaker.)

Second Affirmative Constructive

A third advantage, the weakening of the present Sino-Soviet alliance. Let me make it clear that we do not contend that a policy of recognition will, *ipso facto*, split China from Russia. We do contend that the present policy on non-recognition intensifies the alliance and precludes our taking advantage of any disagreement which may exist between these governments. China's dependence on Russia is furthered by nonrecognition since she is without UN representation and without contact with our government except through Russia. But are there any friction points in this alliance on which we might capitalize after recognition? Authorities such as Harry Schwartz, Arthur Dean, and Sir Alexander Grantham have pointed out five soft spots or friction points in the alliance: one, strong nationalism in both countries; two, the Chinese view of "Asia for the Asiatics"; three, Russia's drive to industrialize limits the amount of economic aid she can give to China; four, Russian resentment of a potential rival on her border; and five, the question of who will lead world communism. We reiterate that nonrecognition intensifies this alliance, while recognition, making contact with the West available to China, would create conditions making it possible for us to take advantage of the friction points in this alliance.

Question

1. Why does the speaker take such pains at the outset to qualify this advantage? Would it have been more or less effective to make more positive claims? Why?

Second Negative Constructive

Now, as to their third advantage, they imply that at the present time we have no alternative but to force Communist China into the Moscow regime, that if we recognize Communist China, all at once they're going to turn around and lean toward the United States. I'd like to point out that Great Britain recognized Communist China and she's still in the sphere with the Russians at the present time. And, further, from the *Department of State Bulletin* of April, 1954, we found that at the very outset the Mao regime declared that it was by choice in the Soviet camp, announcing that it would pursue a lean-to-one-side policy in foreign affairs, one of the greatest understatements of the ages. So we see that the affirmative contentions do not necessarily follow in the debate.

Questions

1. Has the speaker accurately represented the opposition argument? Did the opposition contend that China, if recognized, would "all at once" lean toward the United States?

2. How strong is the point that British recognition has not affected the Sino-Soviet alliance?

3. The point concerning "Mao's lean-to-one-side policy" represents what type of attack on the causal relation of the opposition's argument?

4. What is the over-all effect of the speaker's argument?

Second Affirmative Rebuttal

As to the "Titoism" argument, they told us Britain's recognition hasn't broken her from Russia. But I point out to you, we never contended that the split would occur "all at once." In my constructive speech I indicated that non-recognition was driving Russia and China into a closer alliance and that this was disadvantageous to the United States. I cited five friction points in this alliance upon which we might capitalize by a policy of recognition. Our friends of the negative did not deny the effect of the present policy nor did they deny that it is disadvantageous to us. They chose merely to assert that a split is unlikely and has not been brought about by British recognition. We of the affirmative feel that a positive policy designated to eliminate one of the causes of this alliance is better than the purely negative approach of our friends. And I believe that in conclusion I may use this issue to generalize on the entire debate this afternoon. We have cited evils inherent in the status quo. These evils have not been denied. Our friends have merely stated that recognition is not the solution. They have offered no solution, and yet it is obvious that such pressing problems demand a solution. We give you one: positive, constructive, peaceful recognition. The choice is yours.

Questions

1. What is the defense here against the preceding arguments?
2. What is the significance of the term "the purely negative approach"? Is the use of this term justified?
3. What is the generalization that the speaker is trying to establish? As the concluding remarks of the debate, are they effective?
4. Was the debate close or did one team win quite decisively? Which team deserved the decision? Why?

In conclusion, the great complexity of a debate, as revealed by the foregoing analysis, suggests that evaluating any debate with complete accuracy, particularly in the short time available to a judge, is an unattainable ideal. The best that a judge can hope for is to be right most of the time. However, all judges owe it to the debaters they judge to strive constantly to narrow the margin of potential error.

EXERCISES

1. After reading the analysis, indicate whether you still think the team you originally picked did the better debating. Give your reasons.
2. Read a debate in the *University Debaters Annual* or a similar volume and outline the issues in the manner shown at the beginning of this chapter. After each issue identify the speaker who initiated it. What issues are usually initiated by the affirmative—by the negative?

SPECIAL PROBLEMS

CHAPTER 22

JUDGING DEBATE

When you are studying any matter or considering any philosophy, ask yourself only what are the facts and what is the truth that the facts bear out. Never let yourself be diverted either by what you would wish to believe or by what you think would have beneficent social effects if it were believed. But look only at what are the facts.

Bertrand Russell

1. DECISION VERSUS NONDECISION DEBATING

Why judge debates, why give decisions? Many critics of debate believe that giving decisions puts too much emphasis on winning and thus produces certain undesirable effects, such as overaggressiveness, unethical practices, etc. However, although competition sometimes brings out the worst in debaters, it also brings out the best. If the incentive to win decisions and tournaments were removed, academic debate with all the excellent training it provides would languish and perhaps completely disappear. As Giffin says,[1]

I have never yet found any other device which will motivate students to spend such long hours studying a great public issue, looking up facts in dusty, hidden volumes, poking into inaccessible parts of the library, discussing arguments pro and con with knuckle-headed colleagues, and all the while listening to the advice and instruction of second-class "intellectuals" designated as teachers of speech. To wit, I have never found anything which motivates students to try so hard to learn so much as competitive tournament debating.

If competition produces certain undesirable excesses, the individual directors of debate must accept the responsibility for curbing these. But it would hardly be prudent to eliminate the motivating force that also produces the desirable effects so gratifying to a teacher. This would be like throwing out the baby with the dirty bath water. The desire to win is not incompatible with good debating. Indeed, the point of view expressed throughout this book has been that only good debating—that based on

[1] Kim Giffin, "Non-academic and Academic Debate Through the Eyes of a Student of Public Address," *The Register* (Spring Issue, 1957), p. 9.

361

solid preparation and sound reasoning—is compatible with success and that unethical practices or stratagems are ultimately self-defeating. In sum, the best way to win is to be an excellent debater. Nothing in such a view is inconsistent with sound educational theory.

2. GENERAL CRITERIA FOR JUDGING

Judging debate, like judging anything else, requires first of all certain standards of measurement, or criteria—an ideal with which to compare the thing being judged. Since debate is primarily an activity or a process, the criteria for judging it must be considered in terms of an end–means relationship. Thus, in judging a debater, a judge must decide, first, what is the debater trying to do and, second, how well has he succeeded? At the risk of being repetitious, the primary goal of the debater, from the affirmative standpoint, is to prove the debate resolution (to be probably true) and, from the negative standpoint, either to create doubt that the affirmative has proved the resolution or to disprove the resolution. Since among thinking men the only valid basis for believing that a proposition has been proved or disproved is the type of logical proof offered (and not such irrelevant factors as the manner or disposition of the speaker), the basic question for the judge to decide is: Did the affirmative prove the resolution (to be probably true)? If he decides yes, he is obliged to vote for the affirmative; if no, against the affirmative (and, of course, for the negative).

3. THE JUDGE'S QUALIFICATIONS

To discharge his duties competently, the judge must have certain qualifications, the most important of which are:

1. He must be well versed in logic, since logical reasoning is the means used by both sides to achieve their ends. One cannot very well judge how well a debater has reasoned if he himself doesn't know what sound reasoning is.

2. He must understand the logical development of a policy question and must be thoroughly familiar with the obligations of the affirmative and negative teams in handling such a question. He must also be thoroughly familiar with the particular question being debated. Such knowledge enables him to judge not only accurately but quickly. Because of the multiplicity and complexity of arguments presented in an average debate, even an expert logician could hardly evaluate them properly in the required time unless he were thoroughly familiar beforehand with many of them. As it is, the time available to the judge is often inadequate to enable him to *grasp* certain arguments in all of their implications, let alone to

evaluate them as carefully as he might like. For this reason, no judge should expect to be infallible, but every judge should seek to reduce the possibility of making errors by being as well prepared as possible. It is unfair to debaters, particularly to those taking part in an important tournament, to have to be judged by someone inexperienced or uninformed on the particular question.[2]

3. He must be ever mindful of the universal human failing to believe or disbelieve propositions on other than reasonable grounds; i.e., he must constantly resist the temptation to judge truth on nonrational grounds, such as personality, posture, sincerity, glibness, and intensity of presentation.

Because of this very human tendency to substitute irrelevant criteria in judging debate, a debate team frequently receives widely divergent ratings from different judges.[3] Also, failure to understand and use the proper rationale of academic debate puts debating on a much lower academic level than it deserves. To regard debating as a form of entertainment instead of enlightenment or as a form of psychological persuasion, or salesmanship, is to lose for it the respect that it deserves from serious thinkers. After all, the goals of academic debate and those of higher education itself —to develop the mind and the skill to evaluate and communicate ideas— are synonymous. To substitute for these high goals less worthy and frequently trivial ones is to earn for academic debate suspicion, and frequently contempt, from serious thinkers,[4] and to cause the study of one of the most valuable educational instruments to be traduced and neglected.[5]

[2] Judges at the West Point National Debate Tournament, for example, are sometimes asked to judge in the final rounds even though they have not judged a debate on the particular question all year.

[3] In the Boston University Tournament one year, one team was rated, on the basis of a 100 per cent scale, 33 per cent or "inferior" and 92 per cent or "superior" on the same day by two different judges. In the Dartmouth Tournament one year, a team was rated by five different judges as being in five different categories, ranging from "poor" to "superior," with ratings of 27, 49, 73, 76, and 89 per cent. In the DAPC Tournament one year, one team was placed in five different categories by five different judges, one for each round of debate, from "below average" through "superior." Cf. "Judging the Tournament Debate Judge," The Gavel, XXXVII, 2 (January, 1955), pp. 31ff; "Judging the Judging at Meadville," DAPC Bulletin, XXI, 25 (December, 1955), pp. 30ff; "An Evaluation of Tournament Debate Judging," The Pennsylvania Speech Annual, XIV (June, 1957), pp. 30ff. These three articles were written by the author.

[4] Ruby, for example, in an aside, remarks that debaters are "notorious special pleaders." [Lionel Ruby, Logic: An Introduction (Philadelphia: J. B. Lippincott Company, 1950).] One could cite many other examples if space permitted.

[5] The prejudice against debate is manifested in many institutions of higher learning where debate is either completely disregarded or given only the most token support. Many institutions refuse to appoint a director of debate or to offer a course

4. JUDGING PROBLEMS

Even when one possesses the necessary qualifications, the problems of judging debate are frequently very complex. Some of the difficulties may be seen in the following situations, common in a debate:

1. *Affirmative:* presents proposition A, supporting it with adequate proof. *Comment:* until answered, proposition A merits belief.

2. *Negative:* exaggerates or extends proposition A so that it becomes proposition B, and now proceeds to answer proposition B. *Comment:* since proposition A has not yet been answered, it still merits belief. Thus, the affirmative would be ahead at this point.

3. *Affirmative:* resupports proposition A without showing that the negative has really not answered this proposition. *Comment:* by ignoring the fallacy committed by the negative and by resupporting proposition A, the affirmative implies that the negative did answer proposition A. But since the negative did not answer proposition A, the affirmative's resupport of proposition A is irrelevant. In a sense, the affirmative error may be said to be one of omission, or failing to detect an error, and the negative error, one of commission, or committing an error. Although both teams have committed errors, proposition A, the one at issue, still merits belief; thus the affirmative would still be ahead. However, now consider the following alternative to 3:

4. *Affirmative:* answers proposition B without realizing what the negative has done. *Comment:* by answering proposition B, the affirmative has tacitly accepted the change from its original position. Therefore, the issue now becomes, does proposition B merit belief? If the affirmative has supported proposition B effectively, the answer would be yes, and the affirmative would deserve the judge's vote at this point. But if the affirmative has ineffectively supported proposition B, the reverse would be true and the negative would be ahead. (Actually, in the latter case the affirmative would be guilty of two errors, failing to recognize the negative fallacy and doing a poor job of supporting proposition B.)

When one considers the multitude of arguments involved in an average debate, the many possible complications, like those illustrated above, and the little time available, one can appreciate the magnitude of the judge's task. It is extremely doubtful that any human being could perform this task with complete accuracy, but such accuracy is not required. A well-trained judge can determine with a fairly high degree of accuracy which side has carried the various basic issues, and this is really the important consideration.

in argumentation and debate, even though they offer one in logic, a course not nearly so valuable or vital in the opinion of this writer, who has taught both courses for many years.

Regarding the basic issues, conscientious judges are often disturbed by the problem of how to vote when a negative team carries one issue quite decisively but loses the others. In discussing the truth relations among propositions, we saw that if one basic negative proposition (the affirmative plan could not be enforced, for example) were proved true, the resolution would automatically be proved false. If the affirmative carries the other issues, the judge is confronted with a real dilemma. According to logic, belief in the resolution is not merited and yet, regarding over-all skill as judged by the number of major points carried, the affirmative in a sense has debated more effectively. Since academic debate is more an exercise in reasoning than a means for securing support, through belief, of an actual policy, this writer believes that debating skill should be the primary consideration and that in a situation like that described above a judge should not automatically vote against the affirmative.

An important consideration should be, how decisively has the affirmative lost the issue in question? If the negative has succeeded only in casting doubt on the particular affirmative proposition and if the affirmative has carried its other propositions, the affirmative should be entitled to the decision. If the negative, however, clearly disproves the particular affirmative proposition, the judge cannot very well vote for the affirmative even if it has carried the other issues. In no case, of course, may an affirmative team ignore a basic issue because it regarded the issue as vulnerable or because it felt it could do better by concentrating on the issues it thought it could carry. The affirmative must make a real effort to carry its particular burden of proof. However, it should not be penalized automatically for not being able to carry *every* issue. Unfortunately, many judges vote against the affirmative on the ground that a single flaw renders the entire affirmative hypothesis false, or unworthy of belief—*falsa in uno, falsa in omnibus*. However, as Stebbing points out, a single flaw does not mean that a given hypothesis is entirely false or worthless, for, as she says, "sometimes the negative experiment itself affords a suggestion as to what kind of modification is required." [6] Therefore, on the basis of common sense and logic, in academic debate one is not justified in rejecting the entire affirmative case because there is some doubt about one particular proposition germane to that case.

It should be noted in passing that there is no mechanical rule that can be applied in judging. One does not add up the number of important points carried by each side and then vote for the team which has the larger number. Issues vary in importance; sometimes one issue is enough to carry the day for the negative but not always; each case has to be judged individually, the paramount criterion being the quality of reason-

[6] L. S. Stebbing, *A Modern Introduction to Logic* (New York: Thomas Y. Crowell Company, n.d.), p. 306.

ing shown by each team. It should also be mentioned that a judge should arrive at a decision before giving numerical ratings to the teams and to the individual performers; that is, the decision should determine the individual scoring and not vice versa, as in baseball.

5. FACTORS TO CONSIDER WHEN JUDGING

1. If the negative strategy is to defend a counterplan, the negative must introduce this plan (or at the very least, mention the fact that it intends to introduce such a plan) in its first constructive speech. Since an initial presumption of the affirmative position is that the affirmative proposal is better than the status quo, the fact that the negative is going to defend a counterproposal should, theoretically, be mentioned before the debate starts so that the affirmative need not waste time in discussing a question (Is there a need for changing the status quo?) which will not be an issue. For the negative to defer mention of its counterplan to the second constructive speech is to permit the debate to be almost a waste of time since the affirmative by now has been allowed to spend two-thirds of its time on a nonexistent issue.

2. All major issues and subissues must be introduced in the constructive speeches. However, new evidence for issues already introduced in the constructive speeches may be introduced in the rebuttal speeches. If the negative introduces a new argument in its second constructive speech— for example, the affirmative plan can't be enforced—the affirmative in dealing with this argument in its first rebuttal speech (its first opportunity to do so) is not introducing a new issue, even though it is considering this argument for the first time in its rebuttal speeches. When there is some doubt as to whether or not certain new evidence in the rebuttals constitutes a new argument, the judge should be liberal and give the debater the benefit of the doubt. Examples of new arguments which should be disallowed are claims of new advantages or new disadvantages of the affirmative plan, *unless* these are introduced by way of a retort to the opposition. For example, if the negative has claimed in one of its constructive speeches that the affirmative plan will hamper the peacetime uses of nuclear energy, the affirmative in denying this conclusion for the first time in its rebuttal speech may legitimately claim that its plan will actually promote the peacetime uses of nuclear energy, even though it has not claimed this advantage in its constructive speeches. Thus, in deciding whether or not an argument is new, the judge must always carefully consider its underlying context.

3. The judge should discount all assertions used as arguments. These include certain rhetorical questions which are in effect arguments by

assertion, like "But what guarantee do we have that the Soviet Union will join?" The implication underlying such a question is that the Soviet Union will not join, but no evidence for this proposition is given.

4. During the course of the debate an argument may be considered standing until it is refuted by the opposition. However, at the conclusion of the debate the judge must evaluate the various arguments and consider which side has reasoned more effectively in regard to the various issues which have been introduced. This is an important point to remember, for many debaters erroneously believe that "the last word" given on an issue automatically carries the issue since this last argument "remains standing," i.e., since there has been no answer to it. However, in his final evaluation the judge must consider not only "the last word," or final argument, but also *all* of the preceding arguments which were introduced in connection with that issue. The "last word" may be the one which the judge remembers best, but he must not dismiss or forget all of the preceding "words," or arguments, on that issue.

5. Finally, in arriving at a decision the judge should take into account the following factors, most of which are usually listed on the debate ballot:

a. Analysis. This, as we have seen, consists of picking out and developing the important issues and subissues of the particular debate proposition. Here the judge must consider the significance of the particular issues chosen.

b. Knowledge. The broader, the more detailed, the more comprehensive, and the more recent the knowledge which a team displays, the more highly rated it should be, in contrast to the team whose knowledge is limited or superficial.

c. Evidence. Evidence includes everything that is used as proof: statistics, authoritative opinion, and commonly accepted propositions. An impartial authority carries more weight than one involved in the controversy. Authoritative evidence which includes reasons for the opinions cited is better than authoritative opinion alone. If both sides present conflicting factual evidence, the judge should ask to see this evidence.

d. Reasoning. This, as we have seen, involves drawing conclusions from evidence. Here the judge must consider whether or not the relationship between evidence and conclusion is sound, whether or not the conclusion is justified by the evidence, and whether or not the conclusion is significant or relevant to the over-all case, or consistent with previous conclusions which have been drawn.

e. Organization. The debaters' cases should be developed around the main issues and should create the impression of being a coherent whole. Although one cannot expect the negative to have the same close organization required of the affirmative, the negative case should not consist of disconnected, random attacks but should be organized at least in its general framework.

f. Adaptation to Opponents. Debaters should not present their arguments as if in a vacuum but should adapt them to the issues raised by the opposition. As previously pointed out, adaptation is required in every speech except the first affirmative constructive. Adaptation by the negative, however, does not mean that it need debate only those issues raised by the affirmative. Besides adapting to the affirmative, the negative should raise certain issues of its own (disadvantages, impracticability, etc.), particularly in its first constructive speech, and the affirmative should adapt to these issues throughout its remaining speeches.

g. Language, Delivery, and Platform Manner. The phrasing of arguments should be clear, precise, and grammatical. Elegance is not a requirement. As to delivery, such factors as posture, voice inflections, force, rate of speaking, facial expression, hand and arm gestures, audience contact, and general attitude should be considered. Debaters should be penalized, though moderately, for sarcasm and other forms of discourtesy. However, gentle irony, skillful retort, and a close, vigorous pursuit of opposition arguments should not be regarded as objectionable.

6. JUDGING PITFALLS

Having seen some of the problems involved in judging debate, let us return for the moment to the third requisite of a competent judge, the refusal to judge truth on other than rational grounds. As Stebbing puts it, "Not only do we tend to believe what we wish to believe but, further, this wish to believe often operates in making us suppose that what we believe is a logical consequence of something else that may be taken for granted." [7] In other words, man not only tends to believe without having a rational basis for his belief but in so doing even believes that he is rational. A good judge, as we have said, resists this tendency. More specifically, a debate judge should guard against the following pitfalls:

1. Voting for the side upholding the position he personally believes in. As a rule, it requires a real effort to vote for someone who expresses views which differ radically from one's own. If a judge believes that under no circumstances could he see any merit in the opposing position or if he believes that he could not judge the caliber of the debating dispassionately, he should disqualify himself.

2. Holding preconceived notions on how a particular position should be developed and penalizing a team for not developing it according to these notions. Some important distinctions must be made here. In one

[7] Stebbing, *A Modern Introduction to Logic*, p. 468.

sense a judge must have certain preconceived notions regarding the general development of a policy question and regarding the obligations devolving on both sides; he must have notions concerning the nature of proof and of a logical definition. That is, the judge is not a *tabula rasa,* or blank sheet of paper, upon which debaters register impressions; the very act of judging presupposes preconceived standards and qualifications. However, there are limits beyond which the judge must not go. He must not predetermine what the specific subpoints of a particular issue should be and penalize the debater for not introducing such subpoints. Actually, a good judge will have definite ideas concerning what he thinks are the best subpoints and will find it extremely difficult to dismiss these from consideration when judging the effectiveness of the points that are actually introduced. The best advice is to be as open-minded and as flexible as possible, and, above all, to consider all points introduced by a given team in relation to how they are handled by the opposition. If a team introduces what the judge knows is a weak or illogical argument, he should not mentally refute or discount it but should permit it to stand until the opposition refutes it. Once again, a distinction must be made here. If, at the conclusion of the debate, the judge feels that the affirmative did not present a prima facie case, that is, a case believable on the face of it if there had been no negative refutation, the judge is obliged to vote against the affirmative. (Theoretically, if a judge were asked to render a decision before a debate even got started, he would have to vote against the affirmative.)

Among the unwarranted preconceived notions are those which hold that the negative should not confine itself to a purely "negative" attack, that is, concede the existence of a problem but offer no solution of its own; or that the affirmative should not refute the negative position but concentrate on proving its own. Where the former has some psychological basis, perhaps, the latter rests on a complete misconception of the affirmative position and has nothing at all to recommend it.

One other mistaken notion that some judges have—and this is related to the previous point—is that the first affirmative speaker shows a "defensive" attitude, or "goes on the defensive" (which they consider bad), if in his rebuttal speech he considers certain negative arguments introduced in the second negative constructive speech. Such judges feel that the affirmative speaker in this first rebuttal speech should consider his own case, regardless of the circumstances. However, to do so under the circumstances just mentioned would be poor strategy, since it would permit important negative arguments to go unchallenged until the final five minutes of debate. Therefore, in this first rebuttal the affirmative must consider all new arguments introduced by the negative in its second constructive speech, this being its first opportunity to do so. It is not very sound for the negative to defer the introduction of important arguments to this late stage in the debate, but occasionally it must. Under no circumstances, however, should the affirmative be penalized for "being on the defensive" when it chooses to deal with these arguments at its first opportunity.

3. Being unduly swayed by arguments dealing with subjects of special interest to the judge. If the judge happens to teach economics, for example, he should not be either too critical or unduly impressed if a debater happens to consider certain facets of his case from an economic standpoint or if he happens to introduce an economic theory with which the judge very much agrees or disagrees.

4. Stressing one aspect of the debate process out of all proportion to its importance and then rewarding or penalizing the debater more than he deserves for excellence or weakness in this regard. The most common failing of judges, perhaps, is to place too much emphasis on delivery or personality and not enough on content. Delivery, it must be remembered, is only the vehicle for communicating ideas; of far greater importance are the ideas themselves. Inexperienced judges, particularly, make the mistake of regarding debate as primarily training in public speaking, whereas such training is only an incidental aspect of academic debate. Teachers of public speaking also tend to regard this aspect of debate as more important than it really is. Many of these teachers actually find the subject matter of debate distasteful but tolerate it because debating provides one more medium for public speaking. Many would like to see the emphasis in debate placed more on public speaking skills and would adulterate the content of debate to make it appeal to an "average" audience.[8] And many would combine the pursuit of truth with "entertainment" since the former is dull for most people. This resembles the Horatian formula for art, of making ideas palatable by dressing them up in an attractive garb, of combining profit with pleasure, of making "dry logic" attractive by disguising it with a "psychological" coating. The difficulty here is that the coating tends to obscure and to dilute what it coats, that one usually does not and frequently cannot differentiate between

---

[8] Typical of this point of view is that expressed in an article by Dale D. Drum, "The Debate Judge as a Machine," *Today's Speech*, IV, 2 (April, 1956), pp. 28–31. Complaining because a debate judge has to take notes, Mr. Drum asks, why can't debaters speak so that the man in the street can understand him? Basically, Drum's reasoning is that one doesn't have to take notes when listening to other types of speeches. Overlooked is the fact that a debate "speech" is not like other kinds of speeches, that it is not directed at an average audience but supposedly at an expert, and that it is not intended to entertain or to inspire an audience but primarily to enlighten one. It is significant that Drum refers to the content of debate as "dry logic." *Cf.* A. N. Kruger, "The Debate Judge as Critical Thinker," *Today's Speech* V, 1 (January, 1957), pp. 29–31.

the two, and that in the final analysis one's well-being depends not only upon making the distinction but also upon cultivating the search for truth, unvarnished and unembellished, as an end in itself. Not until people learn to find this activity attractive can we expect to raise the level of our thinking or to find solutions to the many problems which beset us.

5. Being unduly impressed by the last rebuttal or, at the opposite extreme, underestimating the final rebuttal.

6. Being swayed, subconsciously or otherwise, by such factors as the sex, color, religion, or national origin of the speaker; the geographical location, size, or reputation of the school which the speaker represents; personal mannerisms, quality of voice, dress, or looks of the speaker; personal feelings one may have for the speaker's coach; the past performance of a team; or a consideration of how the decision or speaker ratings will affect the standing of one's own team. All such factors are clearly irrelevant in so far as an individual's debating skill is concerned.

7. GENERAL BEHAVIOR: "DO'S" AND "DON'T'S"

The following suggestions are offered primarily for new judges and are based on the assumption that most judges are teachers or debate coaches and that most judging occurs at debate tournaments:

1. Be friendly, cooperative, and dignified at all times; in a word, act like a teacher.

2. Follow the rules laid down by the tournament committee and urge your students to do so. If decisions are not supposed to be announced, don't announce, or even hint at, yours. Try to follow the tournament schedule; try to be on time for each event you are scheduled to judge.

3. In giving a critique, written or oral, never become personal. Be objective and pleasant, and use temperate language. If for one reason or another an individual debater has annoyed you, point out this fact to him discreetly. Don't be condescending or insulting. Instead of saying "You rant like a fishwife" or "Your behavior while the opposition was speaking was obnoxious," say "I think you would be more effective if you modulated your voice more and kept your volume down" or "When a member of the opposition is speaking, don't distract him by talking too loudly with your partner." In other words, be a teacher at all times.

4. In tournaments where oral critiques are permitted, encourage the debaters to ask you questions and then answer them as you would in class. Don't be pontifical or dogmatic, or try to impress the student by casually using technical terms which you think he may not understand. Once again, your purpose is to inform and to encourage the student.

5. If an overzealous student or coach questions your decision, give your reasons calmly and dispassionately; do not lose your temper or be-

come vindictive, and never offer as a reason a remark like "I just wasn't convinced," for this is really no reason at all but only a tautology. (In effect, this says "I wasn't convinced and therefore voted against you because I wasn't convinced.") Such an answer only creates the impression that you had no valid reason for voting as you did.

6. Do not question another judge's decision unless he happens to be a close friend, even when it is quite obvious from his written comments on the ballot that his decision was based on a misconception concerning some aspect of debate. As a rule, you will gain nothing except perhaps a reputation for being contentious or unsportsmanlike. When your own debaters ask you about an adverse comment that you disagree with, don't belittle the judge who made it. Be philosophical about it and your students will also learn to be philosophical about defeats which they think were undeserved. Incidentally, few debaters ever think they really lose.

7. While listening to a debate, don't daydream, look out the window, read a newspaper, clean your nails, play with your glasses, grade papers, read a book, or work crossword puzzles.

Don't look surly, disagreeable, or sluggish; don't glare or act dull. Look pleasant and interested, and change your facial expression from time to time.

Take notes as the debate progresses; the better the debaters, the more copious the notes.

Don't seal your ballot before the rebuttal speeches begin or while they are in progress, even if you think the decision is pretty clear cut; for if the student sees you do so, he will think you are prejudiced and will become discouraged.

8. Above all, reevaluate yourself periodically by reconsidering the standards you use and the way in which you apply them. Try to determine whether or not your standards are in accord with those of certain experienced coaches, whether or not you have a particular bias or "blind spot," and whether or not you are inclined to be too strict or too liberal in your demands. Do not stress delivery instead of content, as inexperienced judges tend to do. As Robert Louis Stevenson once said, "a debate judge needs to judge himself first if he would value others rightly."

8. THE DEBATE BALLOT

Although no ballot is a substitute for knowledge, a good ballot can simplify the judge's task and a poor one, complicate it. Unfortunately, debate ballots are not standardized and some obstruct rather than aid the judge. Most ballots use a statistical scale that varies greatly from that used in the classroom. The ballot used in the West Point Tournament, for example, lists only three categories, "superior," "excellent," and "good," it

AFA ballot

AFA DEBATE BALLOT

ROUND_____ ROOM_____ DATE_____ JUDGE_____

AFFIRMATIVE_____ NEGATIVE_____

Individual Ratings

Check the column on each item which, according to the following scale, best describes your evaluation of the speaker's effectiveness:

1—poor 2—below average 3—average 4—good 5—superior

1st Affirmative_____
(NAME)

	1	2	3	4	5
Analysis					
Evidence					
Argument					
Refutation					
Delivery					

Total _____

1st Negative_____
(NAME)

	1	2	3	4	5
Analysis					
Evidence					
Argument					
Refutation					
Delivery					

Total _____

2nd Affirmative_____
(NAME)

	1	2	3	4	5
Analysis					
Evidence					
Argument					
Refutation					
Delivery					

Total _____

2nd Negative_____
(NAME)

	1	2	3	4	5
Analysis					
Evidence					
Argument					
Refutation					
Delivery					

Total _____

Team Ratings

Assign to each team the rating which best describes your judgment of its performance:

1—poor 2—below average 3—average 4—good 5—superior

Affirmative_____ Negative_____

Decision

In my judgment, the better debating was done by the

_____
(AFFIRMATIVE OR NEGATIVE)

_____
(JUDGE'S SIGNATURE AND SCHOOL)

Reason for decision:

being presumed with some justification that no team qualifying for the tournament is worse than "good." However, the points assigned the respective categories are 50–41, 40–31, and 30–21. Thus, on a team basis, 100–82 represents a "superior" score, 80–62, an "excellent" score, and 60–42, a "good" score. The discrepancy between this and the classroom scale is confusing; some judges find it difficult to accept the idea that 50 points out of a possible 100 is a "good" score. Other examples can be cited where 24 out of 100 points is classed as "fair." [9] This writer favors the classroom scale or one close to it, namely: 40–49, inferior; 50–59, poor, or below average; 60–69, passable, or average; 70–79, fair; 80–89, good; 90–100, excellent or superior. The scale coming closest to this is that used on the American Forensic Association ballot, which is gradually being adopted and a copy of which appears on page 373.

EXERCISES

1. Of what basically do the affirmative and negative speakers try to convince the judge?

2. Must an affirmative team "carry" every issue in order to win? Explain.

3. What are the important criteria for judging a debate? What is the most important criterion and why?

4. What is the relationship between personality and persuasion?

5. What part should personal manners play in a judge's decision? What part should humor play?

6. Does an argument stand if it is not answered? Explain.

7. How should a judge treat a piece of information he knows to be false or an argument which is clearly fallacious?

8. Read a debate in the *University Debaters' Annual* or a similar volume and indicate whether or not you agree with the decision. Give your reasons.

9. Are other than debate coaches and former debaters qualified to judge academic debates?

10. Discuss some of the weaknesses of untrained or unqualified debate judges.

[9] The ballot used at Dartmouth, for example, lists the following categories: 0–23, poor; 24–43, fair; 44–65, good; 66–85, excellent; and 86–100, superior.

CHAPTER 23

DIRECTING A FORENSIC PROGRAM

His [the teacher's] problem is to protect the spirit of inquiry, to keep it from becoming blasé from overexcitement, wooden from routine, fossilized through dogmatic instruction, or dissipated by random exercise upon trivial things.

John Dewey

Much has been written on organizing and directing a forensic program. In the following pages only the highlights of this subject will be touched on. Many of the remarks will pertain to a high school program as well as to a college program.

1. THE DIRECTOR'S QUALIFICATIONS

Any truly interested teacher can initiate and develop a successful forensic program. Usually, however, teachers in the social sciences or in the humanities are most likely to find debate and other forensic activities compatible with their other academic interests. In schools where speech is taught, the task of directing a forensic program usually falls to a teacher of speech, although it might just as well fall to a teacher of logic or English. A teacher completely inexperienced should consult with an experienced director from a nearby school.

2. OBJECTIVES OF A FORENSIC PROGRAM

In carrying out a forensic program, a director should seek the following objectives:

To give as many students as possible an opportunity to participate and to promote opportunities for all who desire them. Of course, not all students will be able to make the varsity debate team or to represent the school in outside events. However, opportunities should be made so that even the inept or inexperienced student may profit. Such opportunities

375

might be provided by encouraging intramural debating; encouraging the student to attend or take part in discussions, and also to collect evidence; and directing him into other forensic events not so demanding as debate, such as persuasive speaking (oratory), oral interpretation, and discussion.

To make the program as varied as possible. Although competitive debate is the cornerstone of any forensic program, variety should be provided by encouraging students to enter other events, such as those mentioned above. Also, every effort should be made to present programs in the form of debate forums or panel discussions before local civic and religious groups, on local radio and TV stations, and possibly at other schools, especially local high schools. Local organizations, always eager for programs, welcome student speakers. As the forensic program becomes known, the director will not have to go out of his way to promote outside programs; he will be asked to provide them.

To make teaching and not winning his primary objective. Although the desire to win is usually the greatest stimulus to hard work for the student debater and therefore should not be discouraged, the director should not make winning *his* primary goal. That is, he should not concentrate his efforts on a few "stars," do research for the squad, or write speeches for his debaters to help them win. On the other hand, effective teaching is not accomplished by the do-it-yourself or laissez-faire method. Teachers who rely on this method usually do not know enough to teach, which after all, involves communicating ideas to students. Thus, the director should teach the principles and techniques of debate as thoroughly as possible without doing the actual research for the student. Teaching should be his goal, although winning may be the debater's.

To make the program fit the needs and resources of the institution. The scope of any forensic program should be commensurate with the size of the institution and with its available resources as to interested students, teaching personnel, and time and money allocated by the administration. A director should not undertake to do so much that he has to neglect his other work. Nor should he schedule more events than the number of available students warrants, except in unusual circumstances. Finally, he should not spend more money than is allotted by the administration, although he may request more as the program grows.

3. OPENING MEETING

As a rule, debate clubs or forensic societies call a meeting or hold a "smoker" at the beginning of the fall semester. Invitations are sent to all active members of the previous year who are still in school, to students recommended by various teachers, to all freshmen who have shown any interest during Freshman or Orientation Week, and to other interested underclassmen. Notices are posted on bulletin boards and in the school bulletin and newspaper; and announcements are made in class and in assembly inviting anyone who is interested. At this first meeting, refreshments (soda, pretzels, peanuts, potato chips) are usually served and an effort is made to get everyone acquainted with one another. The rest of the program usually consists of a mock debate or humorous speeches by some of the older members of the group and a few short speeches by the debate manager, or president, and by the director, extolling the benefits of debate, outlining the year's program, and pointing out the many opportunities offered for self-improvement, leadership, and recreation. At the close of the meeting, all present receive forms to fill in and return. These usually contain such items as name, age, address, phone number, class, major subject, minor subject, organizations (high school and college), activities (high school and college), and speech experience. The regular meeting time and place for the group are announced, and all are urged to attend the next scheduled meeting.

4. TRAINING DEBATERS

Regular Meetings

Most groups meet regularly at least once a week, some twice a week, and a few as often as three times a week. Those meeting once a week usually find it necessary to schedule additional meetings either during the week, in the evening, or on weekends, especially in the early stages of the season and before important events.

Selecting Prospects

In picking prospective debaters, the director may try several techniques, none of which, unfortunately, are entirely satisfactory. Some debate coaches ask the interested students to prepare a five- to ten-minute speech on various aspects of the debate question, and some prefer to lead a cooperative discussion (see p. 418) on the question, with each candidate contributing a three- to five-minute speech before taking part in the discussion. The latter practice unquestionably provides a better gauge of how the student thinks and extemporizes, the two most important debating skills, but it is far from infallible. A good indication of whether or not a student will be able to master the complex techniques of debating is his academic record and scores on intelligence tests. These records, therefore, should be checked before a student is encouraged to debate. If his record indicates that debating will be too difficult for him, a student should be encouraged to concentrate on other phases of the program.

Delegating Responsibility

If the forensic group is large and the director has no faculty or graduate assistants, he should divide the group into subgroups, like those for novice debaters, junior varsity debaters, varsity debaters, and "other events" members, and put his more experienced students in charge of the various groups. Also, a debate manager, or president, a public relations manager, and a corresponding secretary should be elected by the group or appointed by the director. Very large groups would require even more officers.

Teaching Aids

Early in the season mimeographed notes on analysis, strategy, debate terminology, etc., should be distributed to the debaters, particularly to the novices; lectures by other faculty members on the subject matter of the debate should be arranged; and lectures on various aspects of debate technique should be given by the director or his assistants. As soon as possible the new members should be given an opportunity to hear a practice debate by the older members or a recording of an actual debate. If the group owns a tape recorder, it can build up a collection of recordings over a period of years. Recordings of the final rounds of such tournaments as the West Point, Boston, Notre Dame, Northwestern, Georgetown, Harvard, and Johns Hopkins are an excellent training device.

Discussion and Rebuttal Sessions

During the early stages of the season, meetings should be devoted to a discussion of such questions as "What is the meaning of the resolution?" "What are the main issues of the question?" and "How shall we conduct the research for the question?" As more and more is learned about the question, as the evidence files are built up, and as the first scheduled event approaches, perhaps the most important phase of the debater's training begins, participating in rebuttal sessions supervised by the coach. At these sessions every possible issue is debated directly for from two to four minutes, and longer if necessary, with the coach commenting periodically on the strategy, reasoning, evidence, and language used, and suggesting lines of attack and defense. A typical clash might sound like this:

COACH: Fred, give us one disadvantage of the affirmative proposal.
FRED: The affirmative proposal would be disadvantageous to the United States because the development of small nuclear bombs would be prevented. J. Anthony Panuch, former Under Secretary of State, said in a symposium at N.Y.U. December 12, 1958: "It is important that we develop small weapons; therefore, we must continue testing."

COACH: O.K., Jess, how would you answer that?

JESS: First of all, we are not convinced that small weapons are even necessary because we feel that there can be no such thing as a limited war. Since limited wars would lead inevitably to an all-out war, our military leaders would not, in the last analysis, attempt to wage such a limited nuclear war.

COACH: Do you have any evidence, Jess?

JESS: Not right now, but I think I can get it.

COACH: O.K. It's not a bad point. All right, we'll assume that the point has been supported by some important general or other military expert. Now, John, what would you answer?

JOHN: Dr. Kissinger of Harvard, widely accepted authority in the nuclear policy field, wrote a whole book explaining the concept of limited war. He pointed out that the United States, to combat the Soviet Union's conventional armaments' lead, must resort to technological means such as small, complex bombs for tactical use. He also pointed out that Korea was a limited war because atomic weapons were not used; Communist China and the United States reached a tacit agreement—China did not bomb our ports in South Korea, and we did not go into China proper. It also recognized—

COACH: What do you mean by "it"?

JOHN: Kissinger's book.

COACH: Oh, I thought you were talking about the agreement. Remember, you must make your points clearly, and one of the things you have to watch is those vague pronouns. All right, continue.

JOHN: Kissinger also recognized that we must have nuclear warheads for our antimissile missiles, and John McCone, current chairman of the AEC quoted in the New York Times, October 30, 1958, says: "Stopping tests would probably prevent development of atomic weapons which could be used in rockets to stop enemy ballistic missiles."

COACH: Good. What is your answer to this, Jim?

JIM: Well, first of all, we would point out that McCone, since he has a vested interest in the continued development of nuclear bombs as a member of the AEC, would be expected to say such a thing. And, as a matter of fact, we find that he modified his statement with "probably." The American public has never really been told where we stand in regard to the development of small nuclear bombs, but from Hanson Baldwin's article in the New York Times, February 1, 1959, we see that all kinds of tactical weapons are available—nuclear shells fired by cannon and howitzer, large warheads for the Redstone, small ones for the Honest John, and medium-sized ones for the Corporal and the Nike-Hercules antiaircraft missile.

COACH: All right, let's stop for a minute. First, one very minor point. Before introducing a piece of evidence, mention very briefly the general point you're making. For example, in your last answer, Jim, before introducing the Baldwin evidence, say something like "But we do have many small nuclear weapons"; then introduce the evidence to support this assertion.

Do all of you get the point? [Nodding of heads shows they understand the point.] Now, let's consider this last answer. Does anyone see what the affirmative has done?

JIM: I think I see it myself.

COACH: Good. What do you think I'm getting at?

JIM: Well, we may have shifted ground a little. First we say, small weapons aren't necessary. Then, we argue that we have them.

COACH: Precisely. And what does this last argument imply?

NICK: Isn't there a contradiction involved?

COACH: Be more explicit. Where do you think the contradiction is?

NICK: Well, if they argue that we have these weapons, don't they imply that these weapons are necessary? Otherwise, what's the point in arguing that we have them?

JESS: You mean, first we say small weapons aren't necessary and then we imply that they are?

COACH: That seems to be the implication, I think. A sharp team would probably pick you up on it, and you might have trouble holding your ground.

JIM: Well, what do we do, drop one of the arguments?

JESS: Personally, I think that of the two the second argument is the stronger—that we have the weapons.

COACH: Well, I don't know that it's necessary to drop either argument—if the affirmative is careful.

JIM: You mean qualify the second argument by saying "Even if such weapons were necessary—which we deny—we have enough of them"?

COACH: Yes, I think that might do it. What do the rest of you think? (Others, in unison, express various signs of agreement.) All right then, where were we? The last point made by the affirmative is that we have enough small nuclear weapons. Now what does the negative respond? Tom.

TOM: Ah, but the affirmative has really missed the negative point. We contend that we do not now have a missile armed with nuclear bombs capable of stopping enemy ballistic missiles. We have to continue our testing program to develop bombs suitable for antimissile missiles. The *New York Times*, August 24, 1958, says stopping tests "would freeze the design of missiles since increased miniaturization of warheads would be restricted or prevented."

COACH: What do we say to this? Jess.

JESS: If this is true, we ask the negative how their underground modification will meet this objection?

COACH: How does the negative get out of that? Nick.

NICK: Very simple. The missile containing the bomb need not be fired to be tested. If it fits into a workable missile and can be carried by that missile, then the only problem is whether or not it will explode effectively. And this can be tested underground.

COACH: O.K., one last answer by the affirmative. John.

JOHN: Well, it seems to us that not very much in the way of nuclear bombs needs to be tested in order to continue missile development. We see that, according to *U.S. News*, August 8, 1958, the United States launched a nuclear warhead missile in the Pacific August 1. And two weeks later, on August 15, another nuclear weapon was test-fired as an atomic defense against missiles. Thus, we feel that in the field of nuclear antimissile missiles, the real problem is developing an electronic system to deliver the bomb on target, and there is real doubt that this can be accomplished. And we see that the negative claim concerning small nuclear bombs does not hold and is thus not a real disadvantage.

[After a brief recapitulation, the group proceeds to tackle other issues in the same way.]

Practice Debating

After several rebuttal sessions, the squad begins practice debating. After the first practice debate, the coach should give a detailed critique. The squad may now continue practice debating for a while without the coach, the main purpose of these sessions being to give the debaters an opportunity to verbalize the various arguments repeatedly so as to develop fluency. Another important means for developing fluency is *solo practice*. Debaters, particularly novices and those with language difficulties, should be encouraged to practice continually at home against imaginary opponents.

The week or so before the opening event, practice sessions should be stepped up, with the coach sitting in on as many as he has time for and offering last-minute suggestions. Where several squads are getting ready for different events, the director must, of course, delegate many of his responsibilities to assistants.

Critique Sessions

Once the season is underway and the first event is over, meetings should be devoted to self-analysis, reexamination of issues, and discussion of new evidence and arguments encountered in meetings with teams from other institutions. Research and the collecting of new evidence should continue throughout the season; and occasional practice debates should be held, particularly before a tournament.

5. SCHEDULING EVENTS

Although dual or practice meets may be scheduled from time to time with neighboring schools, the event which gives the group the most for its money is the debate tournament. Consequently, most schools these days build their schedule around various tournaments held in their locale. Forensic tournaments of all kinds are held in all sections of the country from October to May. Most tournaments are open events, which any school can enter merely by writing to the director of the event. When it becomes known that a school has an active forensic program, the director usually receives invitations automatically. Besides debating events, most tournaments schedule events in extemporaneous speaking and persuasive speaking (oratory), and some schedule many other kinds of speaking events, such as oral interpretation, after-dinner speaking, etc. At the beginning of the school year the American Forensic Association annually issues a special forensic calendar which contains a list of most of the tournaments scheduled for the coming year, along with information concerning the type of tournament, the different events scheduled, the place where and date when the tournament is to be held, and the person to whom to write for information. Membership in the AFA is open to all directors of debate, annual dues are nominal, and the advantages of membership are many. One may join by writing to its Secretary Treasurer.[1]

6. CLOSING MEETING

At the end of the academic year, many forensic groups hold a final dinner meeting or a smoker (depending upon the budget), at which awards are given out and the accomplishments of the season reviewed. Sometimes parents or friends, or faculty members who have contributed to the program, are invited.

7. MEETING ROOM

If at all possible, the forensic group should have its own special meeting place, where members can feel free to come at any time, to study, to practice, even to eat lunch; where debate materials can be stored; where notices and clippings can be posted, awards displayed, and pictures of the teams of former years hung. Having its own *sanctum sanctorum* unquestionably adds to the *esprit de corps* of any group.

8. STIMULATING INTEREST IN DEBATE

A campus activity usually succeeds in direct proportion to the efforts of its faculty adviser. To stimulate interest in debate, a director of debate can do many things. In an article on this subject Dr. O. J. Wilson discusses fifteen techniques, briefly summarized here.[2]

1. Correct Erroneous Misconceptions Concerning Debate

Such mistaken views as that debating is outmoded, uninteresting, or impractical can be corrected in speech classes and by demonstration debates in assembly.

---

[1] The Secretary Treasurer for 1960 is Robert O. Weiss, Depauw University, Greencastle, Indiana.

[2] O. J. Wilson, "Techniques for Stimulating Interest in Debate," *The Gavel*, XXXVIII (November, 1955), pp. 11–14, 25–26.

2. Win the Administration

A director of debate can gain support from the administration by pointing out the academic and professional values of debating, by inviting administrative officers to witness local debates, and by apprising them of any honors won by his debaters.

3. Secure Cooperation of Other Teachers

Cooperation from other faculty members can be elicited by occasional invitations to address the debate group and to submit the names of promising students, particularly from classes in English, the social sciences, philosophy, and religion.

4. Build a Sound Foundation on the Curriculum

If possible, the debate program should be coordinated with a course in argumentation and debate.

5. Organize a Debating Club

A debating club provides a focus for forensic activities.

6. Aim at Multiple Debate Units

Having different teams and varied forensic activities enables more students to take part.

7. Attend Debate Tournaments

The debate tournament gives the group the most for its money. If possible, deserving debaters should be sent to at least one tournament annually.

8. Initiate a Tournament at Your Own School

Even a small tournament will create considerable interest among the students, faculty, and administration.

9. Employ the Cadre System

The more experienced debaters should be used to interest prospects and assist novices.

10. Obtain Financial Assistance for Deserving Students with Forensic Ability

Efforts should be made to convince the administration that good students with potentialities in forensics are as deserving of financial assistance as athletes.

11. Encourage Local Leaders to Establish Awards and Prizes

Such awards should be listed in the school catalogue and publicized in the school and local papers.

12. Arrange for Debaters to Appear before Community Organizations

This type of activity not only trains students but also wins friends for the school.

13. Invite the Public to All Forensic Competition

An audience usually stimulates debaters to greater efforts.

14. Publicize Debate Activities

The public relations director should be provided with pictures of debaters and information about the various forensic activities, and articles for the school and local papers should be submitted regularly.

15. Be Patient — but Persistent

The director of debate should not become discouraged easily but should persist in overcoming obstacles. He will find that success brings rewards not only to the individual student and the school but also to himself.

9. POSTSCRIPT: TURNING OUT GOOD DEBATERS

Frequently this writer is asked, what makes a superior debater? to what degree is a coach responsible for turning out such a debater? In answer to this question, the superior debater is a compound of four related elements: brains, knowledge, platform personality, and the desire to excel.

Brains

This is an essential which no coach can produce; either the debater has the innate intellectual equipment or he does not. However, a coach can motivate a debater to work to capacity.

Knowledge

This includes knowledge both of the techniques of debating and of the subject debated. As to the former, it is here that the coach can be of greatest service to the debater. Since many students possess the other qualifications, the fact that they do not become superior debaters may be attributed to their coach's inability to teach them the underlying logic and strategy of debating and to their own inability to master these principles by themselves. A thorough knowledge of the subject is usually the product of strong motivation, the desire to excel or to win.

Platform Personality

Whether rightly or wrongly, this is an important factor in persuasive speaking, since most people instinctively respond to a speaker with an attractive platform personality. Like the rest of his personality, it is largely the product of environmental forces operative from birth. A coach can work on separate aspects of a debater's mode of delivery and help to improve the latter considerably, but no coach can guarantee that a debater will react graciously and articulately to a trying situation in the course of a debate; no coach can guarantee that a debater, concentrating on a series of abstractions, will exude the charm calculated to impress a judge. Thus, this element is, to a significant degree, determined before the coach and debater ever meet, and each can only partially control it. Other aspects of a debater's platform personality, such as fluency, confidence, and poise, usually develop with experience.

The Desire to Excel

This gives the debater the drive to work long hours, to probe for evidence, to practice continually, to reevaluate himself periodically, and to strive always for perfection. In a word, it is the quality which makes the debater industrious and dedicated.

EXERCISES

1. In terms of the criteria discussed in this chapter, evaluate the forensic program at your school. Is it adequate, too small, or too ambitious? Is adequate emphasis placed on tournament debating, or is there too much or too little emphasis? Are there any off-campus events before local high schools, service clubs, etc.? If so, are there too few or too many such events? Is there enough variety in the forensic program? Are all students sufficiently encouraged to participate? Is too much responsibility placed on the director or on the students?

2. Does your school have an intramural forensic program? If not, how would you go about getting one started? What events would you include? What motivations would you provide for the students?

3. What type of publicity does the forensic program at your school receive? Could it be improved? If so, how?

4. Discuss the pro's and con's of tournament debating.

CHAPTER 24

CROSS-EXAMINATION DEBATE

Reason and free inquiry are the only effectual agents against error.

Jefferson

1. ORIGIN OF CROSS-EXAMINATION

Cross-examination debate, introduced at the University of Oregon in 1924 by Professor J. Stanley Gray,[1] provides both variety for the student and greater audience appeal. Several cross-exam tourneys are now held annually,[2] and in 1952 this form of debate was adopted by the National Forensic League and introduced into many high schools.

Asking direct questions as a means of getting at the truth, of reducing exaggerations to their true dimensions, of exposing weaknesses in adverse testimony is an ancient device. A classic example is Plato's account of Socrates' cross-examination of Miletus, who had accused Socrates of corrupting the youth of Athens. In the courts cross-examination is often a lawyer's most potent weapon, though a difficult one to master. As Wellman[3] points out, proficiency in the art of cross-examination

requires the greatest ingenuity; a habit of logical thought; clearness of perception in general; infinite patience and self-control; power to read men's minds intuitively, to judge of their characters by their faces, to appreciate their motives; ability to act with force and precision; a masterful knowledge of the subject matter itself; an extreme caution; and, above all, the instinct to discover the weak point in the witness under examination.

[1] The rules used at Oregon were explained by Prof. Gray in an article "The Oregon Plan of Debating," *Quarterly Journal of Speech Education*, XII, 2 (April, 1926), pp. 175–180.

[2] Cross-exam debate tournaments are held annually at the University of Pittsburgh, Illinois State Normal University, Wesleyan University (Connecticut), DePauw University (annual Delta Sigma Rho tourney), Portland State College, Heidelberg University, and the University of Michigan.

[3] Francis L. Wellman, *The Art of Cross-examination*, 4th ed., rev. and enl. (New York: Garden City Publishing Co., Inc., 1948), p. 8.

2. FORMAT

There is no standard format for cross-exam debate though the following seems to be the most popular:

	Time, minutes
First affirmative presents constructive speech	8 or 9
Second negative cross-examines first affirmative	3 or 4
First negative presents constructive speech	8 or 9
First affirmative cross-examines first negative	3 or 4
Second affirmative presents constructive speech	8 or 9
First negative cross-examines second affirmative	3 or 4
Second negative presents constructive speech	8 or 9
Second affirmative cross-examines second negative	3 or 4
Second negative presents rebuttal-summary	4 or 5
Second affirmative presents rebuttal-summary	4 or 5
	52 or 62

For presentation before large audiences, the University of Pittsburgh uses the following modification:

Affirmative presents constructive speech	8
Negative cross-examines	4
Negative presents constructive speech	8
Affirmative cross-examines	4
Negative presents rebuttal-summary	4
Affirmative presents rebuttal-summary	4
	32

Being shorter and less complicated than other formats, this one is particularly good for audience debates.

3. GENERAL RULES AND PROCEDURE

Purpose

The purpose of cross-examination is to expose weaknesses in the opposition's arguments. Cross-examination should not be used, as it often is in court, to discredit both the witness and the testimony. The cross-examiner should confine himself to the testimony, though he may try to discredit authorities introduced by the witness. The cross-examination period itself should be made an integral part of the case, and points covered in this period should be included in the summary-rebuttal speeches.

Attitudes

Both questioner and responder should be courteous, conciliatory, calm, fair-minded, friendly, and anxious to get on with the issues of the debate. Discourtesy, pugnacity, sarcasm, condescension, bullying, and stalling should be especially guarded against since cross-examination tends to encourage such behavior.

The Chairman Judge

The chairman, usually the judge, of cross-exam debate has more power than the judge of orthodox debate. Besides rendering a decision,[4] he has to decide if the questions asked are fair or answerable and if the answers are relevant or over-long. If the participants are inexperienced, he may have to interrupt frequently to insure that the cross-exam period is being conducted properly.

The Cross-examiner

The same traits required in the courtroom are desirable for cross-examination debate. As Wellman [5] says:

> The counsel who has a pleasant personality; who speaks with apparent frankness; who appears to be an earnest searcher after truth; who is courteous to those who testify against him; . . . who seems to know what he is about and sits down when he has accomplished it, exhibiting a spirit of fair play on all occasions—he it is who creates an atmosphere in favor of the side which he represents. . . .

On the other hand, continuing to quote Wellman: [6]

> . . . the lawyer . . . who is constantly losing his temper and showing his teeth to the witness; who wears a sour, anxious expression; who possesses a monotonous, rasping, penetrating voice; who presents a slovenly, unkempt appearance; who is prone to take unfair advantage of a witness. . . . , and seems determined to win at all hazards—soon prejudices a jury against himself. . . .

"Do's" and "Don't's"

1. The examiner controls the question period. He may interrupt the examinee to ask for shorter answers or to indicate that the answer given is sufficient. He should not interrupt very often, however, lest he give the impression of being ill-mannered.

[4] Many cross-exam debates are nondecision; in fact, Prof. Gray's reason for introducing cross-exam debate was "to get away from the decision debate and its attending evils, and yet to escape the . . . fault (lack of motivation for preparation by the debaters) of the no-decision debate. . . ." (Gray, *op. cit.*, p. 178.) O'Brien considers this a surprising reason, for, as he says, "Since cross-examination debate is as completely a mode of advocacy as is the orthodox form, with intensified conflict in the dialectical period, this medium is actually unusually well adapted to use in decision forensics. [Joseph F. O'Brien, "An Appraisal of Contemporary Forms and Phases of Forensics in Pennsylvania," *Bulletin of the Debate Association of Pennsylvania Colleges*, XV, 19 (Dec. 10, 1948), p. 34.]

[5] Wellman, pp. 14–15.

[6] *Ibid.*

2. The examiner should confine himself to asking questions; he should not comment on or rejoin to the answers given.

3. The examiner should not ask a question unless he has a good idea of what the answer will be.

4. The examiner may not consult his colleague before asking a question.

5. The examiner should begin with questions whose answers will indicate the main point or issue of the inquiry.

6. The examiner should develop one major point at a time and not jump around from issue to issue.

7. In framing his questions, the examiner should use the order of verb-subject-complement. He should try to avoid using "not" in the question, for questions phrased negatively are sometimes confusing.

8. The cross-examiner should phrase his questions so clearly that there is no doubt about their meaning. He should speak distinctly and compel the examinee to do so. The cross-exam period, like the speeches, is for the audience's or judge's benefit.

9. The cross-examiner should pursue his questioning with a particular fallacy or weakness in mind.

10. The cross-examiner should exercise self-control. He should not become ruffled or disconcerted by any answer. He should always be patient and good-natured.

11. To indicate that a particular line of inquiry is concluded, the examiner should repeat one of his opening questions, e.g., "In view of, etc., do you still believe, etc.?"

The Examinee: "Do's" and "Don't's"

1. The examinee may not consult his colleague before answering a question.

2. The examinee should answer as briefly and directly as possible.

3. The examinee may refuse to answer a question if he explains why he thinks the question is unfair.

4. The examinee may ask that a question be clarified, or he may rephrase a question and ask if the examiner concurs with the rephrased version.

5. On rare occasions the examinee may ask the examiner to desist from making speeches and to get on with the questions.

6. The examinee may begin his answer with a qualifying phrase, e.g., "Under certain circumstances, yes."

7. The examinee may exert some influence on the question period by slowing down his answers if he feels he is being rushed, or by speeding them up if he thinks the examiner is too slow in asking questions.

8. The examinee should exercise self-control. He should not become flustered by any question or be ashamed to admit that he cannot answer

a given question, particularly a question calling for factual information.

9. The examinee should neither evade nor stall. He should at all times be cooperative and good-natured.

4. EVALUATION OF CROSS-EXAM DEBATE

The requirements for effective cross-exam debating are basically the same as those for orthodox debating—good analysis, plentiful evidence, logical organization, clear thinking, adaptation, and skillful delivery. In addition, cross-examination requires skill in asking pertinent questions, a skill which is difficult to acquire or teach. Thus, cross-exam debating probably lends itself more readily to experienced debaters than to novices.

Because it is less formal than orthodox debating and because the pattern of straight speaking is interrupted by personal clashes, cross-exam debating is more appealing to most audiences than orthodox debating. Also, the opportunities for cross-examination make this type of debating especially valuable for students who plan to enter law or politics.

On the other hand, cross-examination tends to limit the number of points that can be covered effectively. The examiner must not only spend more time developing a point but must cope with the evasive tactics of the examinee. The result is that frequently only one point can be covered in the time that three or four points can be covered in orthodox debating. Also, cross-examination tends to emphasize the personal conflict in debate, to provoke undesirable attitudes, and to stress showmanship instead of the academic values of debate. The purpose of academic debate is, after all, to train students to become thinking individuals, not entertainers. For the sake of variety, however, cross-exam debate is a desirable supplement, though not a substitute, for orthodox debate.

5. SAMPLE CROSS-EXAMINATION

Q: You say that the United States is presently ahead of the Soviet Union in nuclear weapons technology. Is that right?

A: Yes.

Q: And that a test ban at the present time would preserve this advantage?

A: Yes.

Q: Do you consider that this would be a significant advantage for the United States?

A: Yes, I believe that it would be.

Q: This, then, you claim, is one reason why the United States, England, the Soviet Union, and other nations should agree to prohibit nuclear weapons development at the present time?

A: One reason, yes.

Q: Now, then, since the United States would benefit significantly at the expense of the Soviet Union, do you consider this a good reason why the Soviet Union should join the agreement—or should want to join?

A: No, this may not be a good reason for the Soviet Union to join, but there are other good reasons for her wanting to join. As Senator Humphrey recently pointed out, a test ban would ease world tensions and provide the Soviet Union with the necessary breathing spell to solidify her economic base.

Q: You admit, however, that you have shown at least one reason why the Soviet Union should not want to join.

A: Yes, but, as I have said, this must be balanced against other reasons why she should or would want to join.

Q: Very well, then; you say—or Humphrey says—that the Soviet Union wants to solidify her economic position. Is it your contention that she cannot do so unless she enters into an international agreement to prohibit nuclear weapons development?

A: The point is, she could not do it as well under the status quo since the tensions produced by the nuclear armaments race divert her from this objective—that is, they prevent her from concentrating on it.

Q: All right, then, the issue with regard to the Soviet Union seems to be: would she rather speed up her economic development and leave herself vulnerable militarily, or would she prefer to develop economically at a slower pace but secure herself militarily. In view of the Soviet Union's psychotic fear of the West, is it your contention that the leaders in the Kremlin would choose the first course—speedy economic development along with military vulnerability?

A: I don't think I should answer that question since it contains certain assumptions which I don't feel are warranted.

Q: Very well, what assumptions do you object to?

A: In the first place, you assume that if the Soviet Union joins, she will be militarily vulnerable. We never contended this. The United States may enjoy a military advantage in nuclear weapons technology, but this doesn't mean that the Soviet Union would consider herself militarily vulnerable, or militarily weak, over-all. She still has enough big bombs and a superiority in conventional weapons to feel secure that she can destroy any enemy. Secondly, there are other reasons besides her desires for economic development for her wanting to join. After all, she has as much to fear from fallout and from other nations getting nuclear weapons as the United States. Eliminating these hazards would also be good reasons for the Soviet Union's wanting to join.

Q: Are you saying, then, that the Soviet Union would remain militarily powerful?

A: Yes.

Q: Do you agree, then, that the so-called military advantage that the United States would gain—one of your main reasons for wanting to change the status quo—wouldn't really be very significant after all?

A: Not at all. The United States can gain a significant military advantage without the Soviet Union's military position being simultaneously undermined.

Q: What, then, do you mean by "significant"?

A: I would say "substantial" or "important."

Q: Well, if this so-called military advantage is substantial, or important, wouldn't it be with respect to the Soviet Union's development of nuclear weapons?

A: I'm not sure that I understand the question.

Q: All right, let me put it this way: if the United States were significantly superior to the Soviet Union in nuclear weapons technology, would not the Soviet Union be at a distinct disadvantage to the United States?

A: In the area of nuclear weapons technology, yes.

Q: And wouldn't this be a reason for her to feel vulnerable militarily?

A: Not necessarily—as I have already explained.

Q: All right, then, just one more question. Do you admit that either your need for a change here is not significant, or, if significant, that your program would be impracticable since the Soviet Union would not join it?

A: I don't think I need answer this question since there are other choices than the two you offer.

Comment. Here the examiner pursues a major need argument presented by the examinee and by skillful questions succeeds in showing that either the need is insignificant or that the examinee's plan is impracticable. Despite the examinee's efforts to slip between the horns of this dilemma, the examiner persists in pinning him to one or the other horn.

EXERCISES

Exercises for this chapter have been combined with those for Chapter 25.

OTHER DEBATE FORMS

In the last analysis we are governed either through talk or through force.

Felix Frankfurter

Besides orthodox and cross-examination debates, there are many other forms which often prove educational and interesting to participants and audience alike. Desirable as an occasional departure from the regimen of formal debating, they also provide the debater with exercises in argumentation and persuasion that more closely approximate real-life situations and are thus more readily adaptable for use before general audiences than are orthodox debates. The different debate forms appear here in the order of their increasing variance from the orthodox form.

1. THREE-MAN-TEAM DEBATE

As the historical forerunner of current orthodox debate, the three-man-team debate is valuable because it allows greater participation. Although it uses the same stock issues of the orthodox form, the time allotted each speaker may be reduced to allow for the additional speeches. The final rebuttal speakers are occasionally given seven minutes to summarize all the previous speeches. With six speakers and with approaches to the same issue varying among team members, issues are in danger of becoming clouded and arguments forgotten from speech to speech. Because of their general unwieldiness, three-man-team debates have practically disappeared.

2. ONE-REBUTTAL DEBATE

Another variation of the orthodox form, the one-rebuttal debate, provides the first affirmative five minutes to present his case. The next three speakers have the standard ten minutes, and then the first affirmative finishes the debate with a five-minute rebuttal. The main advantage here is supposed to be the reduced time, but it is doubtful if the first affirmative can present very much in only five minutes. Moreover, the other speakers have no opportunity to show their skill in summarizing or integrating important issues as they have in the rebuttal speeches of the orthodox form.

3. THREE-TEAM DEBATE

Despite its complexity and length, the three-team debate has achieved some popularity in meets involving a limited number of friendly schools. Three teams, A, B, and C, defend respectively the status quo, a plan embodied in the proposition, and a counterplan. The following format is used:

Minutes

The first speaker of B attacks the status quo	8
The first speaker of A defends the status quo	8
The first speaker of C attacks the status quo	8
The second speaker of B advocates a plan	12
The second speaker for A defends the status quo against B	12
The second speaker for C advocates a counterplan	12
The first speaker of C attacks B	8
The first speaker of A attacks C	8
The first speaker of B attacks C	8

4. SPLIT-TEAM DEBATE

A simple variation of either orthodox or cross-exam debate, the split-team debate prevents institutional rivalry and, conversely, builds up friendly relations between individual debaters from different schools. Teams from each school are split and individual members are paired with new partners from other schools. The split teams then debate either their combined cases or an entirely new case based on materials dealing with a relatively simple, previously unannounced proposition selected by the tournament sponsors. In the former instance, the case that each team brings to a tournament must be broken up and the materials pooled to achieve a new unity. Original analysis, solid training in fundamentals, and compromise are especially necessary if the newly formed teams are to debate their new case effectively. Unfortunately, such talents and ability are often lacking in debaters. However, several hours are provided before the debates start, and the rounds are widely spaced so that the debaters can reach agreement on their case. Decisions, if any, are given on the basis of team effectiveness and integration. Individual ratings based on effectiveness may also replace team decisions. Since the value of extensive teamwork is consciously destroyed and since there is little time for analysis and no time for solid research, the emphasis is likely to fall on simple persuasive speaking.

5. DIRECT-CLASH DEBATE

Developed by Edwin Paget in 1931,[1] the direct-clash debate seeks to bring the two sides to a quick determination of issues by eliminating unimportant points and weak reasoning. This form holds some interest for debaters for the same reason that cross-exam does: quick thinking, sound preparation, and verbal acuity are at a premium. Debaters also are attracted to the direct clash because it progresses round by round like a boxing match to a final decision. The judge has more opportunity to insert himself into the debate and thus to justify his eventual decision by considering each issue individually.

There are from two to five members on a team. The speaking order is extremely flexible, the only provision being that there be no successive speeches or initiation of successive clashes by one speaker. A typical format is as follows:

The affirmative opens for five minutes, defining terms, outlining arguments, and presenting a plan.

The negative follows for five minutes, accepting or rejecting terms, proposing affirmative and new negative issues, or perhaps introducing a counterplan.

Each side then has an additional three minutes for clarification.

The judge enters the debate, ruling on the relevancy of issues introduced and possibly requiring a clash on definition. He may establish the order of treatment of the issues, and he can rule against a concession if he thinks it concedes the debate. He may also stop the debate at this stage if he thinks that one side is clearly victorious.

If the debate is not stopped:

The affirmative considers a basic subissue for four minutes.

The negative deals with this argument for two minutes.

The negative and affirmative alternate with two-minute speeches on the issue for a total of three speeches on each side.

If the judge has permitted the clash to go full-length, the affirmative gives a two-minute summary.

At any time after the first two speeches, the judge may halt a clash, give a point against a team raising irrelevant issues or employing weak answers, and give his reasons for doing so.

At the end of a clash the judge awards a point to one side.

The negative initiates a clash, and the same procedure is followed.

The final decision can go to the team which either wins three clashes first or proves "decisively the one, all-important issue of the debate."

While this form can be very stimulating for an audience, debaters, and the sometimes bored judge, it is open to several criticisms. Issues

[1] Edwin H. Paget, "The Direct Clash Debate Plan," *Quarterly Journal of Speech*, XVIII, 4 (November, 1932), pp. 648–653; "Revised Direct Clash Debate Rules," *ibid.*, XVII (February, 1941), pp. 125–127.

are not likely to stand out either in specific detail or in their relevance to the broad picture because they are considered separately from other points "irrelevant" to a clash. To quote O'Brien, "There is great question whether the debaters or the audience, at the conclusion of the debate, have the total values at issue in perspective. Breaking a problem up into its subsidiary units militates against the comprehensive view."[2] It is also very unlikely that many judges could be found who were competent to judge such a complex contest. The form, however, is useful as a formalized means of intrasquad analysis of issues before the final case has been agreed upon.

6. DIRECT-QUESTION OR DIALECTIC DEBATE

The direct-question or dialectic debate resembles direct-clash and cross-exam debates. Constructive speeches are replaced by dialogues between colleagues for fifteen minutes, followed by ten minutes of cross-examination by the other side. Each team ends with a two- to five-minute summary. Audience interests would probably be retained by such an interchange, but continuity, unity, and effective use of time would undoubtedly be hard to sustain.

7. HECKLING DEBATE

The heckling debate resembles open-air speech making and thus approximates a real-life speech situation. However, as often happens in such situations, intensified conflicts may degenerate into chaotic wrangling. Formal speeches are interrupted by questions, protests, and comments intended to challenge the speaker's contentions and shake his composure. Typical rules are as follows:

There are four ten-minute speeches and no rebuttals.
One member from each team heckles each speaker of the other team.
No heckling is permitted during the first three minutes and the last two of a speech.
No new arguments may be introduced in the final two minutes of the second affirmative. If new arguments are introduced, the chairman may grant heckling time to the negative.
Usually no more than a half minute and a sentence or two should be used for each heckle. The heckler may demand specific evidence, expose fallacies, and, within bounds, embarrass the speaker. The heckler should aim at main points, not minor or isolated ones.
The judge decides whether any infractions of the rules have occurred. The

[2] Joseph F. O'Brien, "An Appraisal of Contemporary Forms and Phases of Forensics in Pennsylvania," *Bulletin of the DAPC,* XV (December 10, 1948), p. 38.

decision is awarded to the more effective team, with consideration being given to the reasonableness and appropriateness of the heckling.

Drawbacks to this form are that debaters are not likely to have immediately at hand materials to answer every challenge, and the opposition is inclined to make unreasonable challenges. However, the heckling debate has at least one thing to recommend itself to debaters: no side ever finds itself "without rejoinder" to a new issue raised in a last speech.

8. ENGLISH-STYLE DEBATE

American audiences witnessing English debate teams on tour here have been entertained by the English wit, philosophic-literary style, and easy platform manner. The English lack of teamwork and the nonchalant attitude to the contest situation provide a good show and an interesting contrast to serious American debaters. English-style debate stems from procedures patterned after those used in the House of Commons and perfected at the Oxford Union Society, where hundreds of students gather, choose sides, and are addressed formally but without brief by two of their colleagues on each side. Each speaker takes about fifteen minutes, subject to interruptions by the chair and heckling from the floor. An open forum and voting on the question follow.

Formal English debate resembles American legislative debate, but when English debaters on tour graciously engage American college debaters in our more particularized forms of debate, we see a great contrast, both in method and goal. The English are open-minded and ready to concede telling points. Their preparation, on the other hand, is haphazard and perhaps explains why they are not prepared to pursue an argument. They use no briefs or files. They are interested in having a good time while simultaneously perfecting themselves as future leaders able to sway their listeners by brilliant platform performance. They tend to stress emotional more than logical appeals.

9. PROBLEM-SOLVING DEBATE

Theoretically a combination of traditional debate and discussion, the problem-solving debate is employed to solve a difficult problem. Consequently, the resolution is phrased as a question. There are two or three speakers on each team (A and B). The members of A team speak 1-3-6, and the members of B, 2-4-5. If each team has only two members, the first speakers present a complete analysis of the problem. Otherwise, the first speaker of each team speaks ten minutes, analyzing the problem objectively, presenting background information, and establishing criteria for a solution; the second speaker of each team speaks twelve minutes, presenting a solution based on his team's research. The last speakers speak eight minutes, evaluating the solutions of both sides fairly and dispassionately; they may ask the others questions and even disagree with their own colleagues. If a decision is desired, the speakers are ranked in pairs by the judges, who consider primarily (1) scientific research and reasoning, (2) avoidance of prejudice and prejudicial appeals, and (3) effective cooperation. Effective perhaps in early season practice sessions, this form also reduces a debater's contentiousness and is informative for general audiences.

10. SYMPOSIUM-FORUM

The symposium-forum is another complex of informal modifications of orthodox debating. According to the dictionary, a symposium is a meeting for discussion of some controversial subject marked by a collection of varying opinions. It usually takes the form of short formal addresses by several participants, followed by a discussion among them. If a forum is included, questions from the audience are directed to specific speakers through the chairman.

There are obviously several variations of this general arrangement, depending on the audience and the time allowed. If there is to be no decision, the audience may be surveyed before or/and after the presentation to see how many have changed their minds.

Debate Symposium

In the *debate symposium* four two-man teams take part. The first speaker states his team's position, and subsequent speakers amplify the team position, cross-examine, refute preceding arguments, restate, and summarize. After the teams' positions have been stated, there may or may not be a particular order of speaking.

Radio (Television) Forum

In the *radio (television) forum* two opposing speakers are given a short time to establish their respective positions on a particular issue. They then answer back and forth, with the moderator controlling the time used and asking questions to clarify issues.

Intercollegiate Forum

The *intercollegiate forum* calls for four speakers. The first explains the problem, giving its background and present status. Each subsequent speaker continues proposing solutions, withdrawing propositions, refuting, and defending. Any speaker may change his point of view. An opportunity for rejoinder may be given each speaker at the close if he desires it. The chairman finishes with a critical summary of the four speeches.

Two-man Debate Forum

Probably the most effective debate presentation for the after-dinner circuit is the *two-man debate forum*. It provides the flavor of orthodox debating while keeping audience interest through frequent change of speakers, by taking less time, and by providing for audience participation. The moderator takes five minutes or so to give a background of the question and perhaps a simple explanation of the principles of debate. The affirmative speaker then presents his case in eight minutes; the negative answers in ten minutes, trying to anticipate the affirmative defense; the affirmative closes with two minutes of rebuttal. The time division, is, of course, subject to modification, the only requirement being that each side has equal time. After a number of questions from the floor, the moderator closes the program.

Finally, there are those variants of debate that most closely approximate certain real-life situations. The following forms offer a varied speech experience; both group discussion in committees and advocacy of bills on the floor are employed together with the intricacies of parliamentary procedure. Because tournament tensions are absent, such gatherings are also more inclined to promote good fellowship and mutual understanding.

11. PARLIAMENTARY SESSION

As practiced at Penn State University, the parliamentary session is, perhaps, the most informal parliamentary debate form. It involves a chairman, secretary, four discussion leaders, and an audience. The chairman opens the meeting; he states the question and may temporarily adjourn the meeting for committee work on prospective bills. When the meeting is back in full session, the first speaker gives an eight-minute report on "evils" and moves the adoption of a solution. The second speaker speaks eight minutes on the plausibility of the solution. Then, each of the two home-team speakers has eight minutes to support, amend, or offer alternatives to the bill. Discussion is then open to speakers for and against. The effectiveness of each team may be judged by the success or failure of the bill in a vote taken at the end of the discussion period.

12. CONGRESSIONAL-STYLE SESSION

Similar to the parliamentary form, the congressional-style session is a combination of orthodox, cross-question, and heckling, patterned after the operation of Congress. Teams are usually composed of two speakers. Two twelve-minute constructive speeches are allotted to each side, but one-third of this time can be taken up in heckling. Heckling may begin after the first three minutes of each speech and last until the final minute. Only three heckles are allowed per speech, and an attempt to heckle in the last minute will gain the speaker an extra minute. Points of order directed to the judge are permitted at any time on misrepresentation, misquoting, new arguments in rebuttal, and begging the question.

The rebuttals are six minutes each in the same order and are subject to interruptions or cross-examination amounting to one minute. The last rebuttalist may not be interrupted during his final two minutes. A speaker may yield to his colleague on a question he cannot handle himself.

Though very interesting, congressional-style debate may easily get out of control and is thus infrequently used.

13. LEGISLATIVE DEBATE

The most complicated of the three parliamentary forms is the legislative debate. Its elements are (1) a relatively large group of people representing different institutions, (2) a set of generally accepted rules, and (3) a body of officers to direct the group according to those rules. Oral discourse and behind-the-scenes "politicking" leading to election of officers and passage of bills are envisioned.

Problems are usually announced two months or so prior to the meeting, and the schools come prepared to defend their respective bills. The general session is preceded by committee work on the bills and election of officers. At the call to convene, the audience may seat itself according to sentiment on a resolution, with the proponents on the chairman's right and the opposition on the left facing each other. When a number of different bills are to be presented, the assembly may also be seated by geographical area. A typical procedure is:

Two speakers speak for the resolution and two against, without interruption, for seven minutes each.

General debate follows when the chair asks, "Is there further discussion?" Floor speakers are recognized for three minutes each, alternately.

Speakers may be interrupted by anyone addressing the chair, "Mr. Chairman, will the speaker yield for a question?" The chairman then inquires of the speaker, who may or may not yield.

The debate is ended by general consent or by a two-thirds vote.

The bill and amendments are carried by a simple majority.

Roberts' Rules of Order and other typical legislative practices are followed.

14. MOCK-TRIAL DEBATE

Developed by Warren Guthrie,[3] the mock-trial debate is interesting for an audience and especially for debaters intending to become lawyers. The topic is in the form of a court decree, or writ of mandamus.[4] In law schools where the mock trial or moot court is a formal teaching method, actual cases or theoretical points of law are argued before a *banc*, or panel, of judges who may interrupt to question the student advocates at any time. The law students prepare their briefs in teams and give them under rules of court procedure patterned after an appeals court hearing. Guthrie's mock trial, however, is patterned after a lower court. Students represent the judge, the attorney general of the United States, and an attorney seeking a writ. Each attorney may call three witnesses representing prominent authorities, who in turn may cite historical fact or the written testimony of the authorities they represent. A bailiff opens court, swears in witnesses, and keeps time. Twelve members of the audience compose the jury. The following format is used:

The bailiff calls order.

The judge speaks three minutes on background and definitions.

The plaintiff's attorney presents his case in three minutes.

The attorney general speaks for three minutes against the plaintiff.

The plaintiff's attorney calls his witnesses, using four minutes for direct questioning of each.

The attorney general calls his three witnesses and the same pattern is followed.

The attorney general closes with a three-minute summary and final plea.

The plaintiff's attorney does likewise.

The judge instructs the jury.

The jury votes, and discussion from the floor may follow.[5]

Some tournaments, besides giving many schools an inexpensive opportunity to meet in debate, also provide a number of other speaking contests in order to give the debater additional and more varied experience. Besides debate, many tournaments include contests in oratory, extemporaneous speaking, oral interpretation, and discussion. In some tournaments a team's final standing is determined by the total number of points scored in all events.

[3] Warren A. Guthrie, "The Reserve Plan for Intercollegiate Discussion," *Quarterly Journal of Speech*, XXV (February, 1939), pp. 392–396.

[4] Literally, "mandamus" is a Latin word meaning "we command." In law, a writ of mandamus is a court order issued to enforce the performance of some public duty.

[5] In terms of orthodox debate, the plaintiff's attorney represents the affirmative, and the attorney general the negative.

Parliamentary Procedure

Motions Classified According to Precedence

	Interrupt speaker?	Second required?	Debatable?	Amendable?	Vote required?
Privileged motions (in order of precedence)					
Fix time of next meeting	No	Yes	No	Yes	Majority
Adjourn	No	Yes	No	No	Majority
Recess	No	Yes	No	Yes	Majority
Question of privilege	Yes	No	No	No	No vote
Subsidiary motions (in order of precedence)					
Lay on table (postpone temporarily)	No	Yes	No	No	Majority
Previous question (vote immediately)	No	Yes	No	No	⅔
Limit debate	No	Yes	No	Yes	⅔
Postpone definitely (to a certain time)	No	Yes	Yes	Yes	Majority
Refer to committee	No	Yes	Yes	Yes	Majority
Committee of the whole	No	Yes	Yes	Yes	Majority
Amend	No	Yes	Yes	Yes	Majority
Postpone indefinitely	No	Yes	Yes	No	Majority
Main motions (no order of precedence)					
Main motion for general business	No	Yes	Yes	Yes	Majority
Take from the table	No	Yes	No	No	Majority
Reconsider	Yes	Yes	Yes	No	Majority
Rescind	No	Yes	Yes	No	Majority
Make special order of business	No	Yes	Yes	Yes	⅔
Incidental motions (no order of precedence)					
Appeal from decision of chair	Yes	Yes	Yes	No	Tie or majority
Point of order	Yes	No	No	No	No vote
Parliamentary inquiry	Yes	No	No	No	No vote
Withdraw a motion	No	No	No	No	No vote
Suspend rules	No	Yes	No	No	⅔
Object to consideration	Yes	No	No	No	⅔ negative
Division of a question	No	No	No	No	No vote
Division of assembly	Yes	No	No	No	No vote
Request for information	Yes	No	No	No	No vote
To suppress debate or hasten action:					
Previous question	No	Yes	No	No	⅔
Suspend rules	No	Yes	No	No	⅔

Parliamentary Procedure

Motions Classified According to Purpose

	Interrupt speaker?	Second required?	Debat-able?	Amend-able?	Vote required?
Limit debate	No	Yes	No	Yes	⅔
Take from table	No	Yes	No	No	Majority
Make special order of business	No	Yes	Yes	Yes	⅔
To delay action:					
Postpone definitely	No	Yes	Yes	Yes	Majority
Lay on the table	No	Yes	No	No	Majority
Refer to committee	No	Yes	Yes	Yes	Majority
To prevent action:					
Object to consideration	Yes	No	No	No	⅔ negative
Withdraw a motion	No	No	No	No	No vote
Postpone indefinitely	No	Yes	Yes	No	Majority
To consider more carefully:					
Committee of the whole	No	Yes	Yes	Yes	Majority
To prevent log-rolling:					
Division of a question	No	No	No	No	No vote
To change a decision:					
Reconsider	Yes	Yes	Yes	No	Majority
Rescind	No	Yes	Yes	No	Majority
To get an accurate vote:					
Division of assembly	Yes	No	No	No	No vote
To maintain rules and order:					
Question of privilege	Yes	No	No	No	No vote
Point of order	Yes	No	No	No	No vote
Appeal from decision of chair	Yes	Yes	Yes	No	Tie or majority
Parliamentary inquiry	Yes	No	No	No	No vote
Request for information	Yes	No	No	No	No vote
To close a meeting:					
Adjourn	No	Yes	No	No	Majority
Fix time of next meeting	No	Yes	No	Yes	Majority
Recess	No	Yes	No	Yes	Majority

EXERCISE

1. Suggestion to instructor: Of the various types of debate pick six or so of the most interesting and assign various students to conduct an abbreviated debate in class on each of the types chosen. After each demonstration debate, discuss the strengths and weaknesses of the particular type. Consider such questions as: Which provides the best training in analysis and thinking for the student? Which is most adaptable for audience situations, i.e., which is an audience likely to find most interesting? Which stresses extemporaneous speaking and thinking? Which puts a premium on platform manner?

CHAPTER 26

PERSUASIVE SPEAKING CONTESTS

> Speak not at all, in any wise, till you have somewhat to speak; care
> not for the reward of your speaking, but simply and with undivided
> mind, for the truth of your speaking.
>
> *Carlyle*

Besides debate, many forensic tournaments schedule contests in other
types of persuasive speaking, the two most popular being extemporaneous
speaking, popularly known as "extemp" (the term which will be used
here), and oratory, also called "public speaking" or "persuasive speaking."

1. THE EXTEMP CONTEST

The extemp contest is perhaps second in popularity to debate, being
scheduled in most of the larger tournaments. Actually, the term "extemp"
is something of a misnomer, for the type of speaking called for is a cross
between extemporaneous speaking, which requires much preparation, and
impromptu speaking, which requires very little.

Unlike debaters, extemp contestants are usually left to work out their
own formula for success. Although debate training is helpful, the contestant faces some special problems, the chief one being to prepare an
effective speech rapidly. With only a half hour or an hour in which to
prepare a six to ten-minute speech based upon reading a month's back
issues of some periodical like *Time* or *Newsweek*, many contestants become panicky, work without direction, and find themselves speaking
practically impromptu. The successful contestant, on the other hand, not
only uses his preparation time wisely but also learns certain principles
which help prepare him long before the actual contest. We shall now
consider some of these principles.[1]

---

[1] Much of this material first appeared in an article by the writer, "The Extempore
Speaking Contest," *The Speech Teacher*, III (September, 1956), pp. 214–222.

Choosing a Topic

About an hour before he is to speak, the contestant usually draws three subjects, chooses one, and returns the others. The subjects usually pertain to some political, social, or economic problem and call for either advocating or evaluating some policy, explaining some situation, or predicting some event. At a tournament held a few years ago, representative topics were:

Policy: "Should Wire-tapped Evidence Be Permitted in a Court of Law?" "Why Should the United States Congress Establish and Subsidize a National Theater?"

Evaluation: "Was the Celebrated Lawrence of Arabia a Great Hero or a Great Fraud?" "Are the So-called 'Fair Trade Laws' an Aid or Hindrance to Our Economy?"

Explanation: "The 'Tammany Tiger' Is No Longer Really a Tiger, But Rather a Little 'Kitty.' Why?" "What Are the Causes of the Fairly Basic Split in Both the Republican and the Democratic National Political Parties?"

Fact (Prediction): "What Are the Chances of Yugoslavia's Return to the Soviet Union's Orbit of Influence?" "With the Stock Market at an All-time High, What Are the Possibilities of a Crash?"

First, one must choose his subject wisely. The inexperienced contestant unhesitantly picks the subject he knows best, but the more experienced one, realizing that his knowledge will be limited whatever the subject, considers audience interest first and knowledge second. A good rule is, pick the liveliest, most controversial subject, the one closest to the interests of the audience. Also, judges are more inclined to favor an unusual or difficult subject than a commonplace one.

If one chooses a controversial subject and has no strong feelings for either side, he should usually uphold the unpopular side, i.e., the "liberal" rather than the "conservative" one, like the affirmative of the "Communist China Recognition" question or the negative of the "Outlawing Communist Teachers" question. If all other factors are equal, one should choose a subject from his major field of interest.

Getting Started

After deciding upon a topic, the contestant must work calmly and systematically in preparing his speech. He must resist feelings of panic, confusion, and worry, for these only dissipate time, energy, and mental power. Though he must work quickly, he must do so with a definite plan.

Central Idea, or Theme

The contestant should next determine a central idea, or theme, for this provides a focus for the material, determining what should be included and what omitted. One should avoid a factual or pedestrian approach and seek a fresh or novel one, viewing the subject, if possible, as part of a larger or world problem. Anticipating certain topics, one successful contestant used to work up a file of pertinent quotations, typical of which were "Revolt is one of the essential dimensions of mankind" (Camus) and "The devil's cleverest wile is to convince us that he doesn't exist" (Baudelaire). After picking his subject, he would choose an apt quotation to suggest a theme and would then analyze the topic accordingly. Sometimes he would use several quotations.

Climax and Conclusion

A good speech usually works up to a climax, which, being more important than the beginning of the speech, should be decided on next. There is a good reason for working backwards: if the beginning is good but the ending bad, the speech will probably fail; however, if the beginning is poor but the ending good, the speech will probably succeed. Along with the climax, an effective conclusion should be considered, the two often being one and the same. The conclusion generally should sum up the theme of the speech and should be led up to in a way that the audience will grasp in some fifteen or twenty seconds before it is actually stated. The most effective conclusion is usually dramatic; e.g., in a speech assessing Soviet foreign policy, one contestant, a winner of many extemp contests, concluded thus:

> This is my senior year and, with the help of a few professors, I hope to graduate. And, of course, I hope also that I may come back next year to renew these associations which I have enjoyed so much. Those of you who are sophomores and juniors plan to return as debaters. I hope that you will be able to return.

To enhance the dramatic effect, the speaker almost whispered the last line.

A good ending should be short, decisive, and crisp. If the purpose of the speech is to entertain, a good punch line or an anecdote would serve; if the purpose is to inform, a quick summary, perhaps; if the purpose is to persuade, an appeal to action possibly. In any case, the speaker should never trail off but should end on a crisp, definite note.

Typical Thought Patterns

Most topics fall into four categories, each of which has its own special development, or "thought pattern," and knowing these patterns greatly facilitates organizing a speech. Briefly, the four categories and principles of development are as follows:

Straightforward Exposition

This stresses information for the curious about little known or unusual occupations, like a speech on Disneyland or on recent experiments to determine the origin of life. Few topics are of this nature and generally should be avoided. However, since explanation plays an important part in any speech, whether the aim be to inform, interpret, evaluate, or persuade, the following techniques of explanation should be understood:

By Parts and Factors. This consists of breaking an entity down into its component parts and showing the relationship between them, like enumerating the various divisions of the UN and showing how they function to make up the whole. The terms "analysis" and "synthesis" are commonly used for this process.

By Circumstances and Conditions. This consists of showing how an entity is related to other entities, like showing how the heart functions in relation to other organs of the body. The terms "comparison" and "contrast" are often used for this process.

By Cause and Effect. This consists of explaining how some manifestation is an effect of some cause, like showing how certain factors precipitated the Korean conflict. The terms "history" and "diagnosis" are often used in connection with this process.

By Function. This consists of explaining how some entity functions as a cause of some effect, or as a means to some end, like explaining the functions of a college. Such terms as "advantages," "disadvantages," "practicability," and "future" are often used in connection with this process.

Sometimes an effective explanation or definition begins with a statement of what something is not (e.g., a poem is not a sermon in verse, it is not a treatise, etc.), followed by an explanation of what it is.

Interpretation of a Situation or an Event

This involves the proposition of explanation, or causal hypothesis, and consists primarily of explaining through cause-and-effect reasoning why something happened, is happening, or will happen. Typical subjects are "What Is the Meaning of the New Soviet Foreign Policy?" or "Will Arab-Israeli Differences Lead to a Third World War?"

Evaluation

This weighs the good and bad points of a prominent figure or current policy, like "Kennedy—Presidential Aspirant" or "Do Flexible Price Supports Really Help the Farmer?" To evaluate something, one must first establish a standard of measure—a model or ideal, desirable aims or objectives. Then, whatever measures up to the criteria is good; whatever falls short, bad. In a sense, this type of speech is built around the following syllogism:

Major: Anything which measures up to the established criteria (or achieves the desired objectives) is good.
Minor: Such-and-such an individual or policy does (or does not) measure up.
Conclusion: Therefore, such-and-such an individual or policy is (or is not) good.

In a speech titled "Are the Policies of Nehru in Accord with the Foreign Policy of the United States?" one contestant used this syllogism with good effect:

Major: The objectives of United States foreign policy in the Far East are such and such (established by factual reference).
Minor: Nehru's major policies help fulfill these objectives (two or so major policies were considered).
Conclusion: Therefore, Nehru's policies are predominantly in accord with United States foreign policy.

The object evaluated may of course measure up in some respects and fall short in others.

Policy

This advocates adopting or rejecting a policy or program, like most national debate topics. Since most extemp contestants are also debaters, they are familiar with this type of speech, the main points of which are:

1. Considering objectives of present policy.

2. Evaluating the present policy in terms of these objectives. (Do we have a problem or not?)

3. Inquiring into the cause of the situation described in previous step.

4. Explaining the new policy as a solution to the problem or as being superfluous.

5. Considering other advantages or disadvantages which might accrue from the new policy.

For a very short impromptu speech, an easier formula to remember would be "problem, cause, solution."

In highly provocative speeches one should not state his conclusion bluntly at the outset but should reach it gradually through analysis and proof, with the impact coming at the end. Direct questions followed by answers are often effective.

Knowing how to apply the foregoing patterns insures logical development, reassures a speaker psychologically, and stimulates his associative powers of thought even after he has begun speaking.

General Perspective

A good speech usually takes a broad view rather than a narrow one. Thus, the speaker should try to fit his subject into a philosophical or historical framework, treating it as part of some bigger idea rather than in isolation. Apt quotations plus historical background are usually very helpful. Sometimes the speech can even be built around an historical generalization. For example, in a speech on present-day loyalty programs, one contestant devoted at least half of his time to discussing the history of loyalty programs in America and then concluded that, since overzealous loyalty programs in the past were dangerous, they are dangerous today. A simple formula for short speeches might be "past, present, future."

Taking a broad view does not mean covering much ground and saying little. On the contrary, the treatment should be intensive, with only a few ideas thoroughly developed.

Supporting Material, or Evidence

After determining the framework, the contestant must find supporting materials in the assigned magazines. A simple filing system can help here. For example, several days before the contest one might underline the key points of various articles or make notations in the margin. Then, using 4-inch by 6-inch cards, one can take notes and file them alphabetically by topic in a small file. During the contest one may use these notes directly or transcribe desired material in abbreviated form to 3-inch by 5-inch cards.

Although a speech without facts, statistics, details, illustrations, and quotations is anemic, facts must not be used simply as facts but must be interpreted as leading to certain conclusions; i.e., thinking must be stressed.

Opening Remarks

Next in importance to the conclusion perhaps (from the standpoint of audience effectiveness) is the opening. If a speaker fails to catch the audience's attention at the outset, the effect of his subsequent remarks may be lost. Suitable openings consist of an anecdote, an illustration, a rhetorical question, a quotation, or a reference to the timeliness or significance of the topic. Some farsighted contestants build up a file of openings suitable for different subjects, sometimes using two different types in the same speech.

Whenever possible, opening remarks should refer to the particular speaking situation. When the audience laughed when the speaker's subject was announced ("Is Russia Having a Gas Problem as Evidenced by Khrushchev's Recent Seven-hour Talk?"), one contestant began very effectively, "I see that you're all laughing and I'm not at all surprised. Everyone seems to be laughing these days at the antics of Khrushchev and Bulganin, who apparently pride themselves on being the Martin and Lewis of international politics. But while they expect us to laugh, I can assure you that their actions are no laughing matter." He then proceeded to analyze recent manifestations of the Soviet Union's foreign policy, skillfully weaving in the quotation from Baudelaire—"The devil's cleverest wile is to convince us that he doesn't exist"—which, like the introduction, pointed up the theme of his speech.

Pointing Up the Significance of the Topic

Near the beginning of the speech the speaker should try to show how his subject relates to some dominant interest of the audience. Since most people are interested in self-preservation, perpetuation of race, freedom from restraints, and acquisition of property, power, or popularity, one of these may be mentioned. Some topics, like "The Effect of Mad Comics on American Youth," have an obvious appeal, while others, like "Hawaii —Fiftieth State," must be related to some common interest of the audience.

Delivery and Platform Manner

The principles of effective delivery and platform manner are the same for the extemp speech as for any other. For a review of these principles, see Chapter 17.

General Attitude

The best attitude for any contestant is reflected by his being friendly, goodnatured, well-mannered, and sportsmanlike.

Practicing Aloud

About one-half to two-thirds of the preparation time should be devoted to thinking out the pattern and preparing the substance of the speech. The remainder should be used for practicing aloud, at least twice if possible. One should find an empty room and practice first with notes and then without. If no room is available, one should verbalize the speech several times to himself.

Precontest Practice

To become better acquainted with the foregoing principles and procedures, accustomed to working under pressure, and familiar with prospective topics, some students make practice speeches, under tournament conditions, several days before the tournament on subjects drawn from the required reading. They choose a wide range of topics, from the latest fashions to the Berlin crisis, and work whenever possible under a coach's supervision.

2. ORATORY, OR THE PERSUASIVE SPEAKING CONTEST

All of the foregoing principles of speech construction apply to the oratorical speech, the chief difference between extemp and oratory being that oratorical speeches are prepared weeks in advance and are usually delivered from memory. Many teachers of speech regard the memorized speech as being unrealistic and prefer the speech where notes may be used and the delivery is extemporaneous. Many also object to the term "oratory" because of its connotations and prefer the term "public speaking" or "persuasive speaking."

3. A SAMPLE PERSUASIVE SPEECH

Since there is no appreciable difference in content between the extemp, oratorical, and persuasive speech, the following speech may be taken as representative of all three types:

Motion Picture Censorship: The Legislation of Values [2]

The motion picture industry is one of the largest industries in the United States. Because of its size and scope, it has a tremendous influence on the lives of Americans. Even the smallest town has at least one movie theater. The young people work there; they go there on dates. Next to the funnies and the sports pages, the movie section of the newspapers is the most frequently consulted. You can't even stay home and watch television without a movie finding its way into your home.

Yes, the movie industry is big. Partly because of its size and partly because it is an industry, we seem to lose sight of the fact that it is an art form. We forget that the men behind the movies are artists and that most of them are sincere artists who deserve the right to express themselves freely. And yet many are suggesting that there be government suppression of their artistic freedom.

At present, there exists in the United States three main bodies for the purpose of censoring motion pictures: the film industry's own Production Code, the Roman Catholic Legion of Decency, and five state and sixty city bureaus. The Production Code Seal does not appear on movies concerning drug addiction, homosexuality, abortion, or venereal disease. The Legion of Decency is especially reluctant to approve movies dealing with divorce and birth control. The local and state censoring bodies have their own standards.

[2] This speech was delivered by Mary Frances Swigert at the Annual Pennsylvania Forensic Tournament, March, 1957.

The objections of these censors sound reasonable, don't they? The censors merely object to immorality. But may I remind you that a judgment of a work of art based solely on moral standards is not a valid judgment? The most important concern is not the subject of a movie. More important is the treatment of the subject. A subject that is offensive in one film may not be offensive in another. This is a paradox that cannot be controlled by any censoring body with its book of cut-and-dried rules.

Otis Guernsey, Jr., of the *New York Herald Tribune* put this well when he said: ". . . If the emotional force of a movie is stronger than the immediate impact of violence, then the violence is inoffensive. . . . If the emotional force of the film is weaker than the immediate impact of its violence, then violence becomes a sadistic thrill and is offensive. . . ."

Someone else has humorously said, "It depends on whether the incest is treated by Sophocles or by Mickey Spillane."

I believe that the present standards for evaluating motion pictures are not intelligent. A very necessary part of intelligence is an aesthetic sense, an appreciation of art. Of course, this type of intellectual tolerance must be restricted by a moral sense which objects to unmitigated vulgarity. It seems to me that in many cases the censors are giving their hearty approval to examples of very bad art while overlooking the real value of certain movies that have what they term as "immoral" or "suggestive" themes.

The censors objected to "I Am a Camera" because of its theme; it was the psychological study of an immoral girl. "Man with a Golden Arm" was not given the Production Code Seal because it was the story of a narcotics addict. Nobody seemed to care whether the movie put over a good message or if it glorified narcotics addiction. The subject of the picture lost it its approval. A censoring body in Atlanta, Georgia, objected to "Blackboard Jungle" *only* because it showed colored and white students in the same classroom. Right now, there is a great deal of controversy about the film version of Tennessee Williams' "Baby Doll." This is not the first time that Williams and Elia Kazan, the director, have been under fire for their realistic treatment of certain more ugly aspects of life. I understand that "Baby Doll" will not be shown in Pennsylvania. I would like to know if the true objection to this film is to be found behind the hysterical cries of "immoral" and "suggestive," or if perhaps the movie falls short of carrying its intended message—if any—or if it falls short of reaching artistic perfection in some other ways.

Yes, it is our duty to cry out against inartistic and vulgar things that appear in movies. We must encourage the men who make the movies and the theater owners to give the American people entertainment that reflects the art and culture of a growing nation. However, encouragement of this sort should not involve government suppression or censorship by any group.

The culture of America is growing. Americans must be encouraged to discriminate between good art and bad art—between right and wrong. A man doesn't grow in strength of character if all of his decisions are made for him. And neither does a nation! Americans don't need censors; they need good taste. And they need the freedom to develop it.

You say that there are some people who are incapable of making intelligent moral decisions. But no one would dare question their capabilities on election day. Their right to vote is a part of democracy. Their right to choose what they shall see and hear is a part of democracy, too. Moreover, if a man's mind is low enough, he can find ugliness and vulgarity in a fine work of art. The artificial restraints of censorship and government suppression cannot replace the natural restraints of a sound sense of values and strength of character.

Yes, the movies are guilty of some serious infringements of moral practice, but so is the theater, and books, and magazines, and comic books, and newspapers. Can we censor them all? Perhaps, but we would have to revise the Constitution first.

The righteous indignation aroused by the production and release of certain movies could be more effectively channeled into crusades for better schools. In the case of moral and artistic values, *education* will always have more import than *legislation*.

There is a great deal to the idea of overcoming evil with good. But heaven protect this nation when *good* becomes a synonym for *censorship* or for *government suppression!*

4. JUDGING SPEECH CONTESTS

As in judging debate, speech teachers unfortunately tend to consider delivery and platform personality as the most important aspect of a speech. Aware of this misplaced emphasis, the Speech Association of the Eastern States in its "Code for Contests in Public Speaking" reminds its members that a "contest speech is not an exhibition of skill, not a performance *before* people: it must communicate ideas *to* and *with* people." In other words, the Association rightly holds that a speech must be judged mainly in terms of its content, that delivery "is a means to an end" and "should not be adjudged more important than the factors of conception, organization, and development." [3] As a guide, the following criteria should be used in judging a speech:

1. The originality of its theme.
2. The organization of its ideas, or development of the theme.
3. The quality of its supporting or illustrative materials.
4. The quality of language used.
5. The manner of delivery.

To slight or to ignore any one of these factors is to do the contestant an injustice. As the S.A.E.S. observes: "A contestant who diligently . . . prepares a speech acquires an inalienable right to evaluation on the basis of sound, relevant criteria." [4]

[3] *Today's Speech,* IV, 4 (November, 1956), p. 31.
[4] *Today's Speech, op. cit.,* p. 30.

EXERCISES

1. Using the four most recent issues of either *Newsweek, Time,* or *U.S. News,* compose two titles for each of the four basic types of proposition (fact, explanation, value, and policy).

2. Suggestion to instructor: Pool all titles, have each student pick five, select one, return the others, and after a short preparation period give a five-minute extemporaneous speech. For added interest the class may be divided into groups of three or four students each, with one winner being picked from each group. All winners then meet in a final round from which first-, second-, and third-place winners are picked. Using the criteria listed at the end of this chapter, students do all the judging. If each member of the class wishes to contribute a nominal sum, small trophies may be purchased for the top three speakers.

CHAPTER 27

DISCUSSION

Men are never so likely to settle a question rightly as when they discuss it freely.

Macaulay

1. DEFINITION OF DISCUSSION

A discussion is basically a conversation between two or more people, the purpose of which is to analyze and reach a solution to a problem by sound reasoning. Discussion may take many forms and may deal with trivial or important problems; and its quality may range from very bad to very good, depending upon the preparation, reasoning ability, speaking ability, and cooperation of the discussants.

2. DISCUSSION AND DEBATE: SIMILARITIES AND DIFFERENCES

As an activity, discussion resembles debate in several ways:

In the type of subject usually chosen: that is, one involving a problem and possible solutions. Instead of being stated as a proposition, however, the subject of a discussion is phrased as a question, e.g., "Should the Further Development of Nuclear Weapons Be Prohibited by International Agreement?"

In the analysis of the subject: Each issue and subissue of a debate subject becomes a topic of discussion, e.g., "Is radiation from nuclear weapons' tests a serious hazard to people?" If time is limited, one issue may suffice for an entire discussion.

In the preparation required: As we have seen, to reason effectively, one must have knowledge. To discuss a subject intelligently, one must be well informed.

In the way conclusions are reached: The same principles of clear thinking apply to both.

In the need for clear expression: No idea can be accurately evaluated unless it is clearly communicated.

Discussion differs from debate in several areas:

In purpose: The purpose of discussion is to reach agreement among the participants by means of pooling information, exchanging reasons, and critically evaluating the ideas presented. The purpose of debate (nonacademic, particularly) is to secure belief from a third party. In a democracy, debate usually occurs after discussion has failed to secure agreement between the parties involved. Having arrived, on the basis of the available evidence, at diametrically opposite conclusions, the parties to a debate now seek to convince a third party that their particular conclusion is the true one.

In academic debate, it has to be assumed that the parties have reached their conclusions through prior analysis and discussion. Actually, the reverse is true; they are first given the conclusion and then proceed to support it. To say, as some critics do, that academic debate is therefore unrealistic and thus "uneducational" is to overlook all of its other educational values. To make academic debate more realistic, some teachers advocate that discussion should occur before the debate season starts so that debaters can choose the side they believe in. Unfortunately, however, there is just not enough time to do all of the necessary research, to have discussion sessions, and to prepare for tournaments. And to encourage students to form an attachment to a given point of view on the basis of cursory discussions is probably worse than the ill it seeks to remedy. As was pointed out earlier, debating both sides of a question is probably the best way for the student to secure the breadth and understanding of the question that discussion aims at. The discussions which precede the debate season play an important part in preparing for debate. A good coach will conduct discussions on such topics as "What does the resolution mean?" "What seem to be the important issues of this year's topic?" "What is the best way to develop the need?" etc. All rebuttal sessions are in a sense discussions.

In format: Discussion is much less formal than debate. There are no set speeches or time limits. Under the guidance of a leader, the participants converse with one another—questioning, commenting, agreeing, disagreeing, and qualifying points brought up by the others. Individual contributions are usually short.

Since the desire to win is absent from discussions (except for contest discussions), they produce fewer personal conflicts and distractions from the truth-seeking process. For this reason many critics of academic debate prefer discussion to debate as a training device. However, without the incentive to win, relatively few students will do the necessary research for analyzing a complex social, political, or economic problem or keep their interest at a high pitch as successful debaters do. Thus, decision debating, whatever its shortcomings, provides greater motivation and therefore more effectively achieves its end. On the other hand, discussion is more realistic than debate in the sense that in later life far more people participate in discussion than in debate.

3. AN OUTLINE FOR DISCUSSION

Because of the basic similarities between discussion and debate, a good debater usually makes a good discussant, and vice versa. Many of the foregoing chapters on definition, analysis, research, and reasoning, though written from the standpoint of debate, apply to discussion. Therefore, such matters need not be considered in the present chapter. For convenience, however, the reader is reminded of the following outline for analyzing a question of policy:

Preliminary Considerations
A. What is the occasion for the discussion?
B. Do any terms need to be defined?
C. What are the desired goals?

I. Is there a need for changing the status quo?
    A. Are the desired goals being achieved at present?
    B. If not, how significant are existing evils?
    C. What specifically is the cause of existing evils?
    D. How can this cause best be removed?
II. If a change or new policy is required, what type of policy would best solve the problem?
    A. Are there any serious obstacles which might prevent this policy from coming into existence?
    B. Are there any serious obstacles which might prevent this policy from working or from being enforced?
    C. Would this policy effectively remove the cause of the present problem?
    D. Would this policy result in any harmful effects?
    E. If so, how significant would such effects be?
(Note that in Part II the discussants might have to consider several different policies.)

4. TYPES OF DISCUSSION

Discussions may be conducted to enlighten either the participants involved or an audience listening to the discussion. A discussion with the former purpose may be called a private, or closed, discussion, and one with the latter, a public, or open, discussion. Let us consider each type briefly.

Private Discussions

Private discussions are basically of two types, those which occur in real life, or nonacademic situations, and those which occur in academic, or contest, situations. Nonacademic discussions usually take two forms, the informal panel and the cooperative investigation.

The Informal Panel

This is perhaps the most common type of discussion. A small group, rarely more than fifteen persons, informally discusses some problem facing the group. The program may be anything from deciding whether or not a problem exists to deciding on some action. This is the type of discussion which goes on in classes, clubs, the special committee meetings of organizations, and special conferences called to conciliate the differences of the conferees.

The Cooperative Investigation

This type of discussion differs from the informal panel type in that each discussant gathers information on some phase of the problem and presents it to the group in a short talk before the informal discussion gets underway.

Contest, or academic, discussions are usually of two types, the problem-solving panel and the legislative assembly, or student congress. Although a judge or an audience may be present, they are in a sense bystanders, interested primarily in the techniques of the discussion rather than in the subject discussed.

Problem-solving Panel

The procedure here is the same as for the informal panel. As a rule, each member of the panel is from a different school, and the topic discussed is the national college (or high school) discussion topic. Usually, there are two one-hour rounds of discussion, the first being devoted to formulating the problem and the second to considering solutions. Like the informal real-life panel, the discussion is extemporaneous, informal, and conversational. Participants are judged on such factors as analysis, evidence, reasoning, adaptability, cooperativeness, and expression.

Legislative Assembly, or Student Congress

Students attending such an assembly, or congress, are given an opportunity to practice the discussion techniques used in an actual state legislature or in Congress. Students from the different schools are first assigned to committees, where particular bills are drafted; then all the students are brought together in an assembly, either unicameral or bi-cameral, where the various bills are reported out of committee, discussed on the floor, and voted on. The rules of parliamentary procedure are observed. Some congresses use such variations of discussion as in joint committee sessions, party caucuses, and joint conferences of members from both houses. All performances are evaluated by faculty judges, the criteria used being those listed above.

Public Discussions

Public discussions, as we have said, differ from the preceding types in that they are carried on for the edification of an audience. In some types of public discussion the audience participates after a discussion by the panel, this type of program being called a discussion forum. Typical public discussions are those carried on before a television audience or before certain organizations. Usually a panel of from three to five experts sits facing the audience and carries on a rather systematic discussion of some topic which requires special information. The primary purpose of such a discussion is to inform an audience rather than to solve a problem.

5. PHYSICAL ARRANGEMENTS FOR A DISCUSSION

Except for the public discussion, the members of a discussion group should, whenever possible, sit facing each other. This arrangement can be accomplished by placing the chairs in a circle or semicircle, or around a large table. The latter has an advantage in that it can hold books, papers, ash trays, and a pitcher of water. The room should be well lighted and well ventilated. If the members do not know each other, they should be introduced to one another by the leader, who should arrive early enough to greet everyone. Occasionally, name plates are placed in front of each individual. All members should cooperate in creating a cordial, informal atmosphere.

6. PARTICIPATING IN DISCUSSION

Attitudes

To participate effectively in a discussion, one must cultivate the proper attitude toward the task at hand. Most important, perhaps, is remembering the purpose of discussion, that it is primarily inquiry, not advocacy. (This is why discussion subjects are phrased as questions.) Ideas and not personalities are the important consideration; one must be objective and not react emotionally to anything that is said. Discussion might be described as a "thinking-out-loud" process. Thus, it calls for candor and flexibility; one must not be timid about expressing himself nor ashamed to change his mind if he thinks he has been wrong. Finally, as in any cooperative group situation, for best results one should always be friendly, courteous, tactful, and open-minded. To be rude, stubborn, contentious, or ill-humored is to defeat any group effort.

General "Do's" and "Don't's"

1. Listen carefully to what is being said. Make sure you understand a point before commenting on it.

2. Don't interrupt another speaker to make a point. Wait until he has finished speaking.

3. When you have something to say, speak up clearly and distinctly so that all present may hear you without difficulty.

4. Use language that is clear, concrete, neutral, and grammatical. Don't use "loaded," or emotional, terms, like "bureaucrats," "grafters," and "bunk."

5. As a rule, make your comments brief. Don't complicate the discussion by introducing two or more points simultaneously.

6. Speak to the point. Don't obscure the discussion with irrelevancies.

7. Don't exaggerate, distort, or oversimplify what someone else has said.

8. Never be personal in answering a point. Avoid name-calling and don't be insulting because you happen to disagree with what someone else has said. As in debate, attack the argument, never the person who expresses it.

9. Don't monopolize the discussion. Give others a chance to be heard. Don't get involved in a personal conversation with another member of the panel.

10. Don't be dogmatic or contentious in expressing your views. Don't insist upon having your own views prevail, and don't keep repeating the same point in order to make it stick.

11. Don't become moody, irritable, or disagreeable if you are interrupted by the leader or if one of your suggestions is rejected. Always remember why you are participating: to help the group solve a problem in the most effective way.

7. LEADING A DISCUSSION

The Qualifications of a Good Leader

To be a good discussion leader requires considerable intelligence, tact, knowledge, and certain special skills. Let us consider each briefly:

Intelligence

A discussion leader must be able to think and act quickly, not only in handling the various members of the panel but also in analyzing the points made and in guiding the discussion. A good sense of humor, which usually goes with a quick mind, is also a valuable asset.

Tact

A discussion leader must be congenial, friendly, courteous, considerate, impartial, tolerant, self-controlled, firm when necessary, and modest in the sense of being willing to remain in the background once the discussion gets under way.

Knowledge

A discussion leader must have a good knowledge of the discussion process, of the use of evidence and reasoning, and of the topic under discussion.

Special Skills

A discussion leader must know how to speak extemporaneously, to keep the discussion moving on the right track, and to bring out the best from all panel members by means of skillful questions, comments, and suggestions.

The Duties of a Discussion Leader

A discussion leader must plan the discussion, get it started, keep it moving in the right direction, and summarize its conclusions. Let us consider each factor briefly:

Planning the Discussion

In planning a discussion, a leader should study the question carefully, do some research on it, prepare a bibliography, and make an outline which he should follow during the discussion period. He should call the members of the panel together for a prediscussion meeting, at which time he should pass out a copy of the bibliography and the outline he has prepared, and should discuss very briefly with the group the scope of the discussion. This discussion should not be of the question itself but rather of aims and general procedure. If the discussion is to be of the cooperative investigation type, the leader should assign the various members present a phase of the problem to investigate and report on.

In planning, the leader should also investigate the room in which the discussion is to take place and should arrange for the seating, the distribution of materials, and the use of visual aids if required, and do anything else that may contribute to the success of the meeting.

Getting the Discussion Started

If the discussion is a public discussion, the leader should first introduce the members of the panel. If not, he should begin the discussion by commenting briefly on the history of the problem or the occasion which has given rise to it; pointing out its significance, or how it affects those present; and, if necessary, defining key terms. He should then elicit comments by asking direct questions of specific members until the discussion has gained momentum, at which time he can concentrate on its direction.

Keeping the Discussion Moving on the Right Track

A good discussion leader learns to take notes as the discussion progresses so that he can guide the discussion and periodically summarize its progress. Such notes are also valuable as a record of what the discussion accomplished. In keeping the discussion moving on the right track, the leader usually has to perform a variety of tasks, the most common of which are as follows:

Encouraging the Timid Member to Contribute. "I wonder, John, if you agree with this point" or "John, we haven't heard from you yet; what do you think about this?"

Encouraging the Soft-spoken Member to Speak Up. "If you don't mind, Bill, the acoustics here aren't as good as they might be, and I'm afraid all of us can't hear you."

Discouraging the Member Who Would Monopolize the Discussion. "We certainly appreciate your interest, Mark, but I think Tom has been wanting to say something on this point. Perhaps, we can return to you in a little while."

Cutting Off a Long-winded Member. "If I may interrupt at this point, Jack, time is of the essence, and we do want to get as many different views as possible."

Clarifying the Meaning of a Member's Comment. "Am I right in assuming, Henry, that what you mean is . . . ?" or "Could you give us an example, perhaps, of what you mean?"

Pointing Up the Relevancy of a Point Which Seems Irrelevant. "Don't you mean, Joe, that Formosa would be lost and that then, as a consequence, our defenses would be weakened?"

Analyzing the Source of Evidence. "Wouldn't it be better if we knew just who said this, and when and where it was said?"

Analyzing the Reasoning. "But does it necessarily follow, Bill, that because of . . . ?"

Exposing an Assertion. "I wonder if there are any reasons for believing the assertion (or assumption) that . . . ?"

Dismissing an Irrelevant Point. "That's an interesting observation, Bob, but I wonder if it's entirely relevant at this time. Perhaps, we can come back to it."

Keeping the Discussion from Getting Too Involved. "Actually, Bill, you've made three points. Suppose we consider the second one for the time being and come back to the others later on." Incidentally, if a leader says he will come back to a point, he should come back to it. If he is not sure that he will, he should qualify his remark with "perhaps."

Smoothing Over Personal Clashes or Emotional Outbursts. "I don't think we add anything to the discussion by generating heat. Aren't we really interested in generating light?"

Summarizing Periodically. "Am I correct in saying that up to this point we agree that . . . ; we disagree, however, in. . . ." Points of agreement should be put aside and points of disagreement discussed.

Summarizing the Conclusions of the Discussion

In concluding the discussion, the leader should summarize the main points discussed, the accords reached, and the disagreements remaining. Finally, he should thank the members for their participation and cooperation.

8. A SAMPLE DISCUSSION [1]

What Should Be the Role of the United States in the Middle East?

Meyer (moderator): On July 26, Abdul Nasser seized the Suez Canal. Then there came the invasion of the Sinai Peninsula. After that, the intervention by the British and French in the Suez Canal Zone. These events all combine to make the Middle East possibly the most dangerous and the most troubled area in the world today. Now the United States is a world leader. We must act in this crisis. Our topic for discussion today is "What Should Be the Role of the United States in the Middle East?" I think that in view of the conditions, the circumstances, in view of the fact that the Middle East is the most troubled area in the world today, no more vital topic could be found.

The members of our panel today are Dave Shapiro, Jim Clark, Bert Adkins, John Ensle, and Larry Haile. I am Meyer Witt.

Well, gentlemen, here's our problem: what should be the role of the United States in the Middle East?

Dave: Meyer, I think that we ought to bear in mind that we're seeking to find only America's role in this area of the world.

Jim: Well, the question simply means, what should be the policy of the

---

[1] The discussion from which this excerpt was taken was conducted by students at the University of Texas, under the direction of Professor Don Williams, and won first place in the National Discussion Contest in 1957. The topic for discussion was the national college discussion topic; and the discussants were Meyer W. Witt, James W. Clark, Dave Shapiro, Bert B. Adkins, Larry B. Haile, and John F. Ensle. Witt acted as moderator. A duplication of the tape recording of this discussion and other discussions submitted annually in competition for the National Discussion Contest may be obtained for a nominal sum from the Audio-Visual Center, Kent State University, Kent, Ohio.

United States with respect to this area of the world? Basically, our attitude toward the six countries of the Arab bloc and toward Israel.

Larry: Jim, I think we ought to be a little more specific here in mentioning these nations. As the State Department points out, these nations are Lebanon, Syria, Israel, Jordan, Iran, Iraq, Egypt, Sudan, and Saudi Arabia. I think we ought to follow this definition of these nations.

Bert: Then we're not including French North Africa in our discussion?

Larry: No, I don't think, Bert, that you could actually consider them one of the Arab bloc or an Israel State, or in any way concerned really with the basic problems of the Middle East.

John: Yes, I think we ought to stick with the State Department's definition of the area.

Meyer (moderator): Well, I think along this line we might also discuss the role which should include both our unilateral actions and policies, and our policies and actions in support of international organizations.

John: Perhaps our major objective from which all other objectives stem is the combating of communism in this area. What do you think?

Bert: Well, I think first of all we should clarify this concept of combating communism because we have to realize that the nations of the Middle East look at Russia and communism from an entirely different point of view than we in the Western nations. And so we can't go around saying, we're going to fight communism and that's our purpose in the Middle East.

Larry: I agree with you, Bert, but I think that the thing we must keep in mind above all others is this: capitalizing on our past mistakes, whatever the policy is that we decide on, we must make it a firm one; we must be concrete, we must put it before these nations so that they might see our intentions.

Dave: Gentlemen, I think that while we're discussing such broad concepts as keeping peace in the Middle East, we ought to bear in mind that there are immediate problems at hand, such as reestablishing free passage in the Suez Canal, which affects not only the Middle East but our Western allies in Europe, too.

Bert: Well, going back to what Larry said, I think consistency would definitely be advantageous if possible in the Middle East. However, I don't see it's possible, as is shown by past American actions.

John: Consistency in itself I don't think should be our end. We have to handle each of these problems individually as they present themselves; and our policy need not necessarily be the same in each instance.

Larry: Well, I'd agree with you, John, but my point is this: we must take some firm stand. Nasser said, when we withdrew our aid to help him build his Aswan High Dam, that he did not know the intentions of the United States; he did not know how they were going to act, how he should react. And this was, perhaps, one of their major grievances against us.

Jim: Now I'd agree with Larry; and I think perhaps what we could say is that, from the point of view of consistency, we want to be consistent in our goals and in our applications of our general policy to achieve these goals. But certainly our policy is going to have to be kept flexible so that we can adjust to changing situations.

Dave: Well, gentlemen, do you agree that one of the major goals—one of the major broad goals—aside from keeping peace in the Middle East and maintaining free passage in the Suez Canal is to encourage a pro-Western feeling among the people of the Middle East, not necessarily to make the Middle East a part of the American sphere of influence?

Larry: Wait a minute—no, I don't agree with that, Dave, because I think, if we're going to look at the long-term goals, that the best way we can encourage this pro-Western feeling is at the present to encourage the Nationalist spirit that is growing in this area. And not to strive in fact for this pro-Western approach.

Dave: Well, just what do you mean by encouraging nationalism?

Larry: Well, I think we could best go along without trying to win friends by buying them, by trying to sell democracy to them. I think, if we take into consideration their wants and their needs and perhaps in this sense conform our policies to their policy, we could best bring them to our own side.

John: It seems to me that Larry is taking something of the negative view here in keeping these nations away from communism. I think instead we should work to bring them closer to our concept of an international world.

Larry: How?

John: Well, once again, now I don't know if you want— Jim, do you want to answer that question before I go on?

Bert: Well, once again, I think that we have to consider the historical relationship of the West to the Middle East. After all, the influence of the West on the Middle East has been somewhat disrupted. And these countries are going to be nationalistic as a result of colonialism from the West. And as Larry says, we have to learn to work with this force and harness it. These nations aren't ready to turn to the West automatically in opposition to the Soviet Union.

Jim: Bert has a very good point here, I think, and that is that everything is basically relative. Before we can have these nations come over to our side, we must get them in a firm neutral position first of all.

Dave: Well, I don't see how you go about establishing neutralism in an area. I can certainly see how one country would attempt to encourage a sentiment which is favorable to that country. You just don't establish neutralism.

Meyer (moderator): Well, gentlemen, in establishing some of the objectives of the United States in the Middle East, I think we've realized some of the tremendous problems which face us. We've agreed on one thing—that we need to keep peace in the Middle East. Just how we're going to keep peace or how we're going to meet those problems we haven't yet decided. Now in the first place, how did these problems arise?

Comment

Here the panel follows the suggested analysis of a policy question by discussing first a definition of terms and then common objectives. In the remainder of the discussion the panel went on to discuss the nature and cause of the problem, and possible solutions. By means of questions and suggestions, the moderator guided the discussion and led the group systematically from one topic to another; occasionally he clarified points and conciliated differences. The discussants were friendly, cooperative, and desirous of ironing out differences and reaching accords.

EXERCISES

1. What is the relationship between discussion and debate? What are the similarities and differences between the two activities?

2. What are the duties of a discussion leader?

3. Suggestion to instructor: Divide the class into groups of five students each, let each group choose its own discussion leader, and then have each group conduct a cooperative discussion. Sufficient time should be allowed for an oral critique by the rest of the students, who are expected to take notes on each of the discussants and on the leader while the discussion is in progress.

Suggested Topics

What is the role of propaganda in public opinion?

What should be the policy of the United States toward the problems of Africa —of Asia—of the Middle East?

How can the United States best meet foreign economic competition?

What should be the place of the humanities in American higher education?

What should be the role of the Federal government in regulating our economy?

What should be the role of the government in regulating organized labor?

Is our educational system meeting the needs of our youth?

(For other topics see back issues of the *Annals of the American Academy, Congressional Digest,* and *Reference Shelf.*)

SELECTED BIBLIOGRAPHY

Beardsley, Monroe C.: *Practical Logic*, Prentice-Hall, Inc., Englewood Cliffs, N.J., 1950.

———: *Thinking Straight*, 2d ed., Prentice-Hall, Inc., Englewood Cliffs, N.J., 1956.

Black, Max: *Critical Thinking*, 2d ed., Prentice-Hall, Inc., Englewood Cliffs, N.J., 1952.

Courtney, Luther W., and Glenn R. Capp: *Practical Debating*, J. B. Lippincott Company, Philadelphia, 1949.

Ewbank, Henry Lee, and J. Jeffrey Auer: *Discussion and Debate*, 2d ed., Appleton-Century-Crofts, Inc., New York, 1951.

Larrabee, Harold A.: *Reliable Knowledge*, Houghton Mifflin Company, Boston, 1945.

McBurney, James H., James M. O'Neill, and Glenn E. Mills: *Argumentation and Debate*, The Macmillan Company, New York, 1951.

Potter, David, ed.: *Argumentation and Debate*, The Dryden Press, Inc., New York, 1954.

Ruby, Lionel: *Logic: An Introduction*, J. B. Lippincott Company, Philadelphia, 1950.

Stebbing, L. Susan: *A Modern Introduction to Logic*, Thomas Y. Crowell Company, New York, n.d.

———: *Thinking to Some Purpose*, Penguin Books, Inc., Baltimore, 1939.

Thouless, Robert H.: *Straight and Crooked Thinking*, Simon and Schuster, Inc., New York, 1932.

The following contain transcripts of actual debates, discussions, and persuasive speeches:

Congressional Record, Superintendent of Documents, Government Printing Office, Washington, D.C.

Finley, George W.: *Winning Debates, Orations, Speeches*, Noble and Noble, Publishers, Inc., New York.

Nichols, Egbert R., ed.: *Intercollegiate Debates*, Noble and Noble, Publishers, Inc., New York, 1939. Or write to Nichols Publishing House, 814 Campus Ave., Redlands, Calif.

Nichols, Egbert R.: *West Point Debates,* Nichols Publishing House, 814 Campus Ave., Redlands, Calif.

Parliament Debates, Her Majesty's Stationery Office, Yorkhouse, Kingsway, London, W.C. 2, England.

Taft, Robert A., and T. V. Smith: *Foundations of Democracy,* University of Chicago Press, Chicago, 1939. (A collection of thirteen debates on political topics.)

The Reference Shelf, H. W. Wilson Company, New York.

Ulman, Ruth, ed.: *University Debaters' Annual,* H. W. Wilson Company, New York.

Walch, J. Weston: *Debate Handbooks,* Box 1075, Portland, Maine.

INDEX